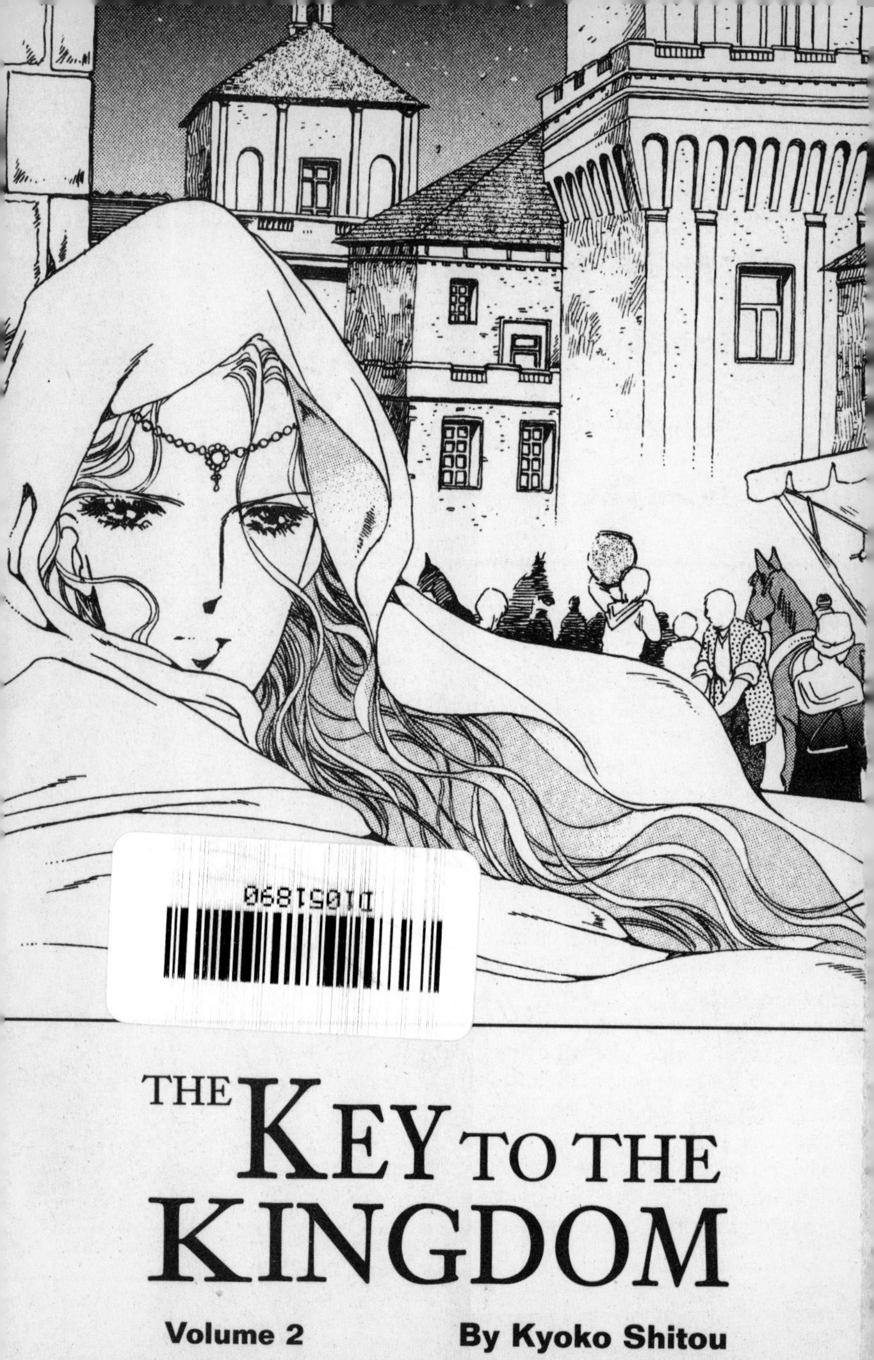

THE KEY TO THE KINGDOM

Volume 2

By Kyoko Shitou

CONTENTS

3   **Episode 5**

51   **Episode 6**

91   **Episode 7**

123   **Episode 8**

163   **Bonus Material**

THE STORY SO FAR:

After the king and his eldest son are killed in a war, a contest is declared to determine the next monarch of the kingdom of Landor. Whoever discovers the fabled "Key to the Kingdom" will ascend Landor's throne. The five contenders, including Asta, the younger prince, and Lady Leticia, begin their journey. Along the way, Asta and Captain Baddorius (his guardian) encounter the mysterious Gaius, who turns out to be one of the immortal Dragon Men who possess extraordinary powers. Gaius also appears to have a deep connection to the legendary Key. But what is the Dragon Man's purpose in desiring Badd's "body and soul"? And what is the "Key to the Kingdom"? Our heroes face more riddles as their quest continues.

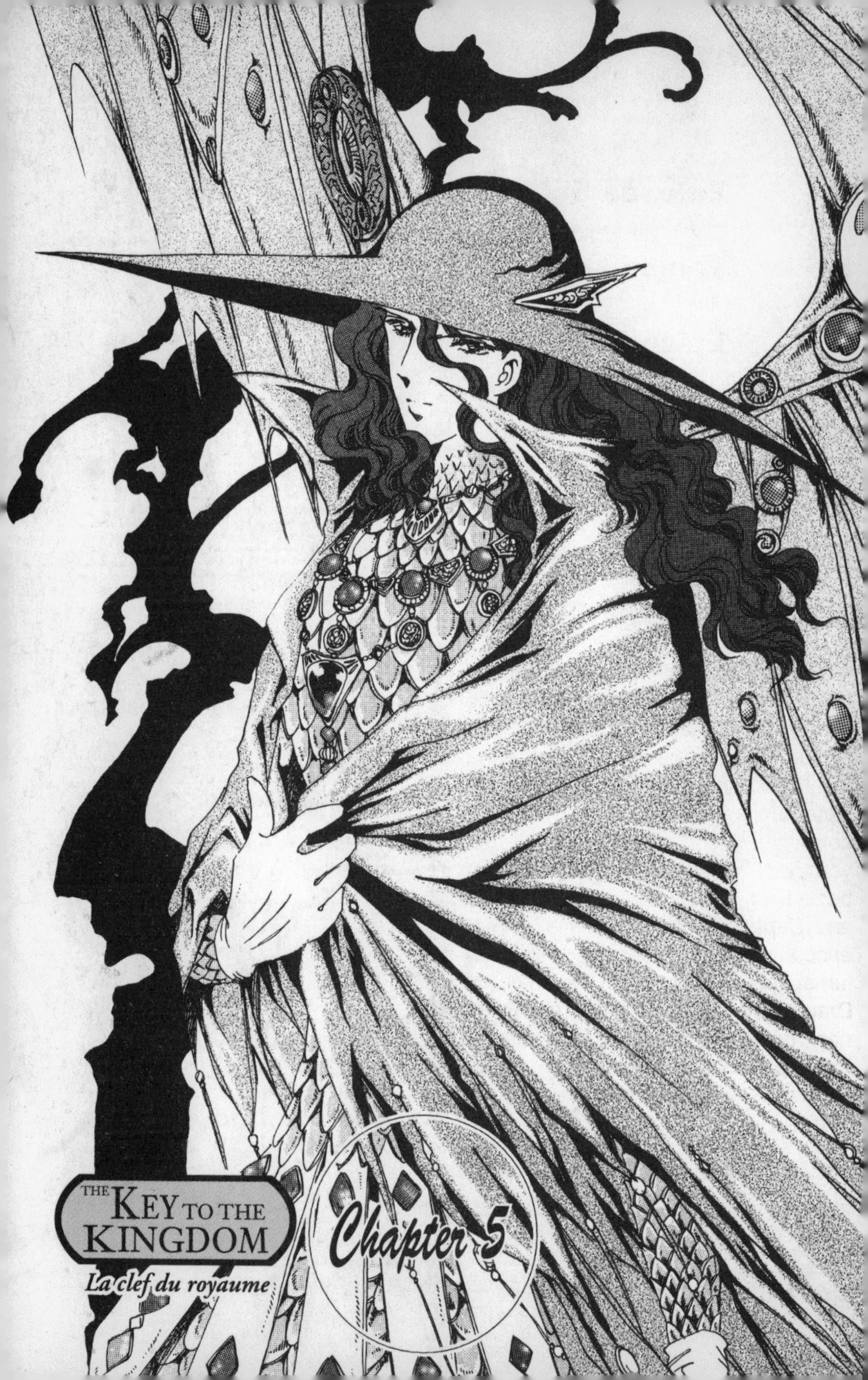
THE KEY TO THE KINGDOM
La clef du royaume
Chapter 5

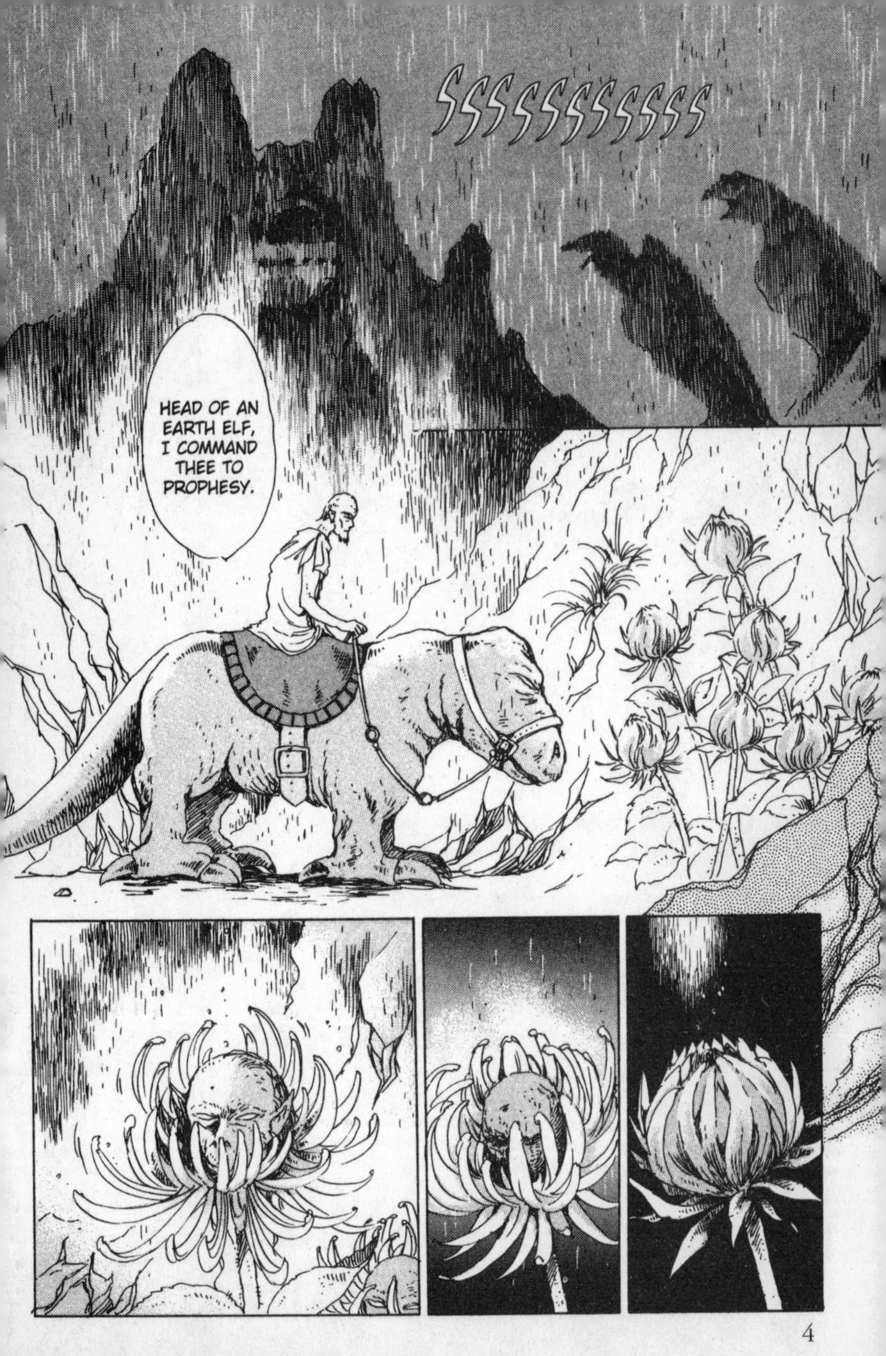
SSSSSSSSSSSS
HEAD OF AN EARTH ELF, I COMMAND THEE TO PROPHESY.

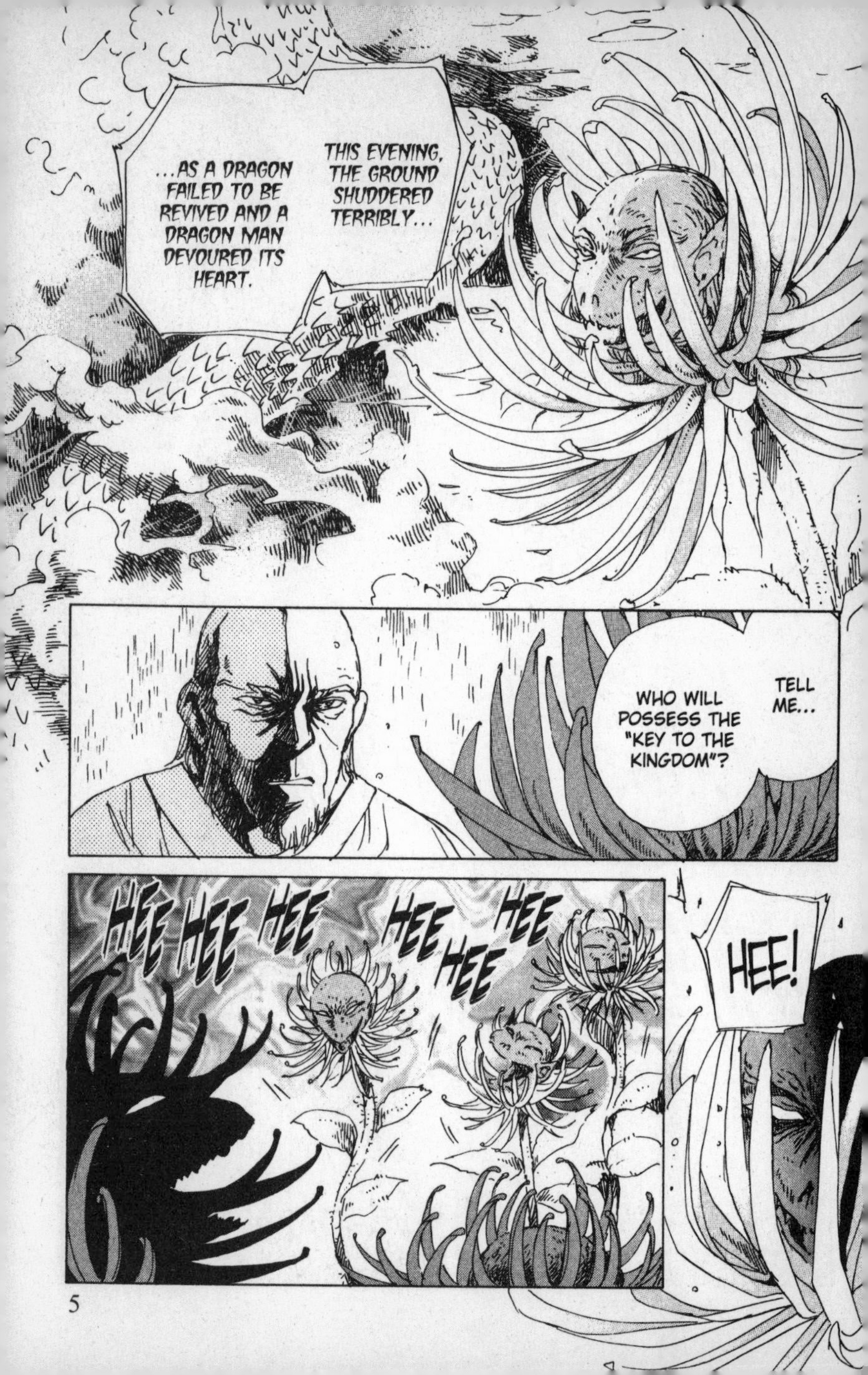
THIS EVENING, THE GROUND SHUDDERED TERRIBLY...
...AS A DRAGON FAILED TO BE REVIVED AND A DRAGON MAN DEVOURED ITS HEART.
TELL ME...
WHO WILL POSSESS THE "KEY TO THE KINGDOM"?
HEE!
HEE HEE HEE HEE HEE HEE

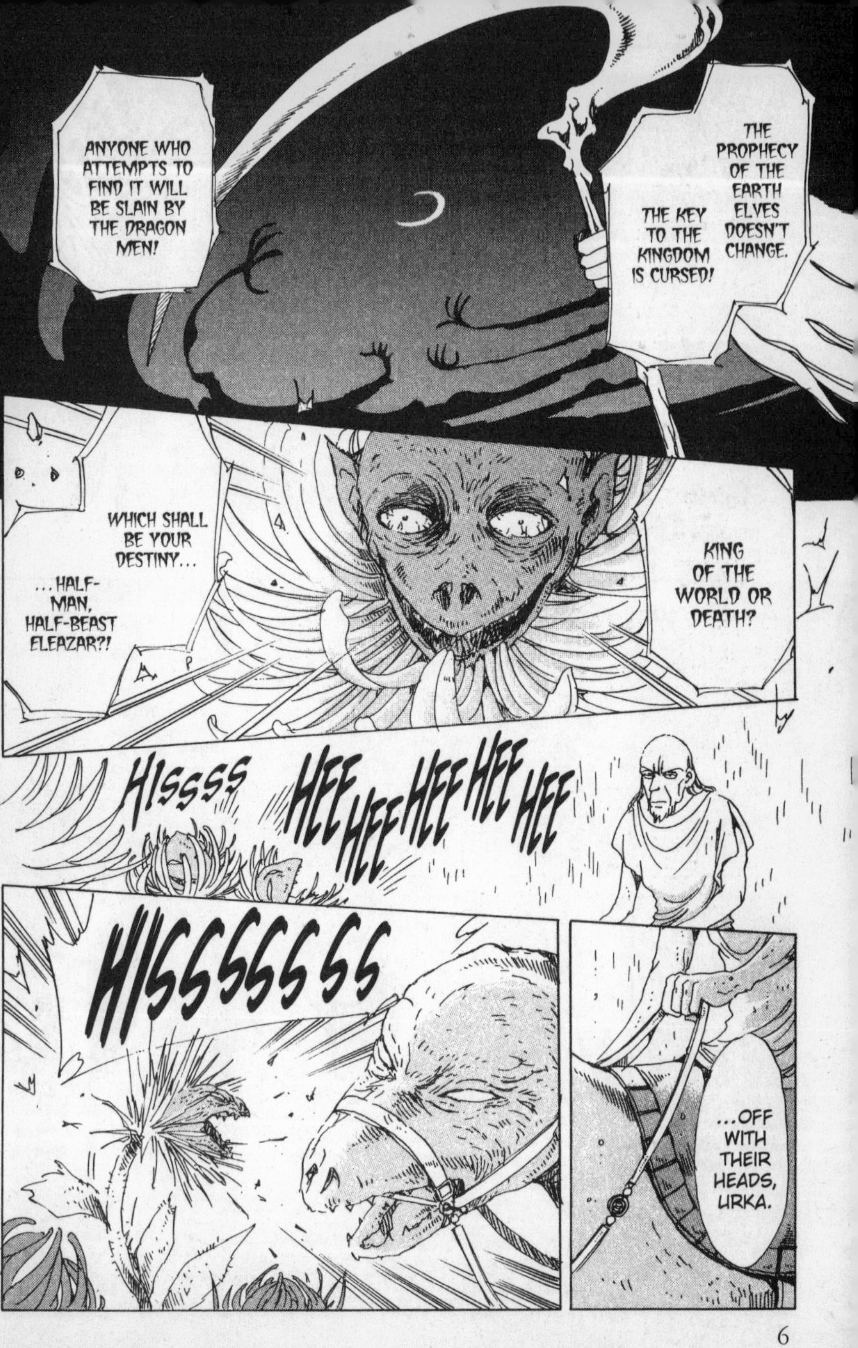
THE PROPHECY OF THE EARTH ELVES DOESN'T CHANGE.
THE KEY TO THE KINGDOM IS CURSED!
ANYONE WHO ATTEMPTS TO FIND IT WILL BE SLAIN BY THE DRAGON MEN!
KING OF THE WORLD OR DEATH?
WHICH SHALL BE YOUR DESTINY...
...HALF-MAN, HALF-BEAST ELEAZAR?!
HISSSS
HEE HEE HEE HEE HEE HEE
...OFF WITH THEIR HEADS, URKA.
HISSSSSSSS

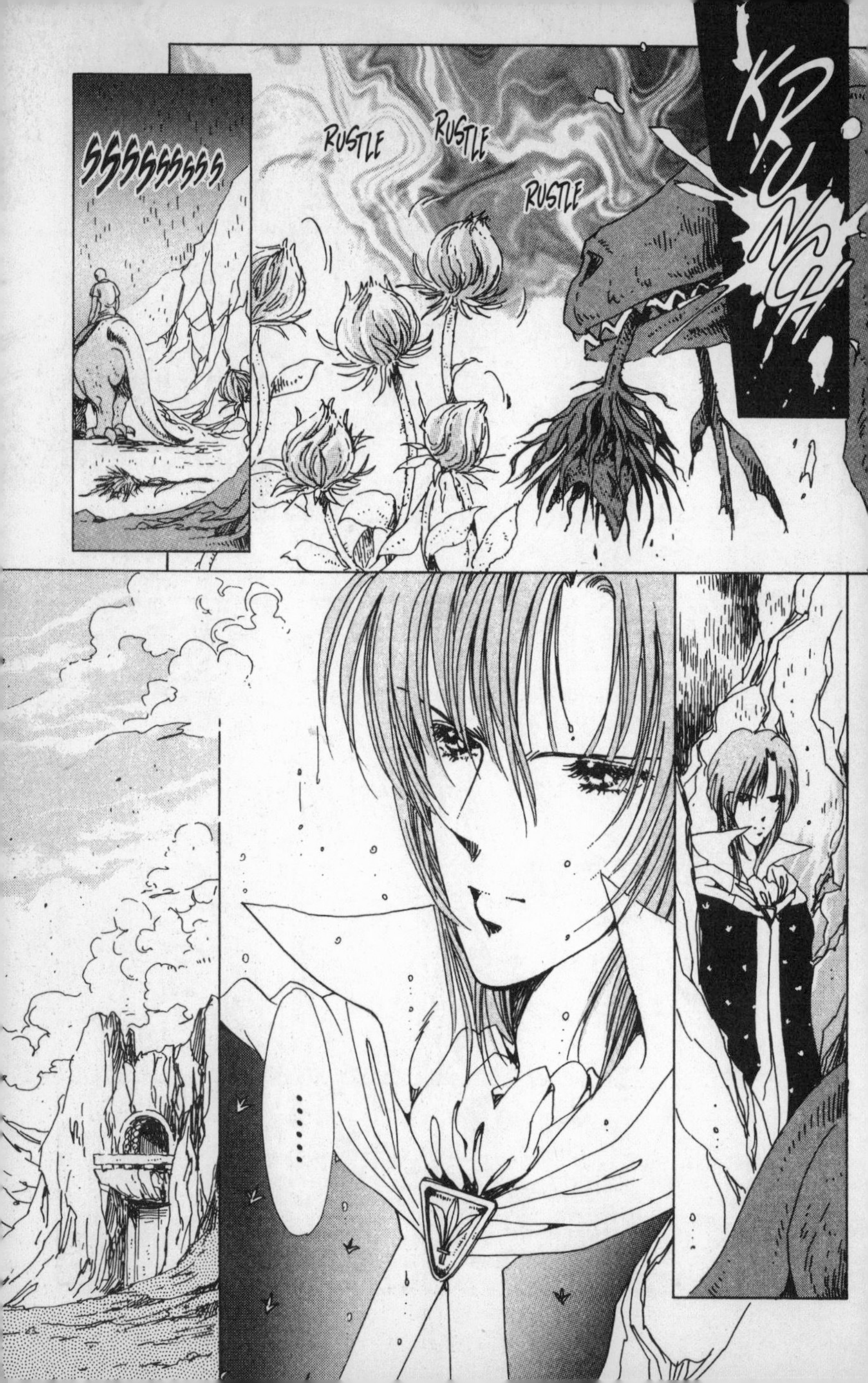
KRUNCH
RUSTLE
RUSTLE
RUSTLE
SSSSSSSSS
......

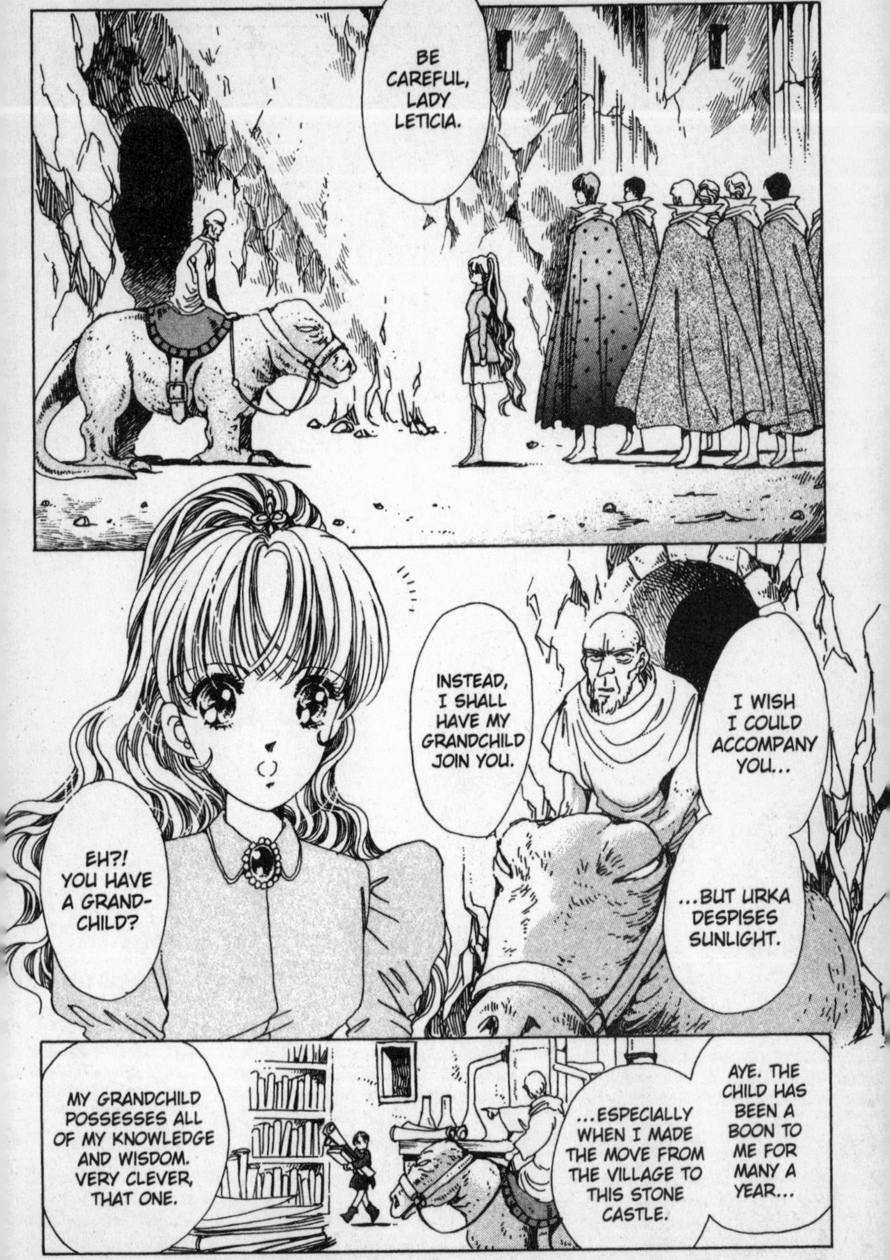
BE CAREFUL, LADY LETICIA.
I WISH I COULD ACCOMPANY YOU...
...BUT URKA DESPISES SUNLIGHT.
INSTEAD, I SHALL HAVE MY GRANDCHILD JOIN YOU.
EH?! YOU HAVE A GRAND-CHILD?
AYE. THE CHILD HAS BEEN A BOON TO ME FOR MANY A YEAR...
...ESPECIALLY WHEN I MADE THE MOVE FROM THE VILLAGE TO THIS STONE CASTLE.
MY GRANDCHILD POSSESSES ALL OF MY KNOWLEDGE AND WISDOM. VERY CLEVER, THAT ONE.

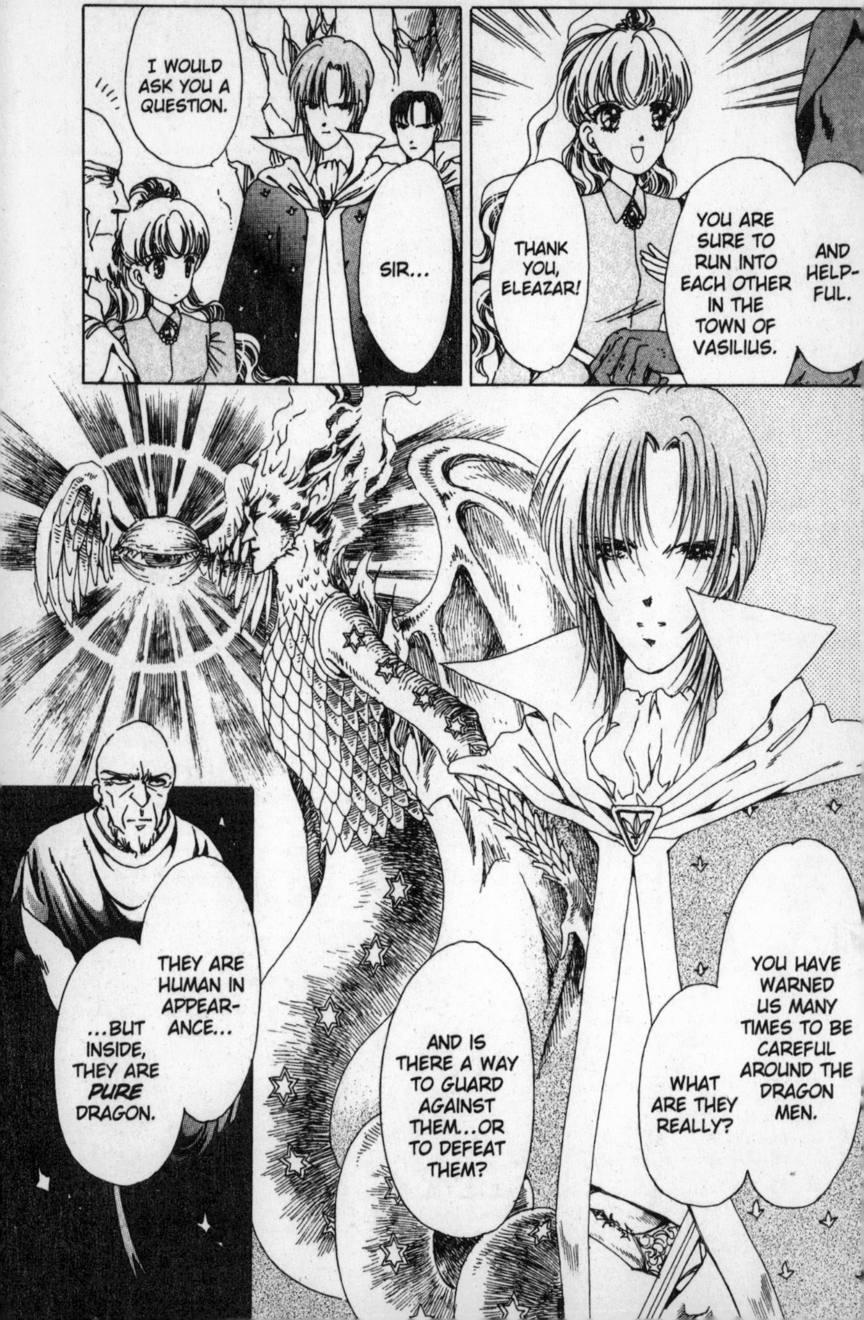
AND HELPFUL.
YOU ARE SURE TO RUN INTO EACH OTHER IN THE TOWN OF VASILIUS.
THANK YOU, ELEAZAR!
SIR...
I WOULD ASK YOU A QUESTION.
YOU HAVE WARNED US MANY TIMES TO BE CAREFUL AROUND THE DRAGON MEN.
WHAT ARE THEY REALLY?
AND IS THERE A WAY TO GUARD AGAINST THEM...OR TO DEFEAT THEM?
THEY ARE HUMAN IN APPEARANCE...
...BUT INSIDE, THEY ARE *PURE* DRAGON.

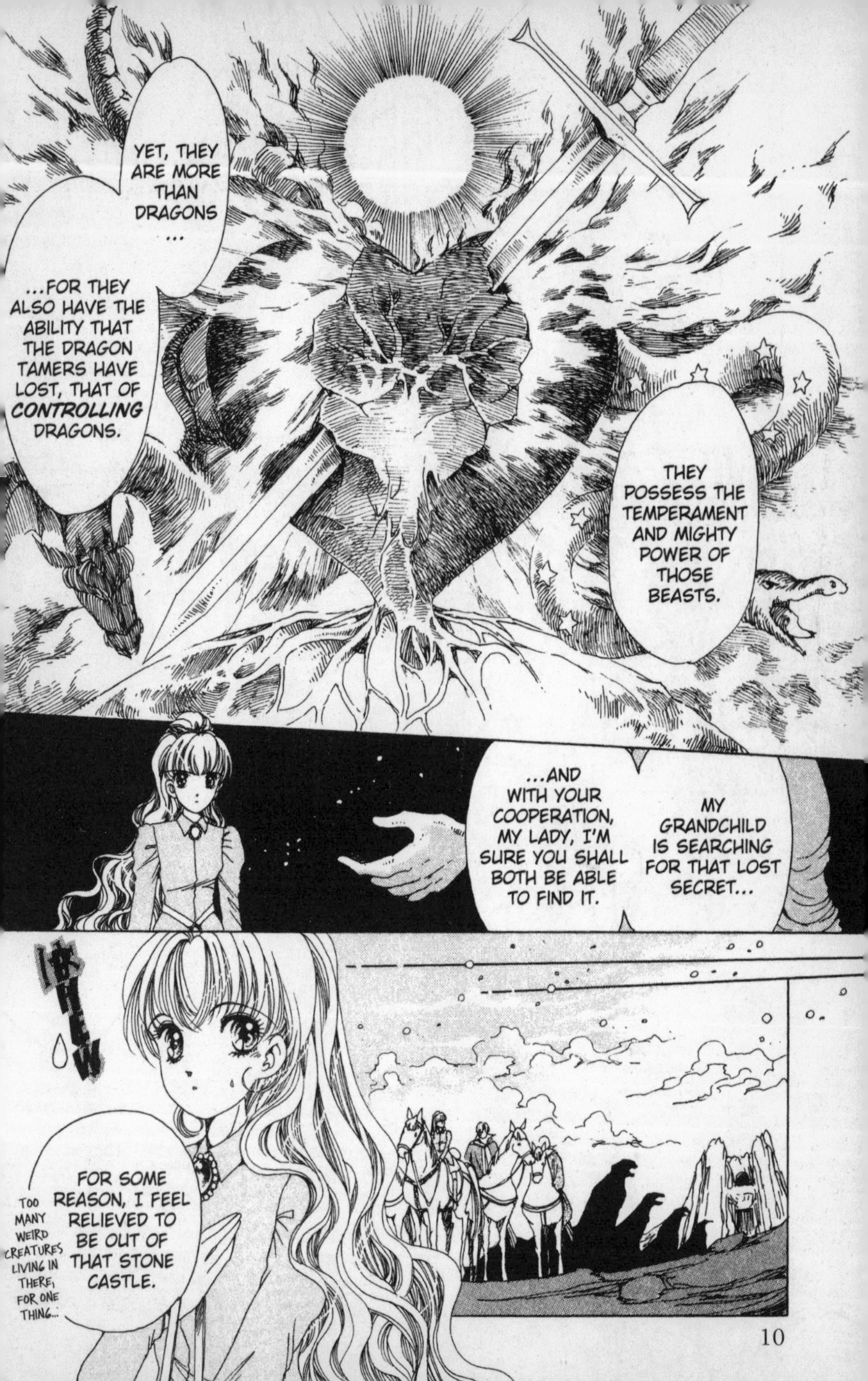
THEY POSSESS THE TEMPERAMENT AND MIGHTY POWER OF THOSE BEASTS.
YET, THEY ARE MORE THAN DRAGONS...
...FOR THEY ALSO HAVE THE ABILITY THAT THE DRAGON TAMERS HAVE LOST, THAT OF *CONTROLLING* DRAGONS.
MY GRANDCHILD IS SEARCHING FOR THAT LOST SECRET...
...AND WITH YOUR COOPERATION, MY LADY, I'M SURE YOU SHALL BOTH BE ABLE TO FIND IT.
FOR SOME REASON, I FEEL RELIEVED TO BE OUT OF THAT STONE CASTLE.
TOO MANY WEIRD CREATURES LIVING IN THERE, FOR ONE THING...

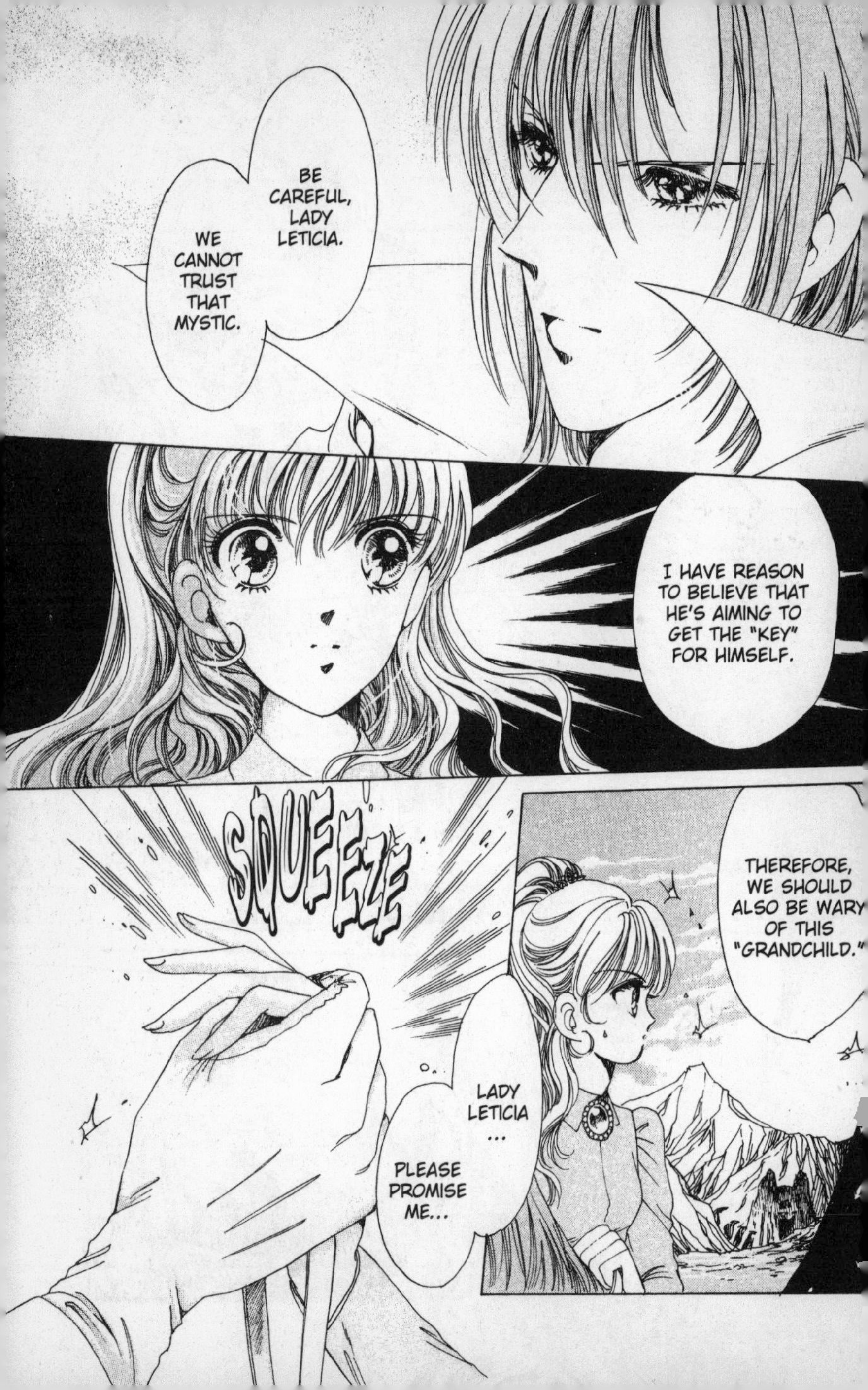
BE CAREFUL, LADY LETICIA.
WE CANNOT TRUST THAT MYSTIC.
I HAVE REASON TO BELIEVE THAT HE'S AIMING TO GET THE "KEY" FOR HIMSELF.
THEREFORE, WE SHOULD ALSO BE WARY OF THIS "GRANDCHILD."
SQUEEZE
LADY LETICIA ...
PLEASE PROMISE ME...

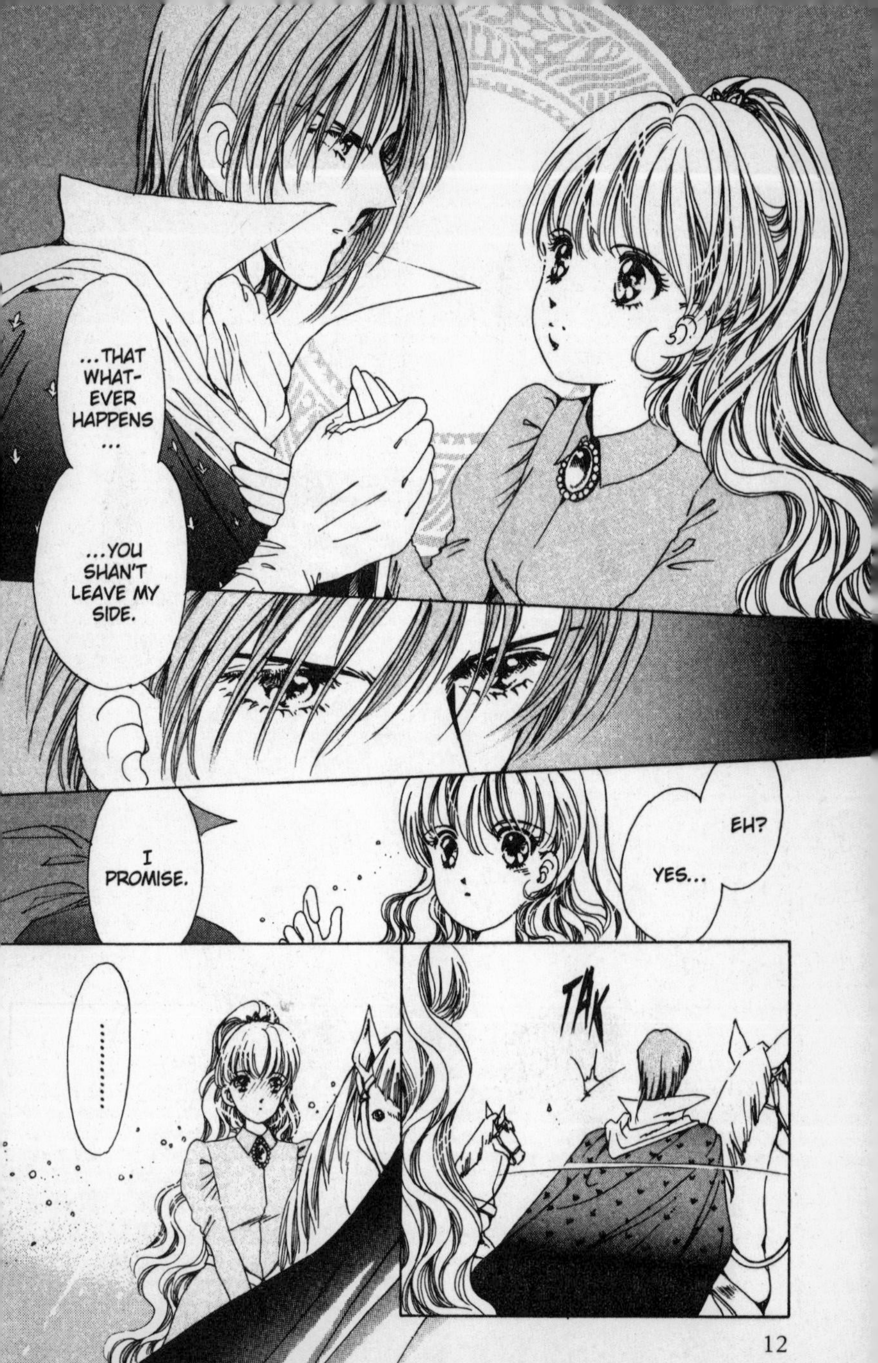
...THAT WHAT-EVER HAPPENS ...
...YOU SHAN'T LEAVE MY SIDE.
EH? YES...
I PROMISE.
TAK
......

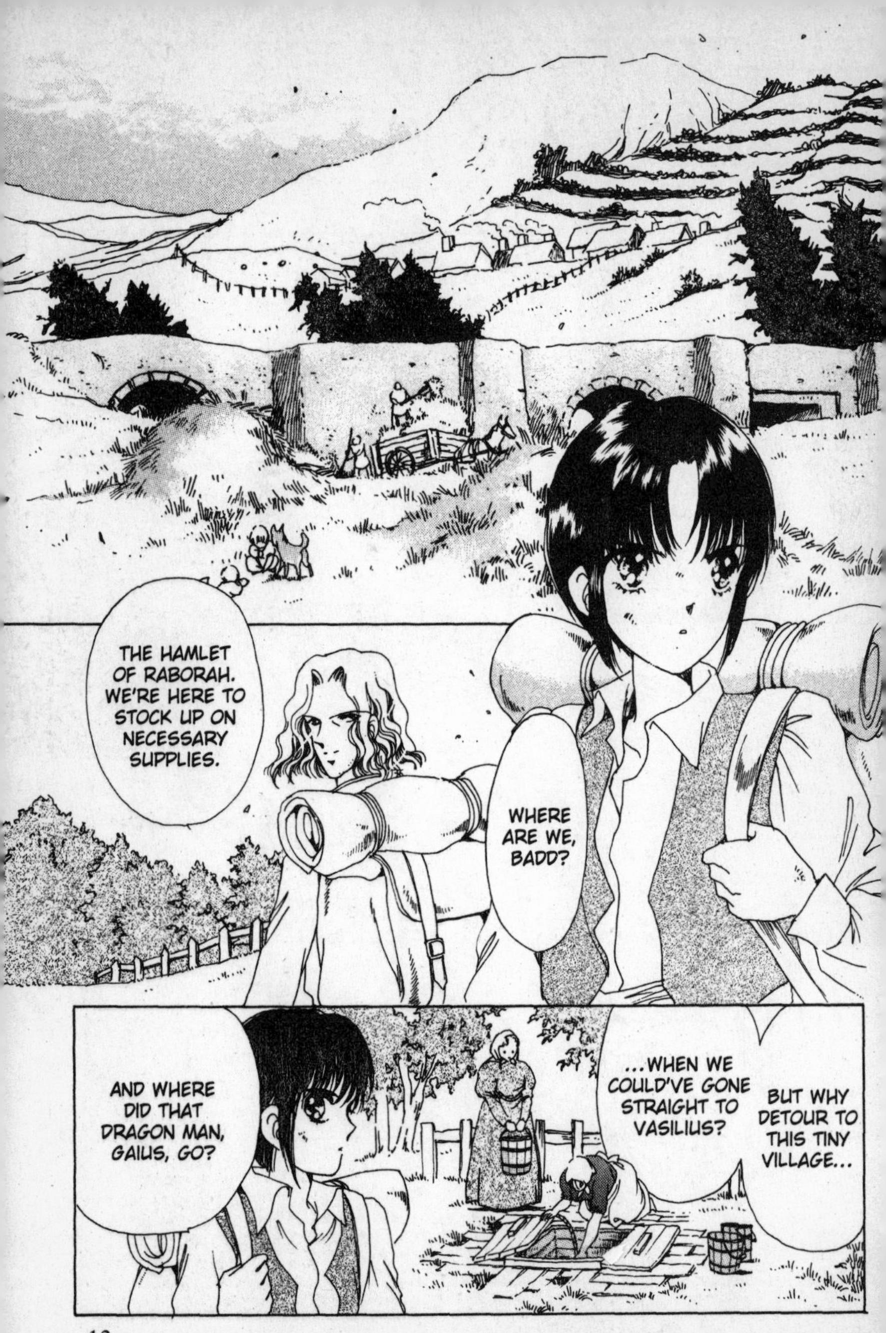
WHERE ARE WE, BADD?
THE HAMLET OF RABORAH. WE'RE HERE TO STOCK UP ON NECESSARY SUPPLIES.
BUT WHY DETOUR TO THIS TINY VILLAGE...
...WHEN WE COULD'VE GONE STRAIGHT TO VASILIUS?
AND WHERE DID THAT DRAGON MAN, GAIUS, GO?

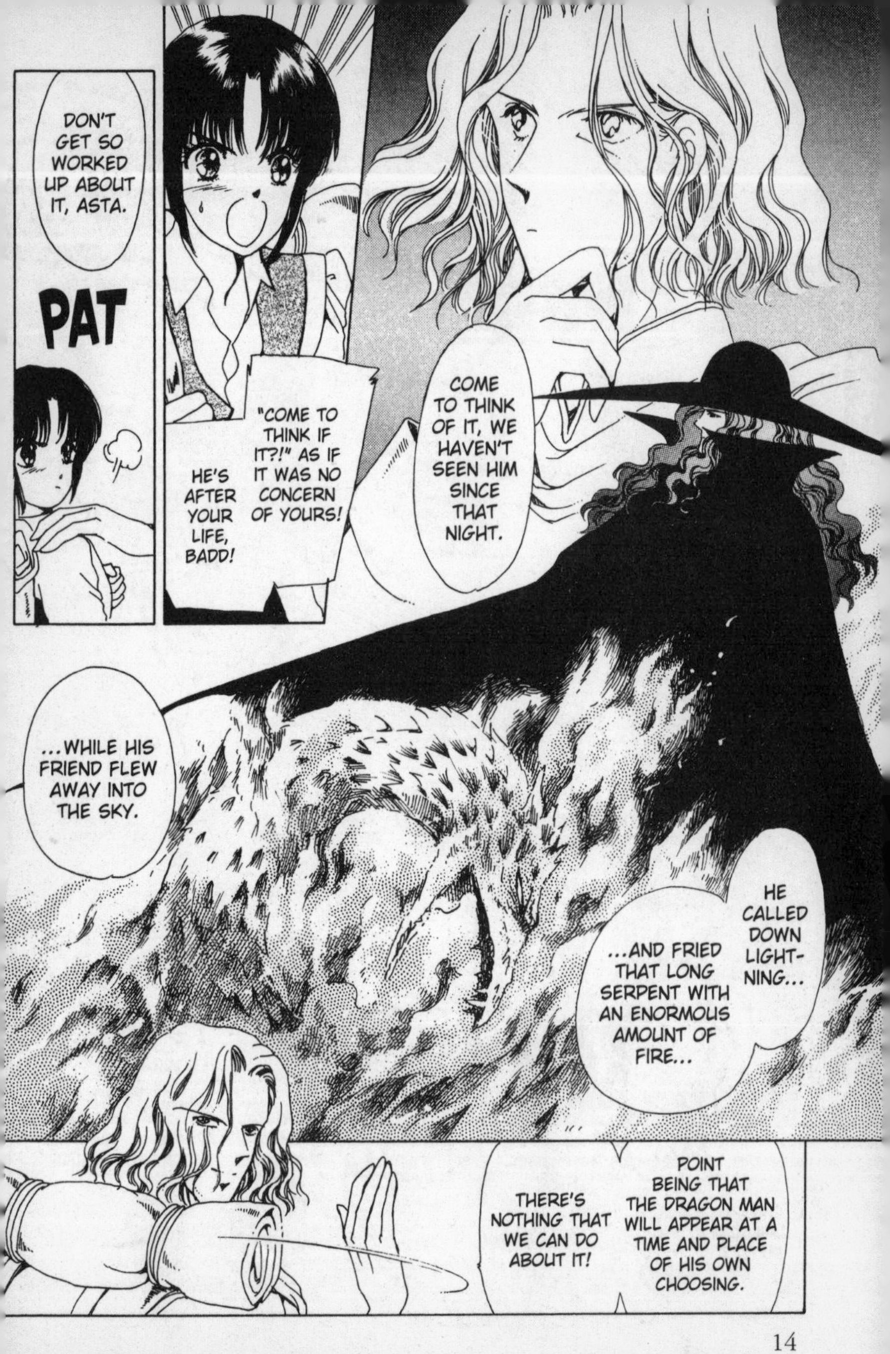
COME TO THINK OF IT, WE HAVEN'T SEEN HIM SINCE THAT NIGHT.
"COME TO THINK IF IT?!" AS IF IT WAS NO CONCERN OF YOURS!
HE'S AFTER YOUR LIFE, BADD!
DON'T GET SO WORKED UP ABOUT IT, ASTA.
PAT
HE CALLED DOWN LIGHT-NING...
...AND FRIED THAT LONG SERPENT WITH AN ENORMOUS AMOUNT OF FIRE...
...WHILE HIS FRIEND FLEW AWAY INTO THE SKY.
POINT BEING THAT THE DRAGON MAN WILL APPEAR AT A TIME AND PLACE OF HIS OWN CHOOSING.
THERE'S NOTHING THAT WE CAN DO ABOUT IT!

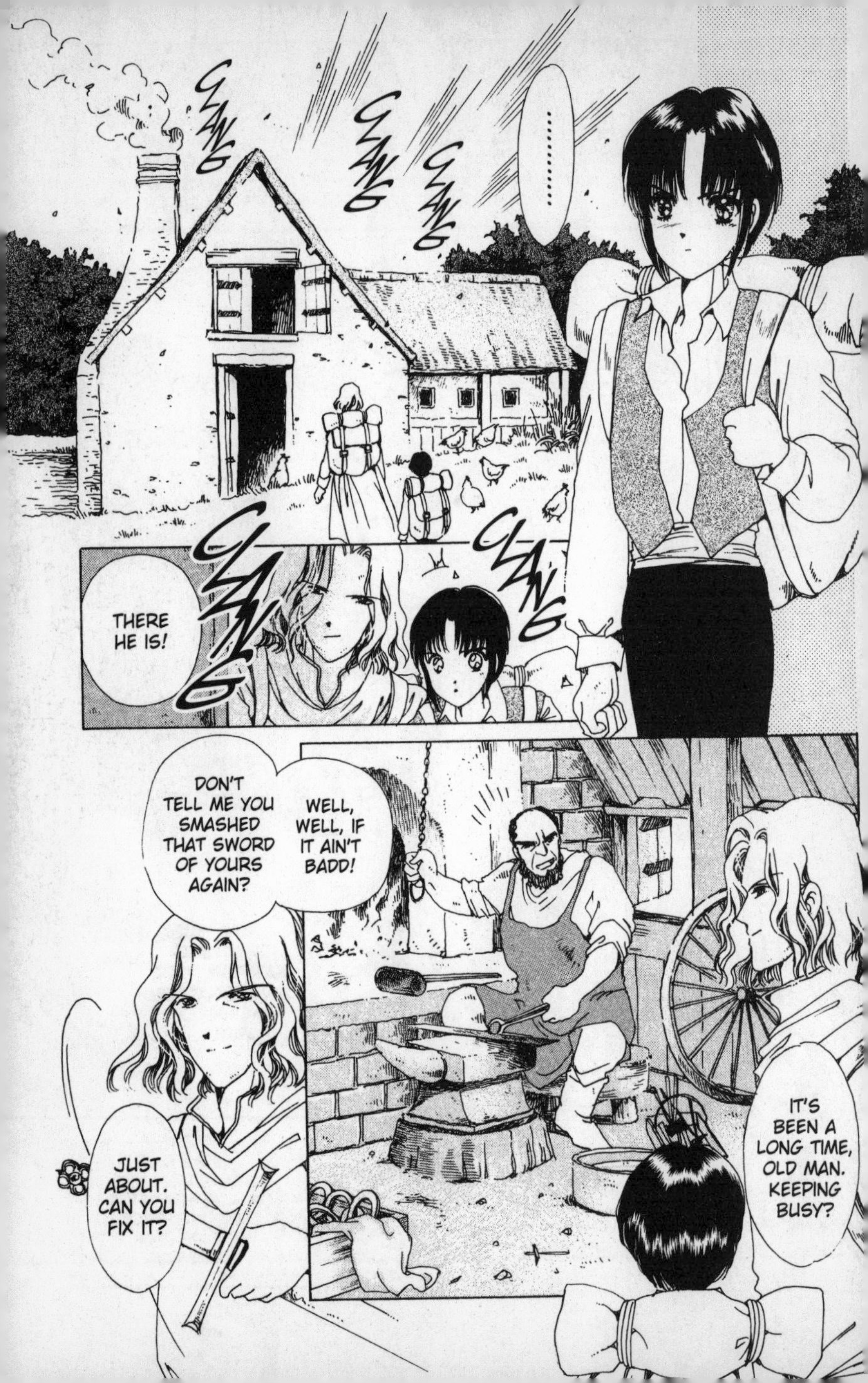
......
CLANG
CLANG
CLANG
CLANG
CLANG
THERE HE IS!
CLANG
IT'S BEEN A LONG TIME, OLD MAN. KEEPING BUSY?
WELL, WELL, IF IT AIN'T BADD!
DON'T TELL ME YOU SMASHED THAT SWORD OF YOURS AGAIN?
JUST ABOUT. CAN YOU FIX IT?

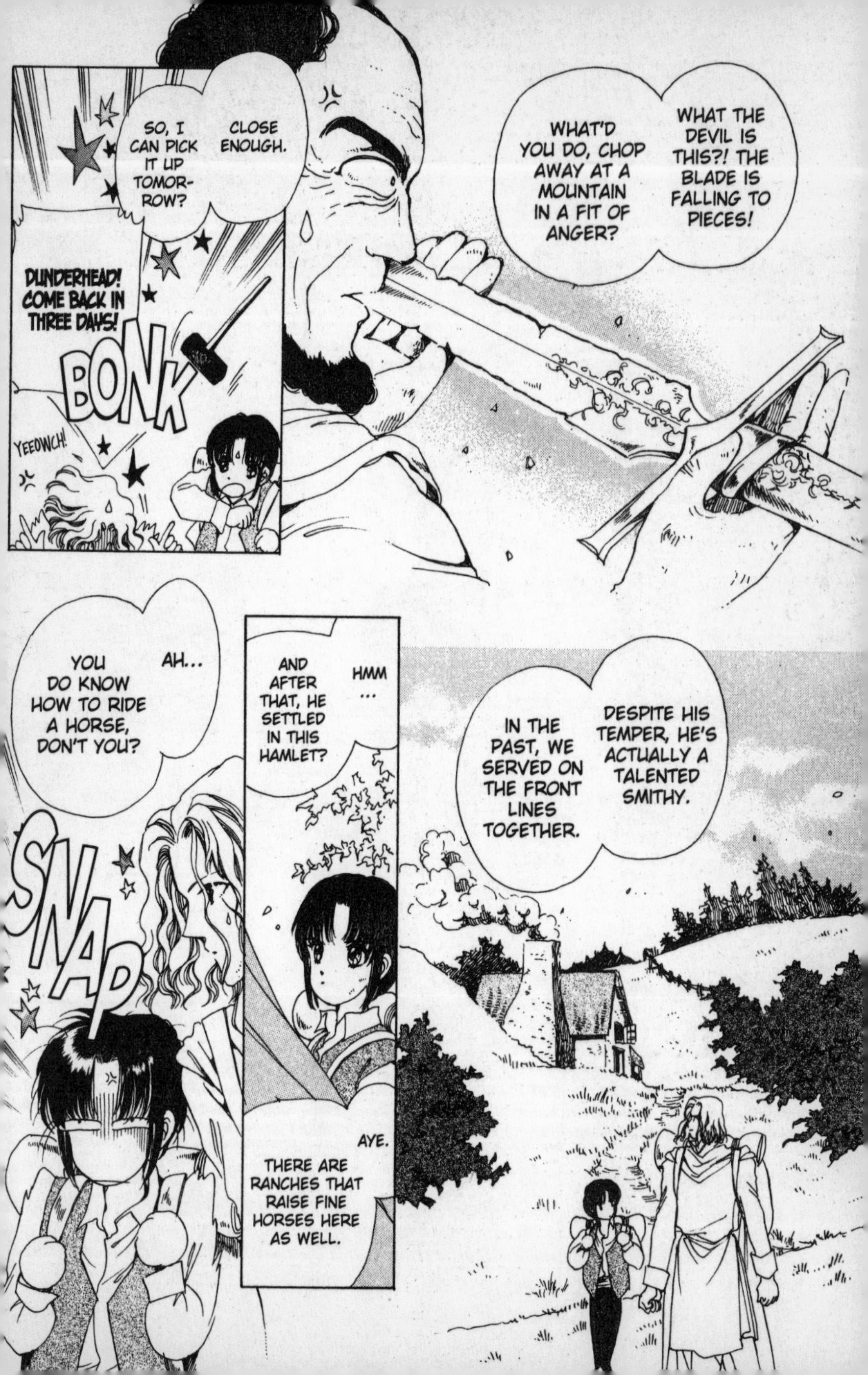
WHAT THE DEVIL IS THIS?! THE BLADE IS FALLING TO PIECES!
WHAT'D YOU DO, CHOP AWAY AT A MOUNTAIN IN A FIT OF ANGER?
CLOSE ENOUGH.
SO, I CAN PICK IT UP TOMORROW?
DUNDERHEAD! COME BACK IN THREE DAYS!
BONK
YEEOWCH!
DESPITE HIS TEMPER, HE'S ACTUALLY A TALENTED SMITHY.
IN THE PAST, WE SERVED ON THE FRONT LINES TOGETHER.
HMM ...
AND AFTER THAT, HE SETTLED IN THIS HAMLET?
AYE.
THERE ARE RANCHES THAT RAISE FINE HORSES HERE AS WELL.
AH...
YOU DO KNOW HOW TO RIDE A HORSE, DON'T YOU?
SNAP

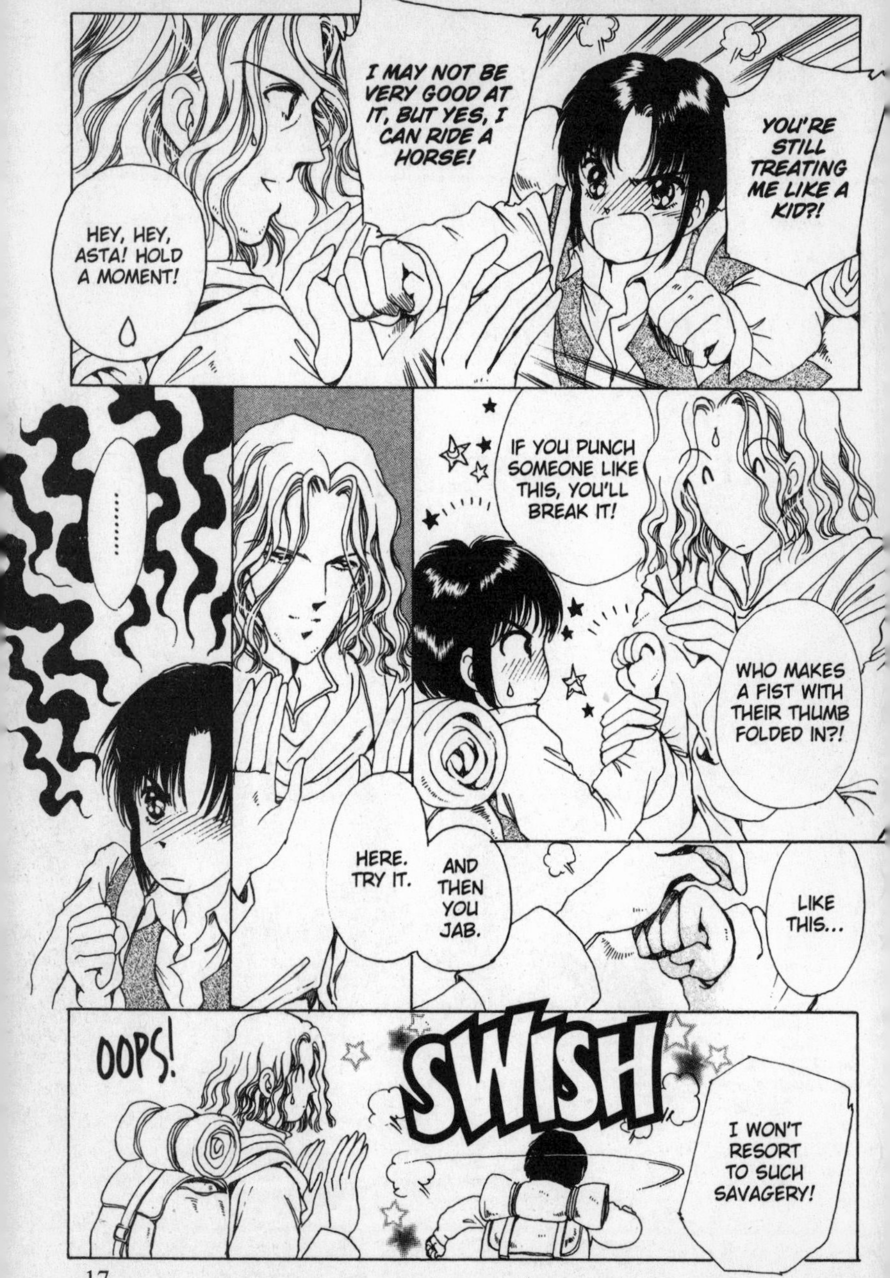
YOU'RE STILL TREATING ME LIKE A KID?!
I MAY NOT BE VERY GOOD AT IT, BUT YES, I CAN RIDE A HORSE!
HEY, HEY, ASTA! HOLD A MOMENT!
IF YOU PUNCH SOMEONE LIKE THIS, YOU'LL BREAK IT!
WHO MAKES A FIST WITH THEIR THUMB FOLDED IN?!
LIKE THIS...
AND THEN YOU JAB.
HERE. TRY IT.
......
I WON'T RESORT TO SUCH SAVAGERY!
SWISH
OOPS!

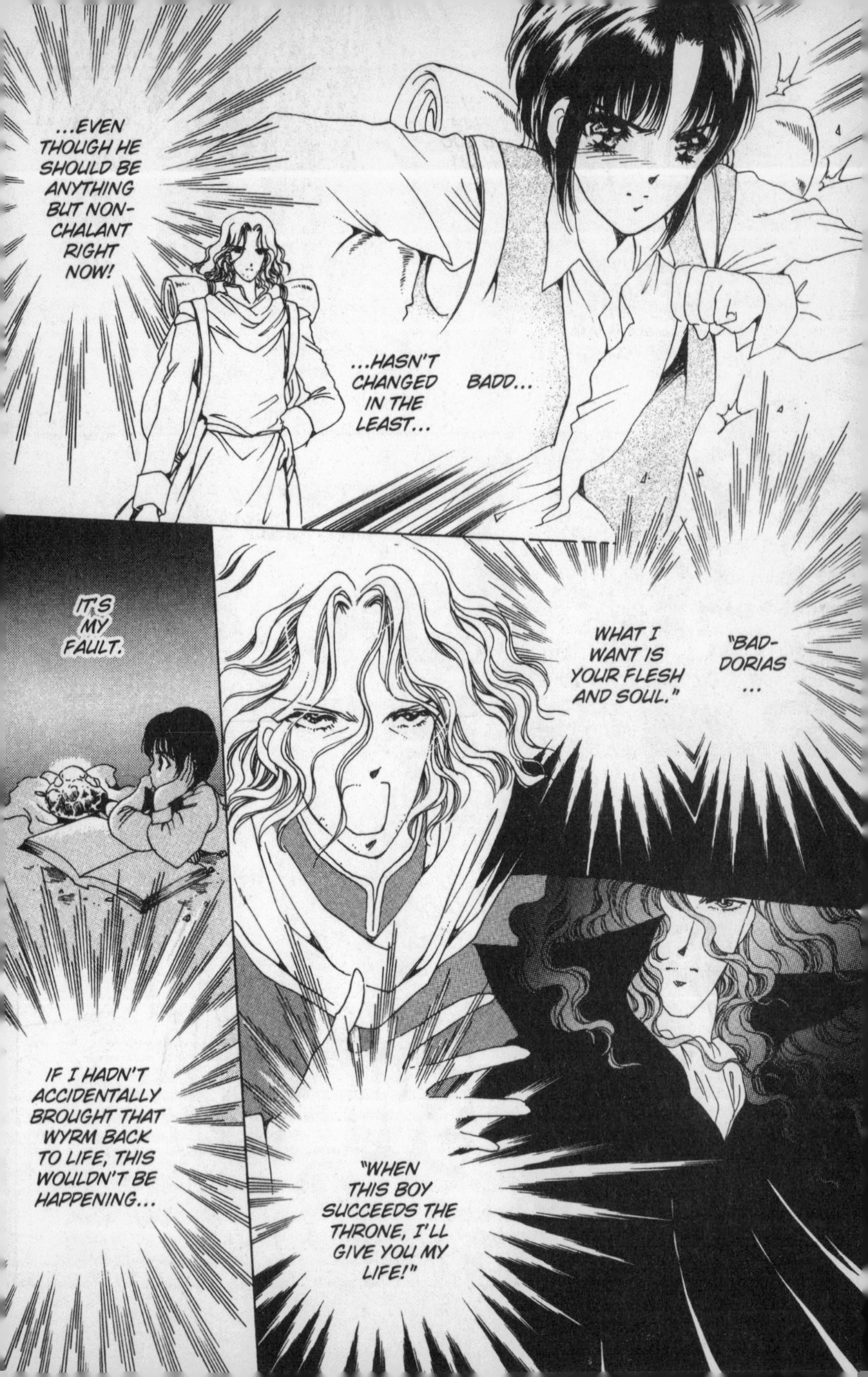
BADD...
...HASN'T CHANGED IN THE LEAST...
...EVEN THOUGH HE SHOULD BE ANYTHING BUT NON-CHALANT RIGHT NOW!
"BAD-DORIAS ...
WHAT I WANT IS YOUR FLESH AND SOUL."
"WHEN THIS BOY SUCCEEDS THE THRONE, I'LL GIVE YOU MY LIFE!"
IT'S MY FAULT.
IF I HADN'T ACCIDENTALLY BROUGHT THAT WYRM BACK TO LIFE, THIS WOULDN'T BE HAPPENING...

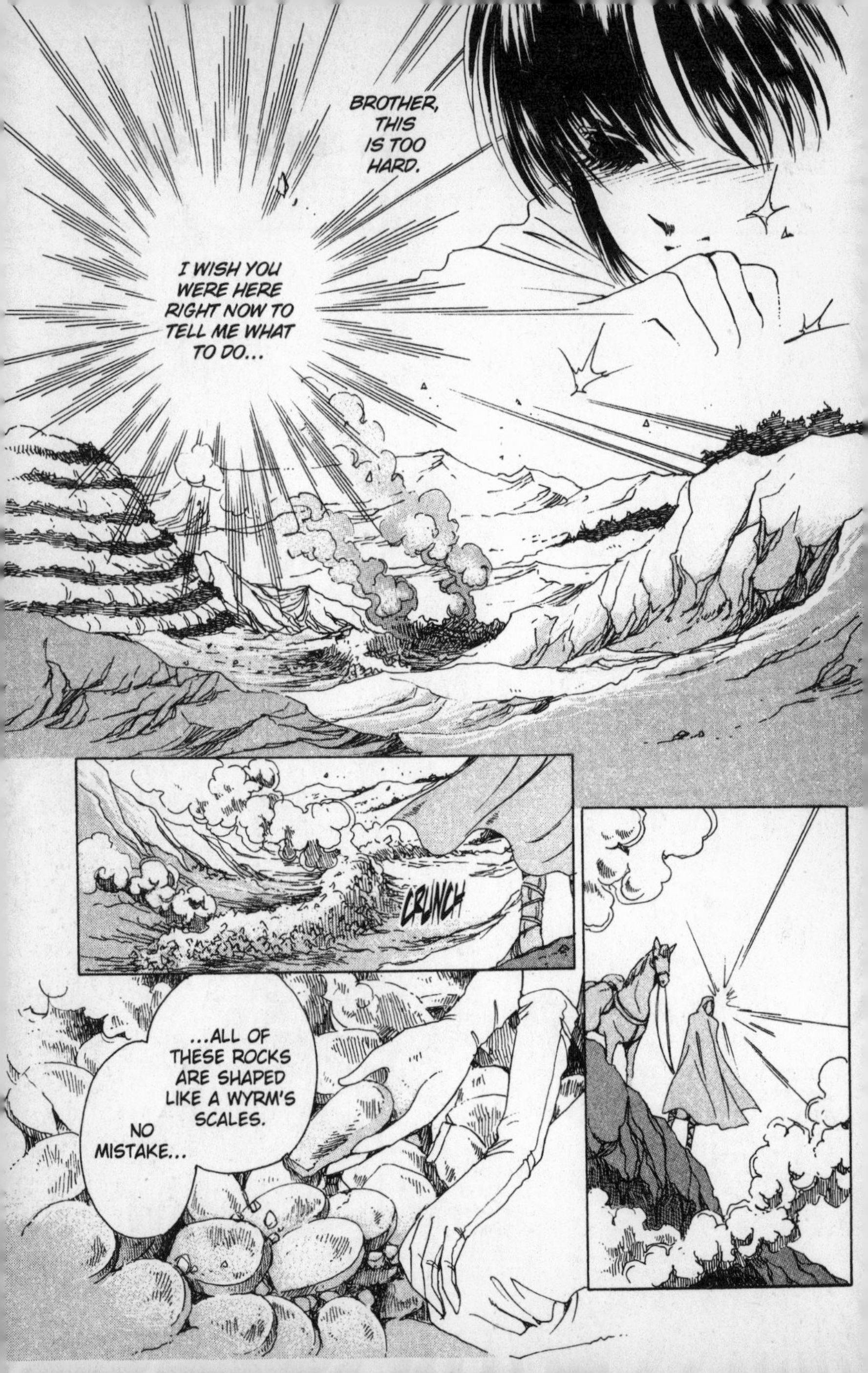
BROTHER, THIS IS TOO HARD.
I WISH YOU WERE HERE RIGHT NOW TO TELL ME WHAT TO DO...
CRUNCH
...ALL OF THESE ROCKS ARE SHAPED LIKE A WYRM'S SCALES.
NO MISTAKE...

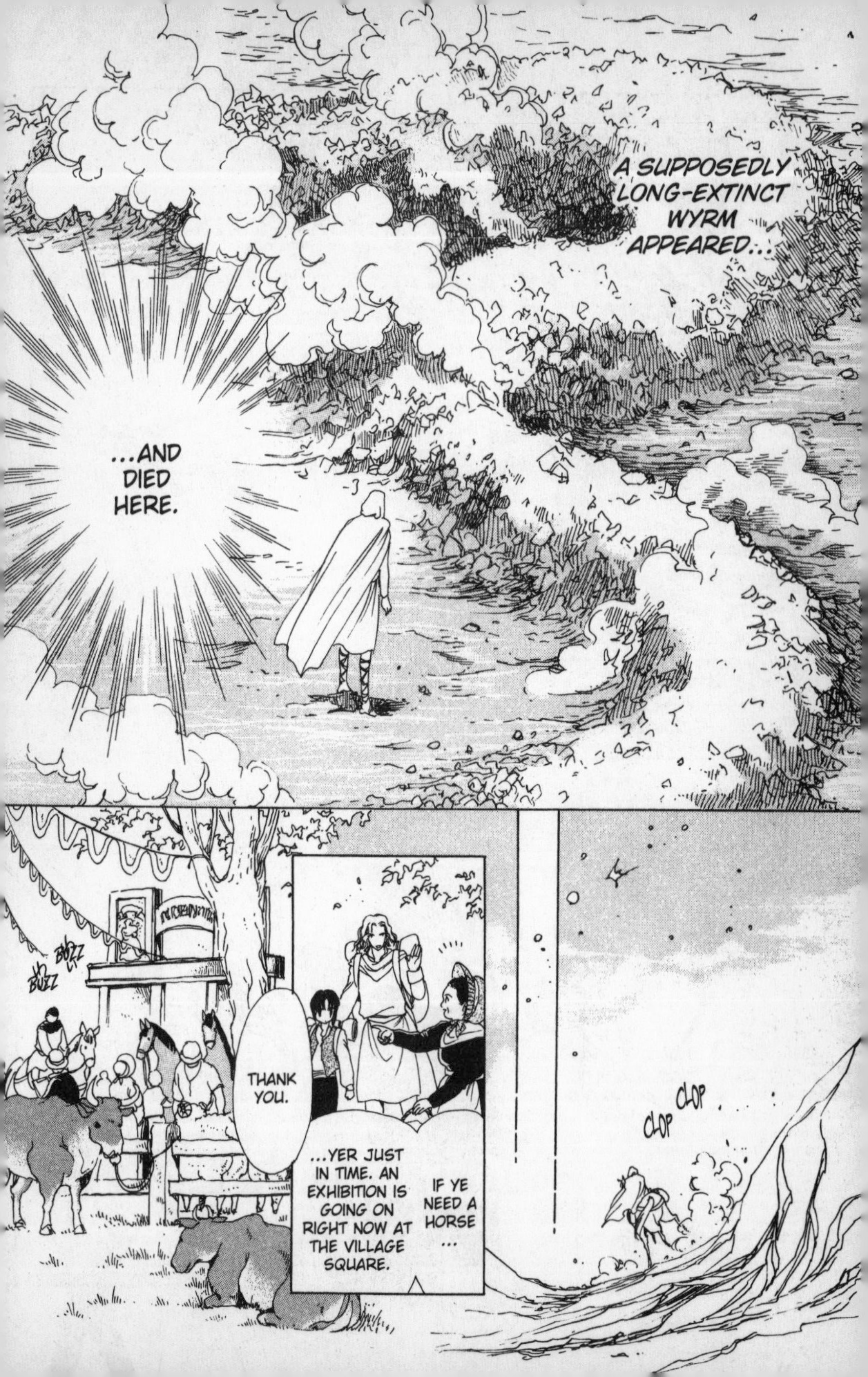
A SUPPOSEDLY LONG-EXTINCT WYRM APPEARED...
...AND DIED HERE.
CLOP
CLOP
IF YE NEED A HORSE ...
...YER JUST IN TIME. AN EXHIBITION IS GOING ON RIGHT NOW AT THE VILLAGE SQUARE.
THANK YOU.
BUZZ
BUZZ

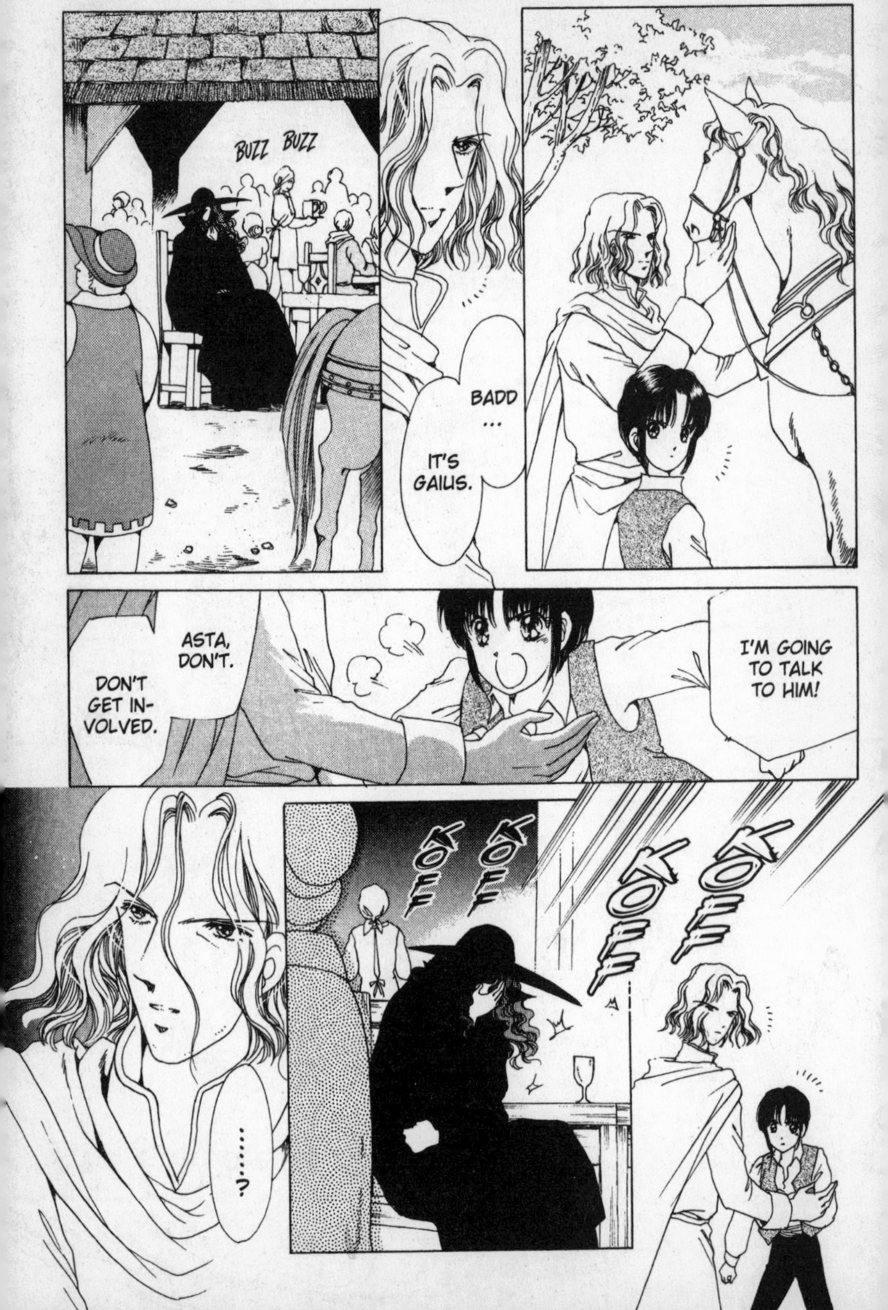
BADD ...
IT'S GAIUS.
BUZZ BUZZ
I'M GOING TO TALK TO HIM!
ASTA, DON'T.
DON'T GET IN-VOLVED.
KOFF KOFF
KOFF KOFF
......?

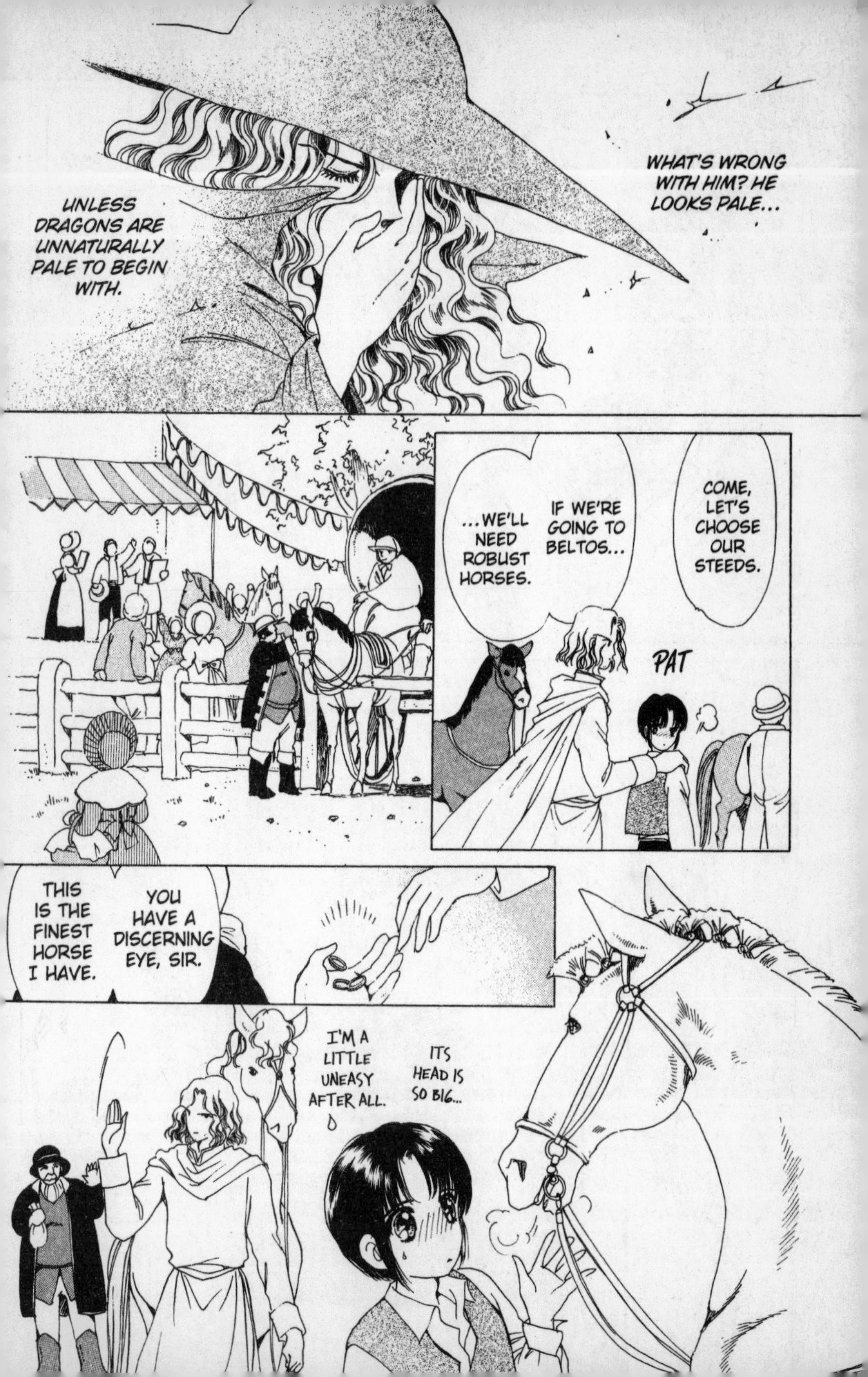
WHAT'S WRONG WITH HIM? HE LOOKS PALE...
UNLESS DRAGONS ARE UNNATURALLY PALE TO BEGIN WITH.
COME, LET'S CHOOSE OUR STEEDS.
IF WE'RE GOING TO BELTOS...
...WE'LL NEED ROBUST HORSES.
PAT
YOU HAVE A DISCERNING EYE, SIR.
THIS IS THE FINEST HORSE I HAVE.
ITS HEAD IS SO BIG...
I'M A LITTLE UNEASY AFTER ALL.

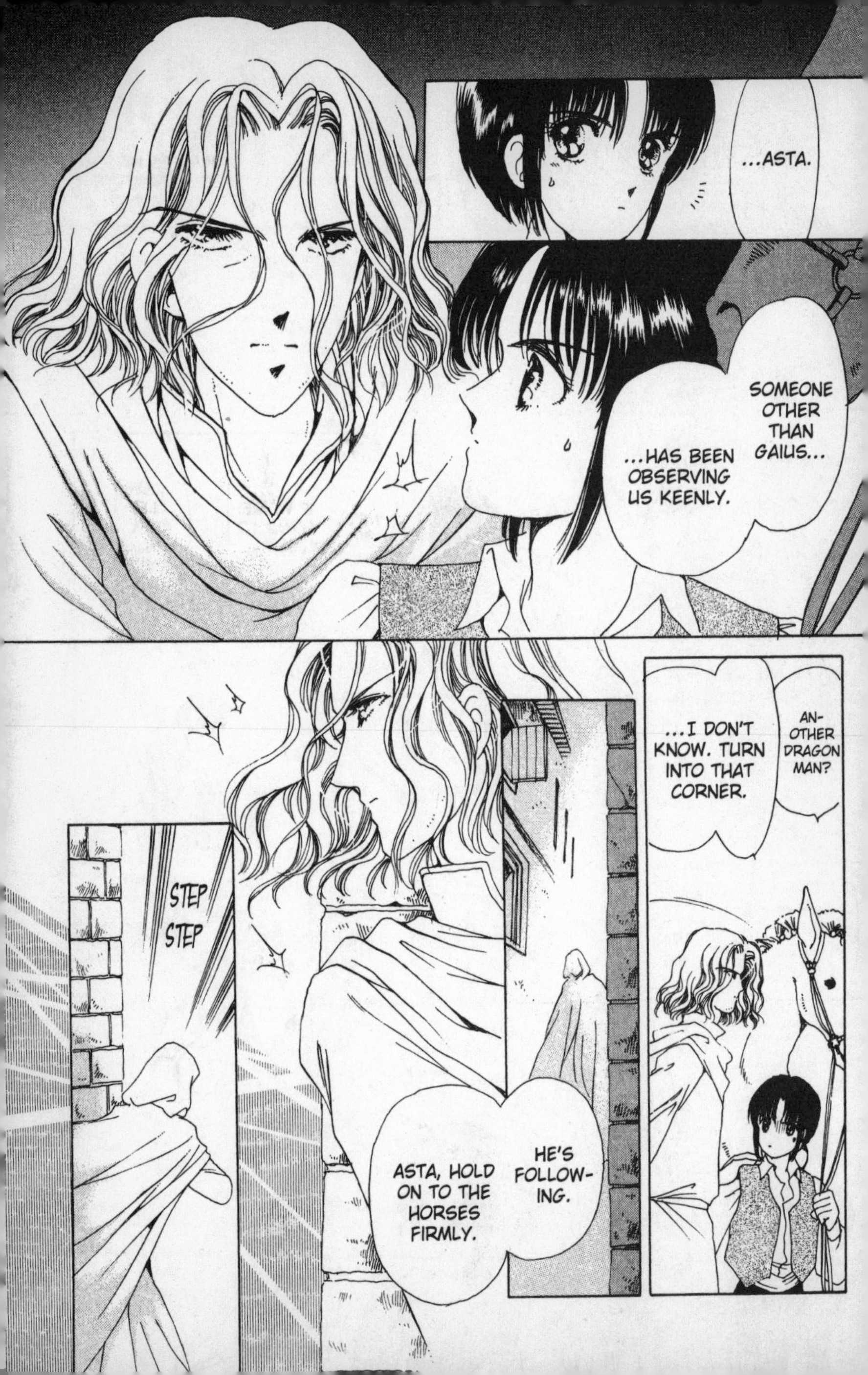
...ASTA.
SOMEONE OTHER THAN GAIUS...
...HAS BEEN OBSERVING US KEENLY.
AN-OTHER DRAGON MAN?
...I DON'T KNOW. TURN INTO THAT CORNER.
HE'S FOLLOW-ING.
ASTA, HOLD ON TO THE HORSES FIRMLY.
STEP STEP

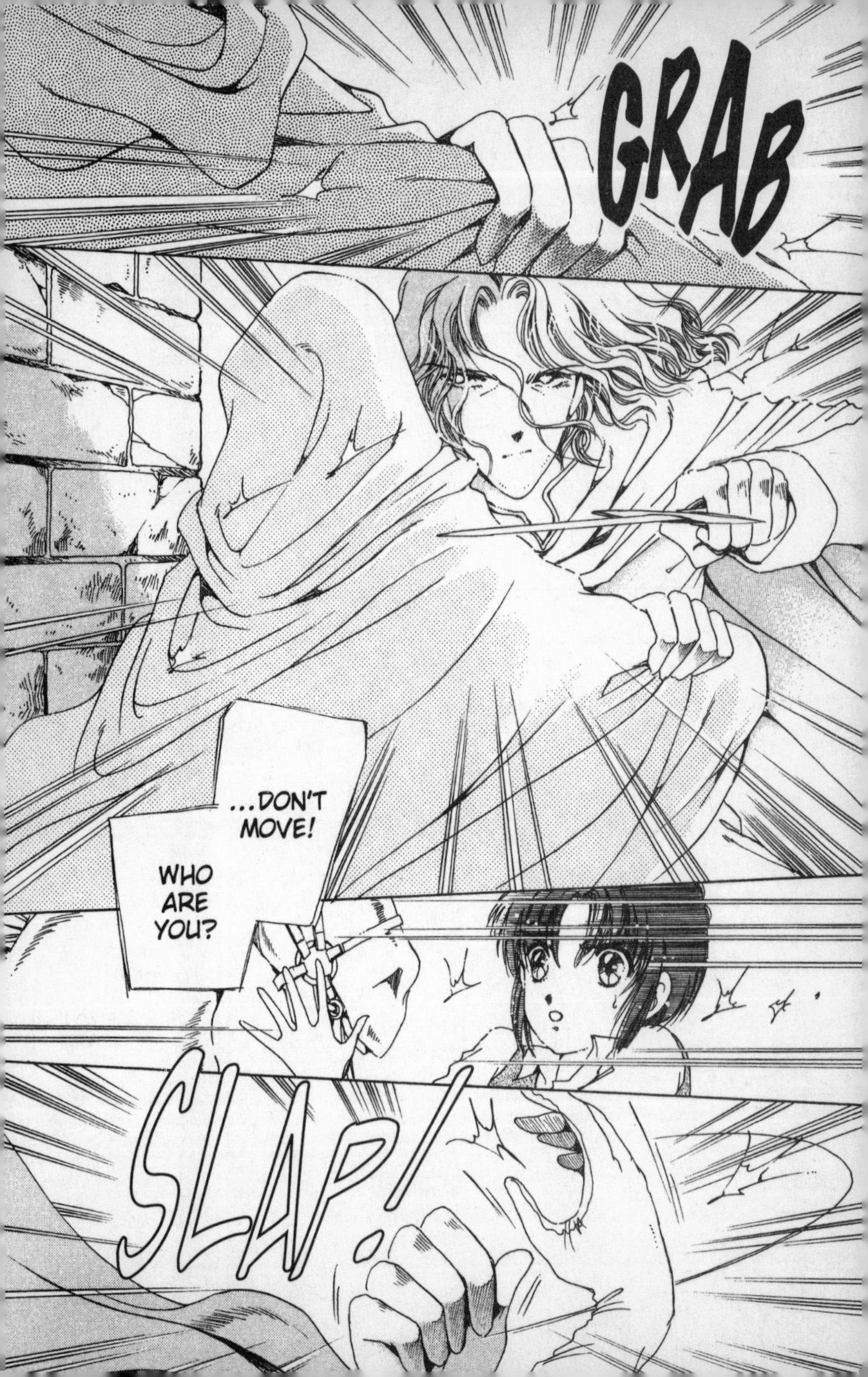
GRAB
...DON'T MOVE!
WHO ARE YOU?
SLAP!

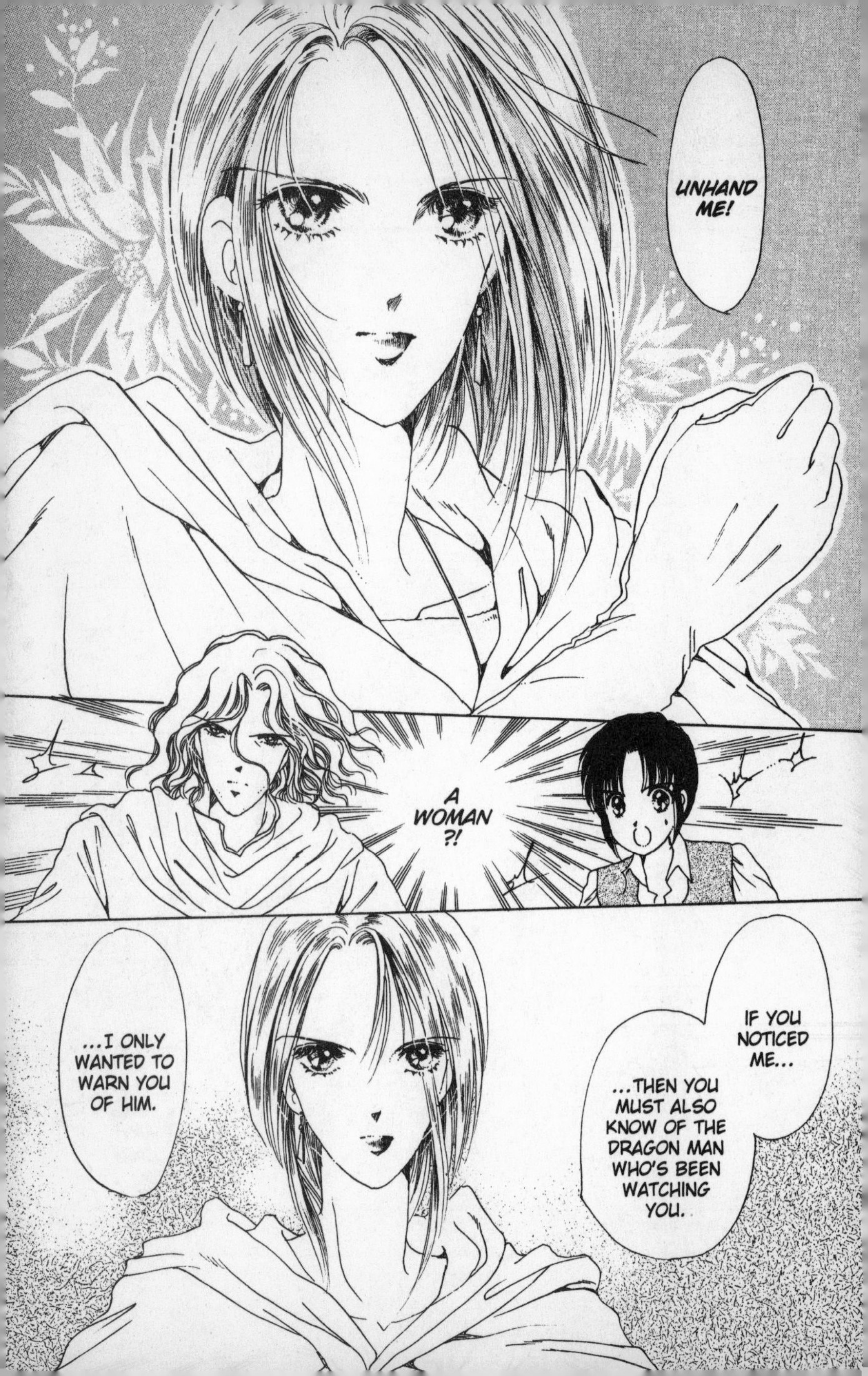
UNHAND ME!
A WOMAN?!
IF YOU NOTICED ME...
...THEN YOU MUST ALSO KNOW OF THE DRAGON MAN WHO'S BEEN WATCHING YOU.
...I ONLY WANTED TO WARN YOU OF HIM.

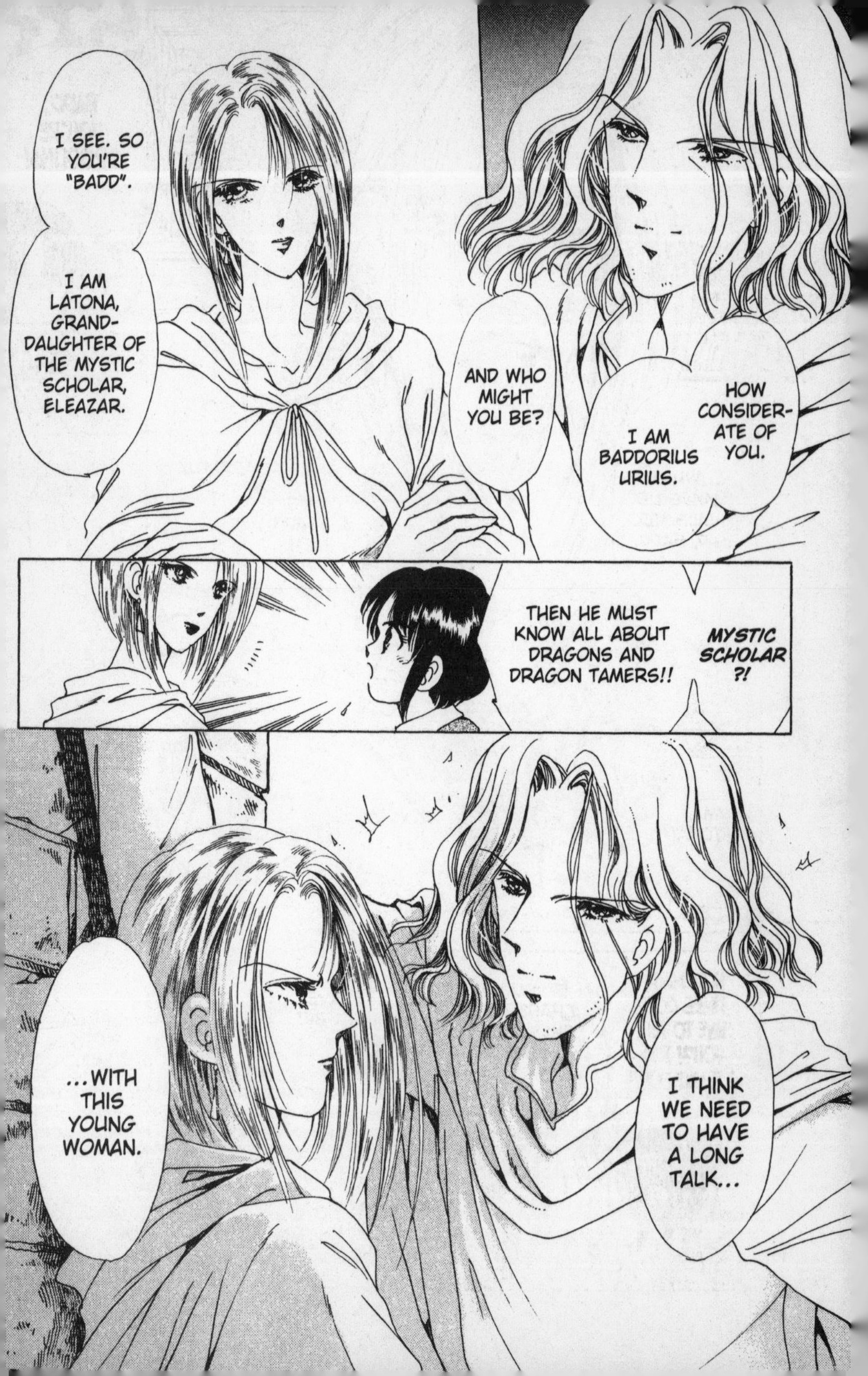
HOW CONSIDERATE OF YOU.
I AM BADDORIUS URIUS.
AND WHO MIGHT YOU BE?
I SEE. SO YOU'RE "BADD".
I AM LATONA, GRAND-DAUGHTER OF THE MYSTIC SCHOLAR, ELEAZAR.
MYSTIC SCHOLAR ?!
THEN HE MUST KNOW ALL ABOUT DRAGONS AND DRAGON TAMERS!!
I THINK WE NEED TO HAVE A LONG TALK...
...WITH THIS YOUNG WOMAN.

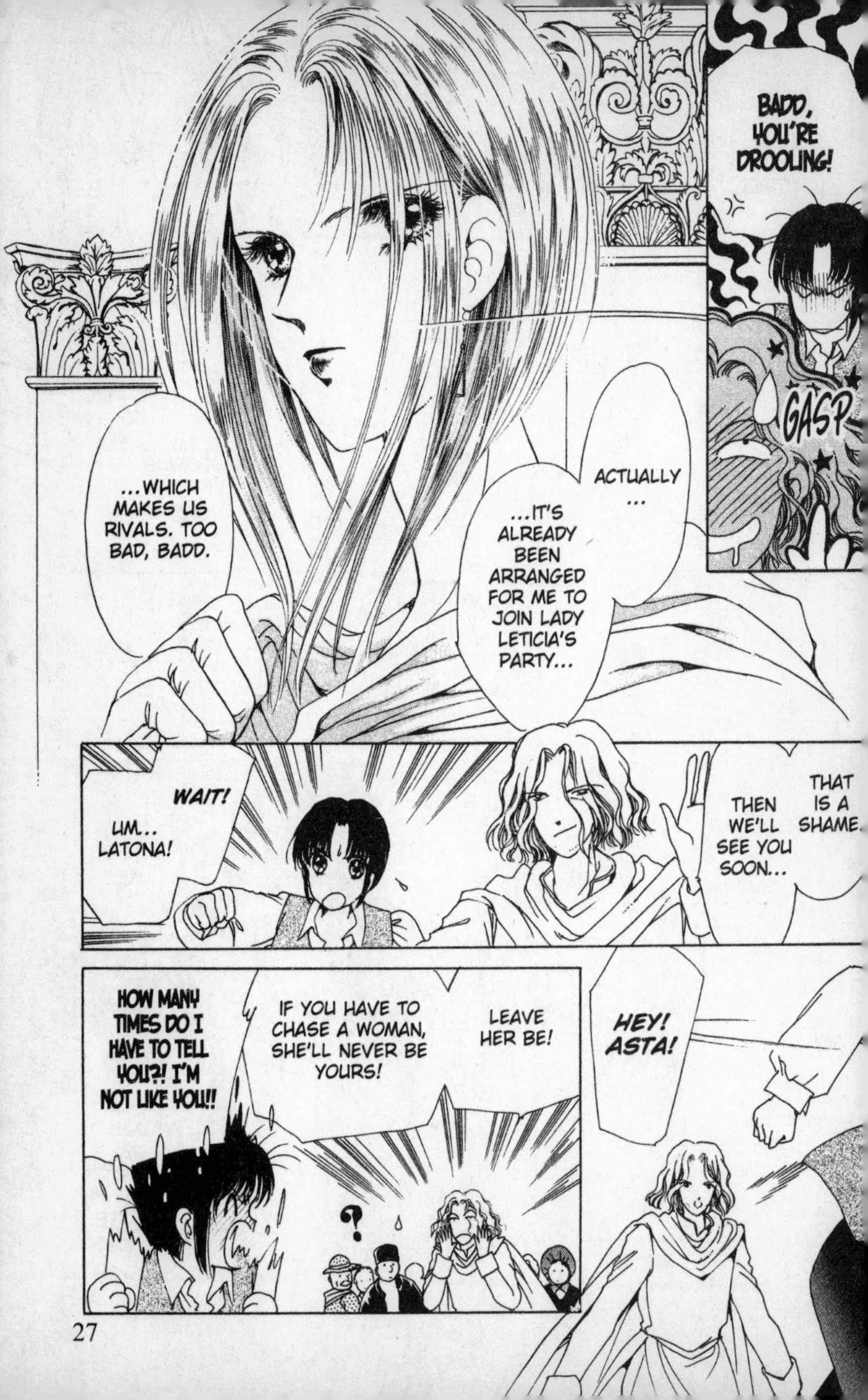
BADD, YOU'RE DROOLING!
GASP
ACTUALLY...
...IT'S ALREADY BEEN ARRANGED FOR ME TO JOIN LADY LETICIA'S PARTY...
...WHICH MAKES US RIVALS. TOO BAD, BADD.
THAT IS A SHAME.
THEN WE'LL SEE YOU SOON...
WAIT!
UM... LATONA!
HEY! ASTA!
LEAVE HER BE!
IF YOU HAVE TO CHASE A WOMAN, SHE'LL NEVER BE YOURS!
HOW MANY TIMES DO I HAVE TO TELL YOU?! I'M NOT LIKE YOU!!

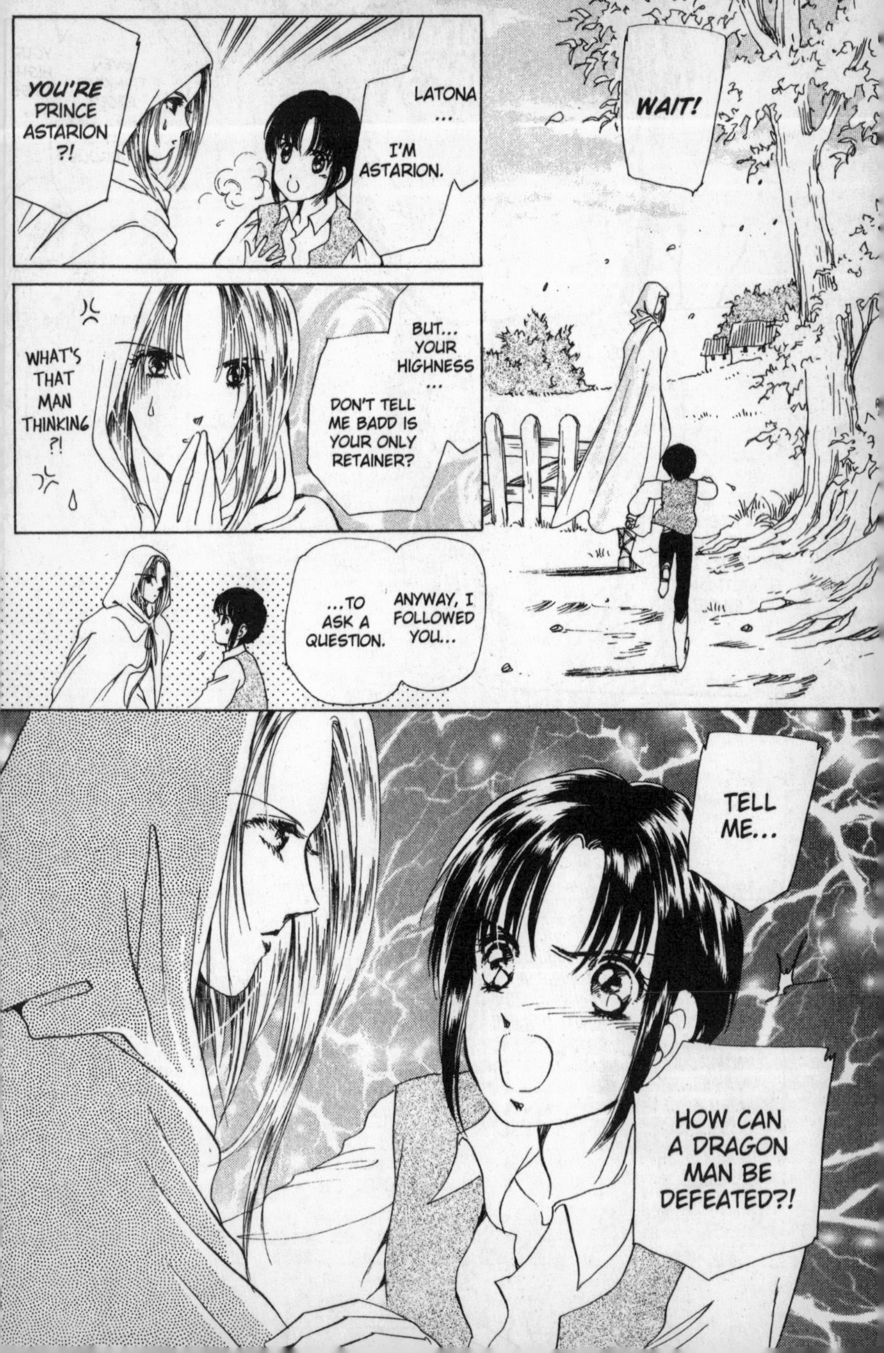
WAIT!
LATONA ... I'M ASTARION.
YOU'RE PRINCE ASTARION?!
BUT... YOUR HIGHNESS ... DON'T TELL ME BADD IS YOUR ONLY RETAINER?
WHAT'S THAT MAN THINKING?!
ANYWAY, I FOLLOWED YOU... ...TO ASK A QUESTION.
TELL ME...
HOW CAN A DRAGON MAN BE DEFEATED?!

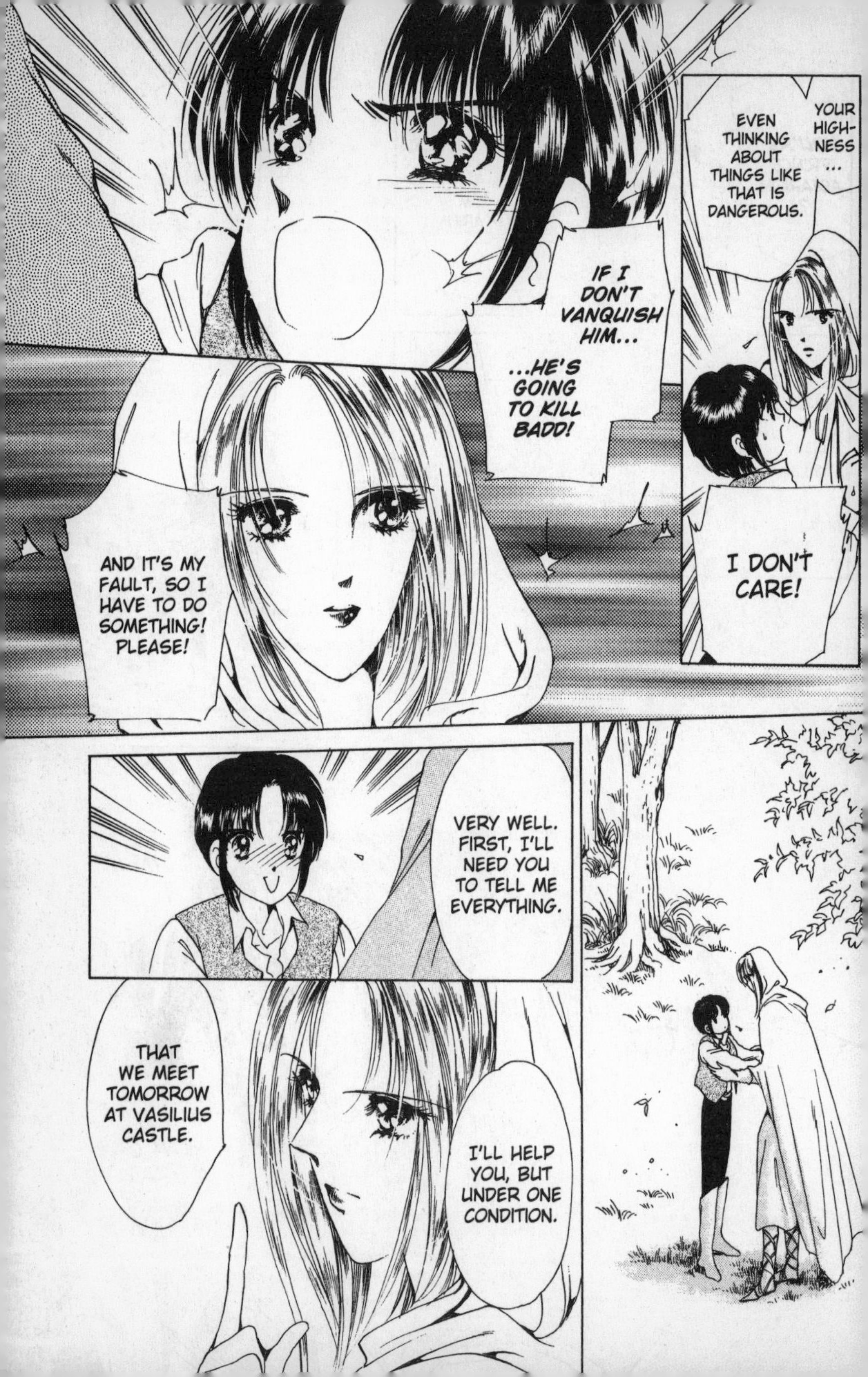
YOUR HIGHNESS...
EVEN THINKING ABOUT THINGS LIKE THAT IS DANGEROUS.
I DON'T CARE!
IF I DON'T VANQUISH HIM...
...HE'S GOING TO KILL BADD!
AND IT'S MY FAULT, SO I HAVE TO DO SOMETHING! PLEASE!
VERY WELL. FIRST, I'LL NEED YOU TO TELL ME EVERYTHING.
I'LL HELP YOU, BUT UNDER ONE CONDITION.
THAT WE MEET TOMORROW AT VASILIUS CASTLE.

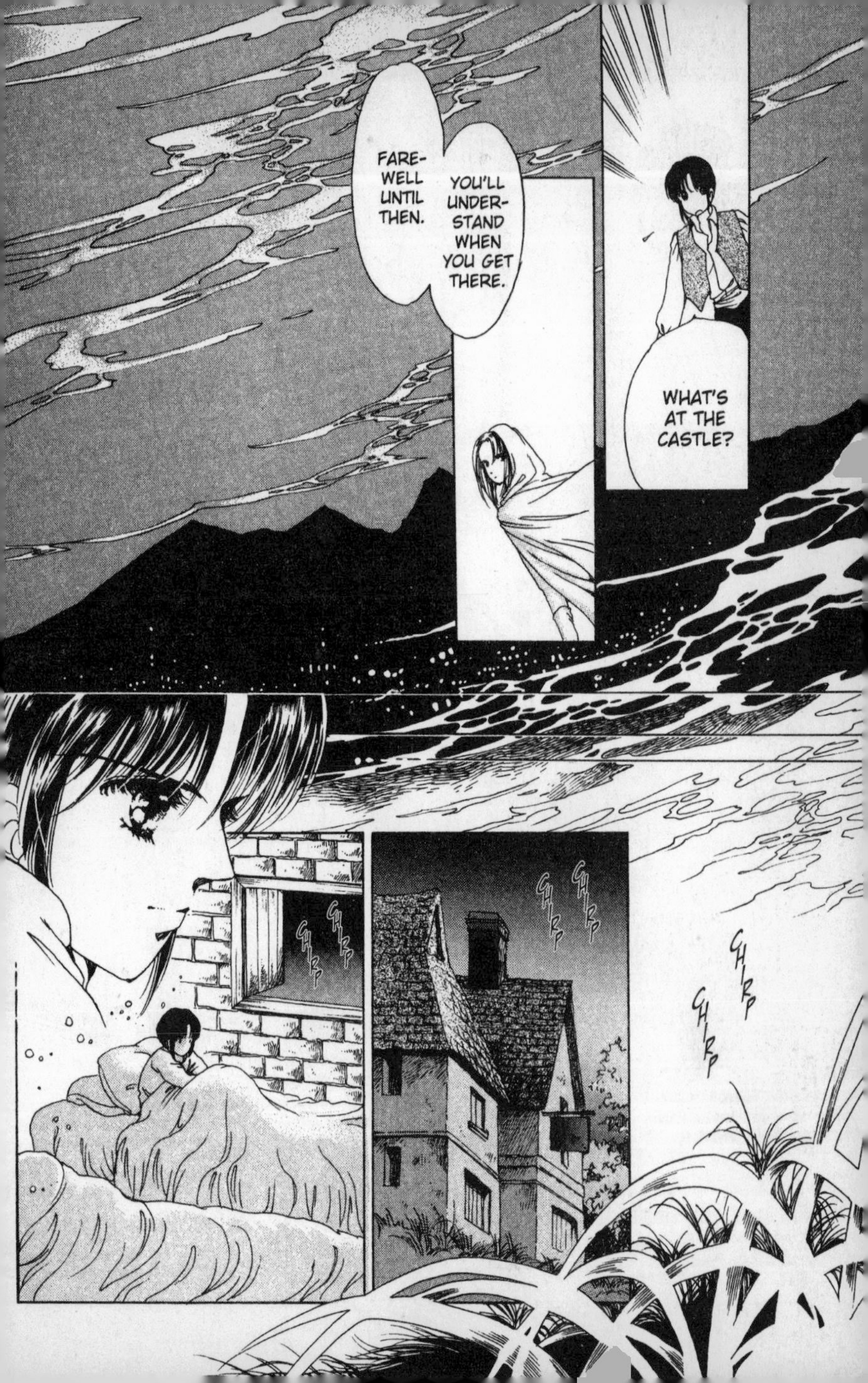
WHAT'S AT THE CASTLE?
YOU'LL UNDER-STAND WHEN YOU GET THERE.
FARE-WELL UNTIL THEN.
CHIRP CHIRP
CHIRP CHIRP
CHIRP CHIRP

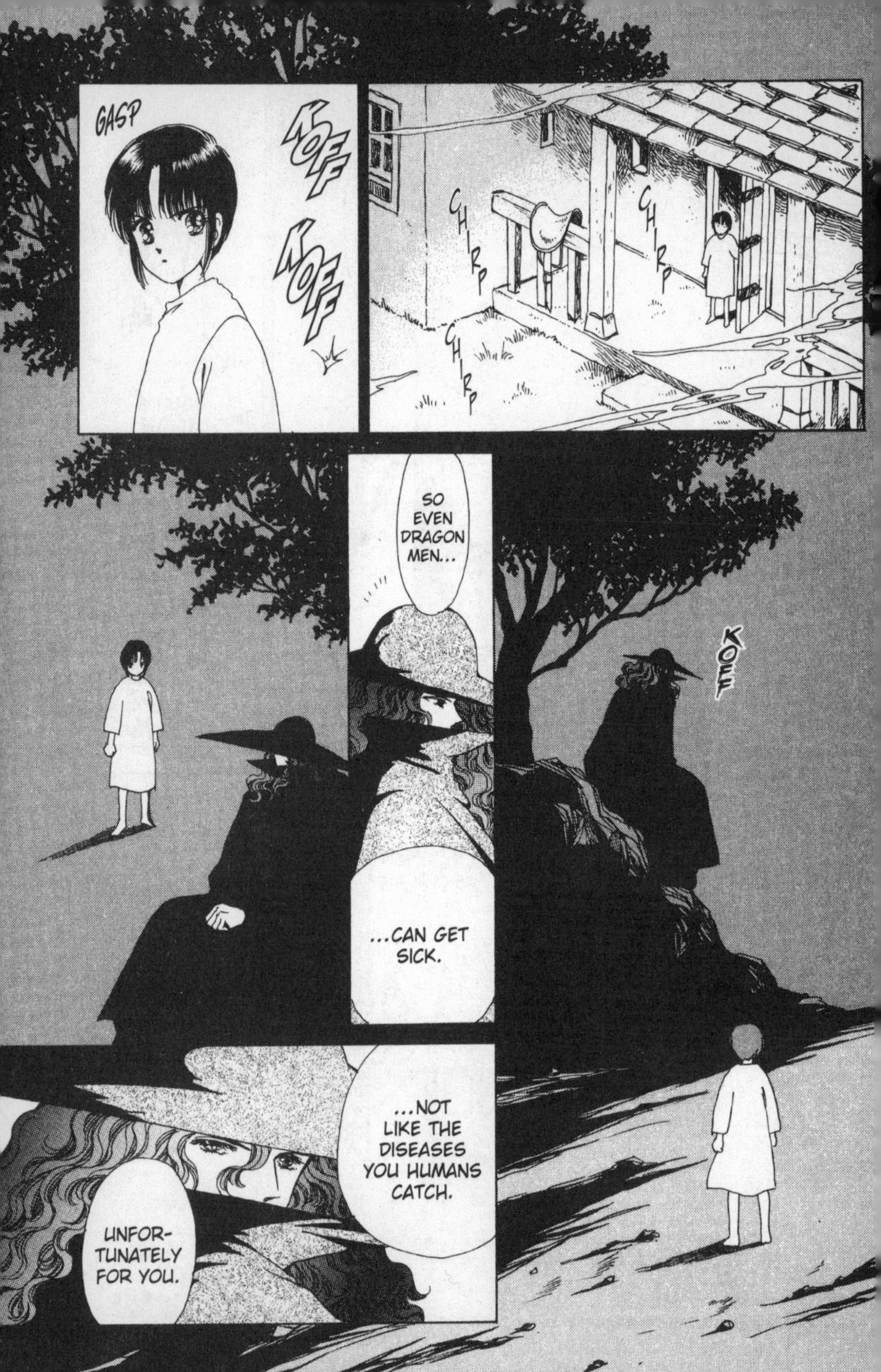
CHIRP
CHIRP
CHIRP
GASP
KOFF
KOFF
KOFF
SO EVEN DRAGON MEN...
...CAN GET SICK.
...NOT LIKE THE DISEASES YOU HUMANS CATCH.
UNFOR-TUNATELY FOR YOU.

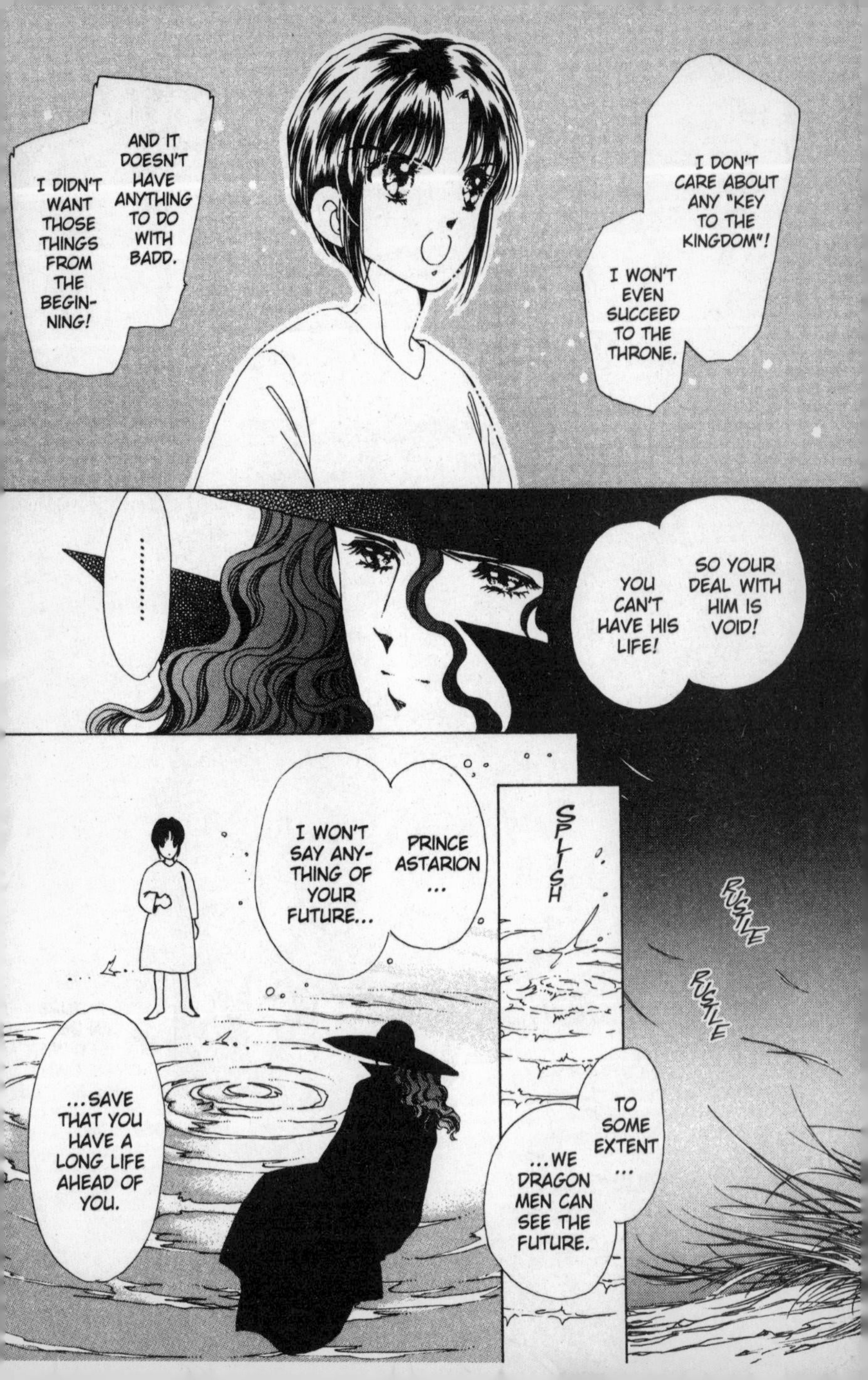
I DON'T CARE ABOUT ANY "KEY TO THE KINGDOM"!
I WON'T EVEN SUCCEED TO THE THRONE.
AND IT DOESN'T HAVE ANYTHING TO DO WITH BADD.
I DIDN'T WANT THOSE THINGS FROM THE BEGINNING!
SO YOUR DEAL WITH HIM IS VOID!
YOU CAN'T HAVE HIS LIFE!
......
RUSTLE
RUSTLE
SPLISH
TO SOME EXTENT ...
...WE DRAGON MEN CAN SEE THE FUTURE.
PRINCE ASTARION ...
I WON'T SAY ANYTHING OF YOUR FUTURE...
...SAVE THAT YOU HAVE A LONG LIFE AHEAD OF YOU.

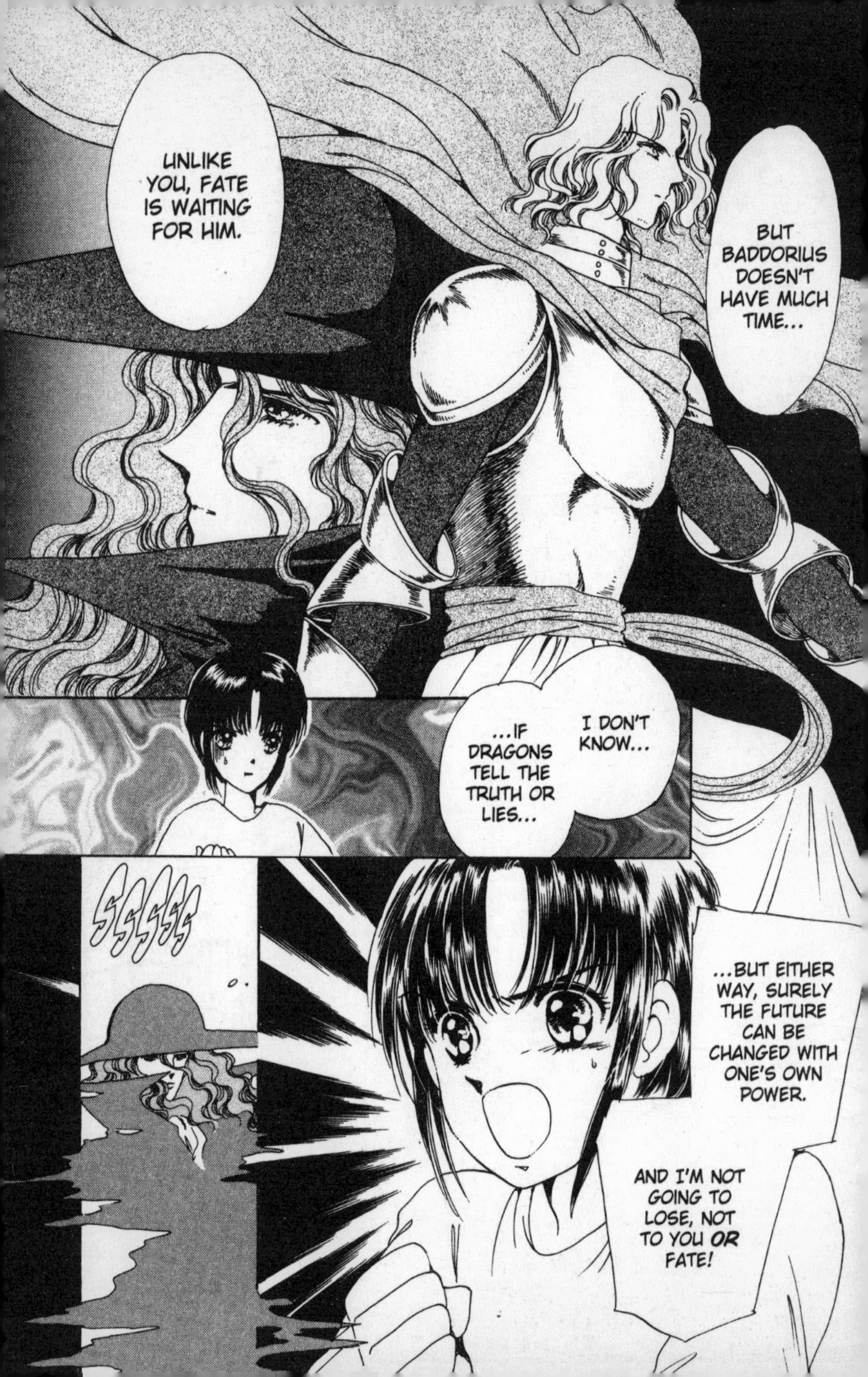
BUT BADDORIUS DOESN'T HAVE MUCH TIME...
UNLIKE YOU, FATE IS WAITING FOR HIM.
I DON'T KNOW...
...IF DRAGONS TELL THE TRUTH OR LIES...
...BUT EITHER WAY, SURELY THE FUTURE CAN BE CHANGED WITH ONE'S OWN POWER.
AND I'M NOT GOING TO LOSE, NOT TO YOU ***OR*** FATE!
SSSSS

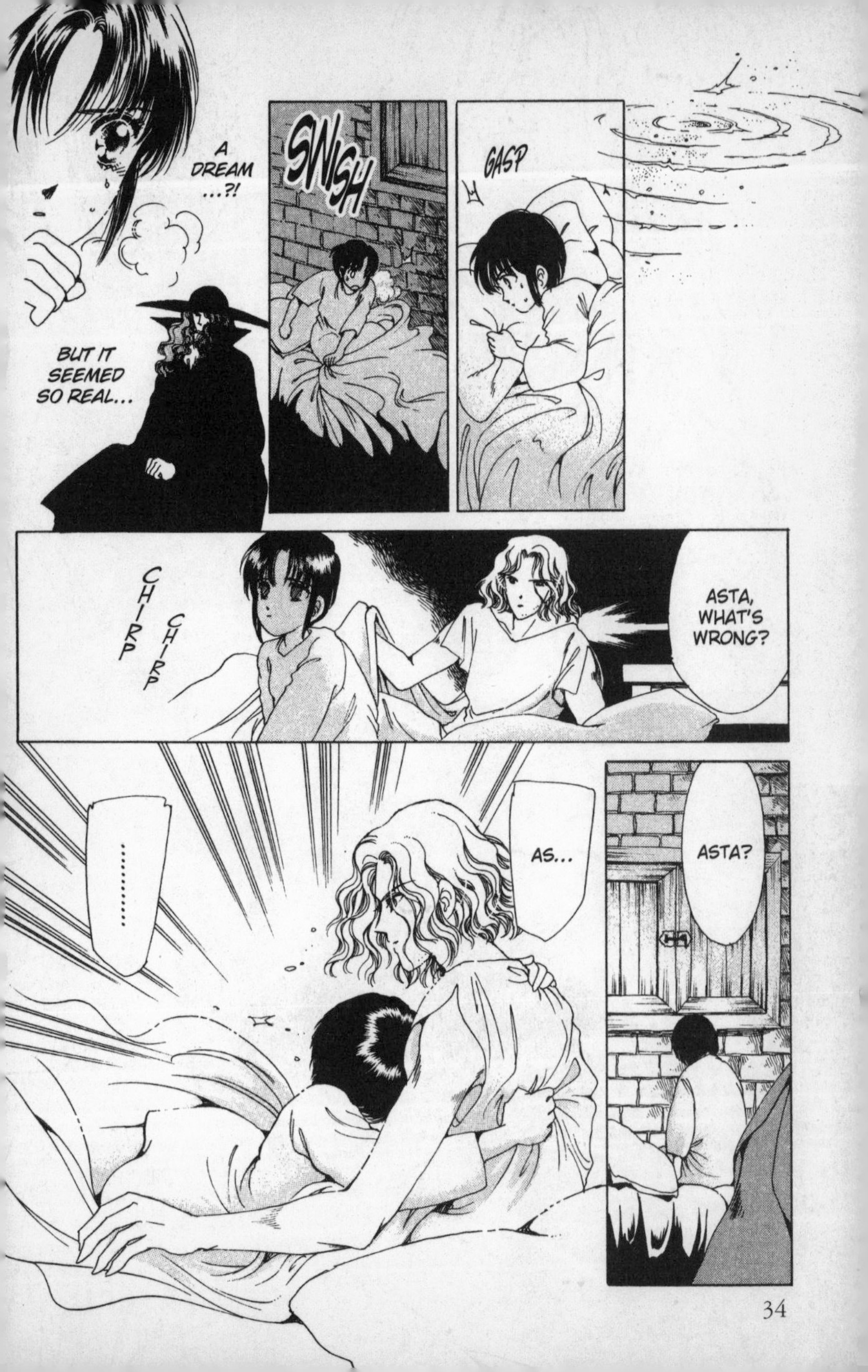
GASP
SWISH
A DREAM ...?!
BUT IT SEEMED SO REAL...
ASTA, WHAT'S WRONG?
CHIRP CHIRP
ASTA?
AS...
......

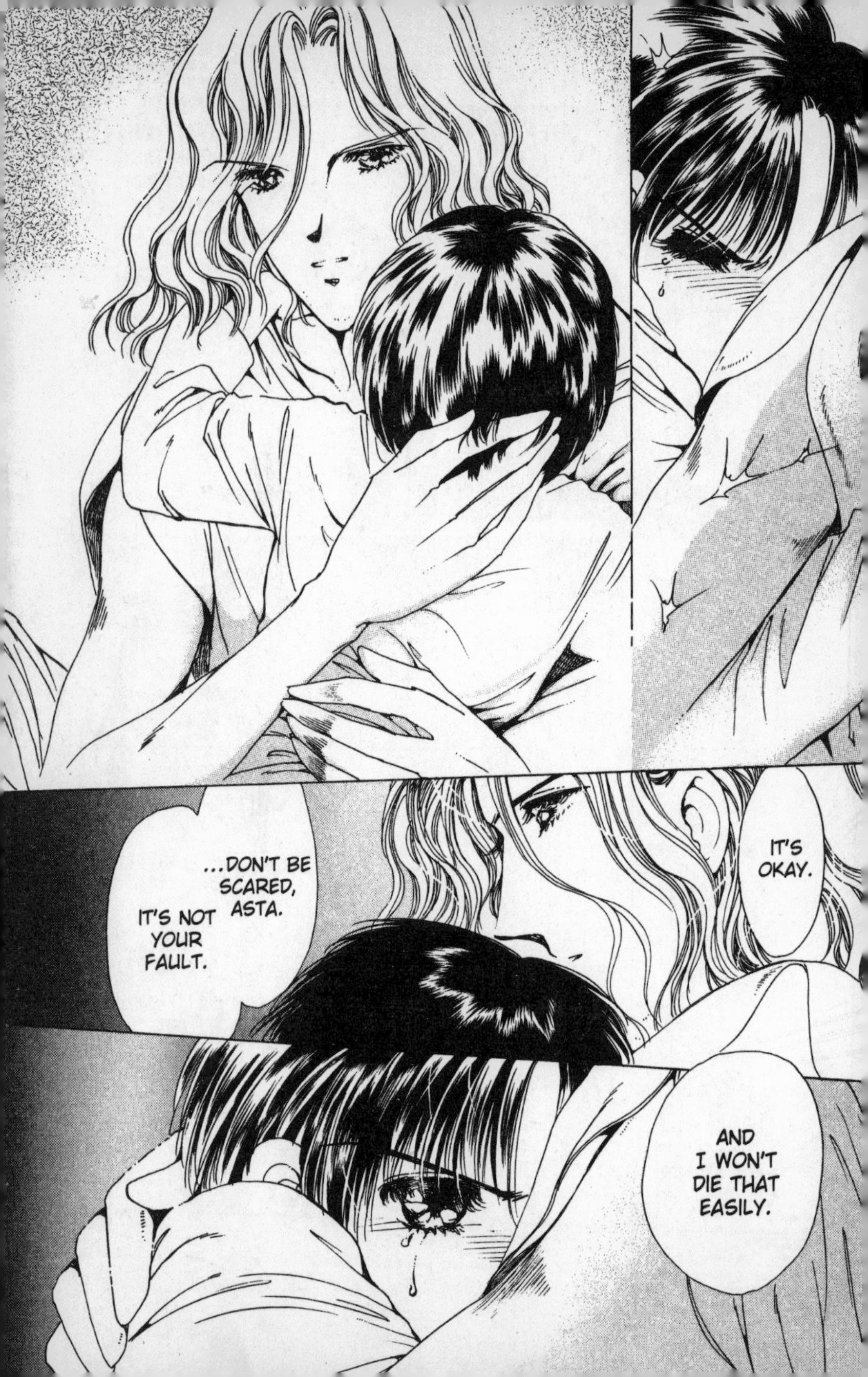
IT'S OKAY.
...DON'T BE SCARED, ASTA.
IT'S NOT YOUR FAULT.
AND I WON'T DIE THAT EASILY.

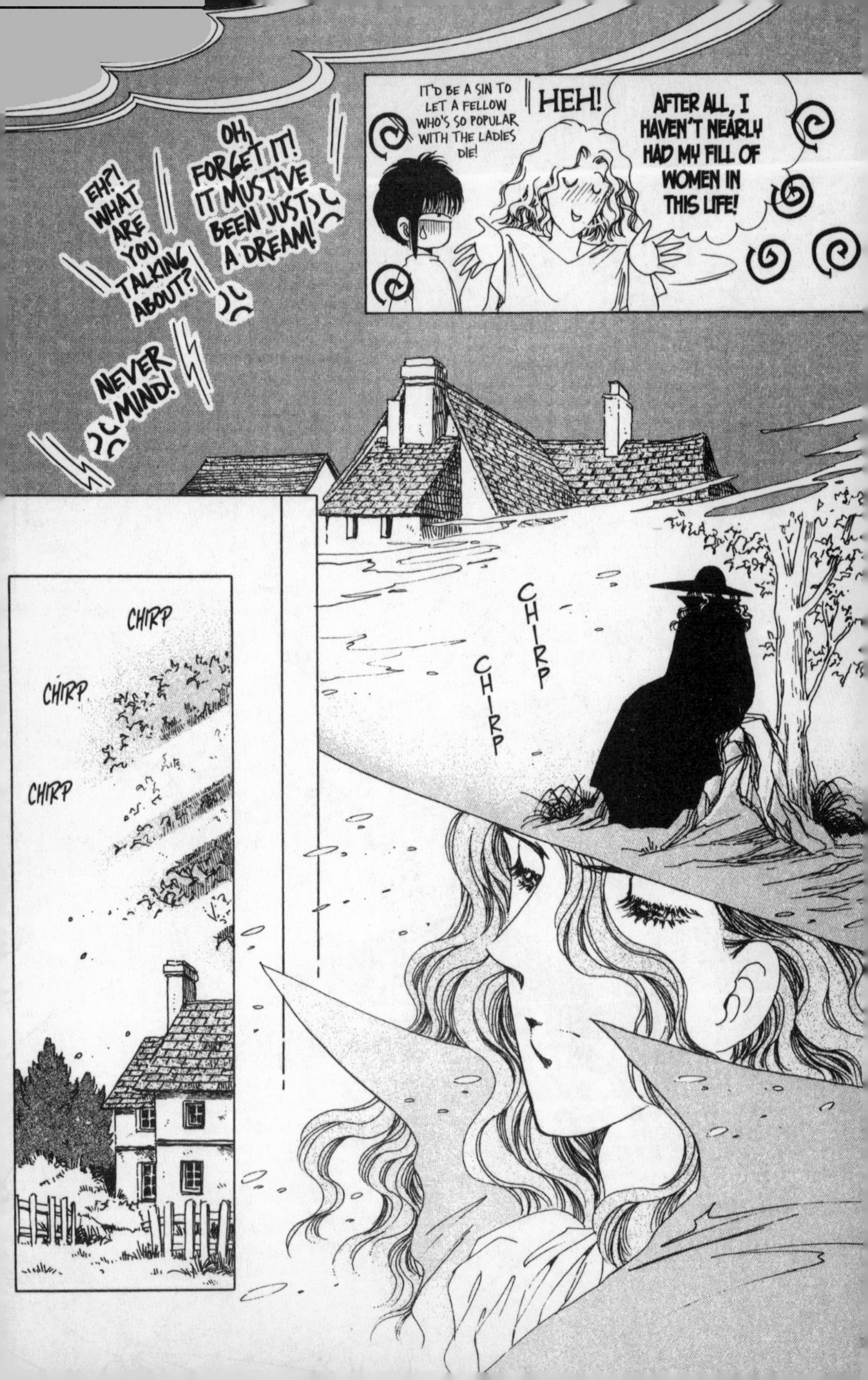
AFTER ALL, I HAVEN'T NEARLY HAD MY FILL OF WOMEN IN THIS LIFE!
HEH!
IT'D BE A SIN TO LET A FELLOW WHO'S SO POPULAR WITH THE LADIES DIE!
OH, FORGET IT! IT MUST'VE BEEN JUST A DREAM!
EH?! WHAT ARE YOU TALKING ABOUT?
NEVER MIND!
CHIRP
CHIRP
CHIRP
CHIRP
CHIRP

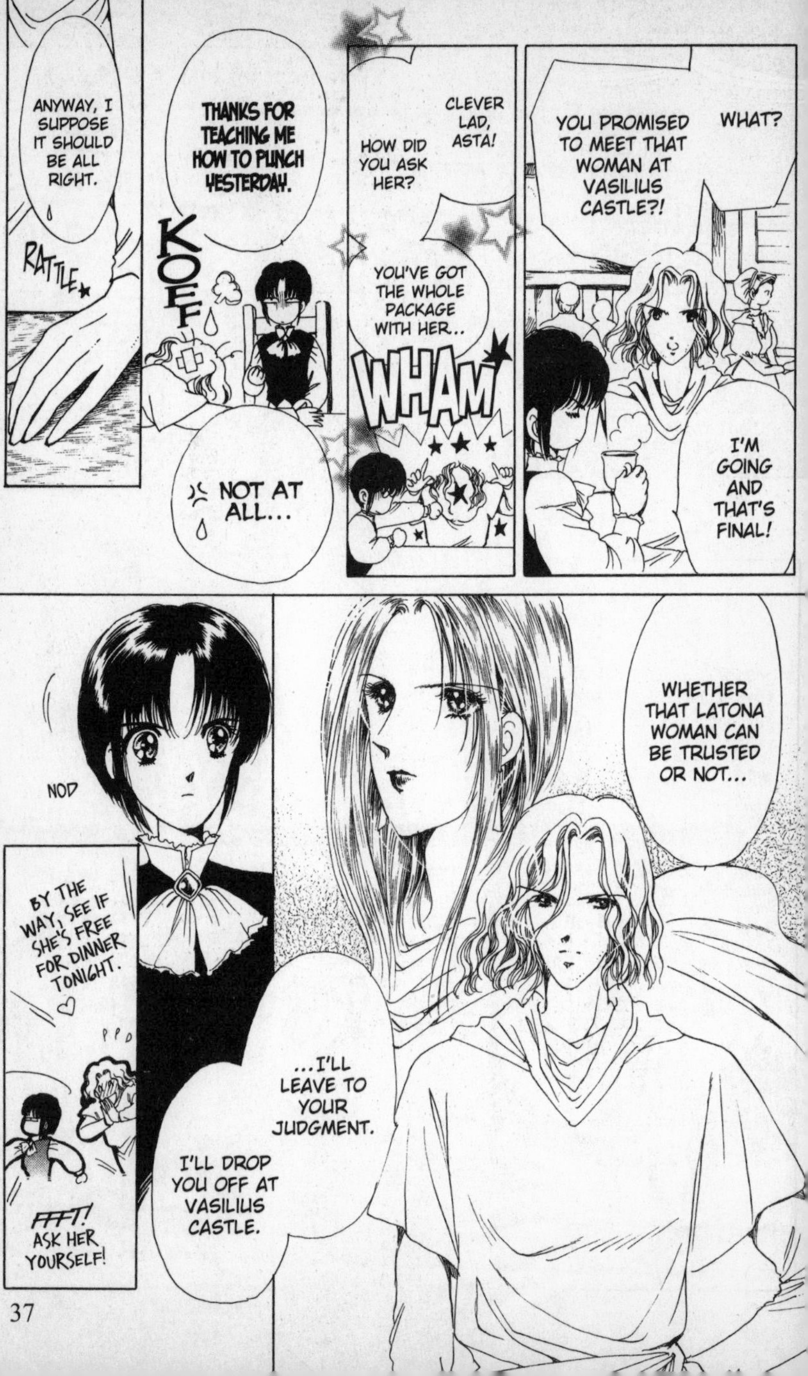
WHAT?
YOU PROMISED TO MEET THAT WOMAN AT VASILIUS CASTLE?!
I'M GOING AND THAT'S FINAL!
CLEVER LAD, ASTA!
HOW DID YOU ASK HER?
YOU'VE GOT THE WHOLE PACKAGE WITH HER..
WHAM
THANKS FOR TEACHING ME HOW TO PUNCH YESTERDAY.
KOFF
NOT AT ALL...
ANYWAY, I SUPPOSE IT SHOULD BE ALL RIGHT.
RATTLE
WHETHER THAT LATONA WOMAN CAN BE TRUSTED OR NOT...
...I'LL LEAVE TO YOUR JUDGMENT.
I'LL DROP YOU OFF AT VASILIUS CASTLE.
NOD
BY THE WAY, SEE IF SHE'S FREE FOR DINNER TONIGHT.
FFFT! ASK HER YOURSELF!

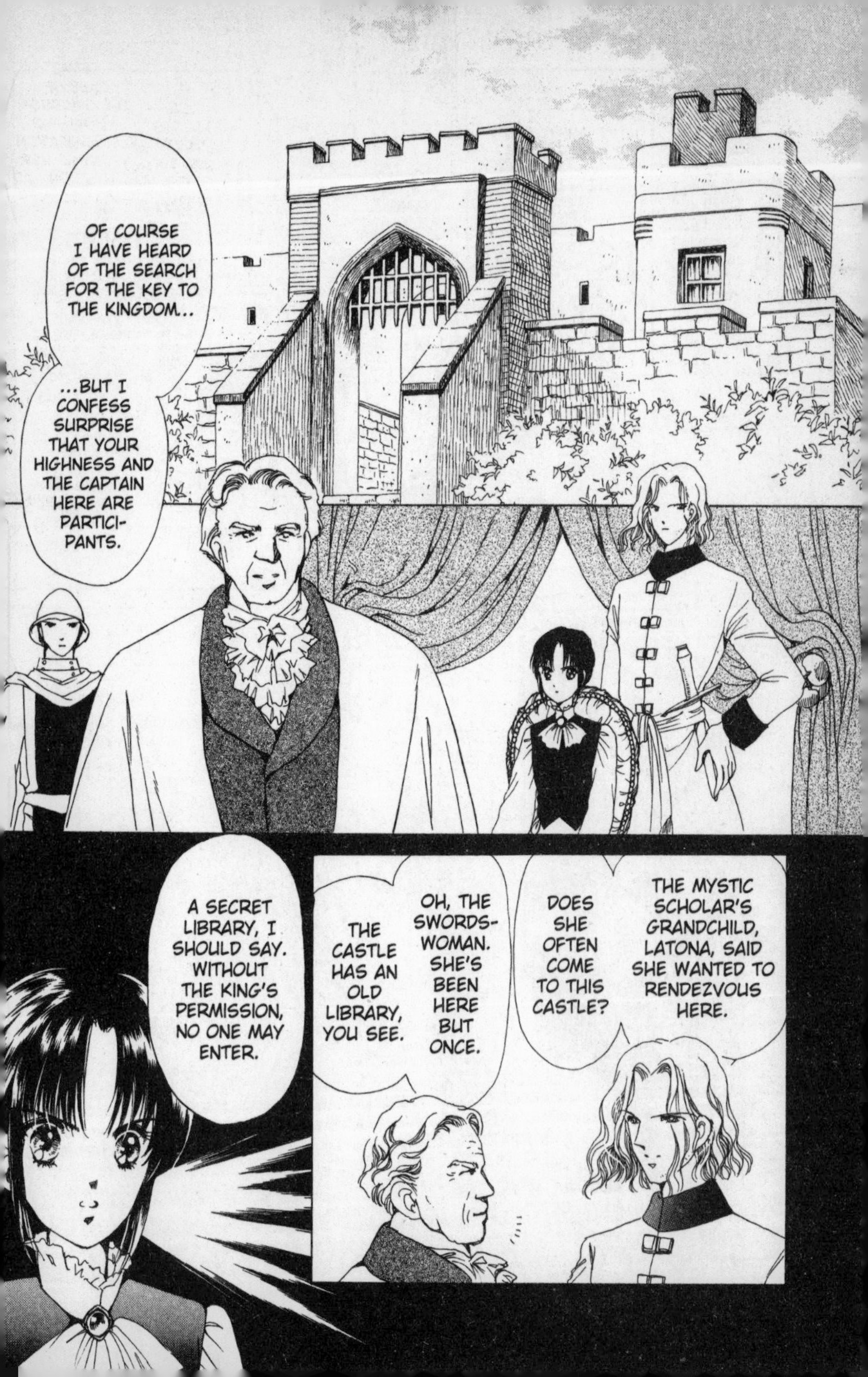
OF COURSE I HAVE HEARD OF THE SEARCH FOR THE KEY TO THE KINGDOM...
...BUT I CONFESS SURPRISE THAT YOUR HIGHNESS AND THE CAPTAIN HERE ARE PARTICI-PANTS.
THE MYSTIC SCHOLAR'S GRANDCHILD, LATONA, SAID SHE WANTED TO RENDEZVOUS HERE.
DOES SHE OFTEN COME TO THIS CASTLE?
OH, THE SWORDS-WOMAN. SHE'S BEEN HERE BUT ONCE.
THE CASTLE HAS AN OLD LIBRARY, YOU SEE.
A SECRET LIBRARY, I SHOULD SAY. WITHOUT THE KING'S PERMISSION, NO ONE MAY ENTER.

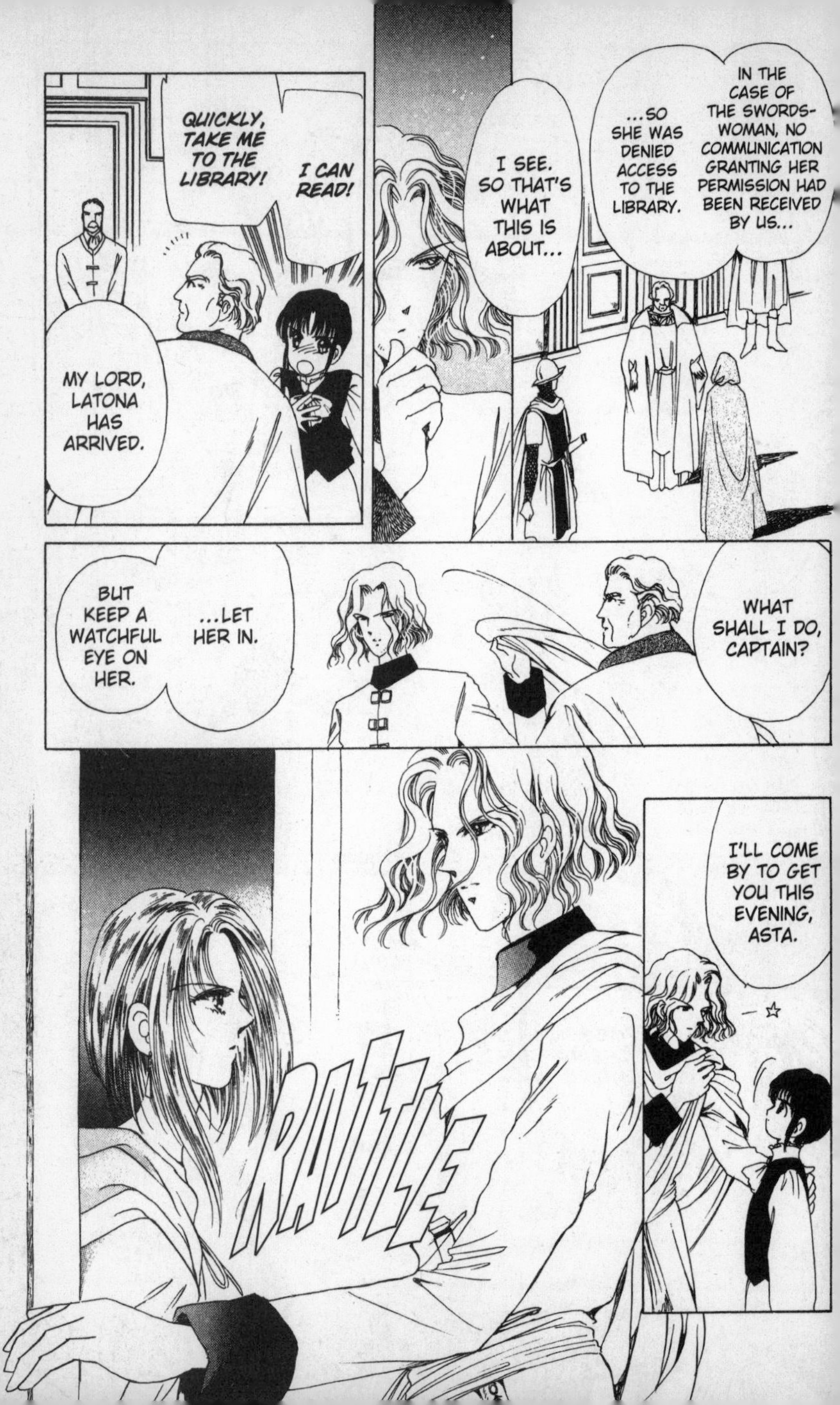
IN THE CASE OF THE SWORDS-WOMAN, NO COMMUNICATION GRANTING HER PERMISSION HAD BEEN RECEIVED BY US...
...SO SHE WAS DENIED ACCESS TO THE LIBRARY.
I SEE. SO THAT'S WHAT THIS IS ABOUT...
QUICKLY, TAKE ME TO THE LIBRARY!
I CAN READ!
MY LORD, LATONA HAS ARRIVED.
WHAT SHALL I DO, CAPTAIN?
...LET HER IN.
BUT KEEP A WATCHFUL EYE ON HER.
I'LL COME BY TO GET YOU THIS EVENING, ASTA.
RATTLE

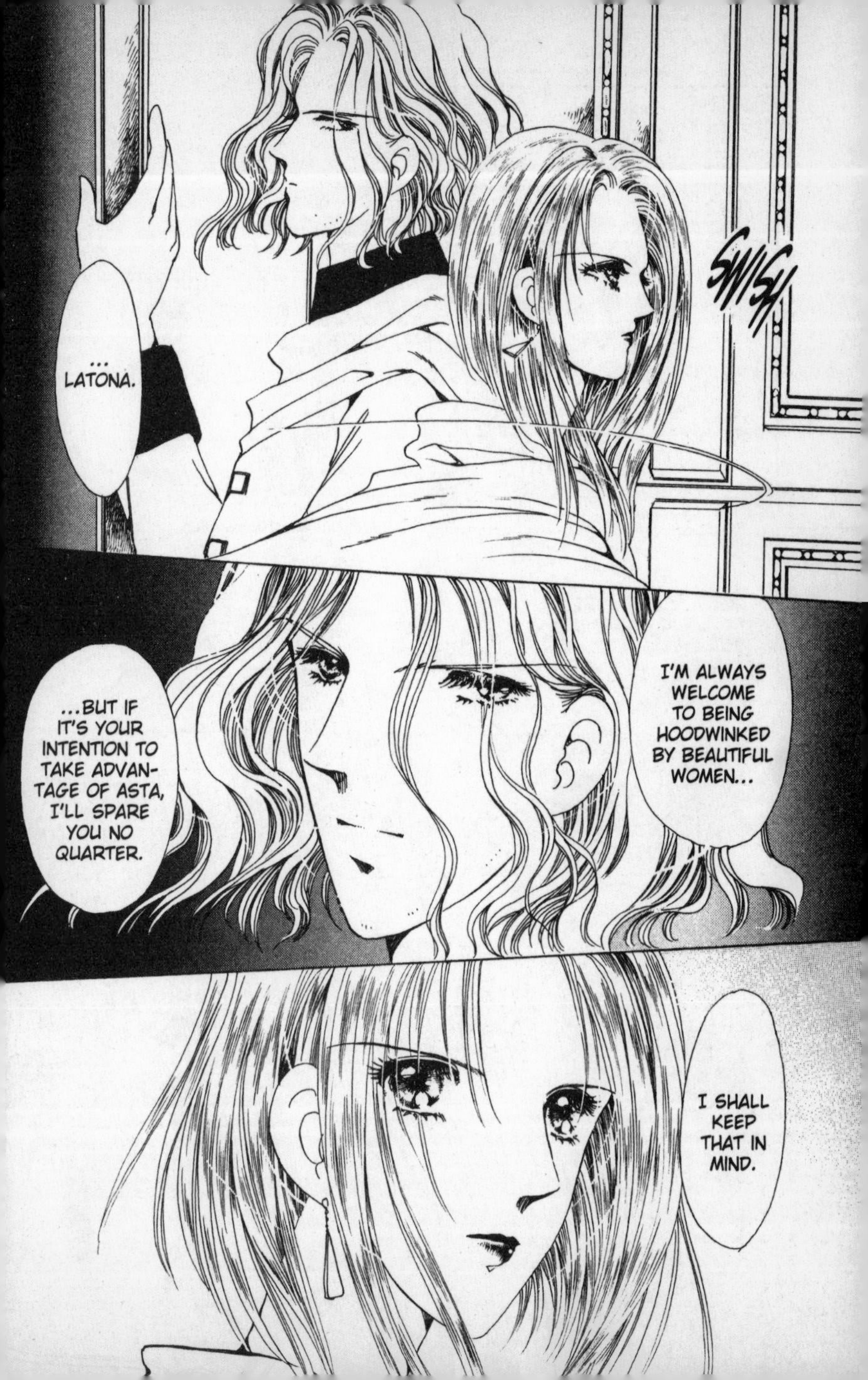
SWISH
... LATONA.
I'M ALWAYS WELCOME TO BEING HOODWINKED BY BEAUTIFUL WOMEN...
...BUT IF IT'S YOUR INTENTION TO TAKE ADVAN-TAGE OF ASTA, I'LL SPARE YOU NO QUARTER.
I SHALL KEEP THAT IN MIND.

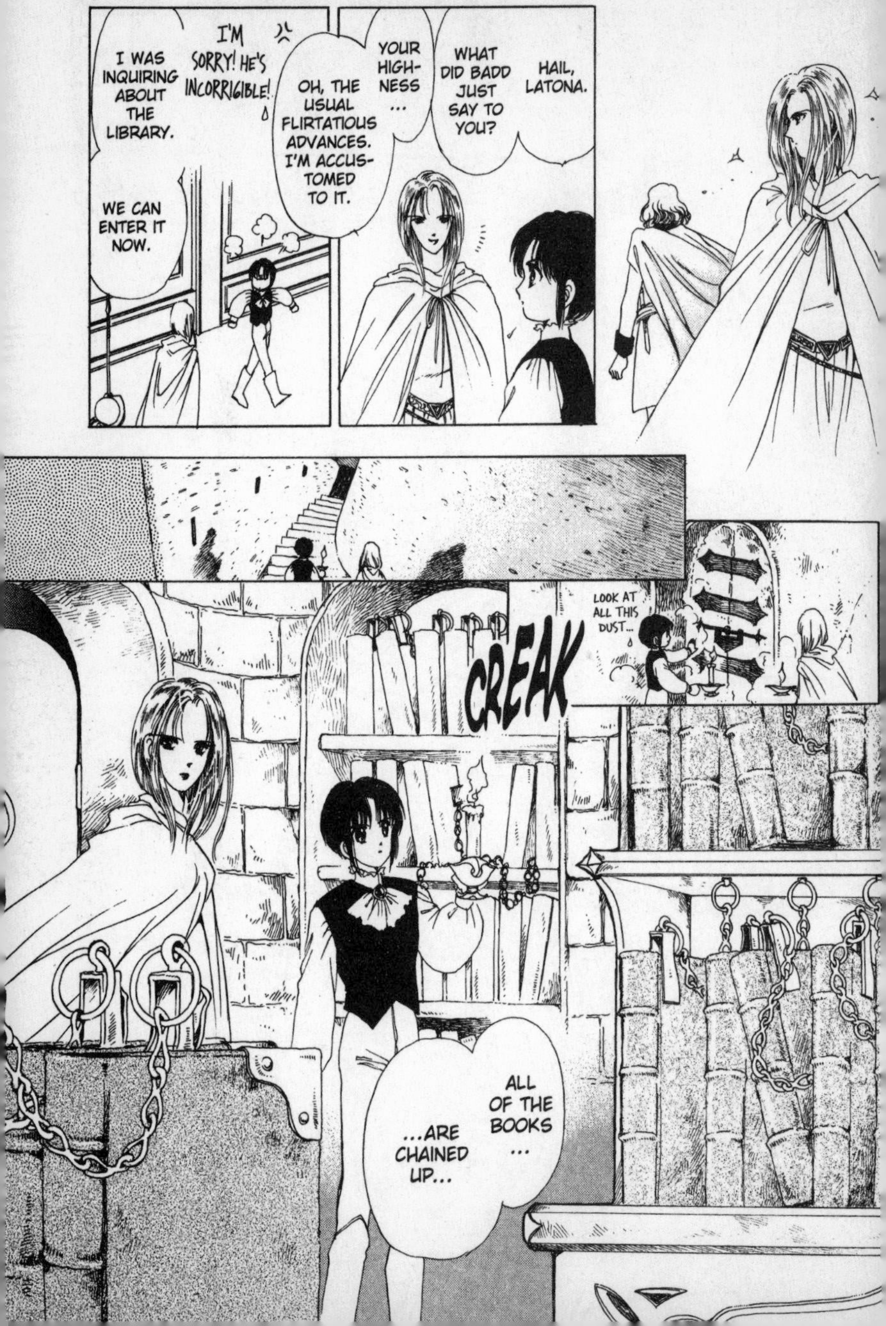
HAIL, LATONA.
WHAT DID BADD JUST SAY TO YOU?
YOUR HIGHNESS...
OH, THE USUAL FLIRTATIOUS ADVANCES. I'M ACCUSTOMED TO IT.
I'M SORRY! HE'S INCORRIGIBLE!
I WAS INQUIRING ABOUT THE LIBRARY.
WE CAN ENTER IT NOW.
LOOK AT ALL THIS DUST...
CREAK
ALL OF THE BOOKS...
...ARE CHAINED UP...

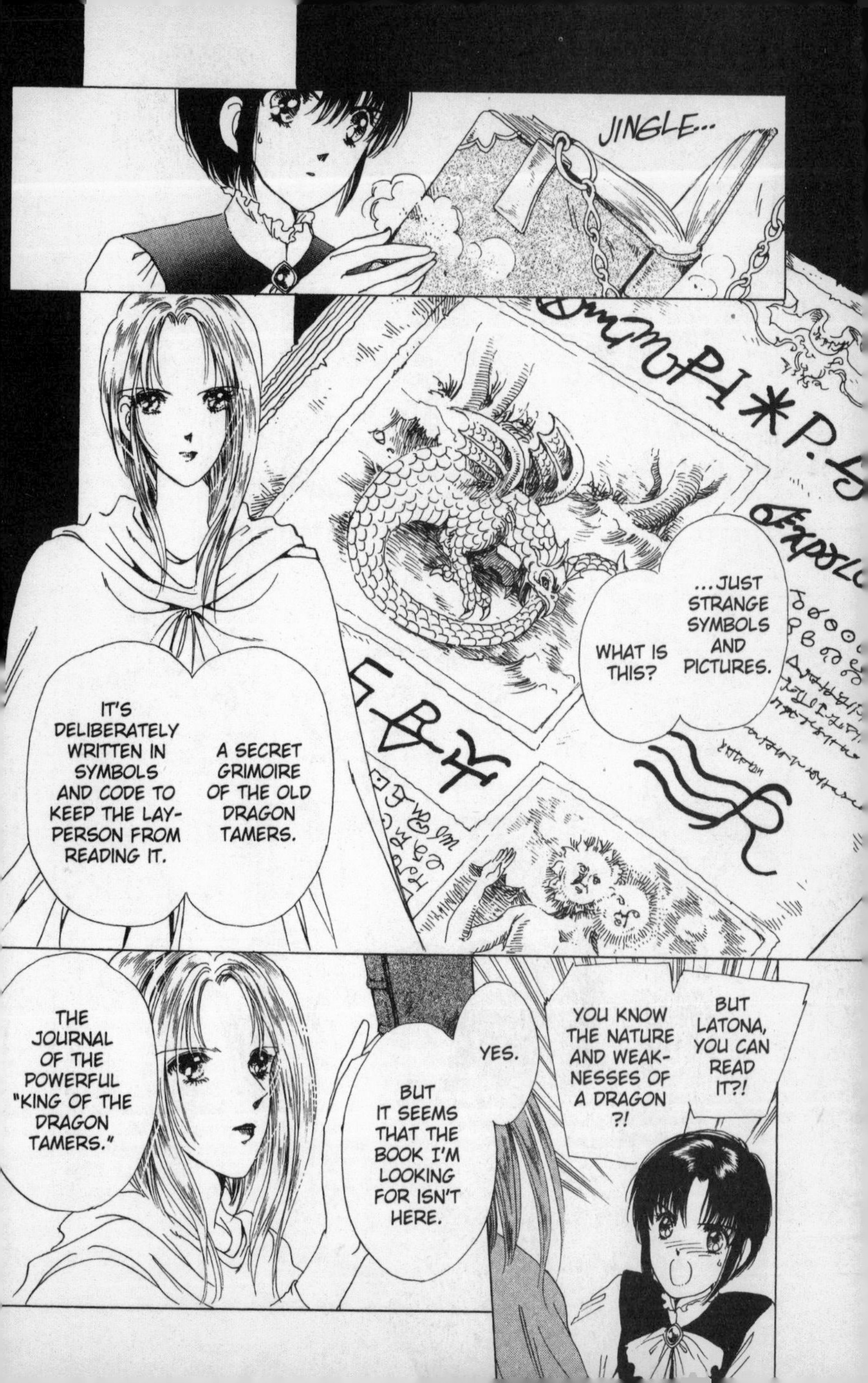
JINGLE...
...JUST STRANGE SYMBOLS AND PICTURES.
WHAT IS THIS?
A SECRET GRIMOIRE OF THE OLD DRAGON TAMERS.
IT'S DELIBERATELY WRITTEN IN SYMBOLS AND CODE TO KEEP THE LAY-PERSON FROM READING IT.
BUT LATONA, YOU CAN READ IT?!
YOU KNOW THE NATURE AND WEAK-NESSES OF A DRAGON ?!
YES.
BUT IT SEEMS THAT THE BOOK I'M LOOKING FOR ISN'T HERE.
THE JOURNAL OF THE POWERFUL "KING OF THE DRAGON TAMERS."

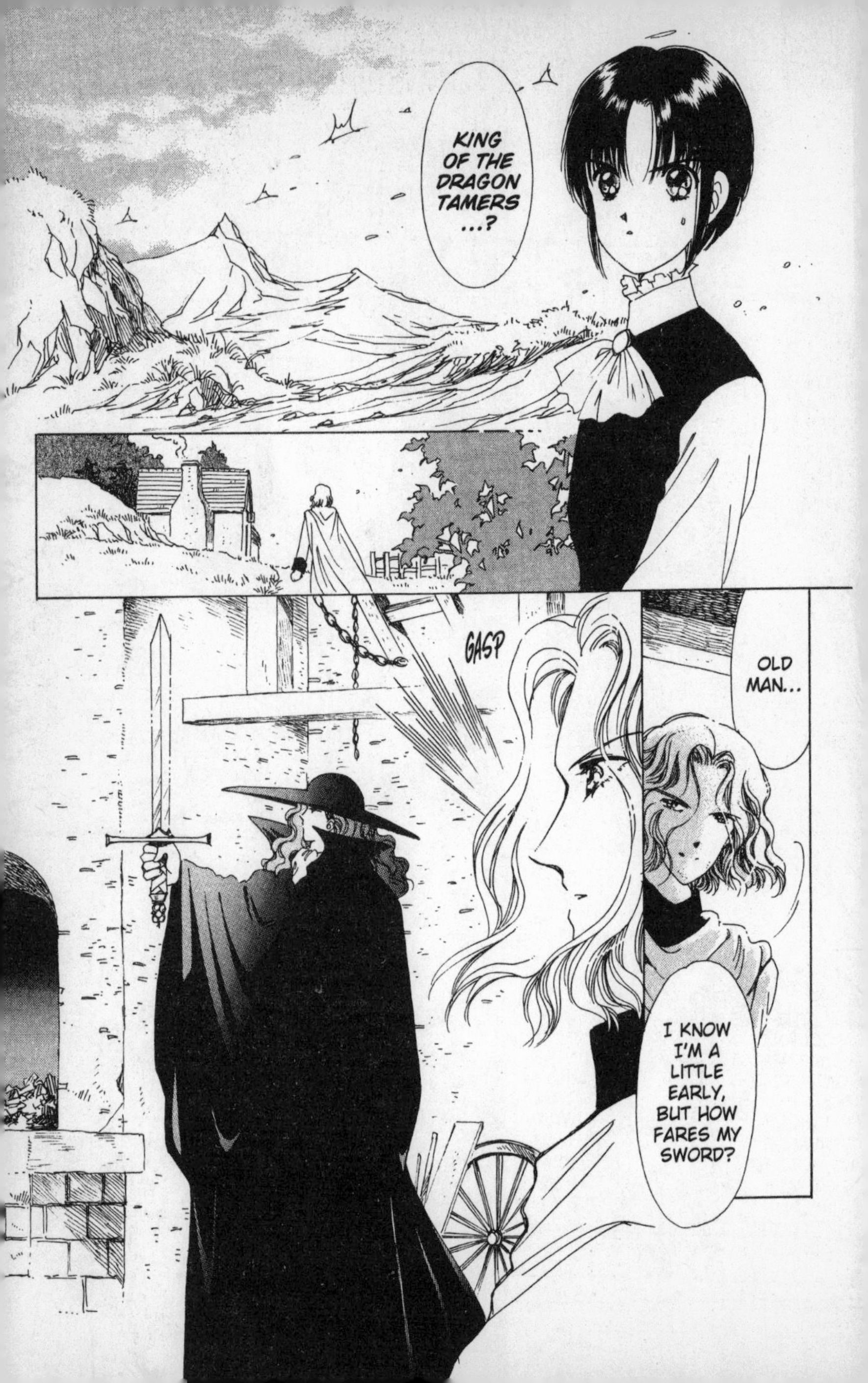
KING OF THE DRAGON TAMERS ...?
GASP
OLD MAN...
I KNOW I'M A LITTLE EARLY, BUT HOW FARES MY SWORD?

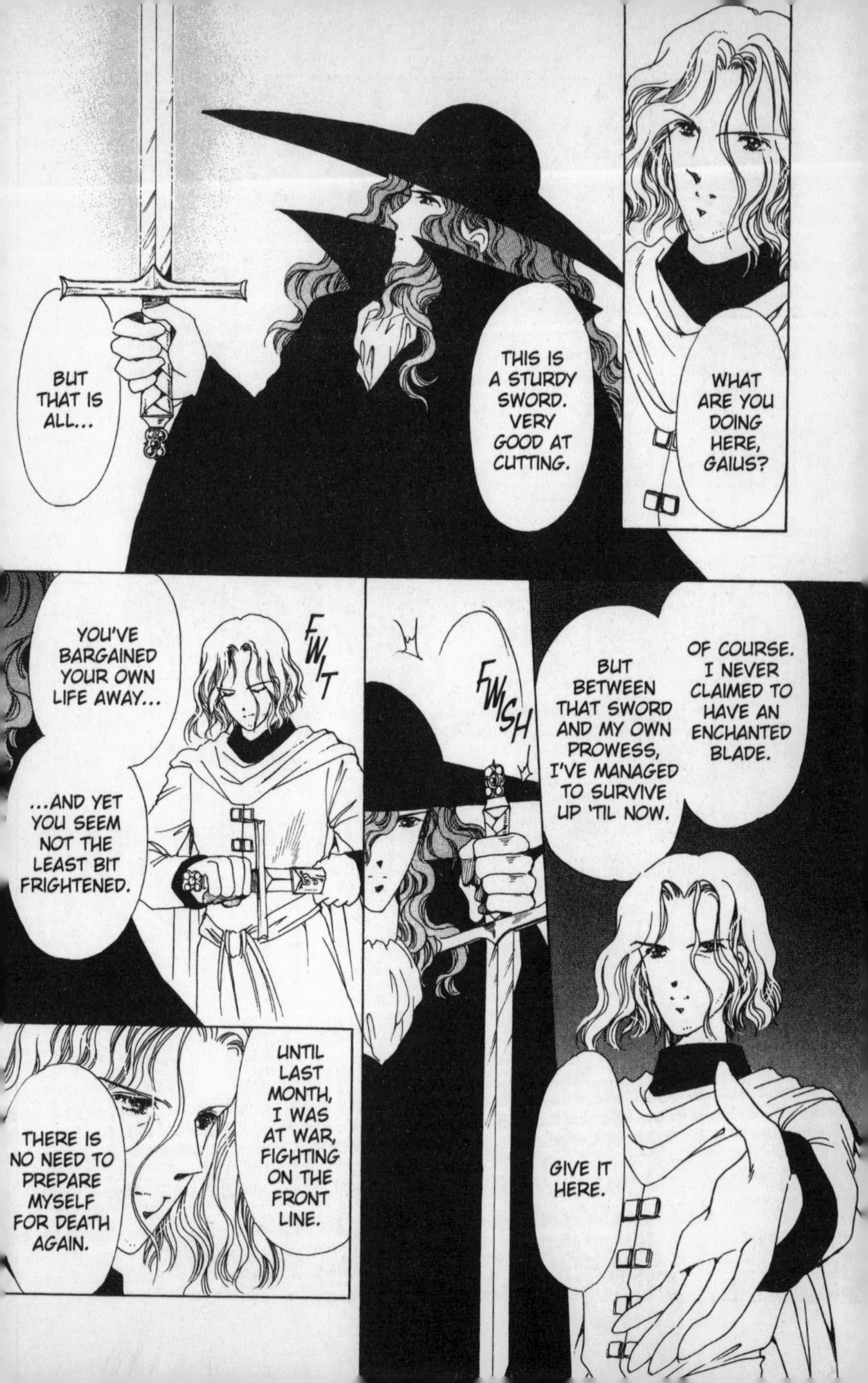
WHAT ARE YOU DOING HERE, GAIUS?
THIS IS A STURDY SWORD. VERY GOOD AT CUTTING.
BUT THAT IS ALL...
OF COURSE. I NEVER CLAIMED TO HAVE AN ENCHANTED BLADE.
BUT BETWEEN THAT SWORD AND MY OWN PROWESS, I'VE MANAGED TO SURVIVE UP 'TIL NOW.
GIVE IT HERE.
FWISH
FWIT
YOU'VE BARGAINED YOUR OWN LIFE AWAY...
...AND YET YOU SEEM NOT THE LEAST BIT FRIGHTENED.
UNTIL LAST MONTH, I WAS AT WAR, FIGHTING ON THE FRONT LINE.
THERE IS NO NEED TO PREPARE MYSELF FOR DEATH AGAIN.

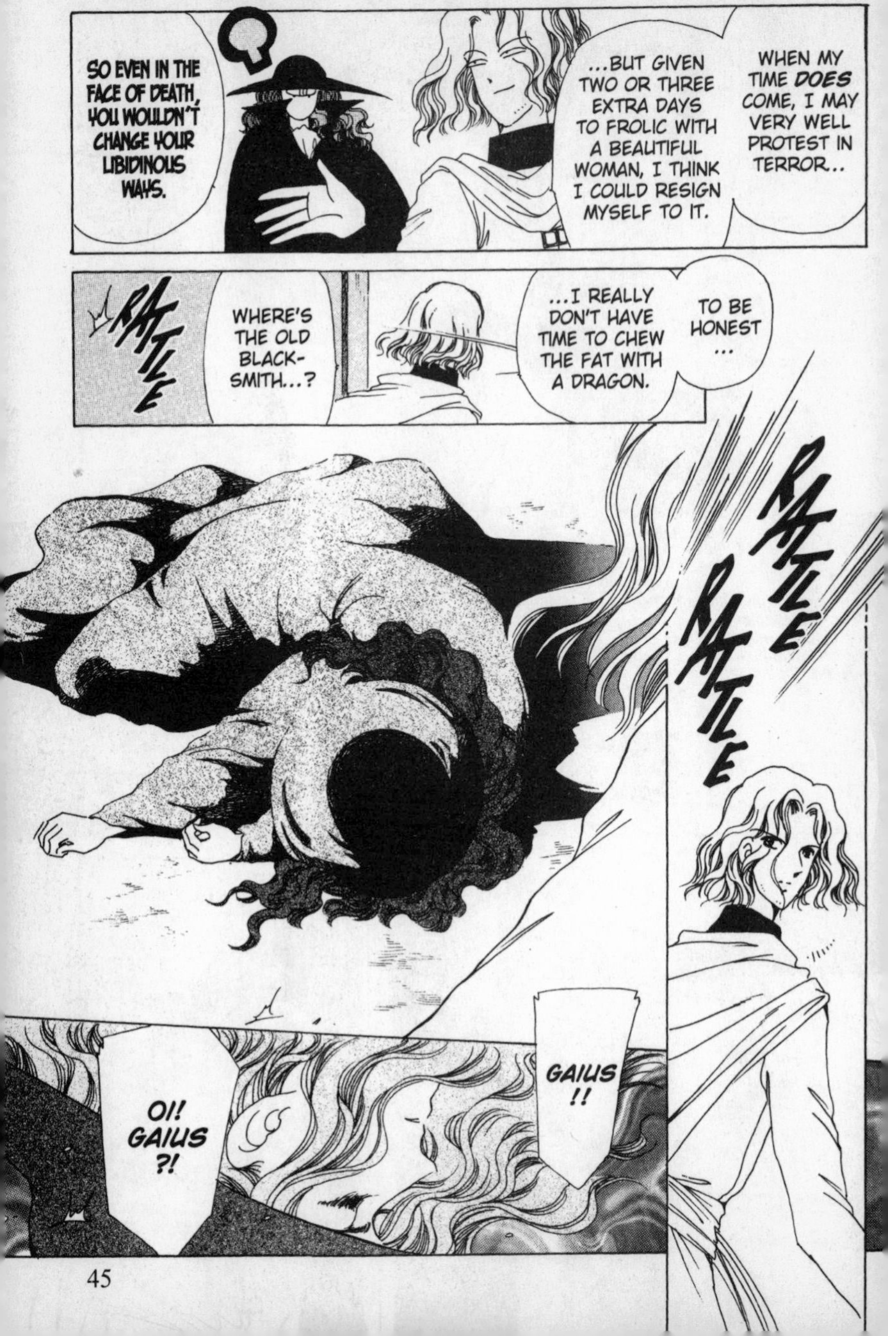
WHEN MY TIME **DOES** COME, I MAY VERY WELL PROTEST IN TERROR...
...BUT GIVEN TWO OR THREE EXTRA DAYS TO FROLIC WITH A BEAUTIFUL WOMAN, I THINK I COULD RESIGN MYSELF TO IT.
SO EVEN IN THE FACE OF DEATH, YOU WOULDN'T CHANGE YOUR LIBIDINOUS WAYS.
TO BE HONEST ...
...I REALLY DON'T HAVE TIME TO CHEW THE FAT WITH A DRAGON.
WHERE'S THE OLD BLACKSMITH...?
RATTLE
RATTLE
RATTLE
GAIUS !!
OI! GAIUS ?!

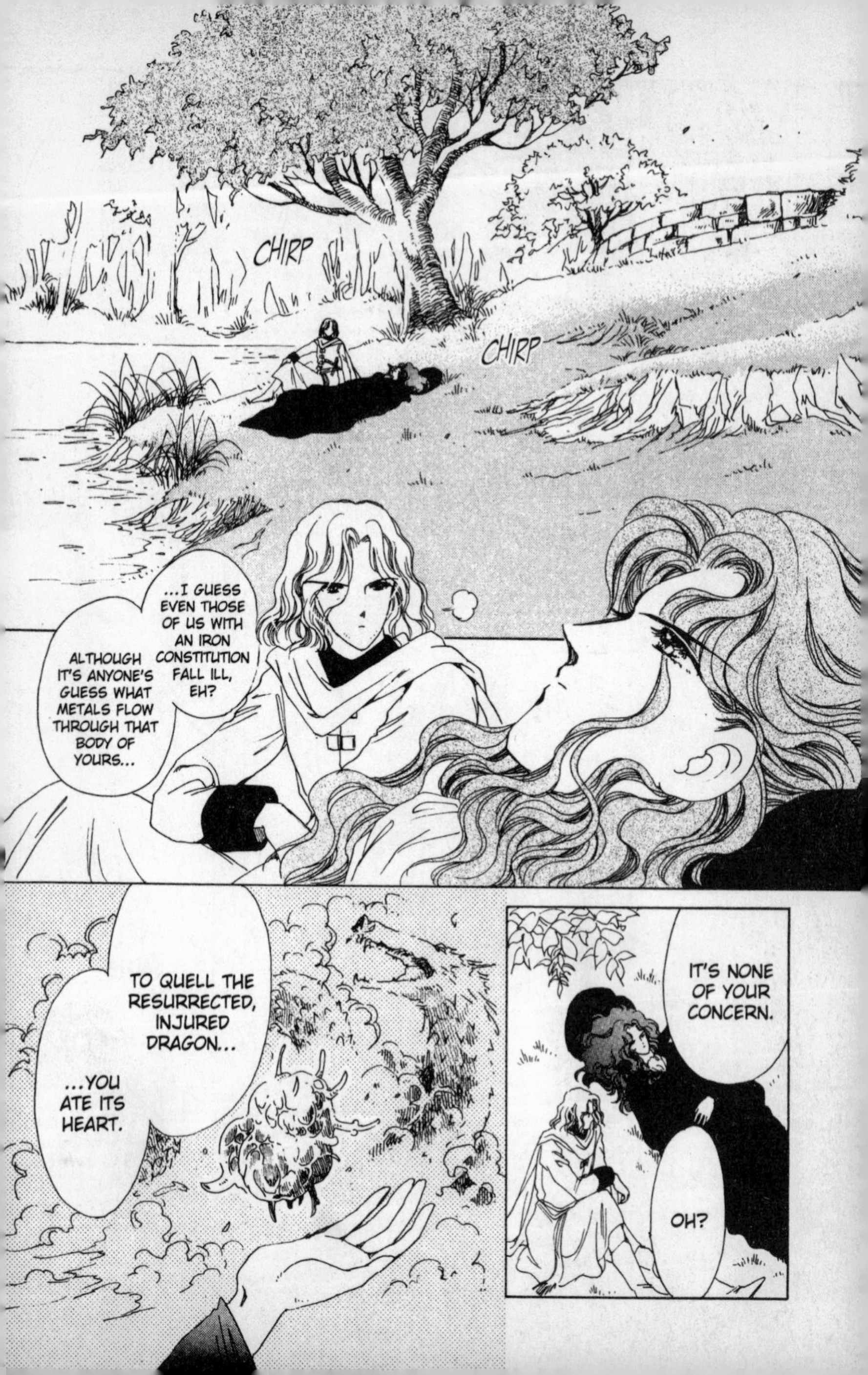
CHIRP
CHIRP
...I GUESS EVEN THOSE OF US WITH AN IRON CONSTITUTION FALL ILL, EH?
ALTHOUGH IT'S ANYONE'S GUESS WHAT METALS FLOW THROUGH THAT BODY OF YOURS...
IT'S NONE OF YOUR CONCERN.
OH?
TO QUELL THE RESURRECTED, INJURED DRAGON...
...YOU ATE ITS HEART.

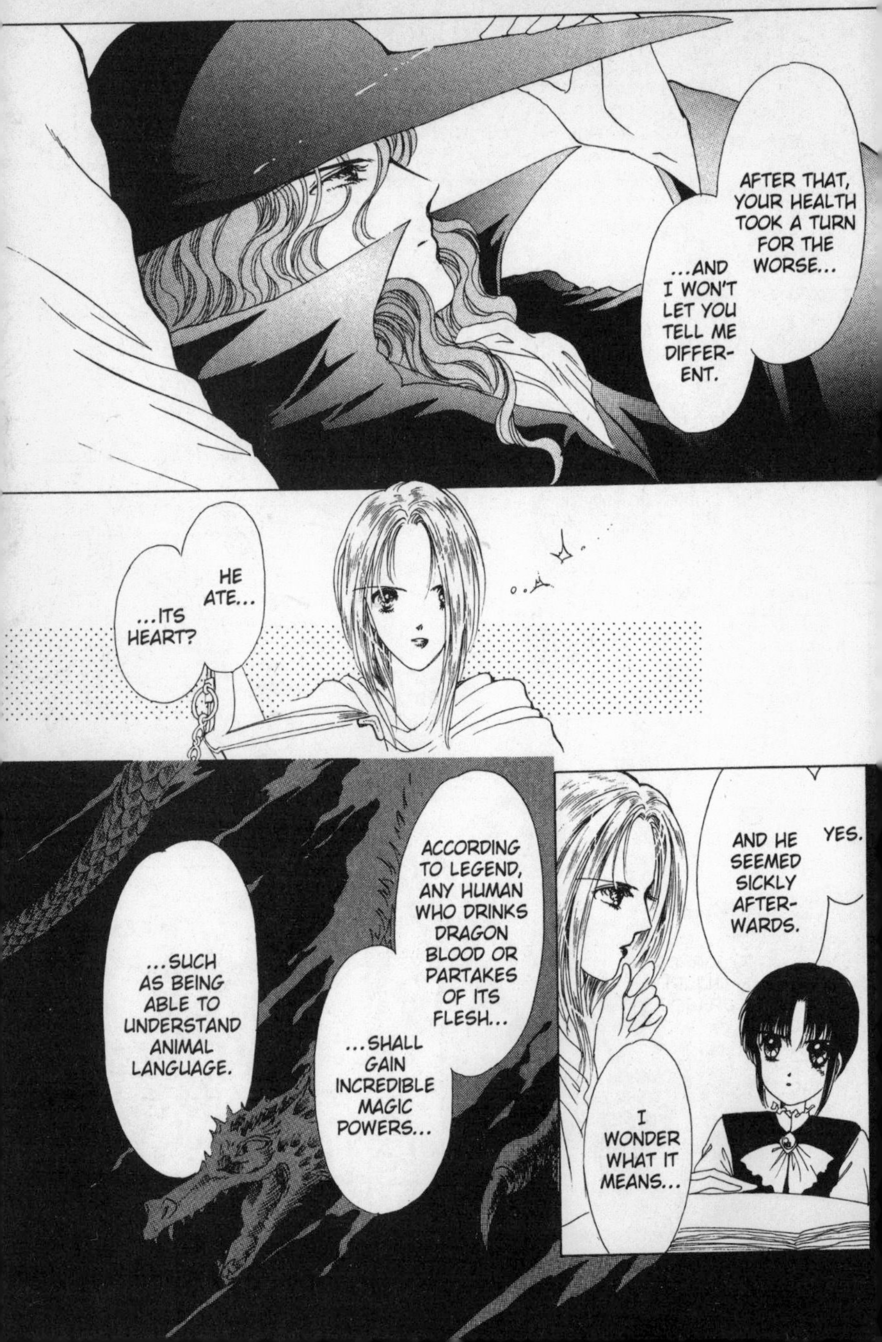
AFTER THAT, YOUR HEALTH TOOK A TURN FOR THE WORSE...
...AND I WON'T LET YOU TELL ME DIFFERENT.
HE ATE...
...ITS HEART?
YES.
AND HE SEEMED SICKLY AFTER-WARDS.
I WONDER WHAT IT MEANS...
ACCORDING TO LEGEND, ANY HUMAN WHO DRINKS DRAGON BLOOD OR PARTAKES OF ITS FLESH...
...SHALL GAIN INCREDIBLE MAGIC POWERS...
...SUCH AS BEING ABLE TO UNDERSTAND ANIMAL LANGUAGE.

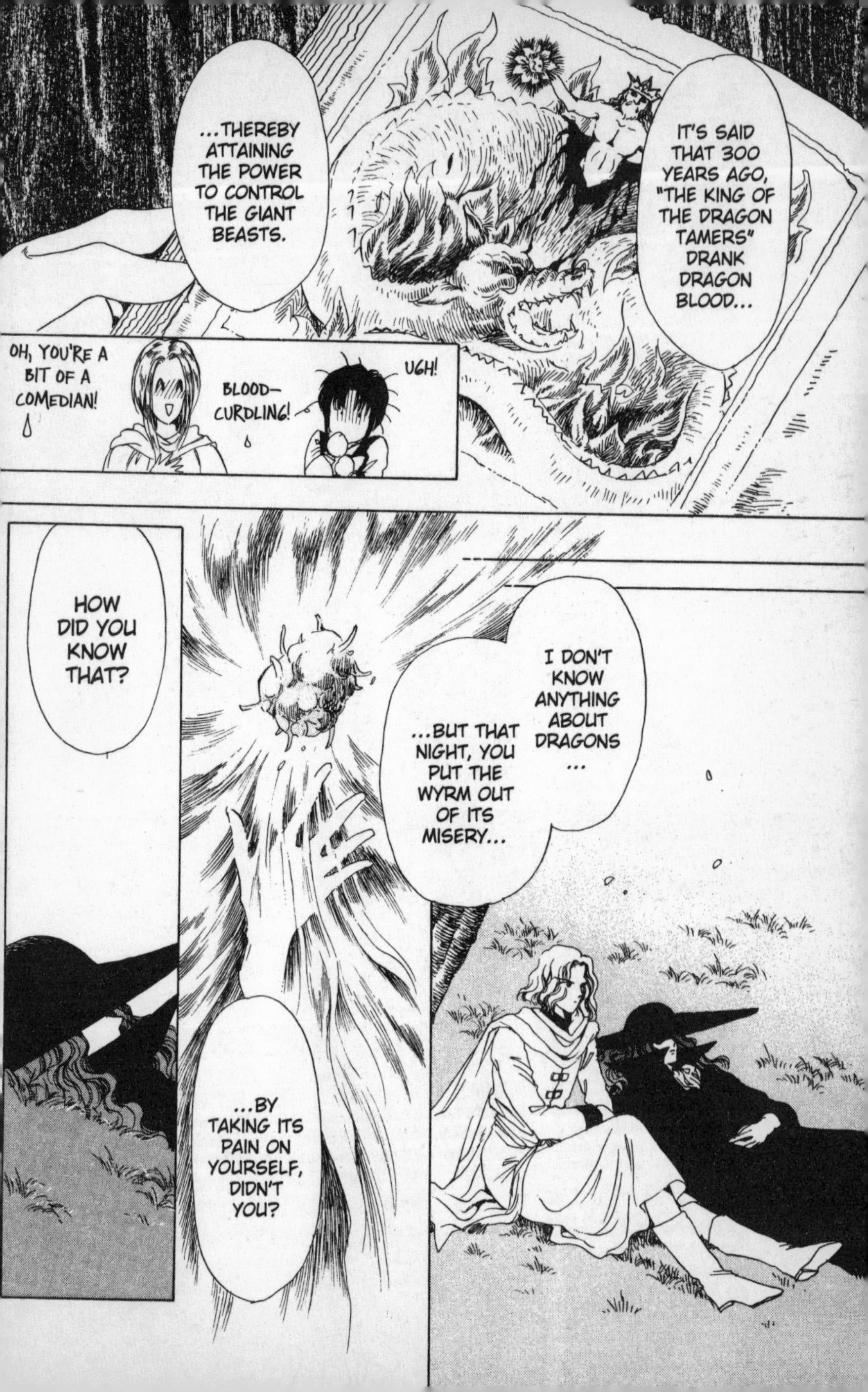
IT'S SAID THAT 300 YEARS AGO, "THE KING OF THE DRAGON TAMERS" DRANK DRAGON BLOOD...
...THEREBY ATTAINING THE POWER TO CONTROL THE GIANT BEASTS.
UGH!
BLOOD-CURDLING!
OH, YOU'RE A BIT OF A COMEDIAN!
I DON'T KNOW ANYTHING ABOUT DRAGONS...
...BUT THAT NIGHT, YOU PUT THE WYRM OUT OF ITS MISERY...
...BY TAKING ITS PAIN ON YOURSELF, DIDN'T YOU?
HOW DID YOU KNOW THAT?

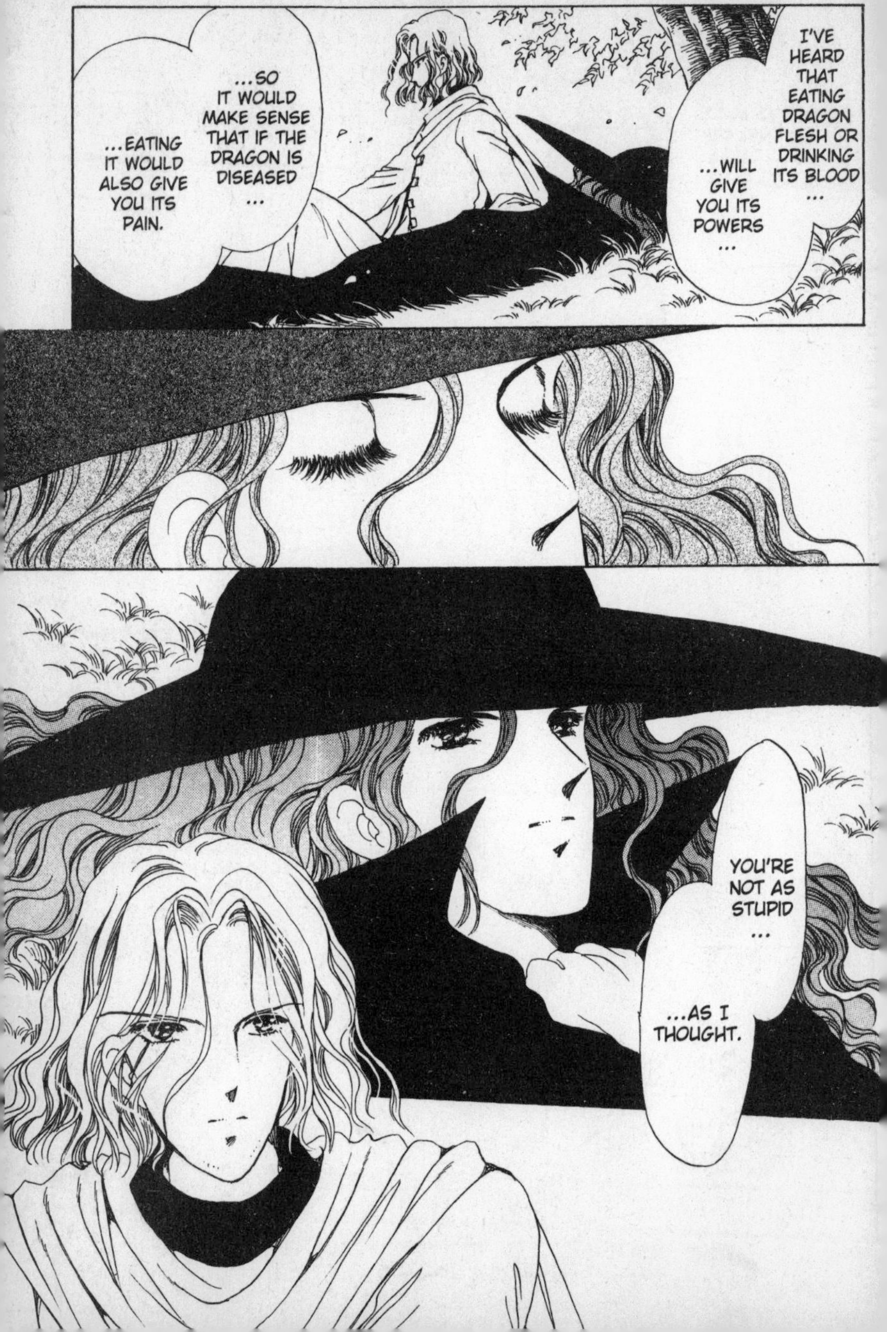
I'VE HEARD THAT EATING DRAGON FLESH OR DRINKING ITS BLOOD ...
...WILL GIVE YOU ITS POWERS ...
...SO IT WOULD MAKE SENSE THAT IF THE DRAGON IS DISEASED ...
...EATING IT WOULD ALSO GIVE YOU ITS PAIN.
YOU'RE NOT AS STUPID ...
...AS I THOUGHT.

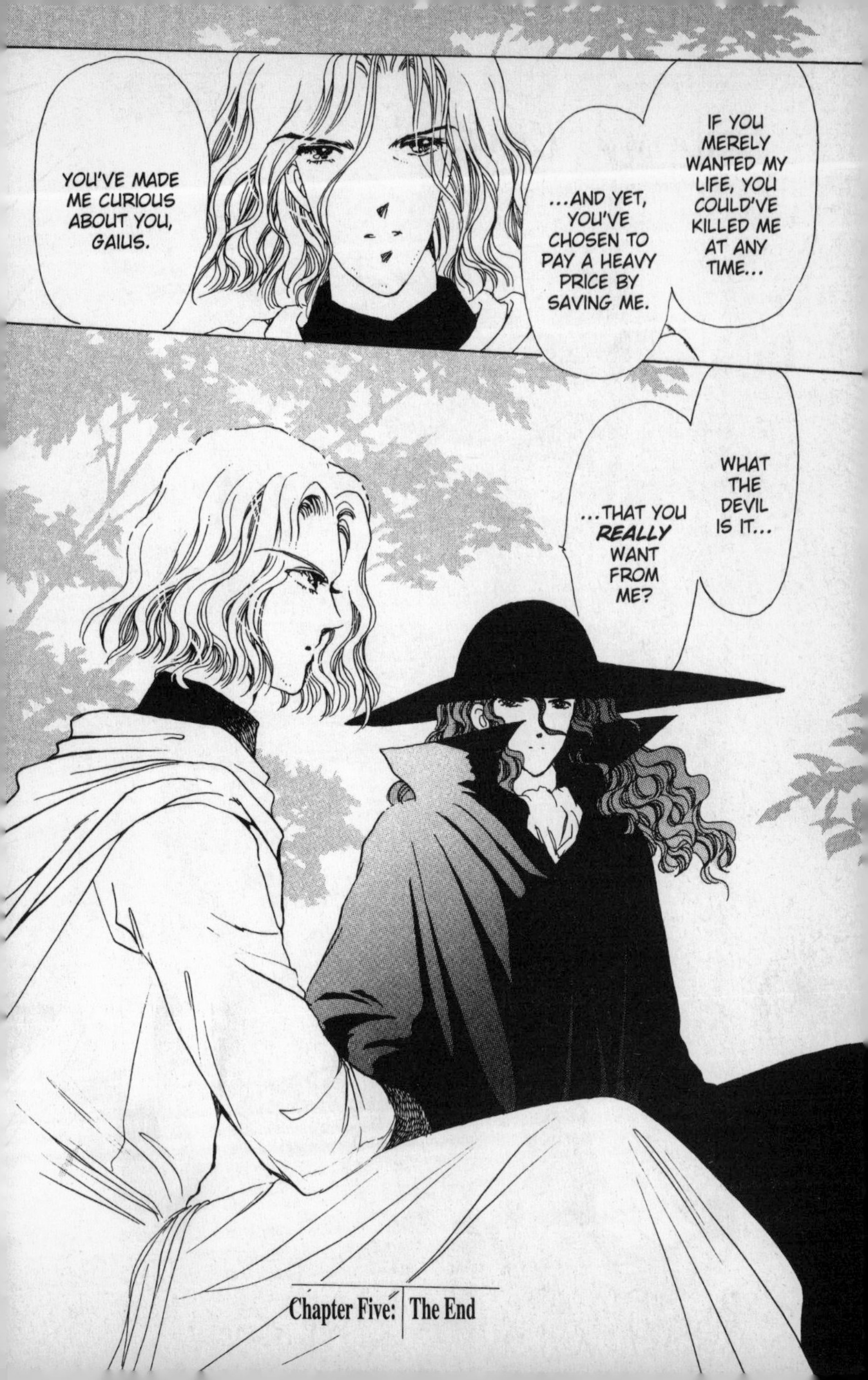
IF YOU MERELY WANTED MY LIFE, YOU COULD'VE KILLED ME AT ANY TIME...
...AND YET, YOU'VE CHOSEN TO PAY A HEAVY PRICE BY SAVING ME.
YOU'VE MADE ME CURIOUS ABOUT YOU, GAIUS.
WHAT THE DEVIL IS IT...
...THAT YOU *REALLY* WANT FROM ME?
Chapter Five: The End

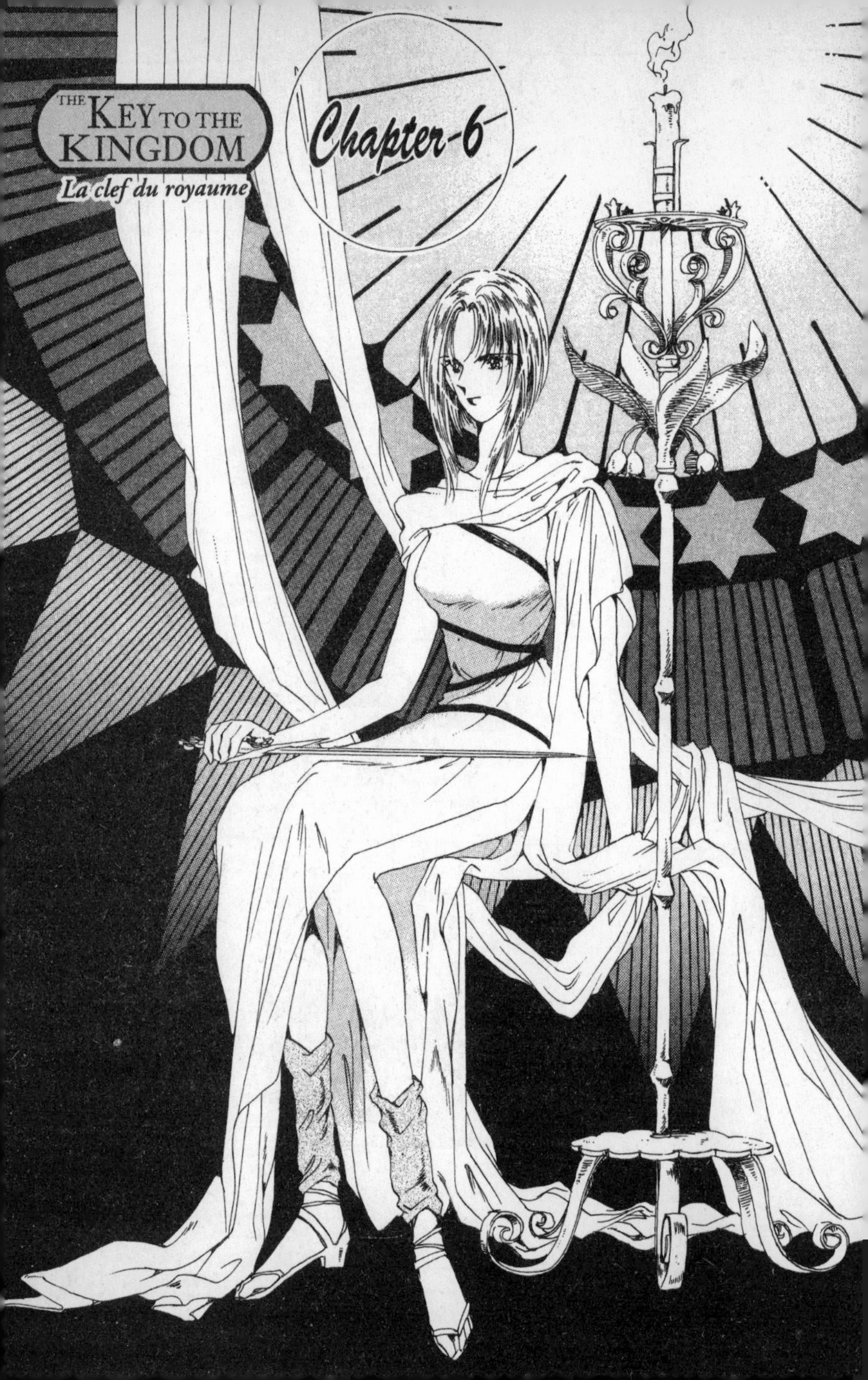
THE KEY TO THE KINGDOM
La clef du royaume
Chapter-6

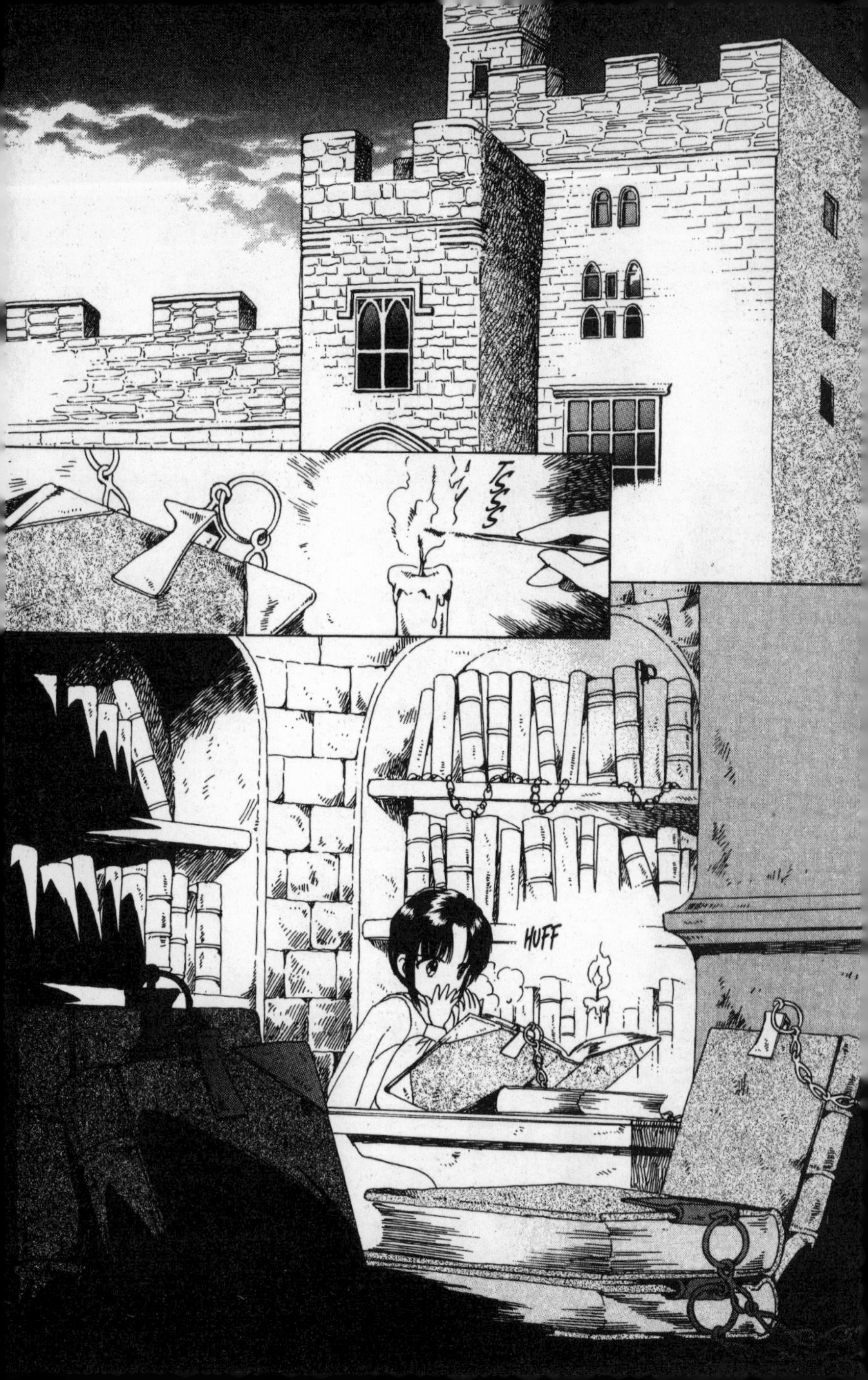
TSSS
HUFF

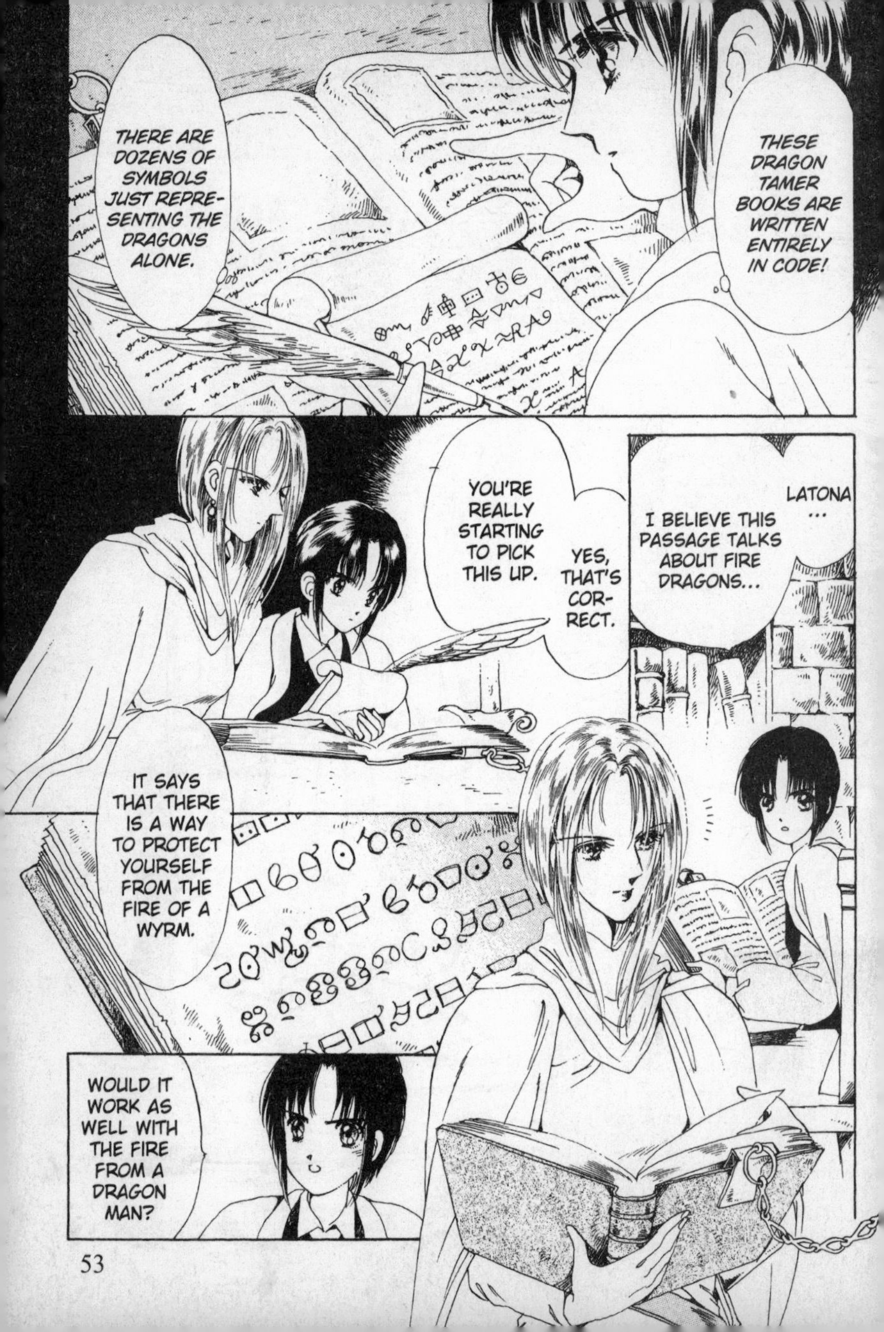
THESE DRAGON TAMER BOOKS ARE WRITTEN ENTIRELY IN CODE!
THERE ARE DOZENS OF SYMBOLS JUST REPRESENTING THE DRAGONS ALONE.
LATONA ...
I BELIEVE THIS PASSAGE TALKS ABOUT FIRE DRAGONS...
YES, THAT'S CORRECT.
YOU'RE REALLY STARTING TO PICK THIS UP.
IT SAYS THAT THERE IS A WAY TO PROTECT YOURSELF FROM THE FIRE OF A WYRM.
WOULD IT WORK AS WELL WITH THE FIRE FROM A DRAGON MAN?

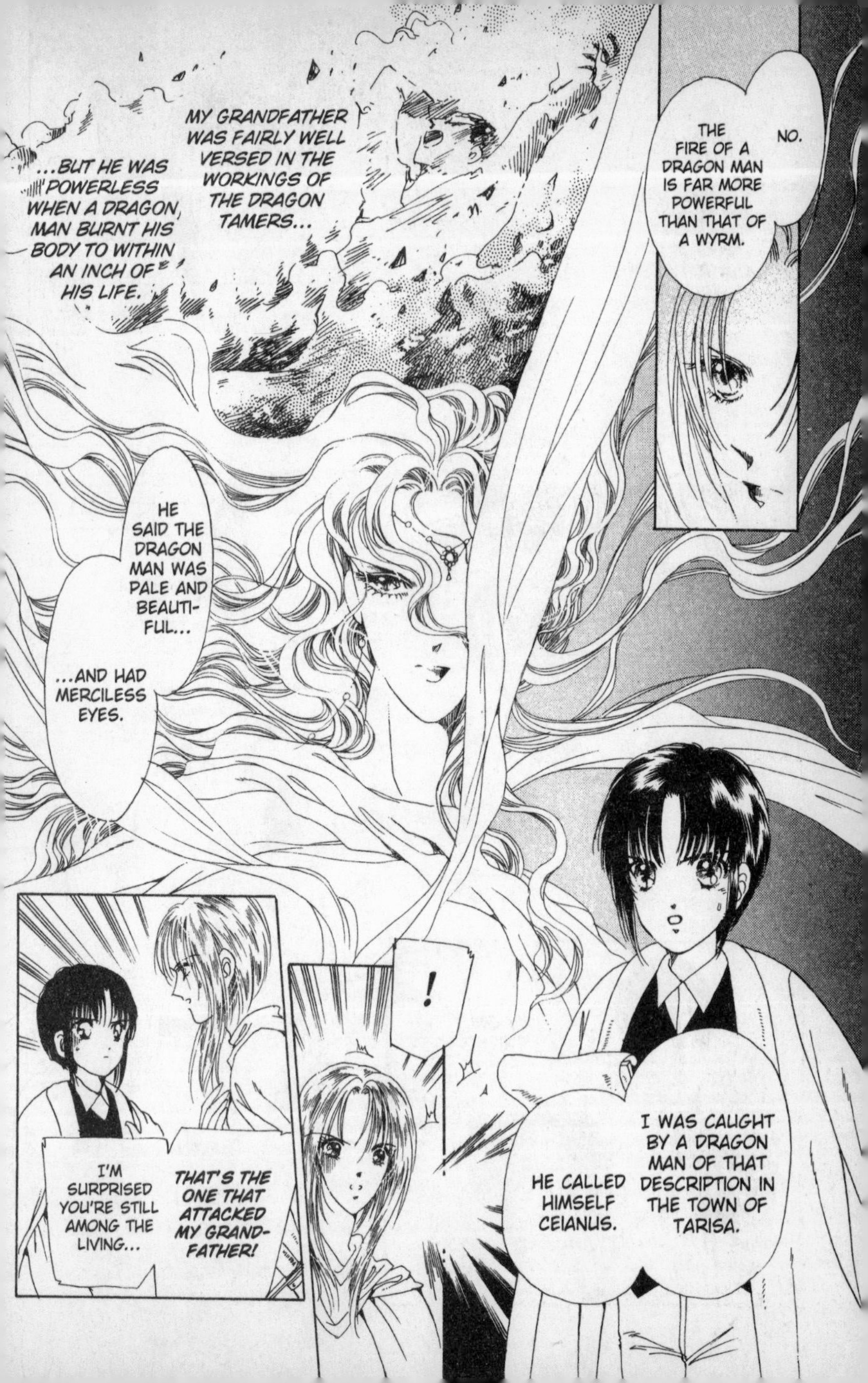
NO.
THE FIRE OF A DRAGON MAN IS FAR MORE POWERFUL THAN THAT OF A WYRM.
MY GRANDFATHER WAS FAIRLY WELL VERSED IN THE WORKINGS OF THE DRAGON TAMERS...
...BUT HE WAS POWERLESS WHEN A DRAGON MAN BURNT HIS BODY TO WITHIN AN INCH OF HIS LIFE.
HE SAID THE DRAGON MAN WAS PALE AND BEAUTI-FUL...
...AND HAD MERCILESS EYES.
I WAS CAUGHT BY A DRAGON MAN OF THAT DESCRIPTION IN THE TOWN OF TARISA.
HE CALLED HIMSELF CEIANUS.
!
THAT'S THE ONE THAT ATTACKED MY GRAND-FATHER!
I'M SURPRISED YOU'RE STILL AMONG THE LIVING...

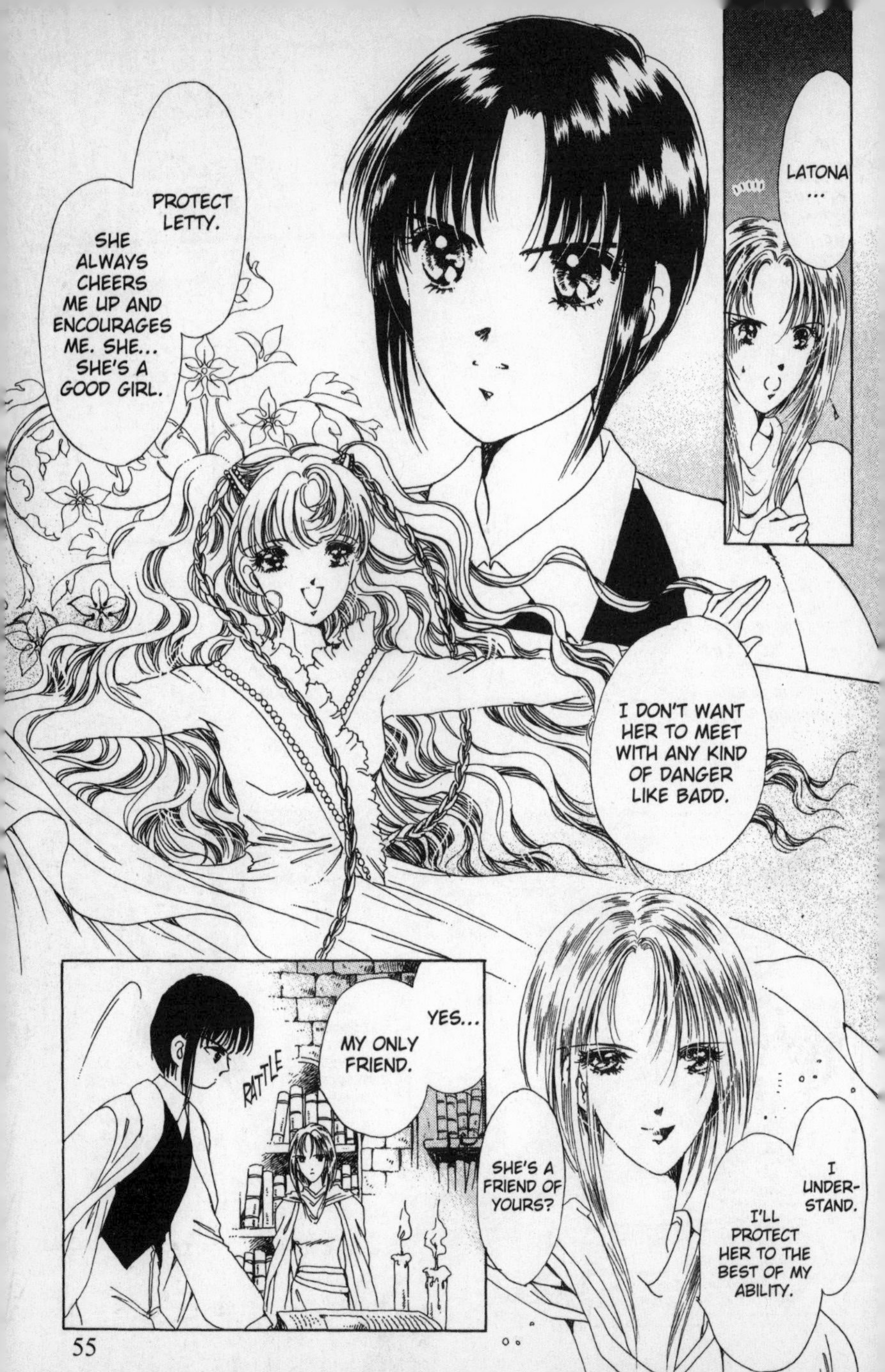
LATONA ...
PROTECT LETTY.
SHE ALWAYS CHEERS ME UP AND ENCOURAGES ME. SHE... SHE'S A GOOD GIRL.
I DON'T WANT HER TO MEET WITH ANY KIND OF DANGER LIKE BADD.
SHE'S A FRIEND OF YOURS?
YES... MY ONLY FRIEND.
RATTLE
I UNDERSTAND.
I'LL PROTECT HER TO THE BEST OF MY ABILITY.

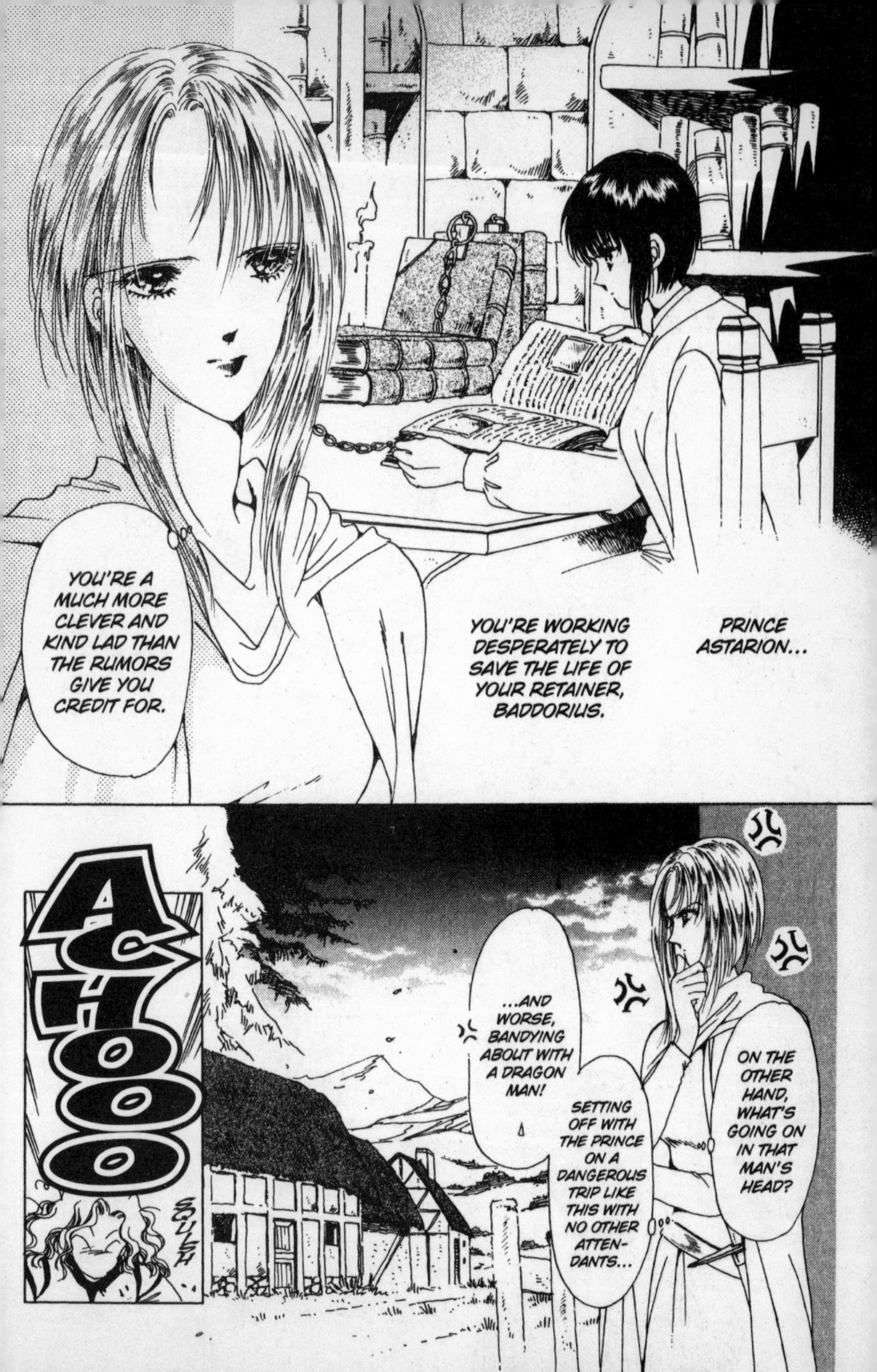
PRINCE ASTARION...
YOU'RE WORKING DESPERATELY TO SAVE THE LIFE OF YOUR RETAINER, BADDORIUS.
YOU'RE A MUCH MORE CLEVER AND KIND LAD THAN THE RUMORS GIVE YOU CREDIT FOR.
ON THE OTHER HAND, WHAT'S GOING ON IN THAT MAN'S HEAD?
SETTING OFF WITH THE PRINCE ON A DANGEROUS TRIP LIKE THIS WITH NO OTHER ATTEN-DANTS...
...AND WORSE, BANDYING ABOUT WITH A DRAGON MAN!
ACHOOO

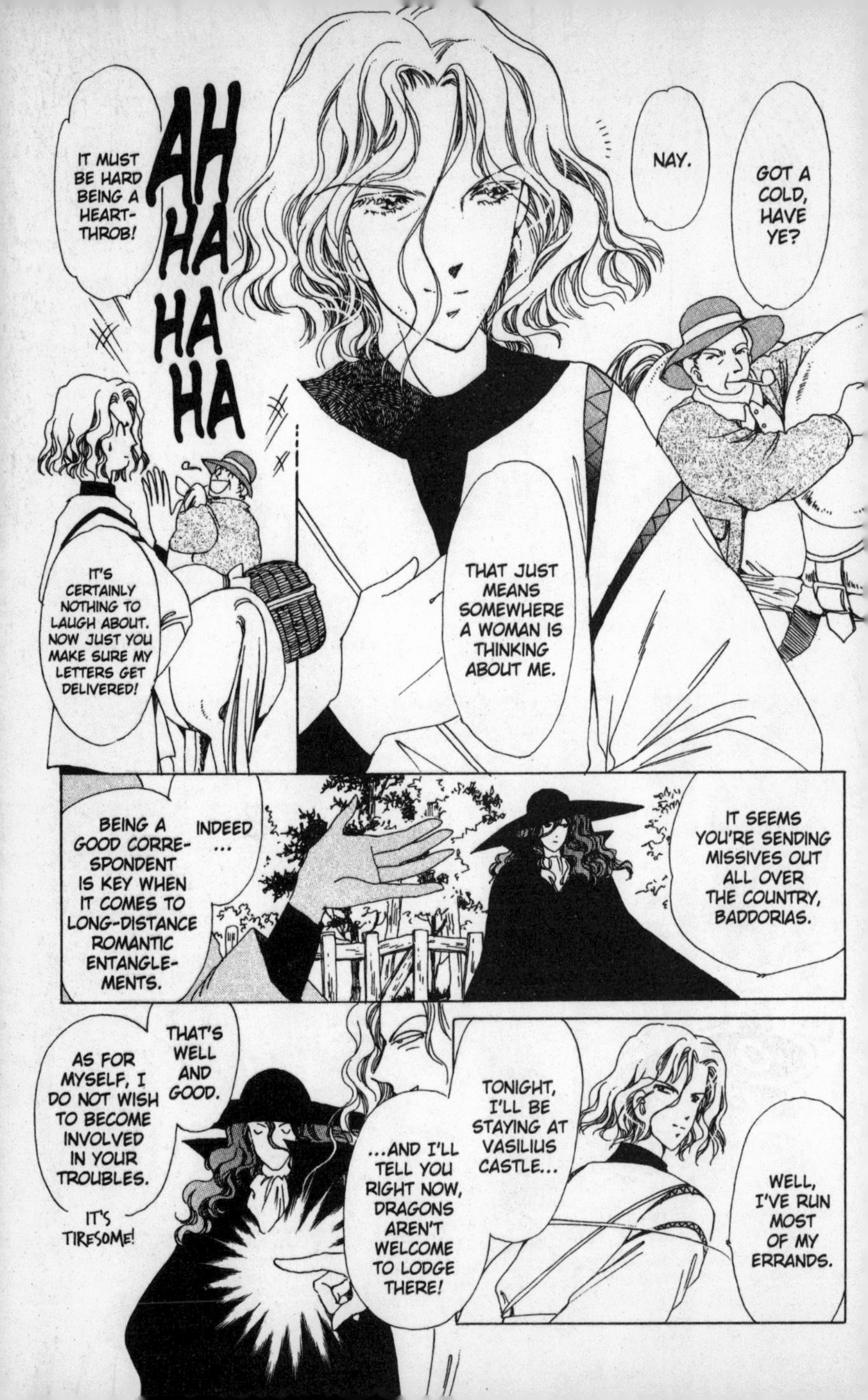
GOT A COLD, HAVE YE?
NAY.
THAT JUST MEANS SOMEWHERE A WOMAN IS THINKING ABOUT ME.
AH HA HA HA HA
IT MUST BE HARD BEING A HEART-THROB!
IT'S CERTAINLY NOTHING TO LAUGH ABOUT. NOW JUST YOU MAKE SURE MY LETTERS GET DELIVERED!
IT SEEMS YOU'RE SENDING MISSIVES OUT ALL OVER THE COUNTRY, BADDORIAS.
INDEED...
BEING A GOOD CORRE-SPONDENT IS KEY WHEN IT COMES TO LONG-DISTANCE ROMANTIC ENTANGLE-MENTS.
WELL, I'VE RUN MOST OF MY ERRANDS.
TONIGHT, I'LL BE STAYING AT VASILIUS CASTLE...
...AND I'LL TELL YOU RIGHT NOW, DRAGONS AREN'T WELCOME TO LODGE THERE!
THAT'S WELL AND GOOD.
AS FOR MYSELF, I DO NOT WISH TO BECOME INVOLVED IN YOUR TROUBLES.
IT'S TIRESOME!

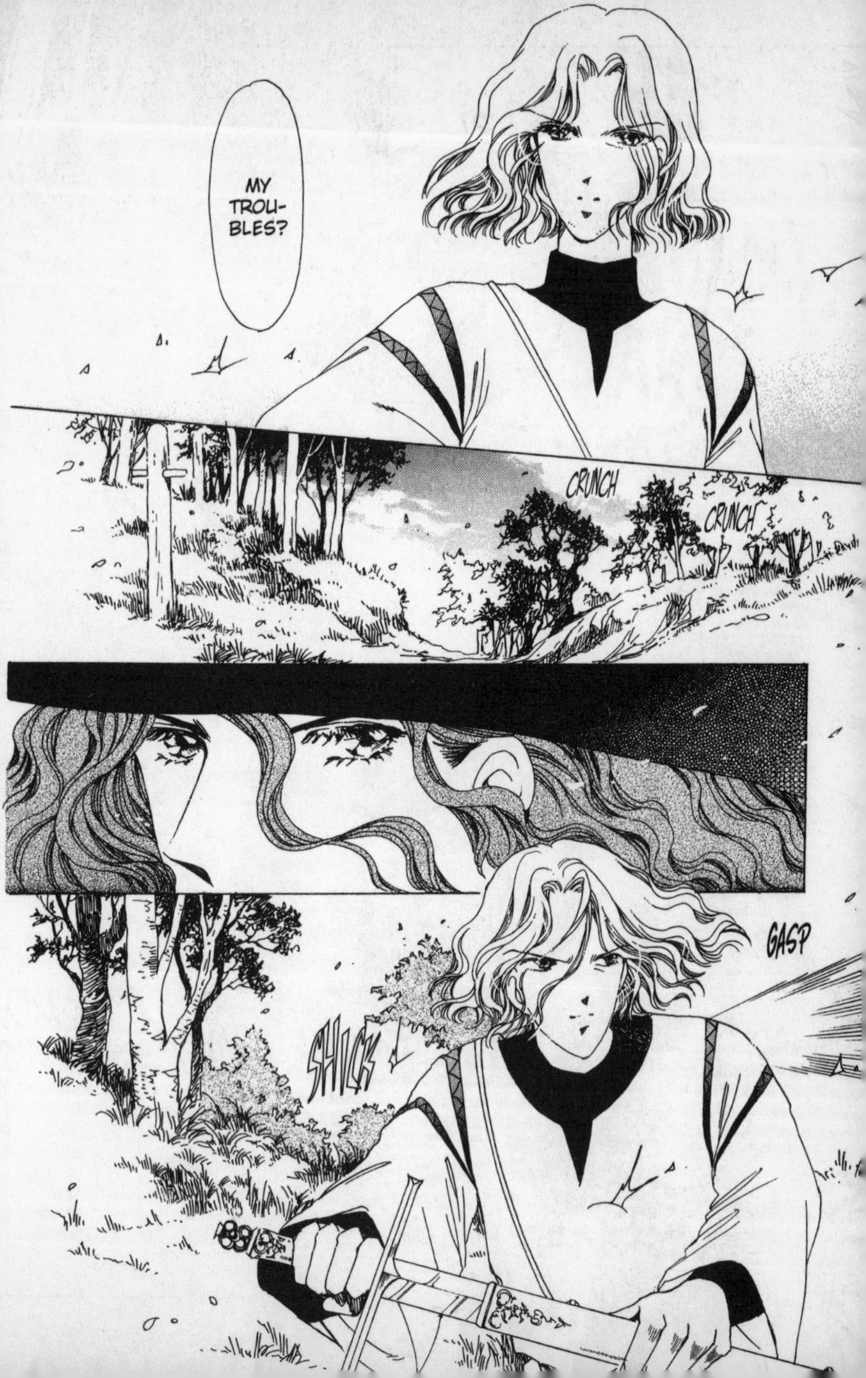
MY TROUBLES?
CRUNCH
CRUNCH
GASP
SHICK

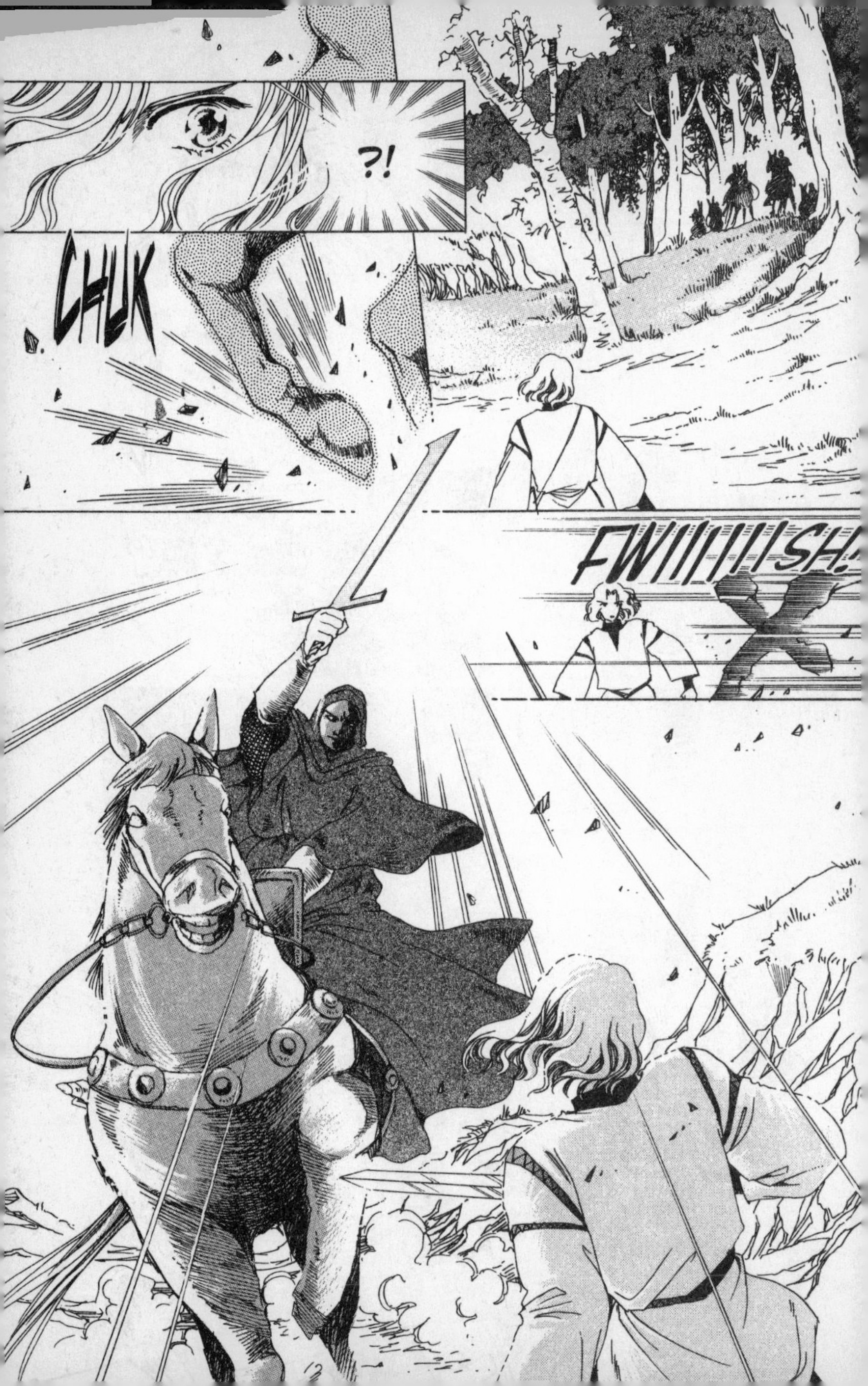
?!
CHUK
FWIIIIIISH!

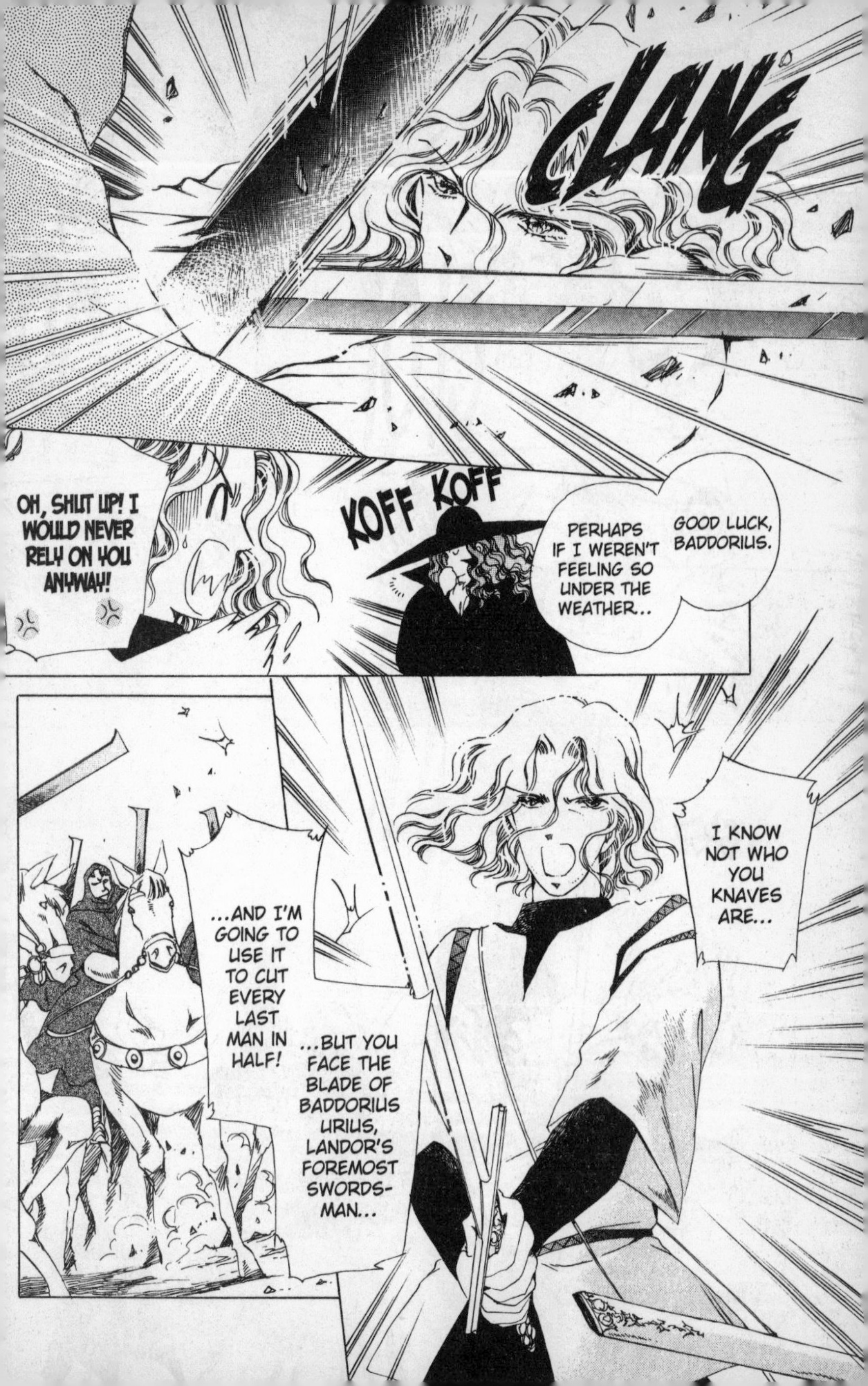
CLANG
GOOD LUCK, BADDORIUS.
PERHAPS IF I WEREN'T FEELING SO UNDER THE WEATHER...
KOFF KOFF
OH, SHUT UP! I WOULD NEVER RELY ON YOU ANYWAY!
I KNOW NOT WHO YOU KNAVES ARE...
...BUT YOU FACE THE BLADE OF BADDORIUS URIUS, LANDOR'S FOREMOST SWORDS-MAN...
...AND I'M GOING TO USE IT TO CUT EVERY LAST MAN IN HALF!

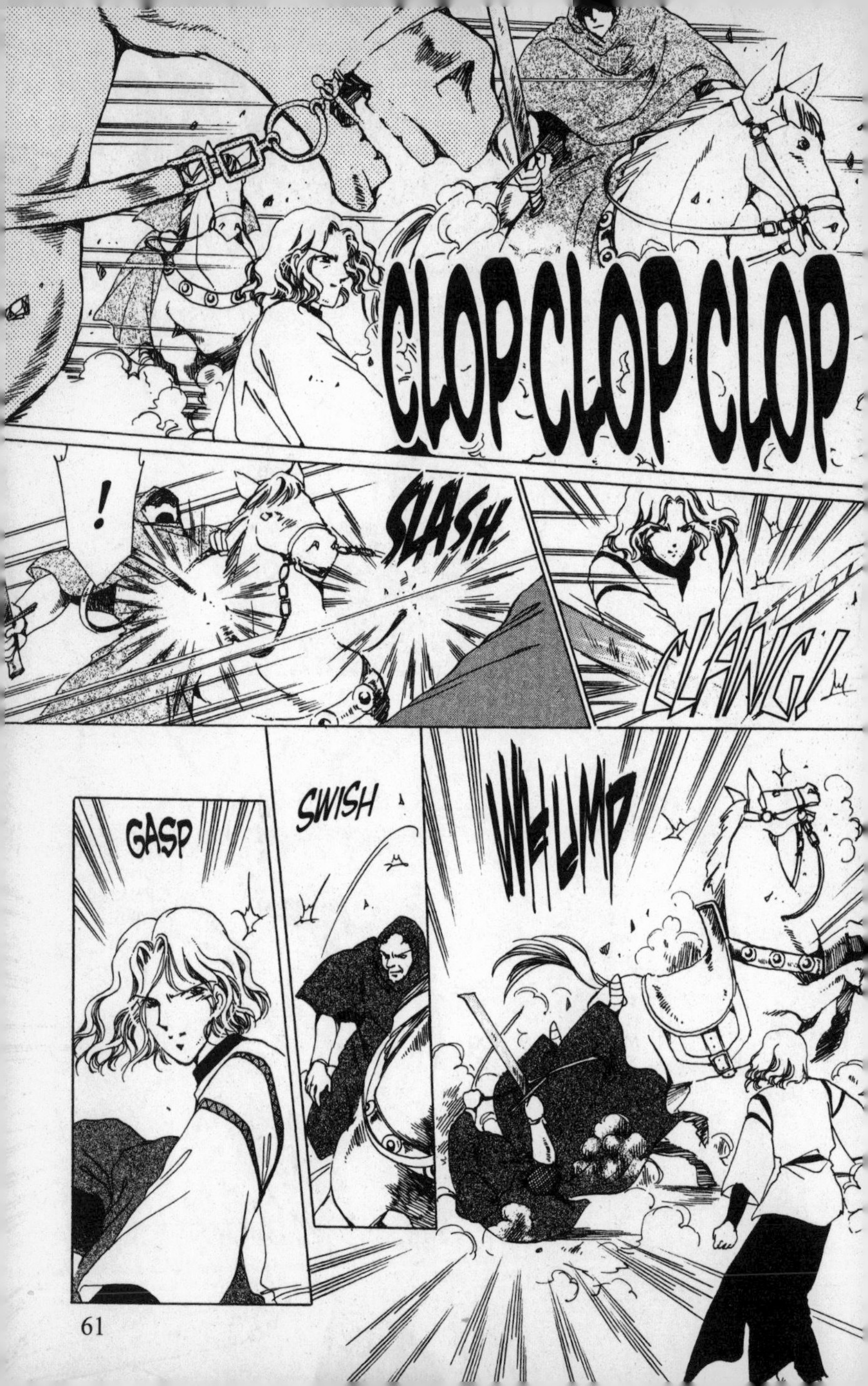

CLOP CLOP CLOP
CLANG!
SLASH
!
WHUMP
SWISH
GASP

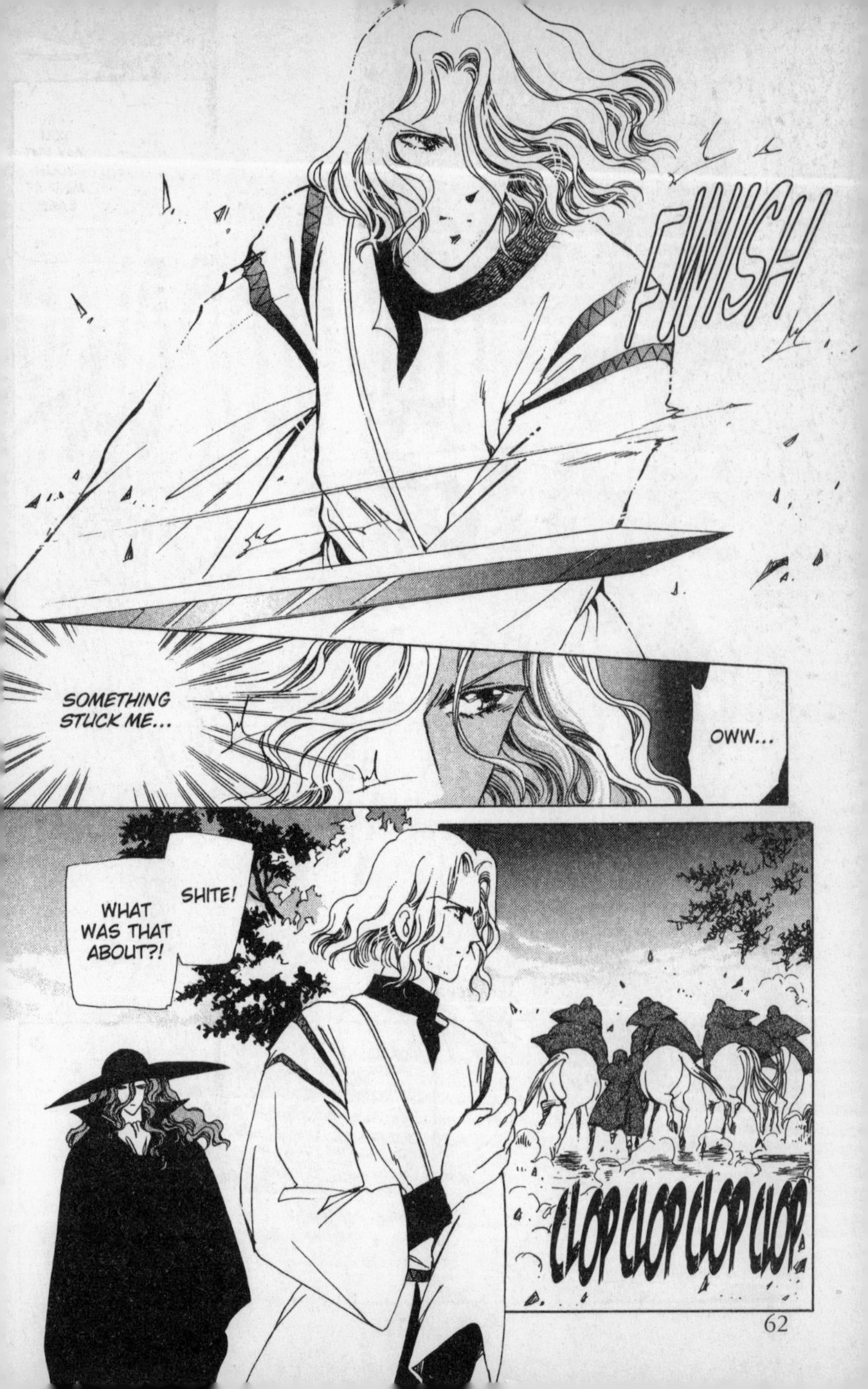
FWISH
OWW...
SOMETHING STUCK ME...
SHITE!
WHAT WAS THAT ABOUT?!
CLOP CLOP CLOP CLOP

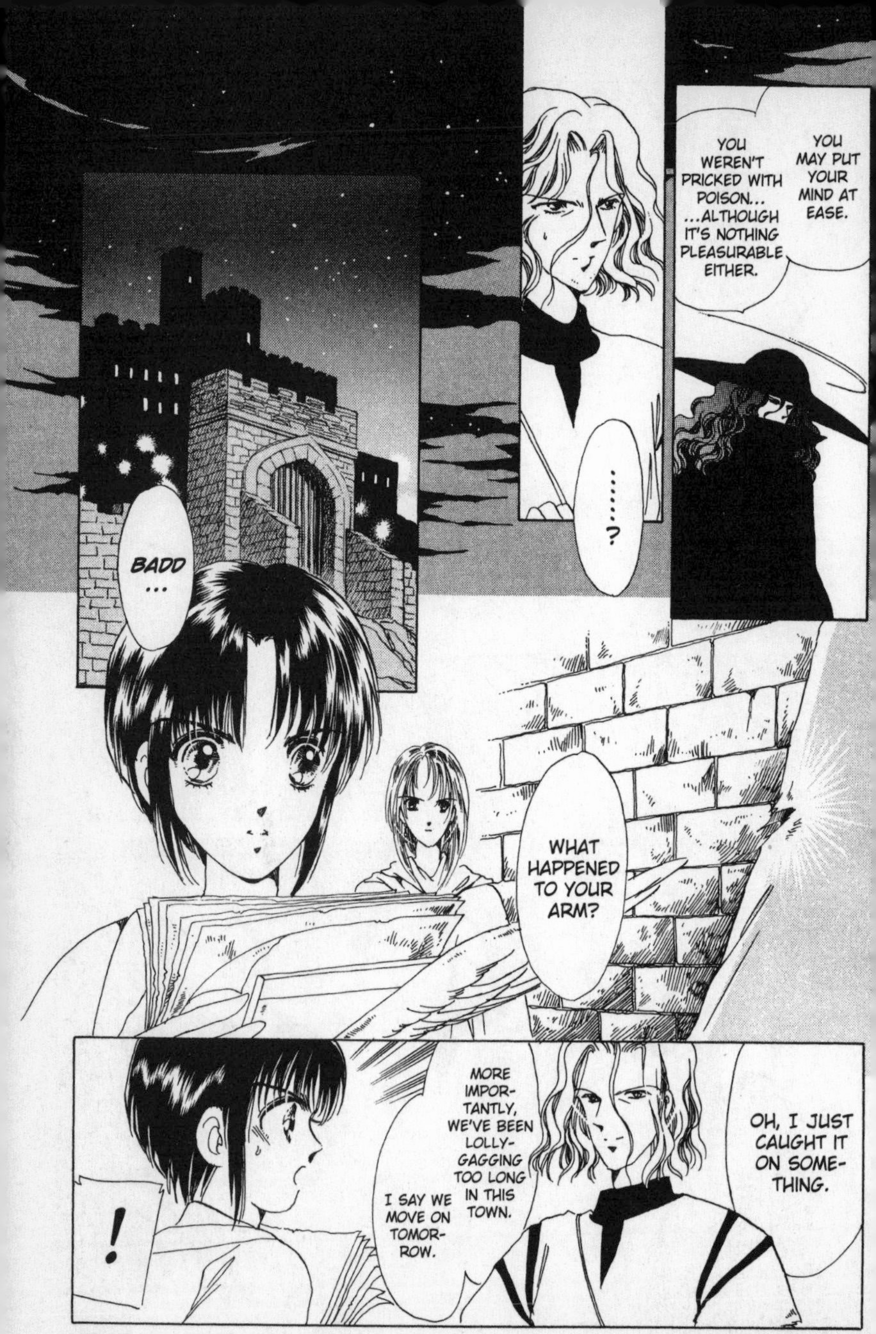
YOU MAY PUT YOUR MIND AT EASE.
YOU WEREN'T PRICKED WITH POISON... ...ALTHOUGH IT'S NOTHING PLEASURABLE EITHER.
......?
BADD ...
WHAT HAPPENED TO YOUR ARM?
OH, I JUST CAUGHT IT ON SOMETHING.
MORE IMPORTANTLY, WE'VE BEEN LOLLYGAGGING TOO LONG IN THIS TOWN.
I SAY WE MOVE ON TOMORROW.
!

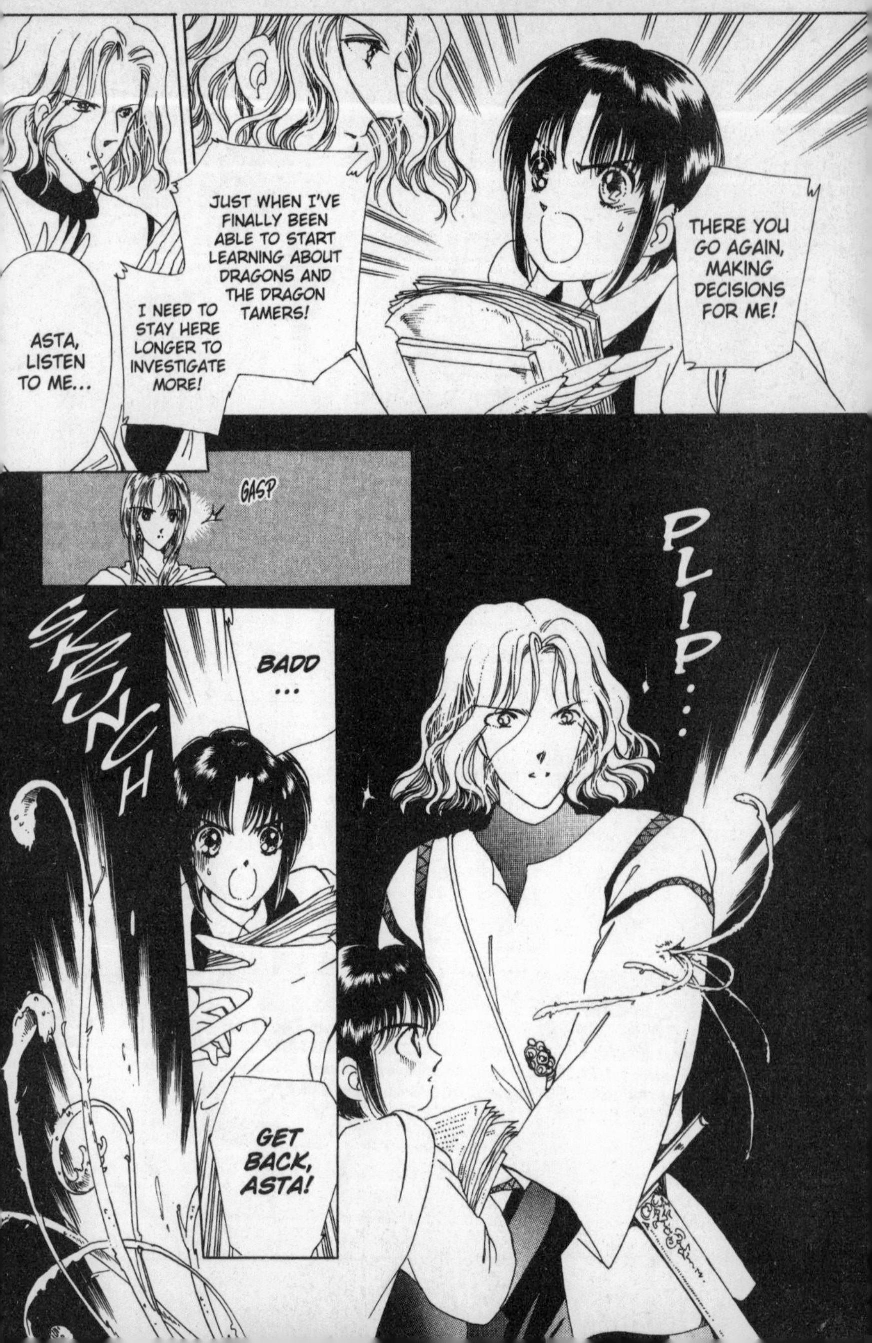
THERE YOU GO AGAIN, MAKING DECISIONS FOR ME!
JUST WHEN I'VE FINALLY BEEN ABLE TO START LEARNING ABOUT DRAGONS AND THE DRAGON TAMERS!
I NEED TO STAY HERE LONGER TO INVESTIGATE MORE!
ASTA, LISTEN TO ME...
PLIP...
GASP
BADD...
GET BACK, ASTA!
SKRUNCH

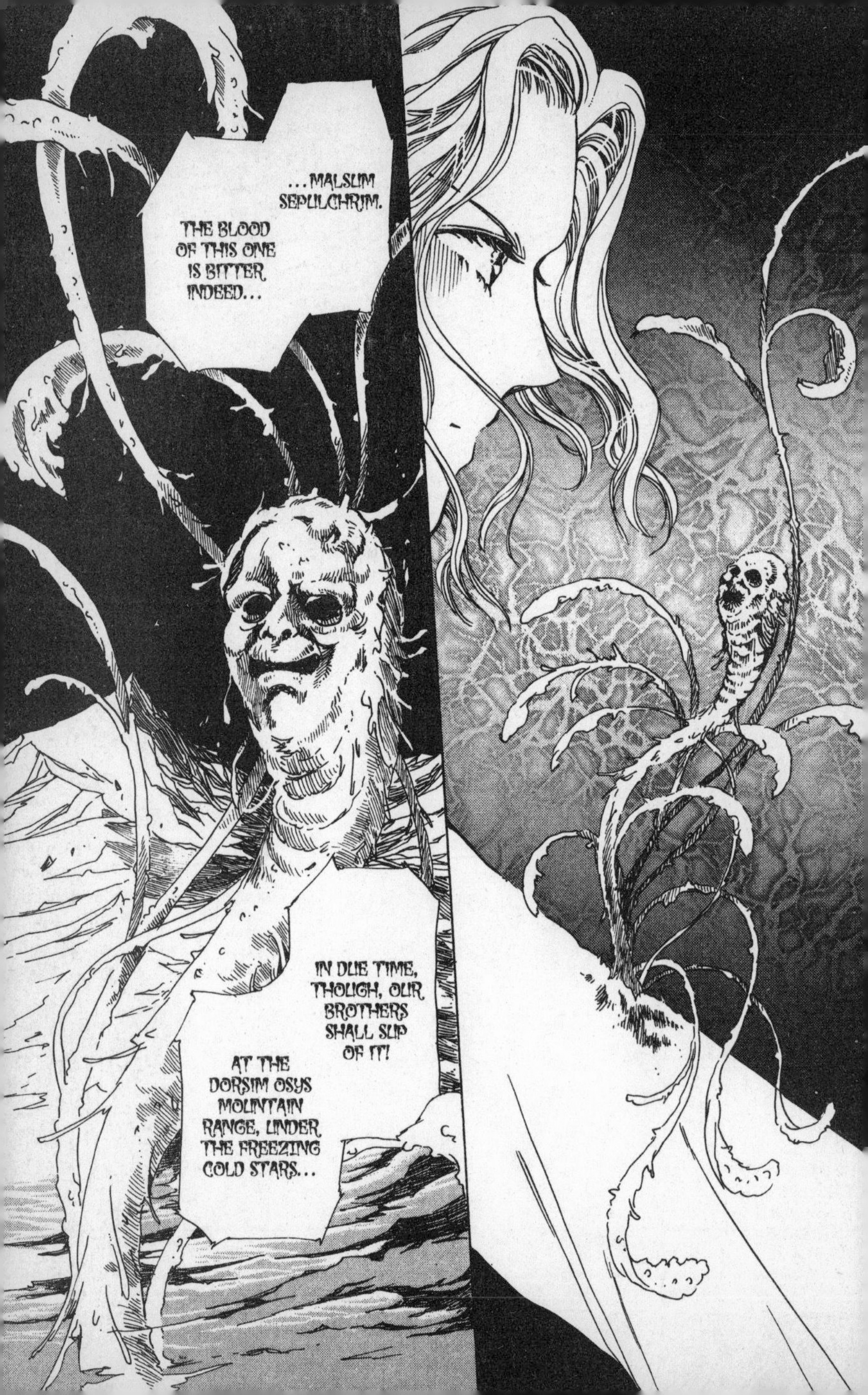
...MALSUM SEPULCHRIM.
THE BLOOD OF THIS ONE IS BITTER INDEED...
IN DUE TIME, THOUGH, OUR BROTHERS SHALL SUP OF IT!
AT THE DORSIM OSYS MOUNTAIN RANGE, UNDER THE FREEZING COLD STARS...

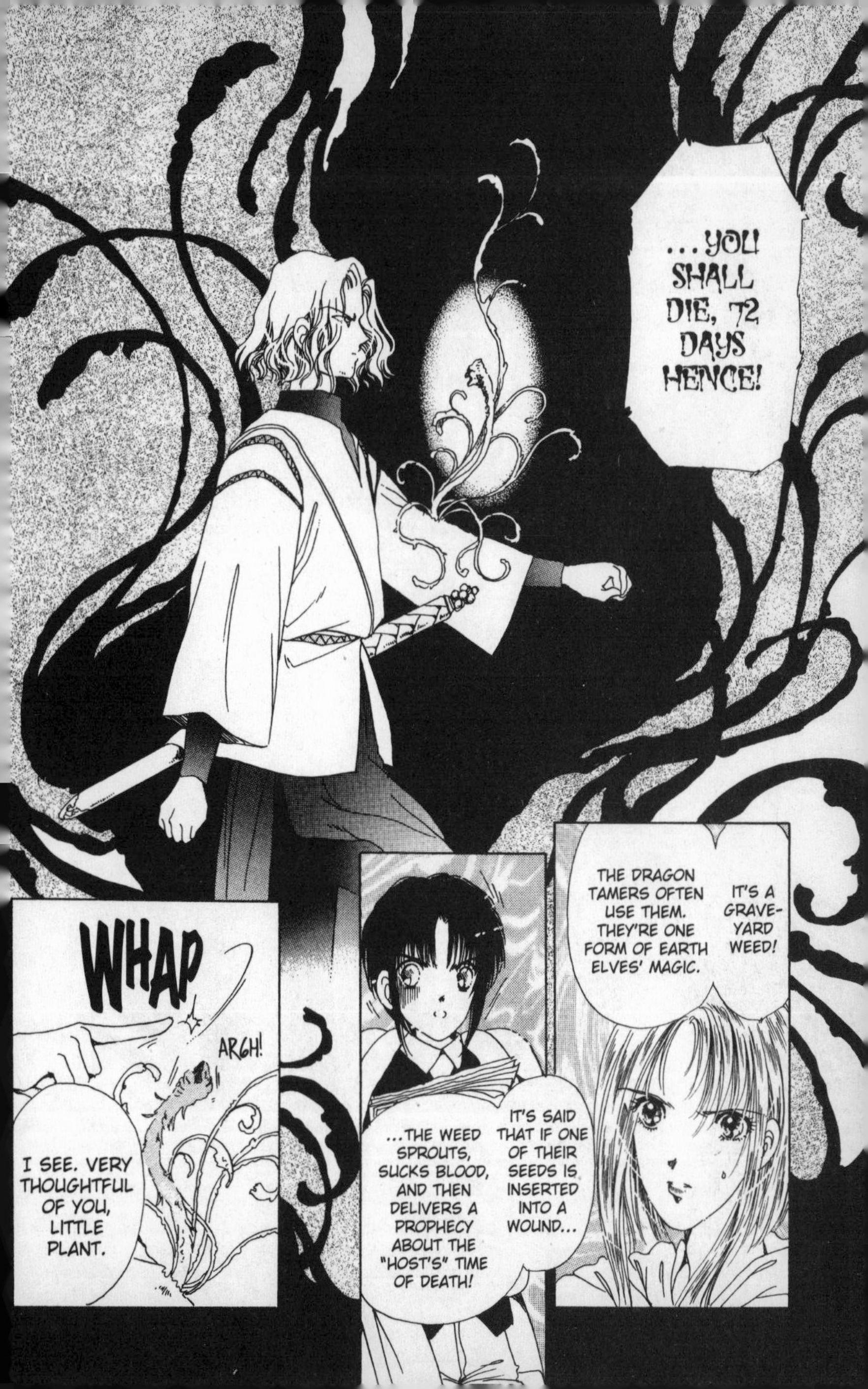
...YOU SHALL DIE, 72 DAYS HENCE!
IT'S A GRAVE-YARD WEED!
THE DRAGON TAMERS OFTEN USE THEM. THEY'RE ONE FORM OF EARTH ELVES' MAGIC.
IT'S SAID THAT IF ONE OF THEIR SEEDS IS INSERTED INTO A WOUND...
...THE WEED SPROUTS, SUCKS BLOOD, AND THEN DELIVERS A PROPHECY ABOUT THE "HOST'S" TIME OF DEATH!
WHAP
ARGH!
I SEE. VERY THOUGHTFUL OF YOU, LITTLE PLANT.

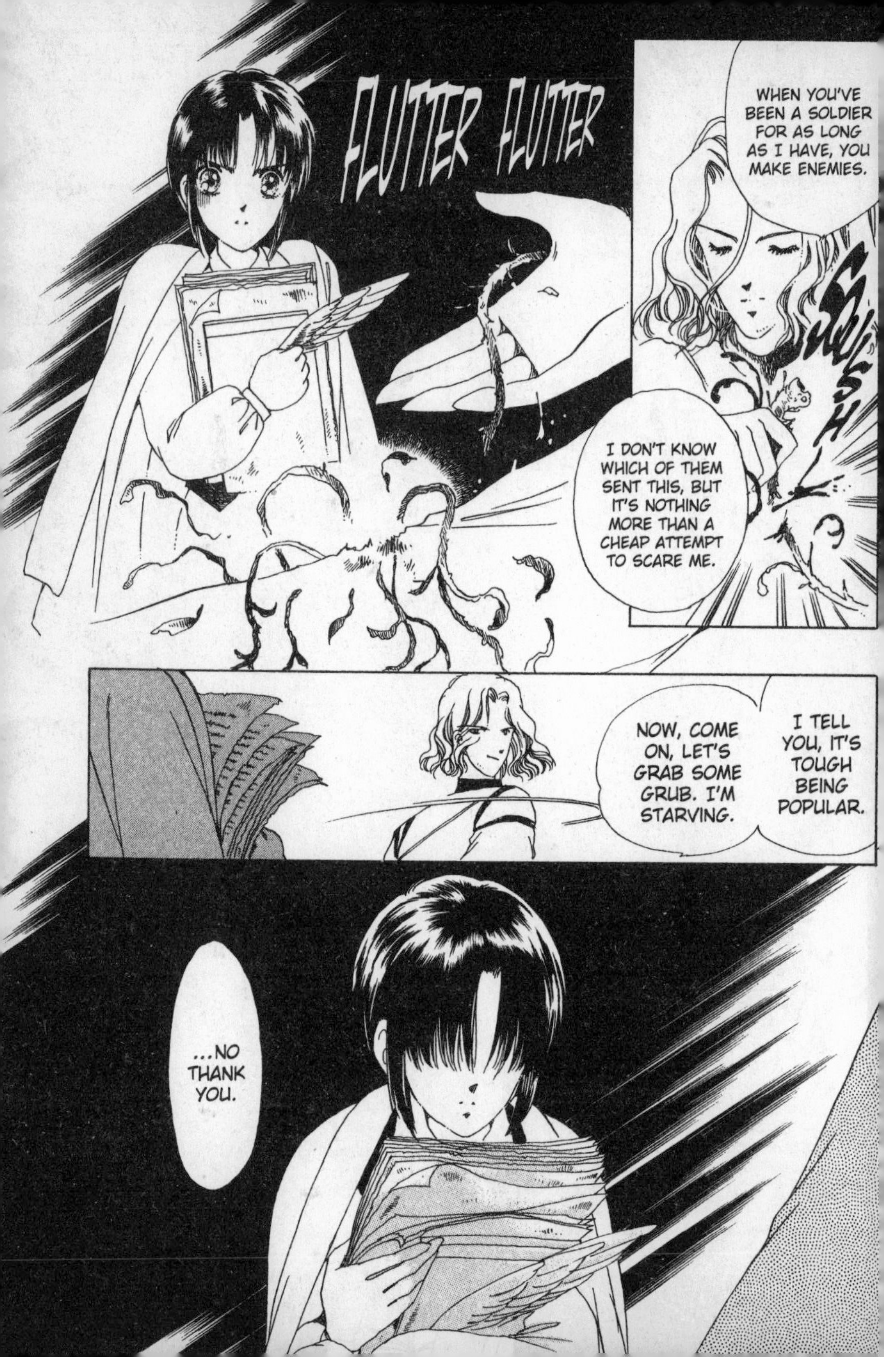
WHEN YOU'VE BEEN A SOLDIER FOR AS LONG AS I HAVE, YOU MAKE ENEMIES.
SWISH
I DON'T KNOW WHICH OF THEM SENT THIS, BUT IT'S NOTHING MORE THAN A CHEAP ATTEMPT TO SCARE ME.
FLUTTER FLUTTER
I TELL YOU, IT'S TOUGH BEING POPULAR.
NOW, COME ON, LET'S GRAB SOME GRUB. I'M STARVING.
...NO THANK YOU.

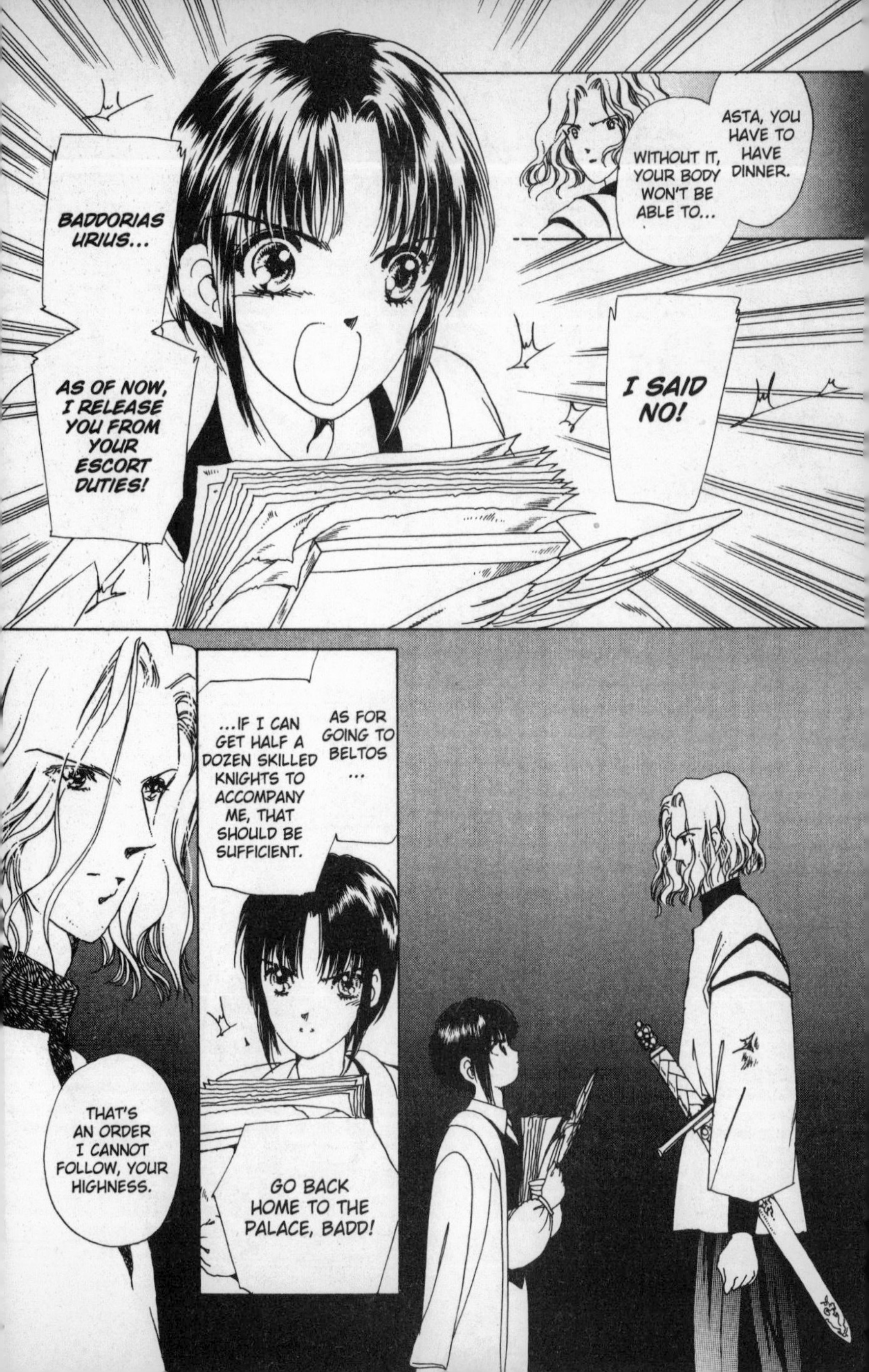

ASTA, YOU HAVE TO HAVE DINNER.
WITHOUT IT, YOUR BODY WON'T BE ABLE TO...
I SAID NO!
BADDORIAS URIUS...
AS OF NOW, I RELEASE YOU FROM YOUR ESCORT DUTIES!
AS FOR GOING TO BELTOS ...
...IF I CAN GET HALF A DOZEN SKILLED KNIGHTS TO ACCOMPANY ME, THAT SHOULD BE SUFFICIENT.
GO BACK HOME TO THE PALACE, BADD!
THAT'S AN ORDER I CANNOT FOLLOW, YOUR HIGHNESS.

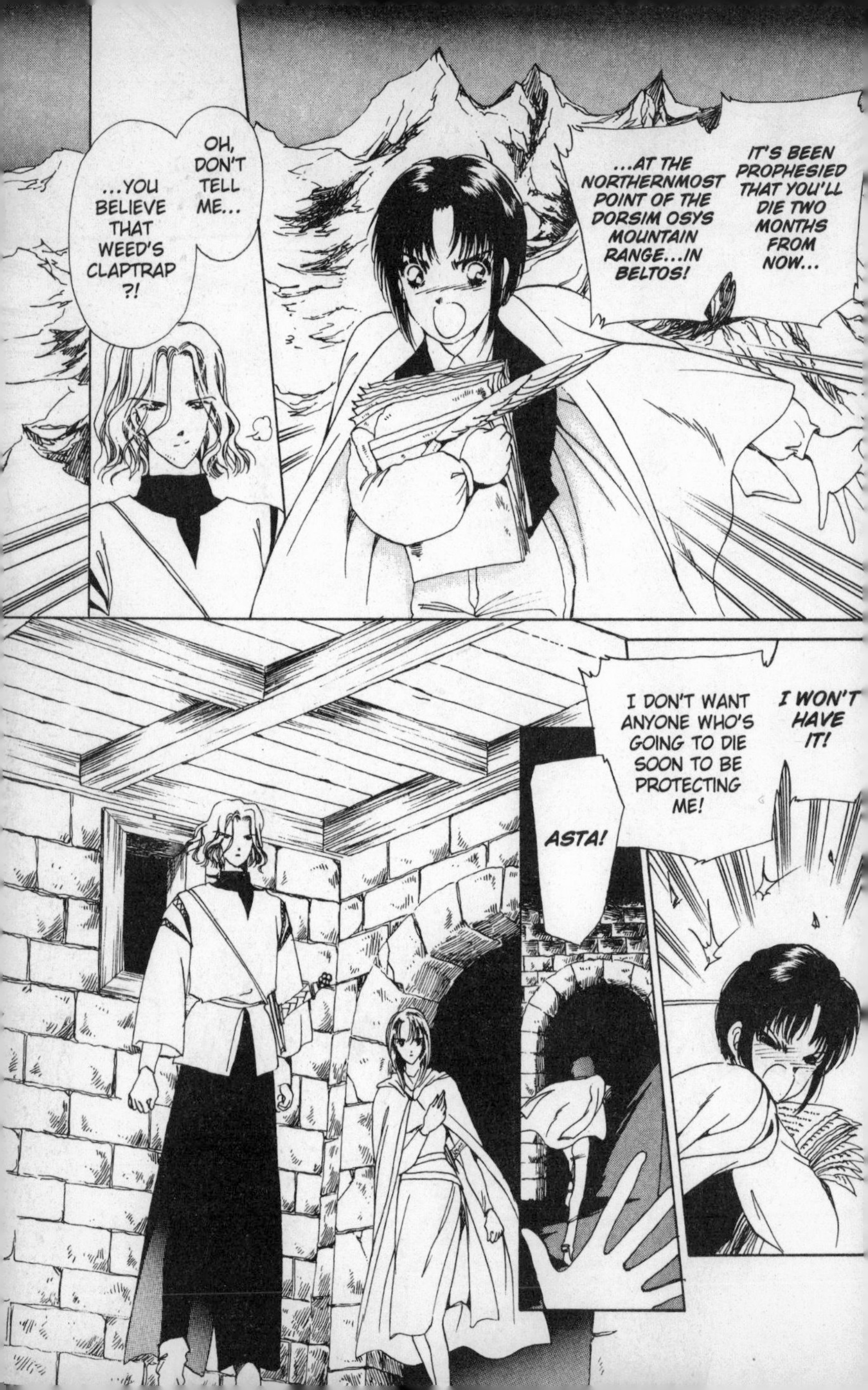
IT'S BEEN PROPHESIED THAT YOU'LL DIE TWO MONTHS FROM NOW...
...AT THE NORTHERNMOST POINT OF THE DORSIM OSYS MOUNTAIN RANGE...IN BELTOS!
OH, DON'T TELL ME...
...YOU BELIEVE THAT WEED'S CLAPTRAP ?!
I WON'T HAVE IT!
I DON'T WANT ANYONE WHO'S GOING TO DIE SOON TO BE PROTECTING ME!
ASTA!

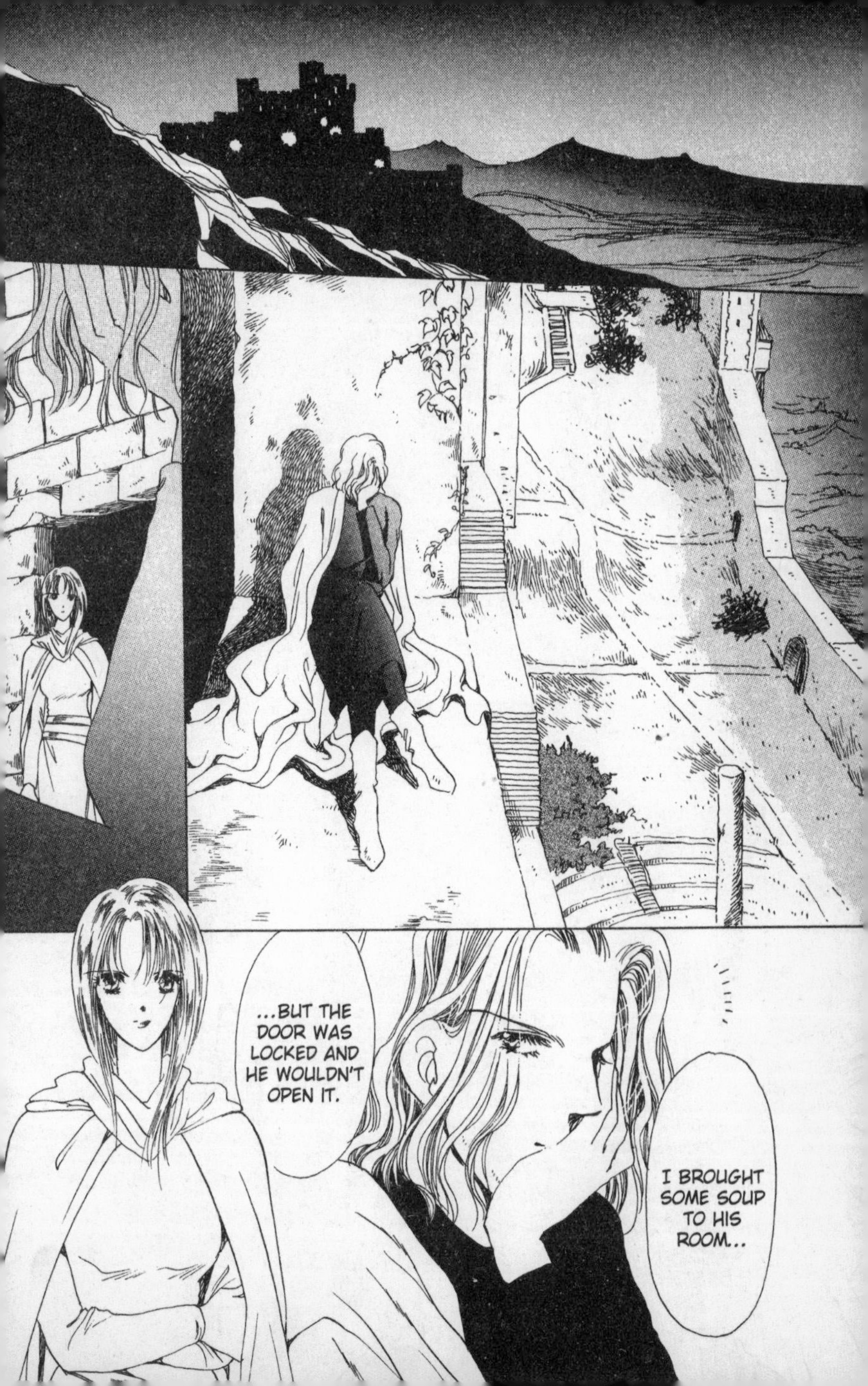
I BROUGHT SOME SOUP TO HIS ROOM...
...BUT THE DOOR WAS LOCKED AND HE WOULDN'T OPEN IT.

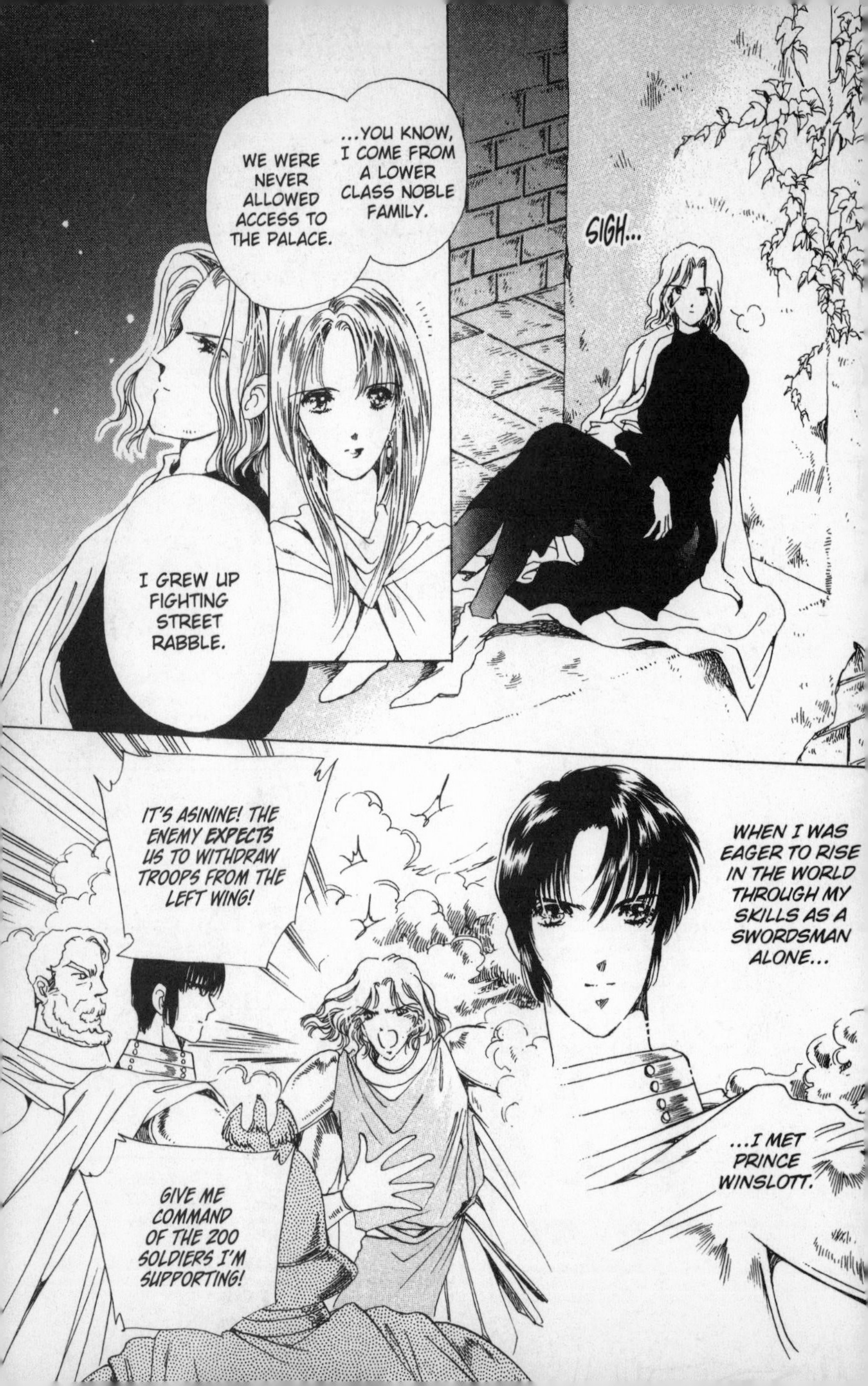
SIGH...
...YOU KNOW, I COME FROM A LOWER CLASS NOBLE FAMILY.
WE WERE NEVER ALLOWED ACCESS TO THE PALACE.
I GREW UP FIGHTING STREET RABBLE.
WHEN I WAS EAGER TO RISE IN THE WORLD THROUGH MY SKILLS AS A SWORDSMAN ALONE...
...I MET PRINCE WINSLOTT.
IT'S ASININE! THE ENEMY EXPECTS US TO WITHDRAW TROOPS FROM THE LEFT WING!
GIVE ME COMMAND OF THE 200 SOLDIERS I'M SUPPORTING!

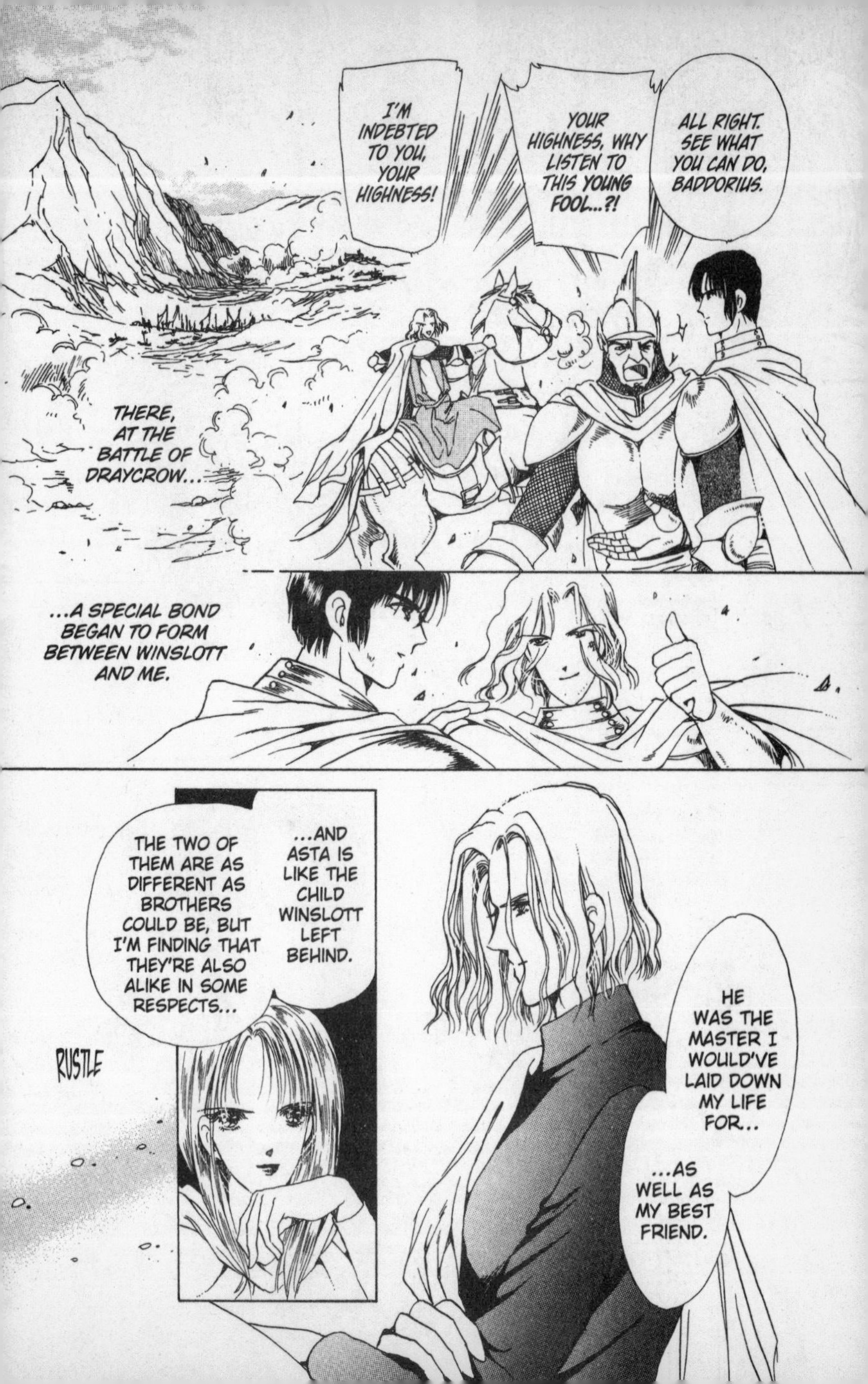
ALL RIGHT. SEE WHAT YOU CAN DO, BADDORIUS.
YOUR HIGHNESS, WHY LISTEN TO THIS YOUNG FOOL...?!
I'M INDEBTED TO YOU, YOUR HIGHNESS!
THERE, AT THE BATTLE OF DRAYCROW...
...A SPECIAL BOND BEGAN TO FORM BETWEEN WINSLOTT AND ME.
HE WAS THE MASTER I WOULD'VE LAID DOWN MY LIFE FOR...
...AS WELL AS MY BEST FRIEND.
...AND ASTA IS LIKE THE CHILD WINSLOTT LEFT BEHIND.
THE TWO OF THEM ARE AS DIFFERENT AS BROTHERS COULD BE, BUT I'M FINDING THAT THEY'RE ALSO ALIKE IN SOME RESPECTS...
RUSTLE

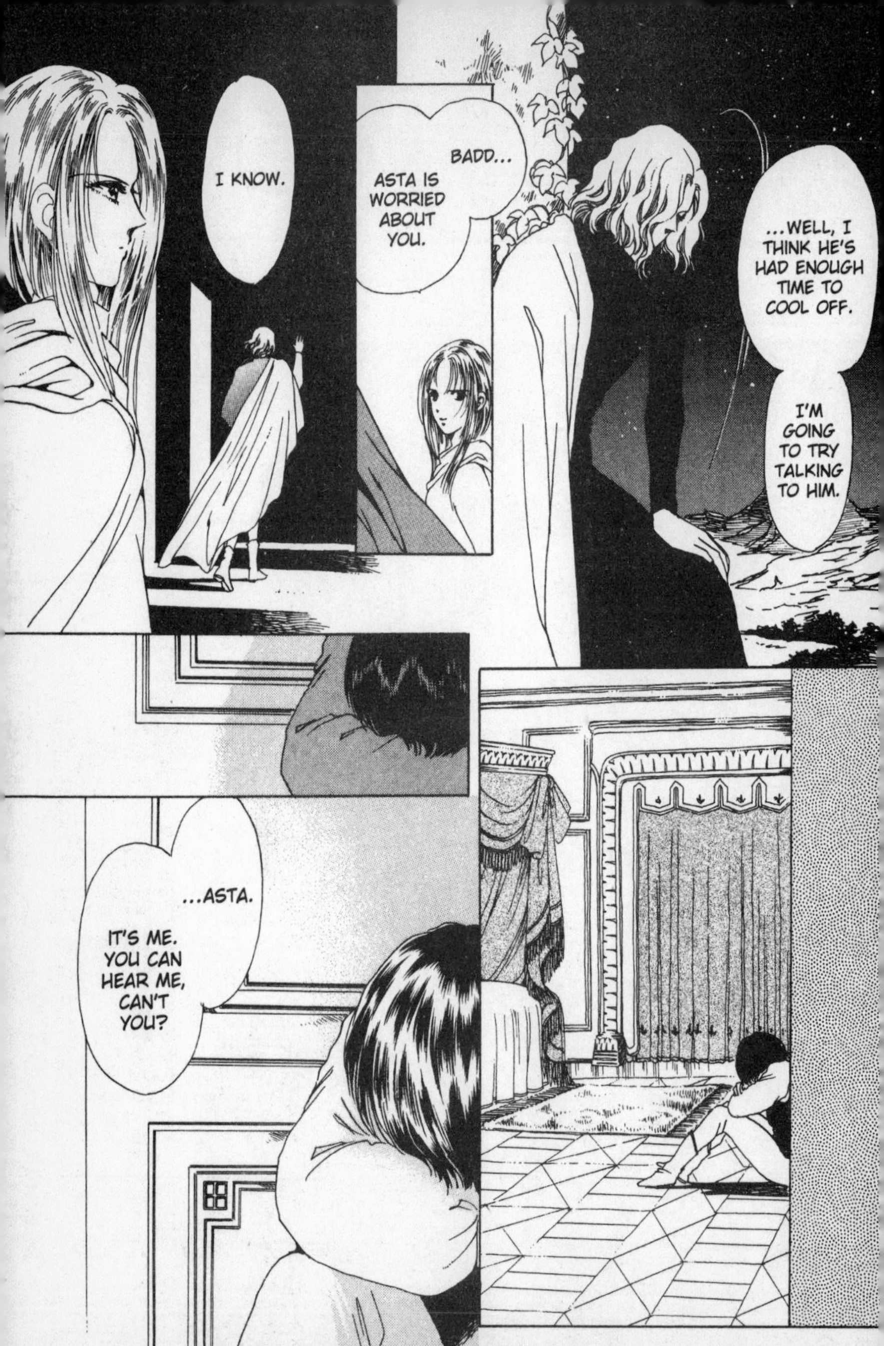
...WELL, I THINK HE'S HAD ENOUGH TIME TO COOL OFF.
I'M GOING TO TRY TALKING TO HIM.
BADD...
ASTA IS WORRIED ABOUT YOU.
I KNOW.
...ASTA.
IT'S ME. YOU CAN HEAR ME, CAN'T YOU?

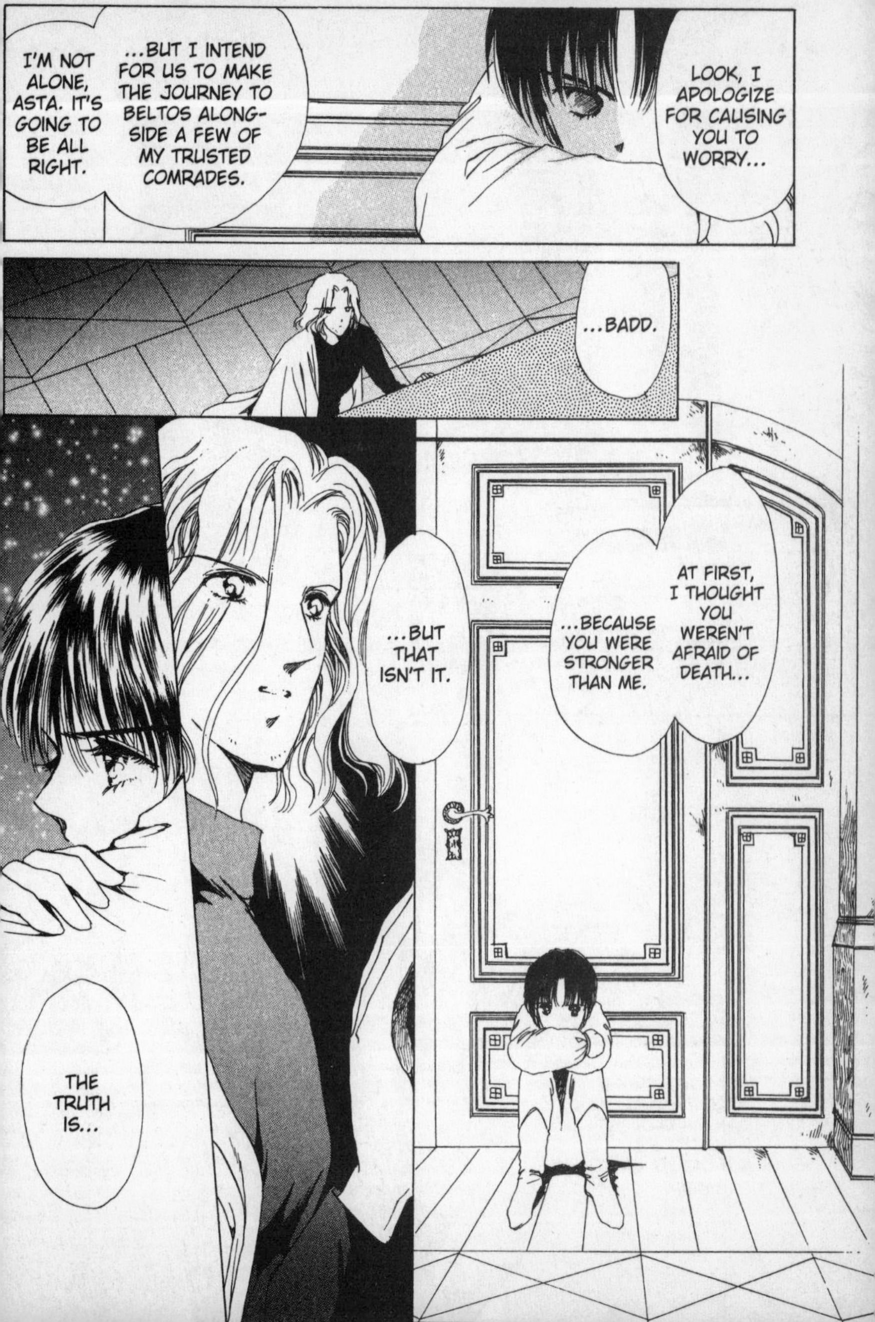
LOOK, I APOLOGIZE FOR CAUSING YOU TO WORRY...
...BUT I INTEND FOR US TO MAKE THE JOURNEY TO BELTOS ALONG-SIDE A FEW OF MY TRUSTED COMRADES.
I'M NOT ALONE, ASTA. IT'S GOING TO BE ALL RIGHT.
...BADD.
AT FIRST, I THOUGHT YOU WEREN'T AFRAID OF DEATH...
...BECAUSE YOU WERE STRONGER THAN ME.
...BUT THAT ISN'T IT.
THE TRUTH IS...

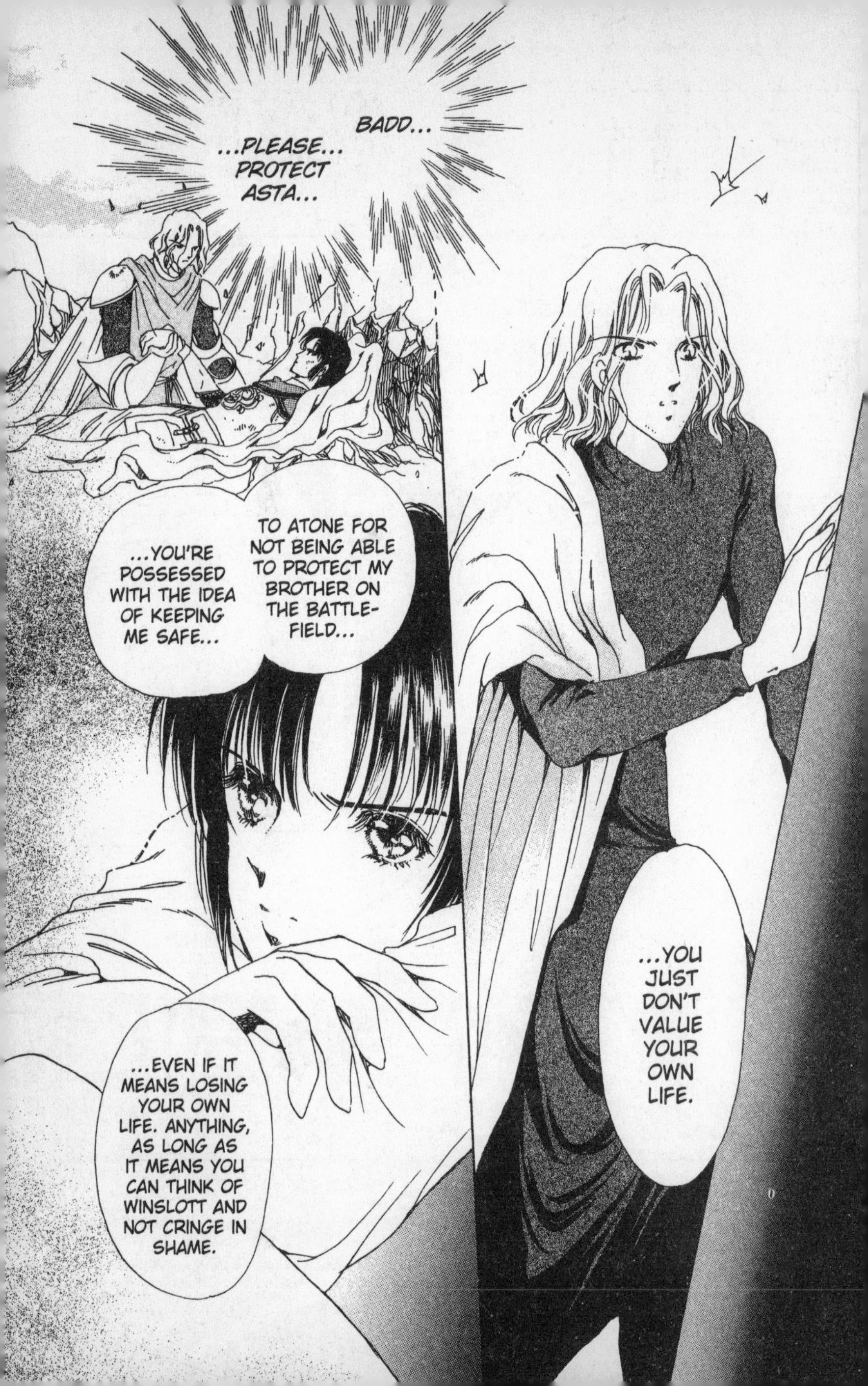
...YOU JUST DON'T VALUE YOUR OWN LIFE.
BADD...
...PLEASE... PROTECT ASTA...
TO ATONE FOR NOT BEING ABLE TO PROTECT MY BROTHER ON THE BATTLE-FIELD...
...YOU'RE POSSESSED WITH THE IDEA OF KEEPING ME SAFE...
...EVEN IF IT MEANS LOSING YOUR OWN LIFE. ANYTHING, AS LONG AS IT MEANS YOU CAN THINK OF WINSLOTT AND NOT CRINGE IN SHAME.

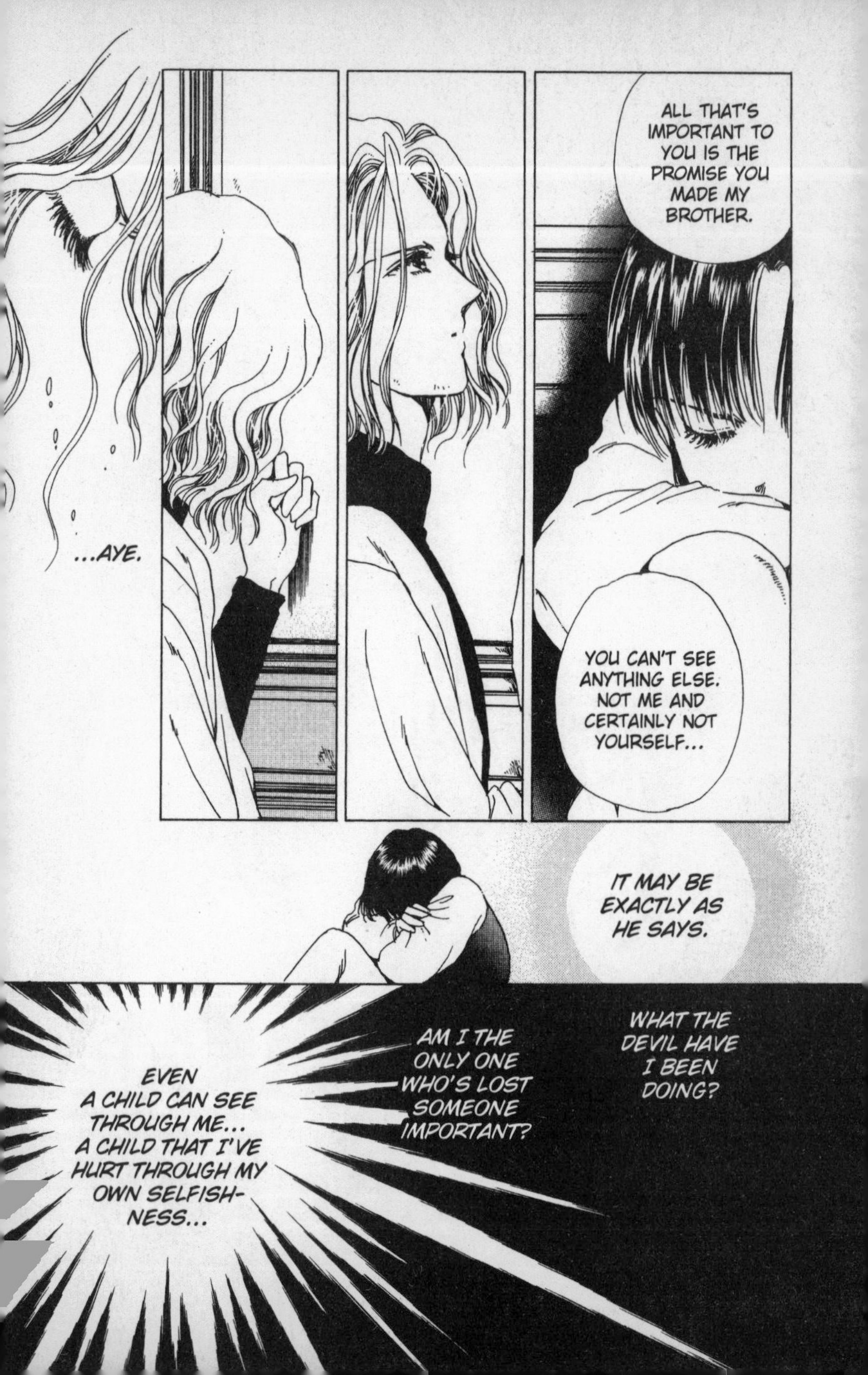
ALL THAT'S IMPORTANT TO YOU IS THE PROMISE YOU MADE MY BROTHER.
YOU CAN'T SEE ANYTHING ELSE. NOT ME AND CERTAINLY NOT YOURSELF...
...AYE.
IT MAY BE EXACTLY AS HE SAYS.
WHAT THE DEVIL HAVE I BEEN DOING?
AM I THE ONLY ONE WHO'S LOST SOMEONE IMPORTANT?
EVEN A CHILD CAN SEE THROUGH ME... A CHILD THAT I'VE HURT THROUGH MY OWN SELFISH-NESS...

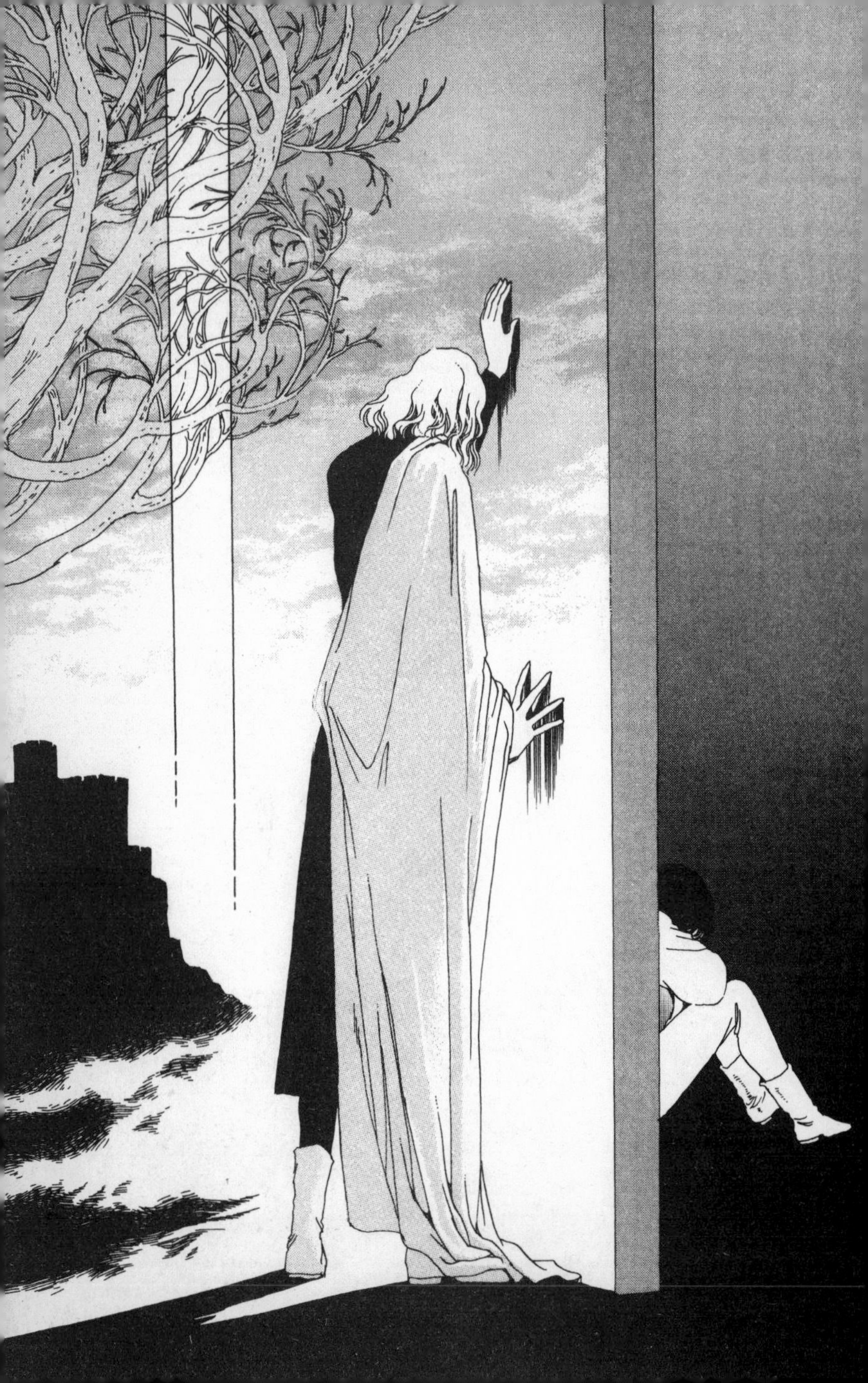

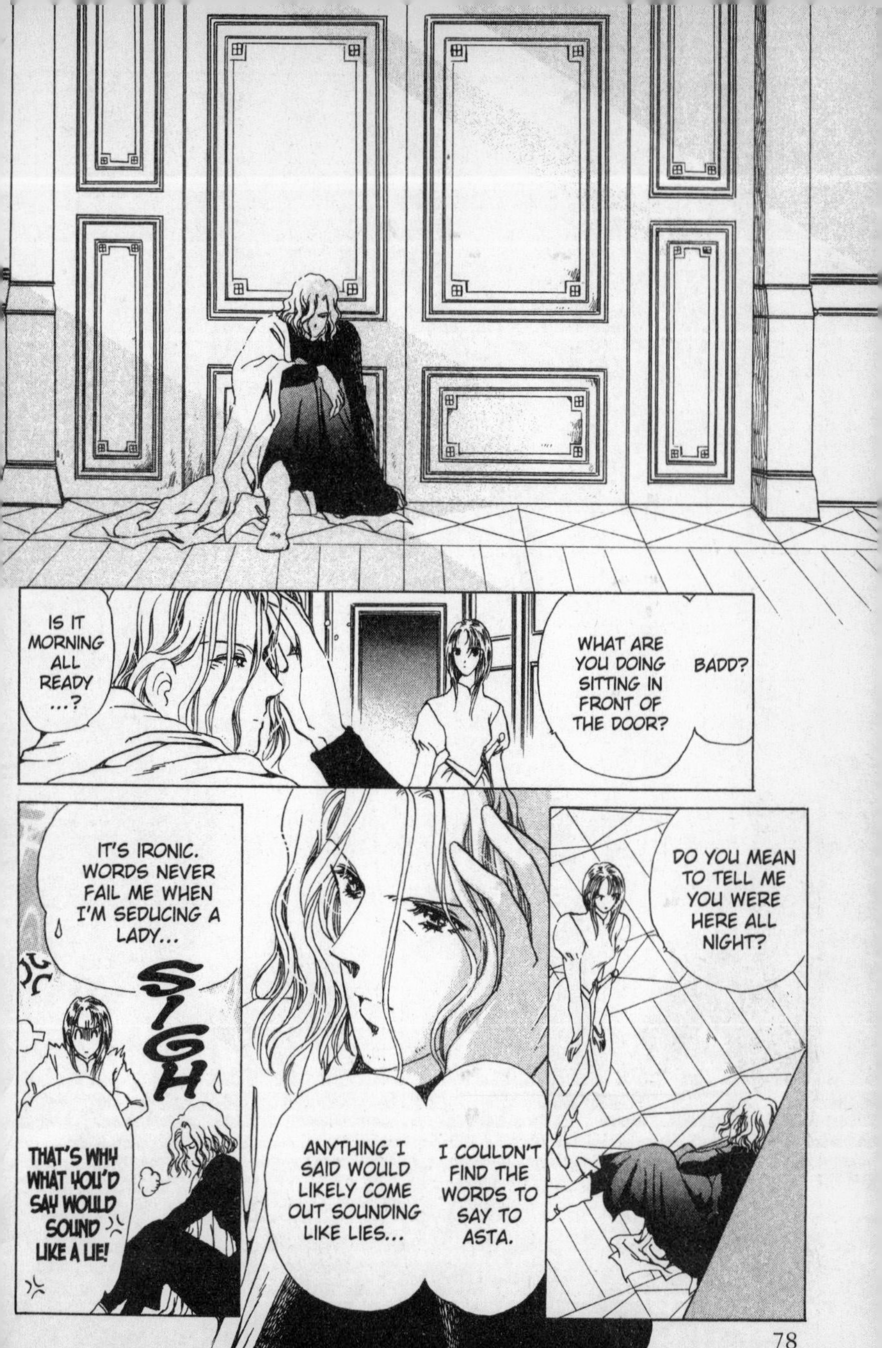
WHAT ARE YOU DOING SITTING IN FRONT OF THE DOOR?
BADD?
IS IT MORNING ALL READY ...?
DO YOU MEAN TO TELL ME YOU WERE HERE ALL NIGHT?
I COULDN'T FIND THE WORDS TO SAY TO ASTA.
ANYTHING I SAID WOULD LIKELY COME OUT SOUNDING LIKE LIES...
IT'S IRONIC. WORDS NEVER FAIL ME WHEN I'M SEDUCING A LADY...
SIGH
THAT'S WHY WHAT YOU'D SAY WOULD SOUND LIKE A LIE!

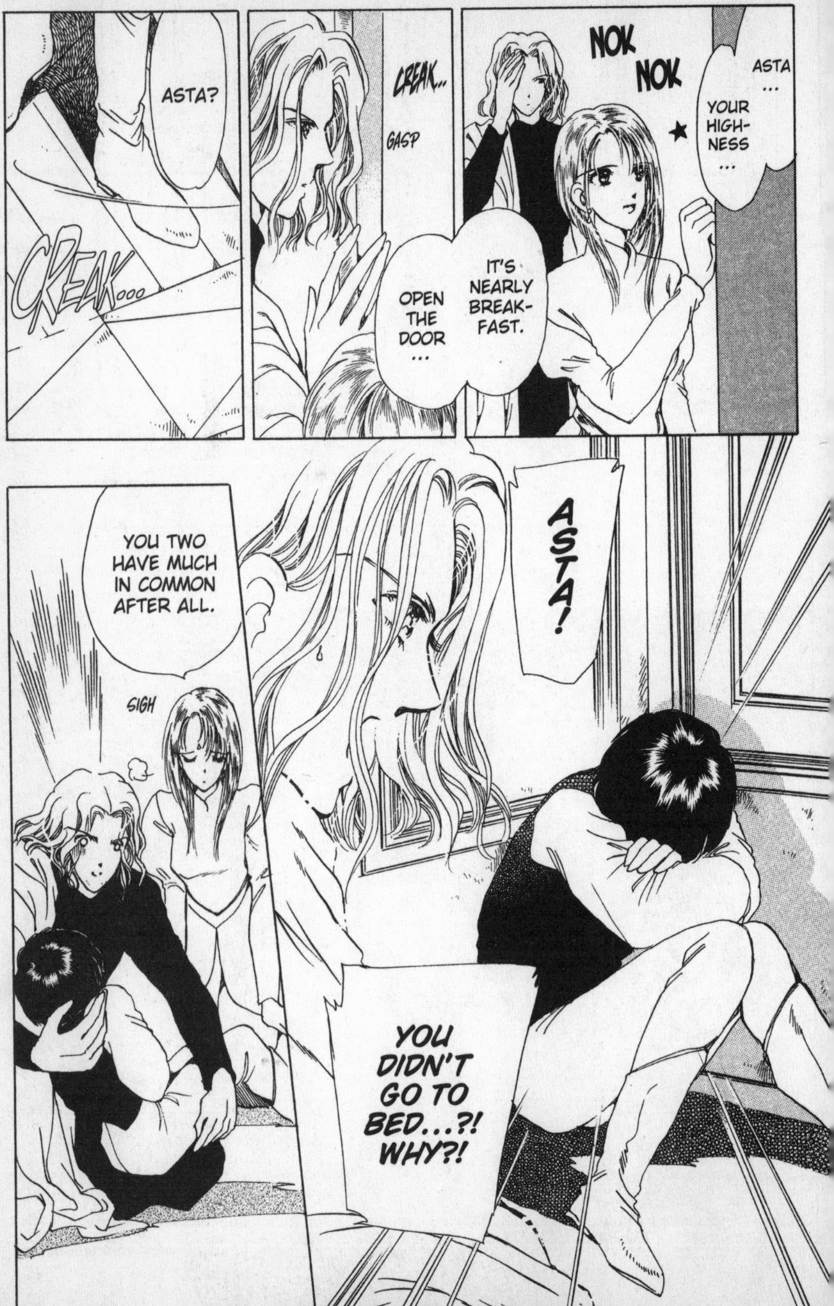
NOK NOK
ASTA... YOUR HIGHNESS...
IT'S NEARLY BREAKFAST.
OPEN THE DOOR...
CREAK...
GASP
ASTA?
CREAK...
ASTA!
YOU DIDN'T GO TO BED...?! WHY?!
YOU TWO HAVE MUCH IN COMMON AFTER ALL.
SIGH

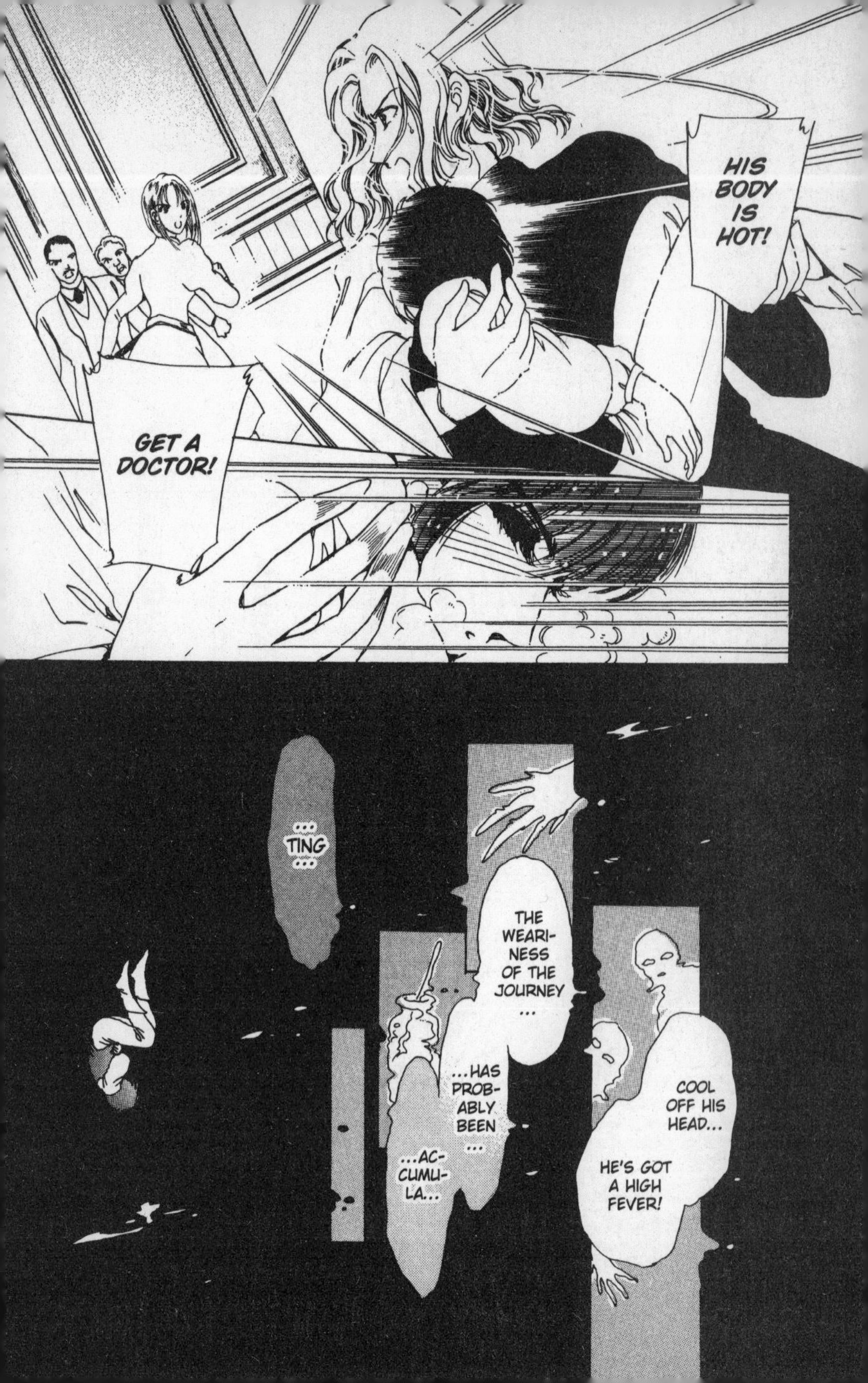
HIS BODY IS HOT!
GET A DOCTOR!
COOL OFF HIS HEAD...
HE'S GOT A HIGH FEVER!
THE WEARI-NESS OF THE JOURNEY ...
...HAS PROB-ABLY BEEN ...
...AC-CUMU-LA...
... TING ...

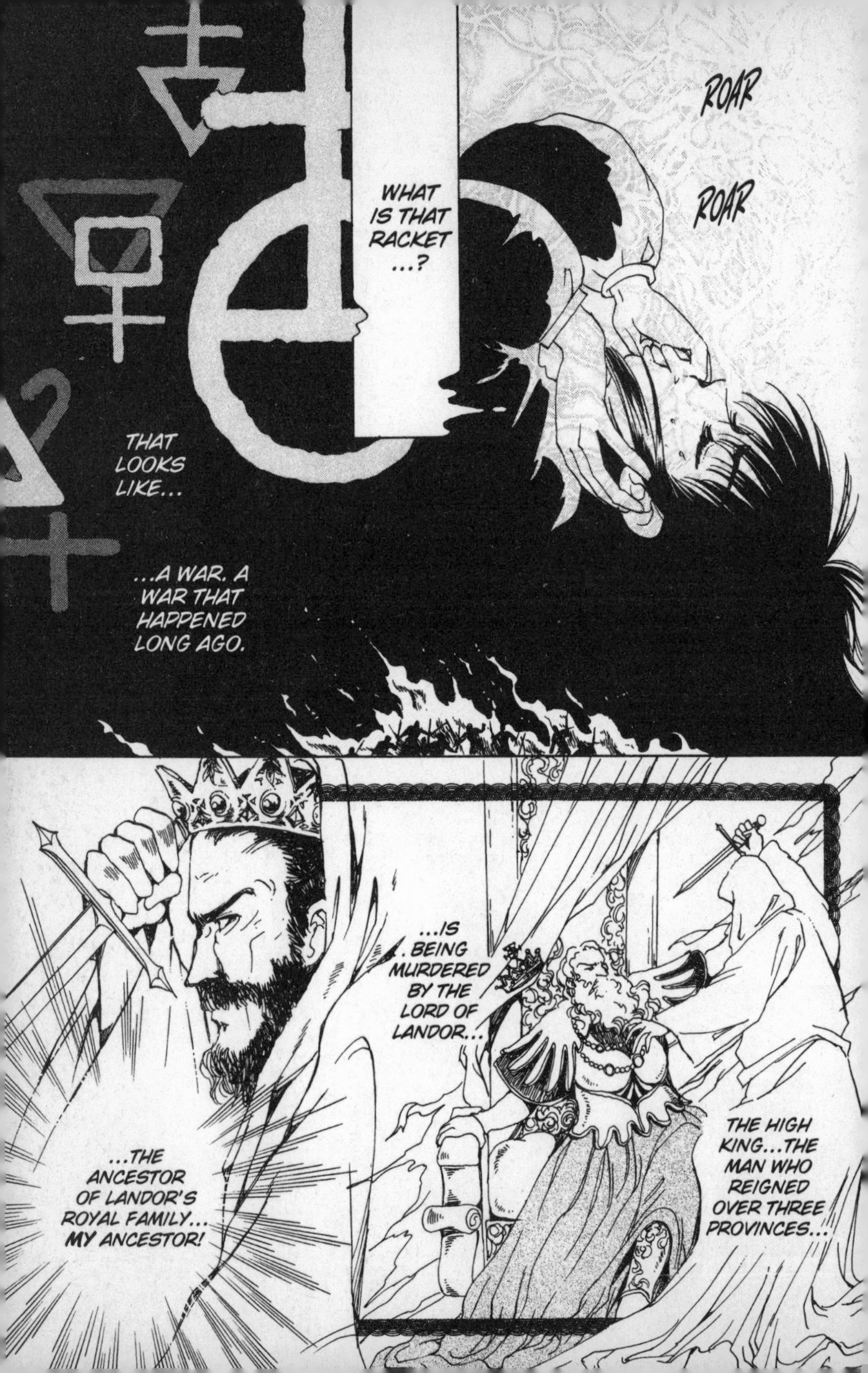
ROAR
ROAR
WHAT IS THAT RACKET ...?
THAT LOOKS LIKE...
...A WAR. A WAR THAT HAPPENED LONG AGO.
THE HIGH KING...THE MAN WHO REIGNED OVER THREE PROVINCES...
...IS ...BEING MURDERED BY THE LORD OF LANDOR...
...THE ANCESTOR OF LANDOR'S ROYAL FAMILY... MY ANCESTOR!

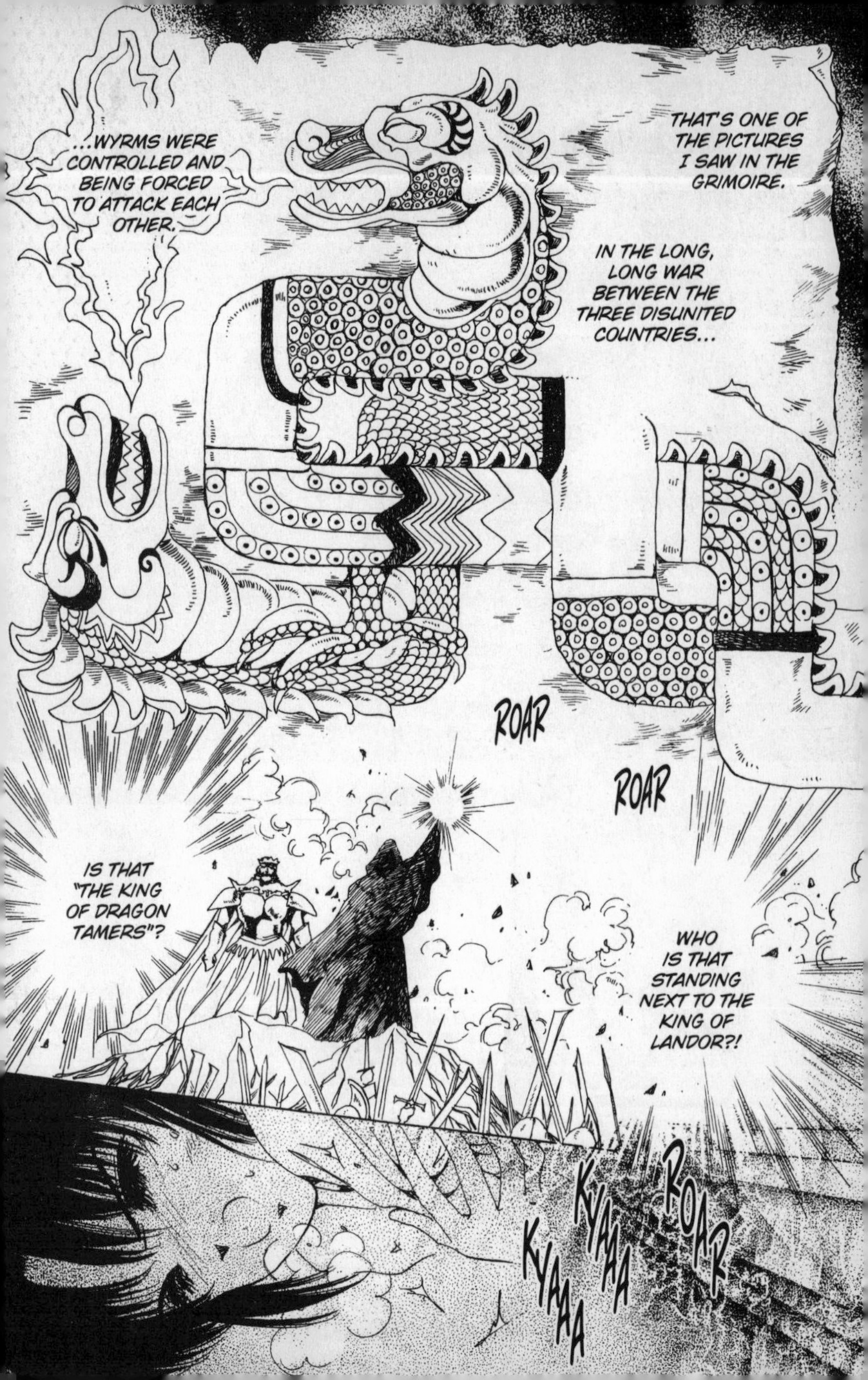
THAT'S ONE OF THE PICTURES I SAW IN THE GRIMOIRE.
IN THE LONG, LONG WAR BETWEEN THE THREE DISUNITED COUNTRIES...
...WYRMS WERE CONTROLLED AND BEING FORCED TO ATTACK EACH OTHER.
ROAR
ROAR
WHO IS THAT STANDING NEXT TO THE KING OF LANDOR?!
IS THAT "THE KING OF DRAGON TAMERS"?
ROAR
KYAAAA
KYAAAA

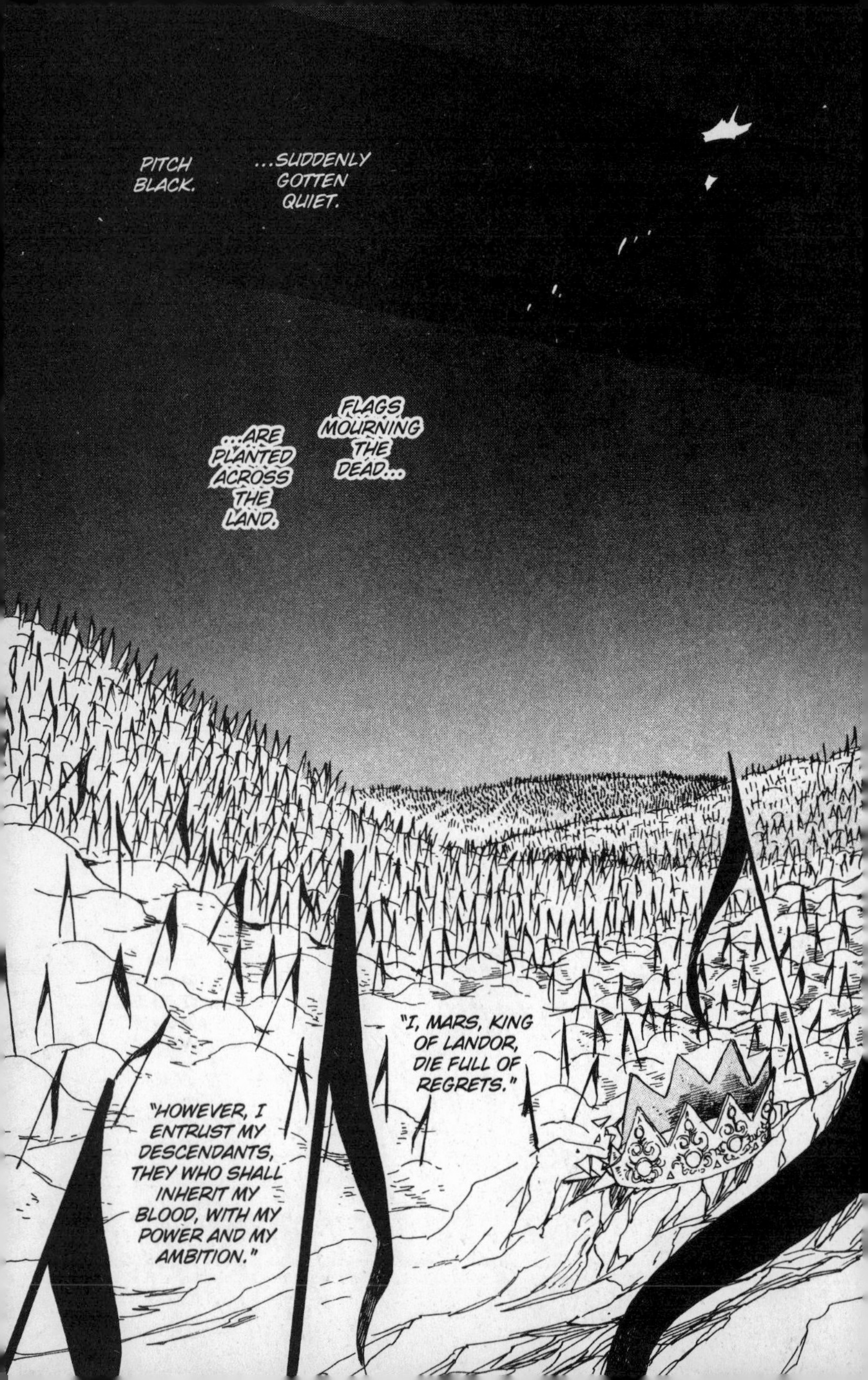
...SUDDENLY GOTTEN QUIET.
PITCH BLACK.
FLAGS MOURNING THE DEAD...
...ARE PLANTED ACROSS THE LAND.
"I, MARS, KING OF LANDOR, DIE FULL OF REGRETS."
"HOWEVER, I ENTRUST MY DESCENDANTS, THEY WHO SHALL INHERIT MY BLOOD, WITH MY POWER AND MY AMBITION."

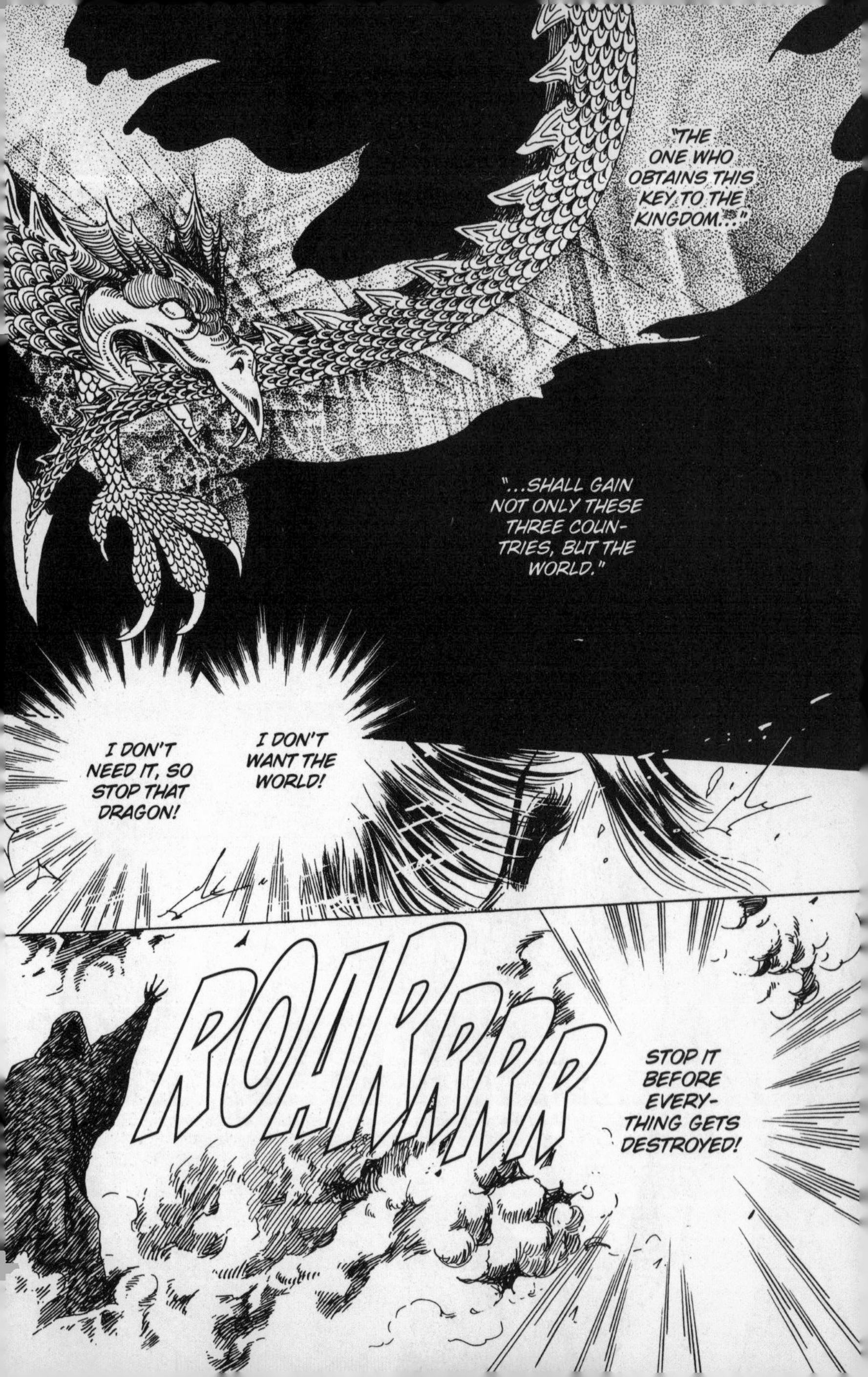
"THE ONE WHO OBTAINS THIS KEY TO THE KINGDOM..."
"...SHALL GAIN NOT ONLY THESE THREE COUN-TRIES, BUT THE WORLD."
I DON'T WANT THE WORLD!
I DON'T NEED IT, SO STOP THAT DRAGON!
ROARRRR
STOP IT BEFORE EVERY-THING GETS DESTROYED!

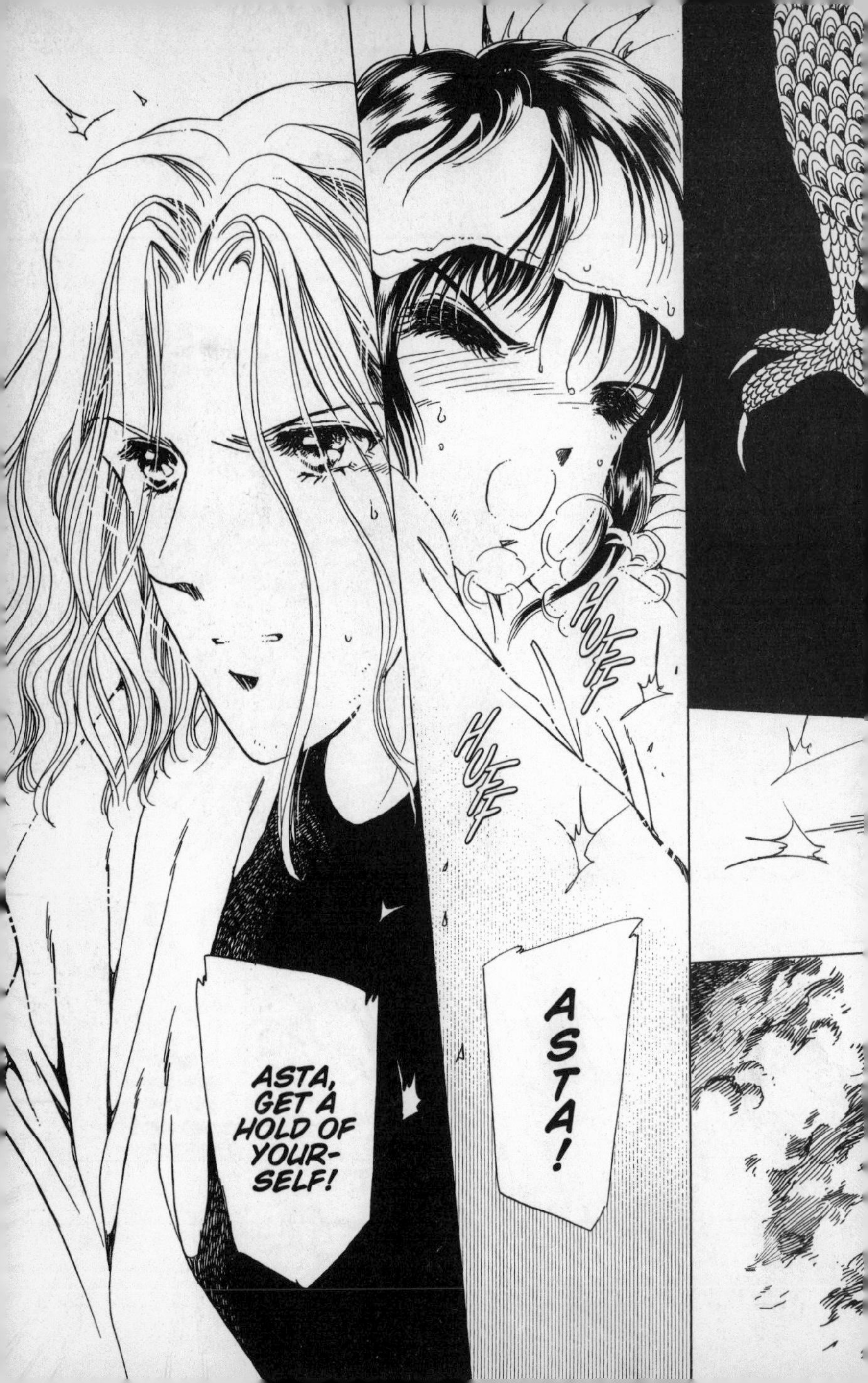
HUFF
HUFF
ASTA!
ASTA, GET A HOLD OF YOURSELF!

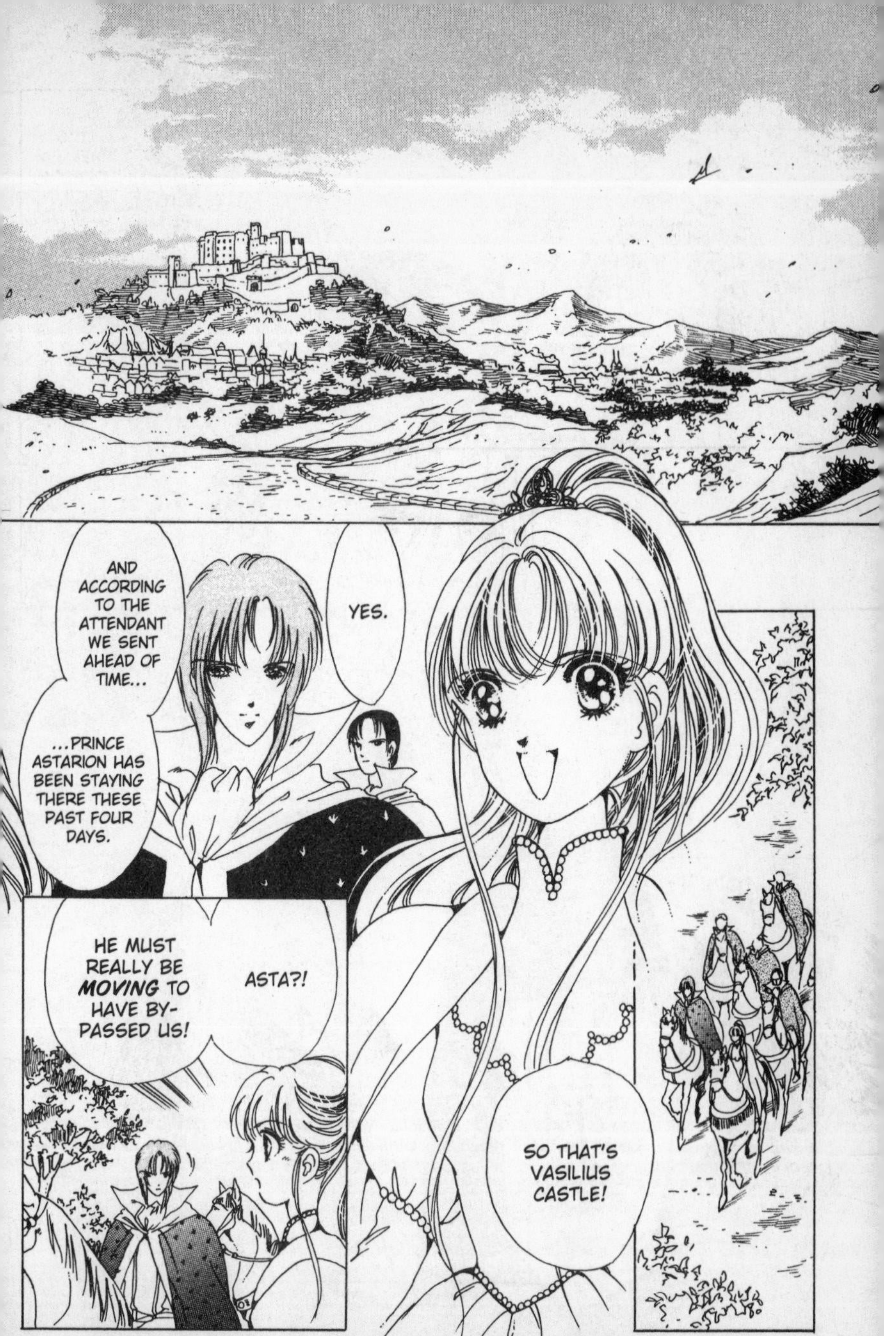
SO THAT'S VASILIUS CASTLE!
YES.
AND ACCORDING TO THE ATTENDANT WE SENT AHEAD OF TIME...
...PRINCE ASTARION HAS BEEN STAYING THERE THESE PAST FOUR DAYS.
ASTA?!
HE MUST REALLY BE *MOVING* TO HAVE BY-PASSED US!

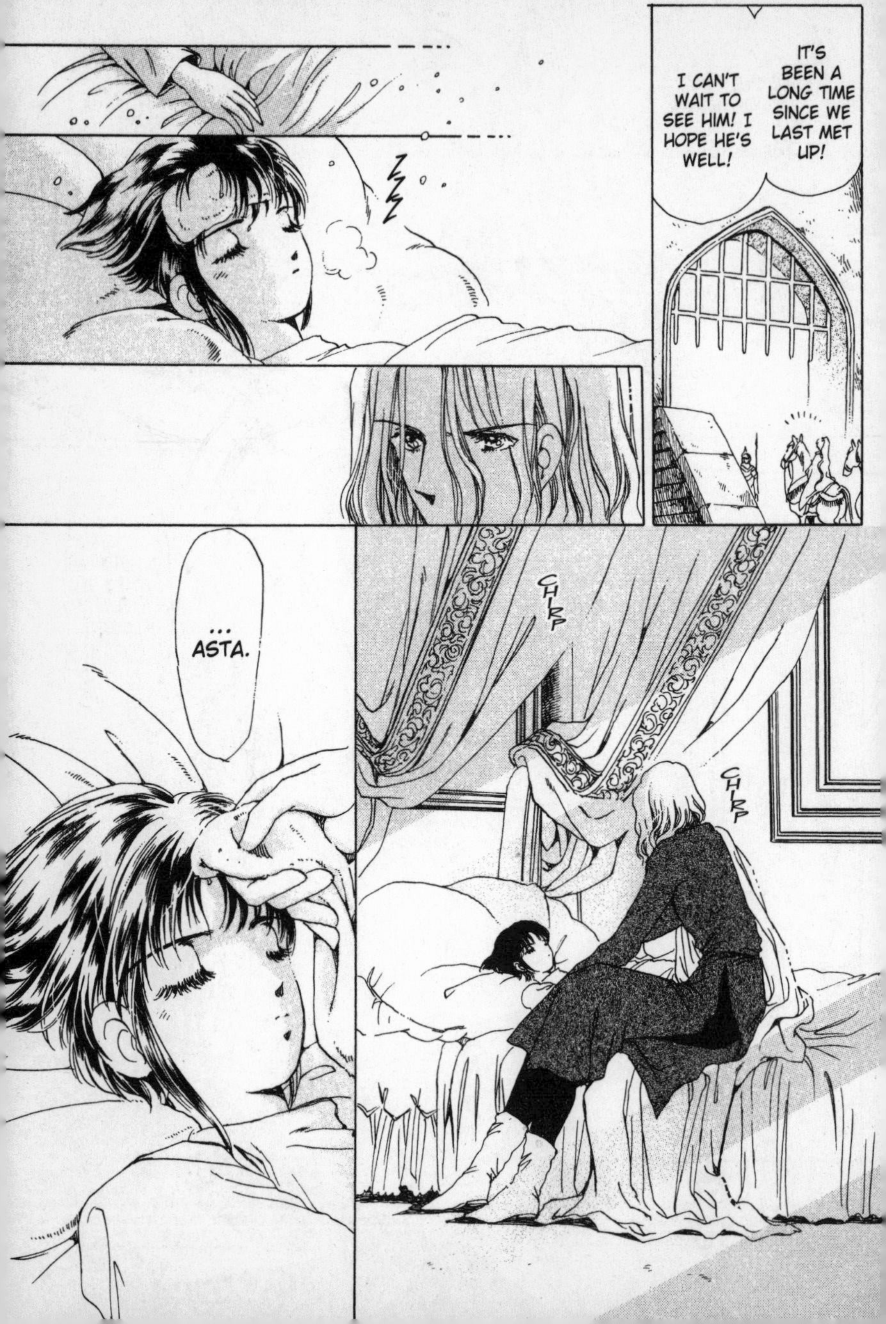
IT'S BEEN A LONG TIME SINCE WE LAST MET UP!
I CAN'T WAIT TO SEE HIM! I HOPE HE'S WELL!
CHIRP
CHIRP
... ASTA.

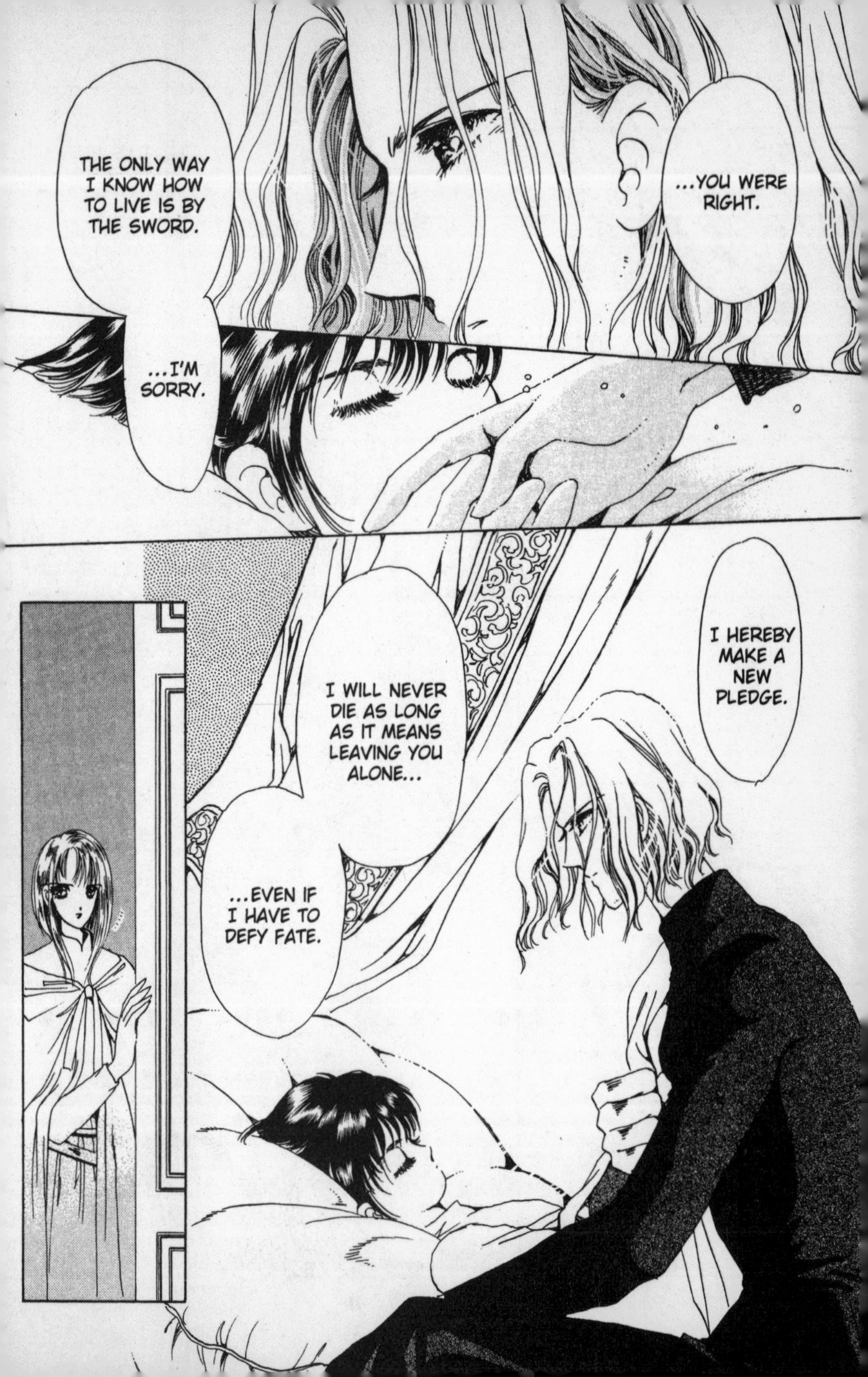
...YOU WERE RIGHT.
THE ONLY WAY I KNOW HOW TO LIVE IS BY THE SWORD.
...I'M SORRY.
I HEREBY MAKE A NEW PLEDGE.
I WILL NEVER DIE AS LONG AS IT MEANS LEAVING YOU ALONE...
...EVEN IF I HAVE TO DEFY FATE.

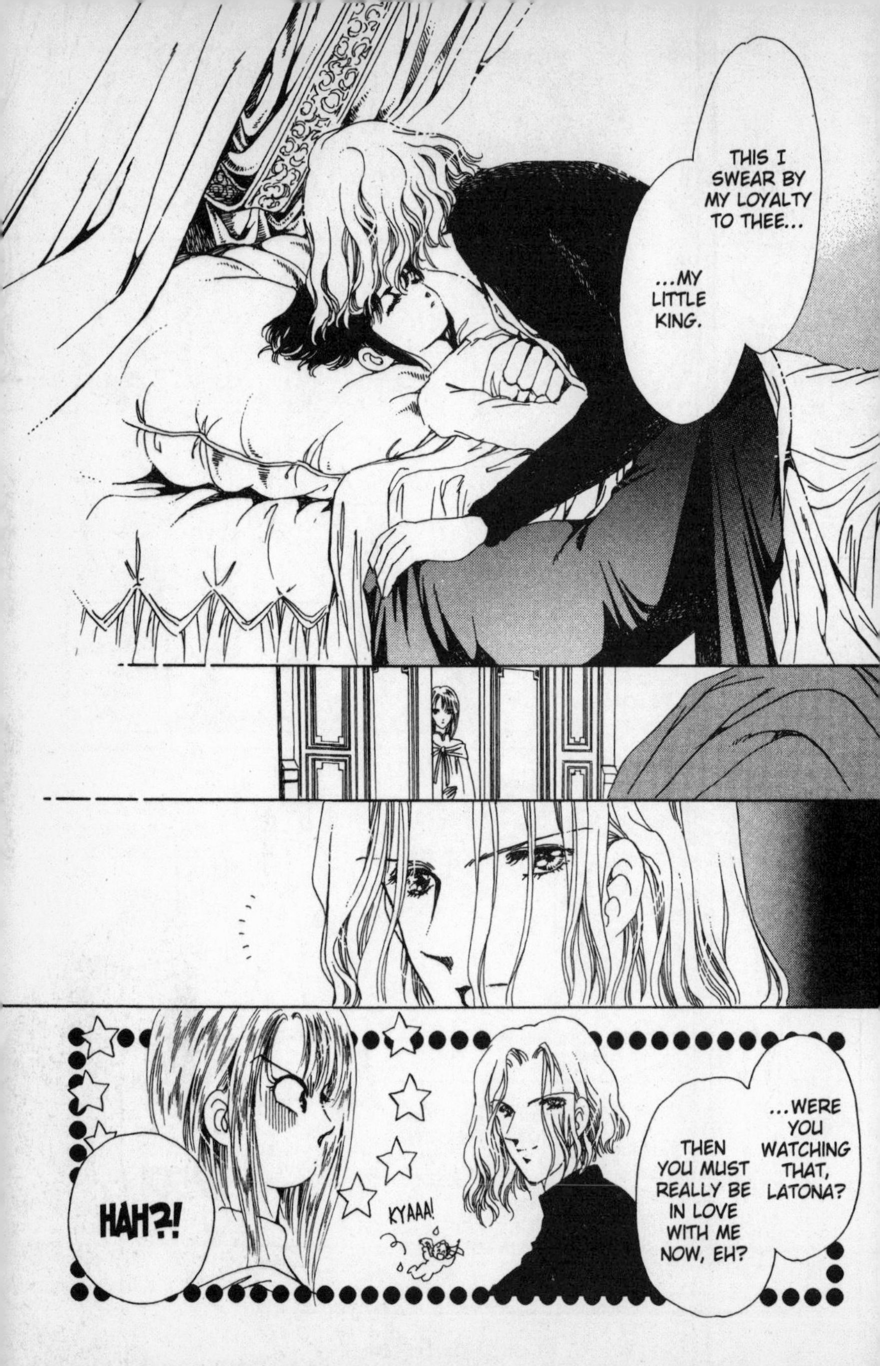
THIS I SWEAR BY MY LOYALTY TO THEE...
...MY LITTLE KING.
...WERE YOU WATCHING THAT, LATONA?
THEN YOU MUST REALLY BE IN LOVE WITH ME NOW, EH?
KYAAA!
HAH?!

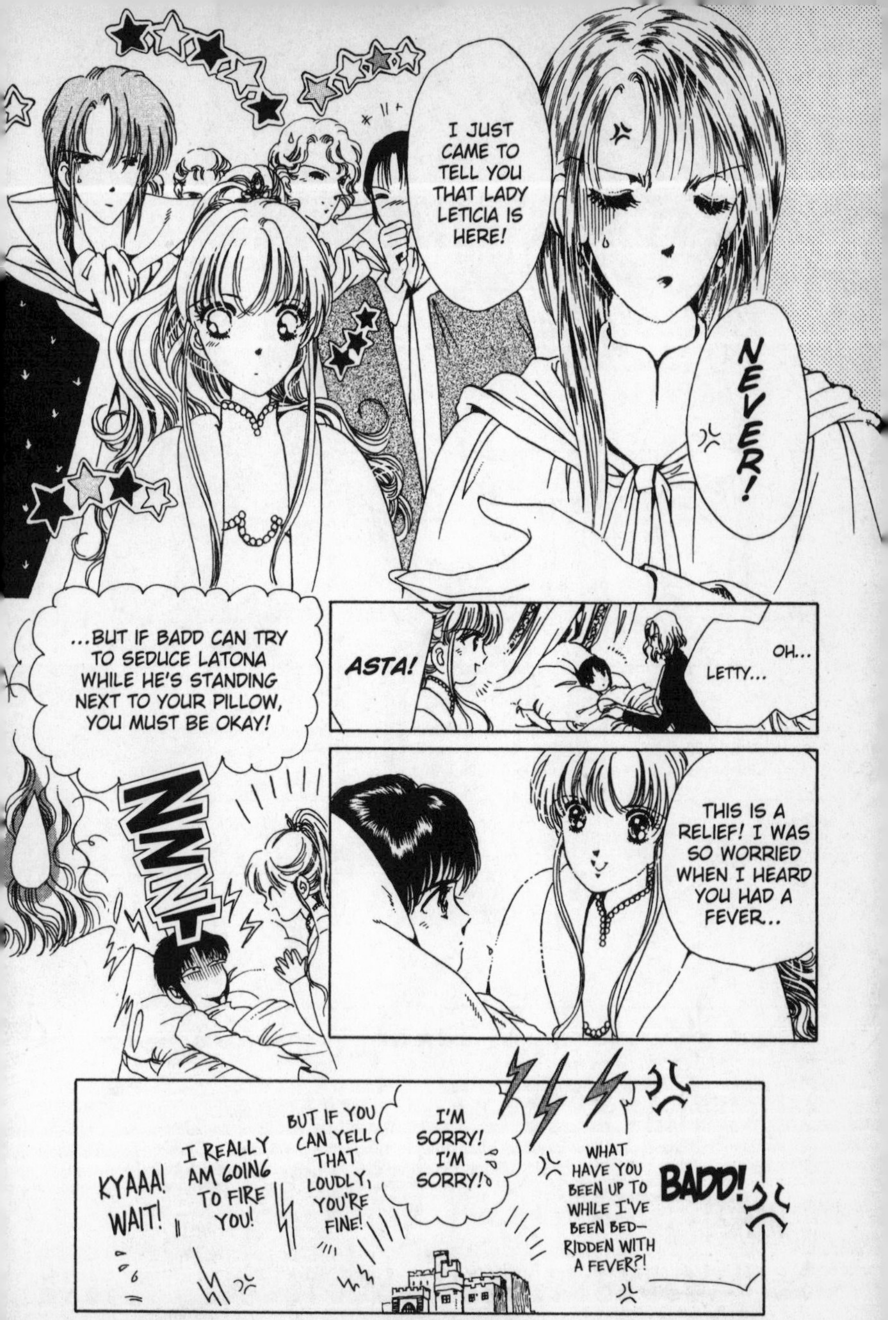
I JUST CAME TO TELL YOU THAT LADY LETICIA IS HERE!
NEVER!
OH... LETTY...
ASTA!
THIS IS A RELIEF! I WAS SO WORRIED WHEN I HEARD YOU HAD A FEVER..
...BUT IF BADD CAN TRY TO SEDUCE LATONA WHILE HE'S STANDING NEXT TO YOUR PILLOW, YOU MUST BE OKAY!
NNNT
BADD!
WHAT HAVE YOU BEEN UP TO WHILE I'VE BEEN BED-RIDDEN WITH A FEVER?!
I'M SORRY! I'M SORRY!
BUT IF YOU CAN YELL THAT LOUDLY, YOU'RE FINE!
I REALLY AM GOING TO FIRE YOU!
KYAAA! WAIT!

Chapter Six: The End

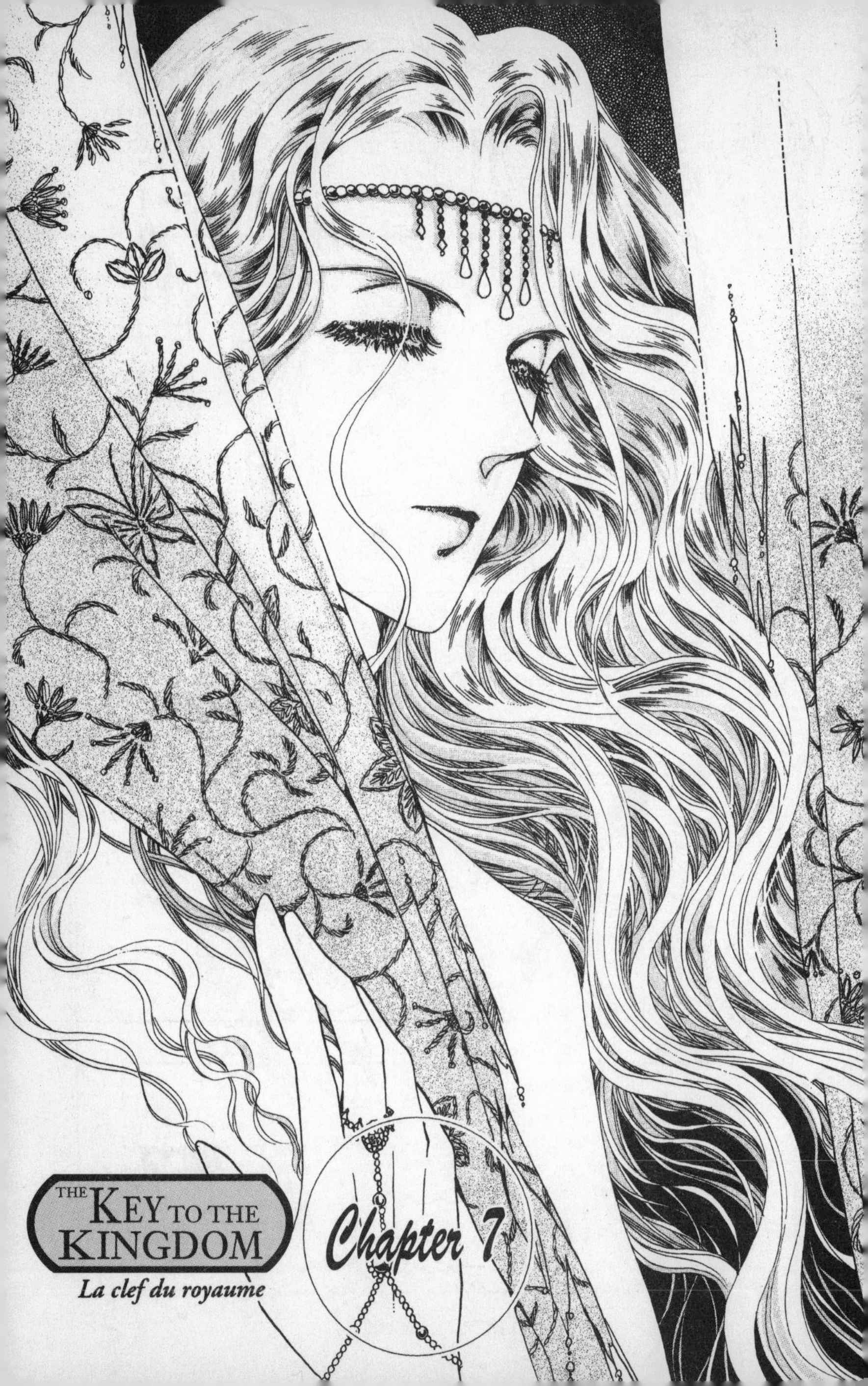
THE KEY TO THE KINGDOM
La clef du royaume
Chapter 7

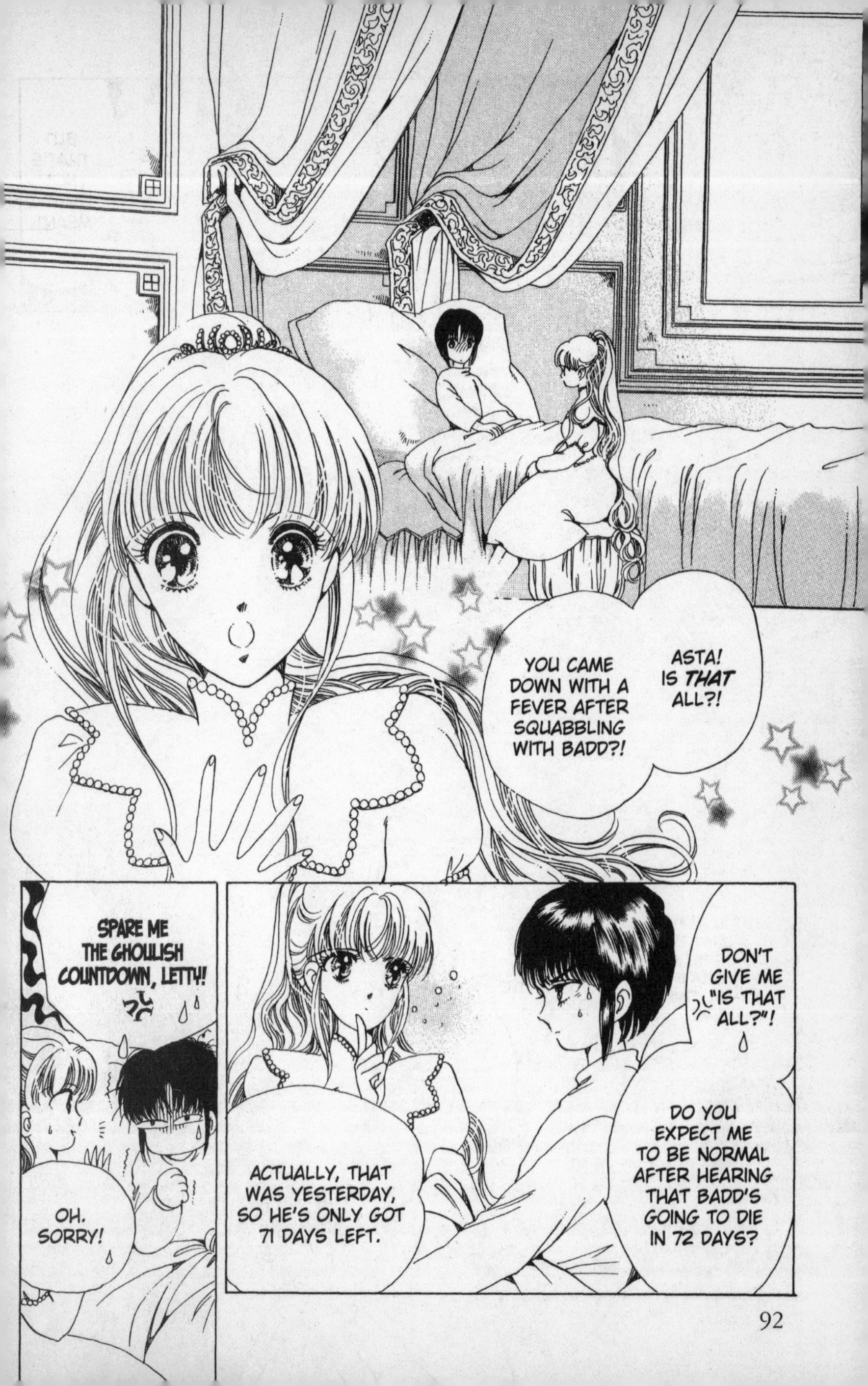
ASTA! IS *THAT* ALL?!
YOU CAME DOWN WITH A FEVER AFTER SQUABBLING WITH BADD?!
DON'T GIVE ME "IS THAT ALL?"!
DO YOU EXPECT ME TO BE NORMAL AFTER HEARING THAT BADD'S GOING TO DIE IN 72 DAYS?
ACTUALLY, THAT WAS YESTERDAY, SO HE'S ONLY GOT 71 DAYS LEFT.
SPARE ME THE GHOULISH COUNTDOWN, LETTY!
OH. SORRY!

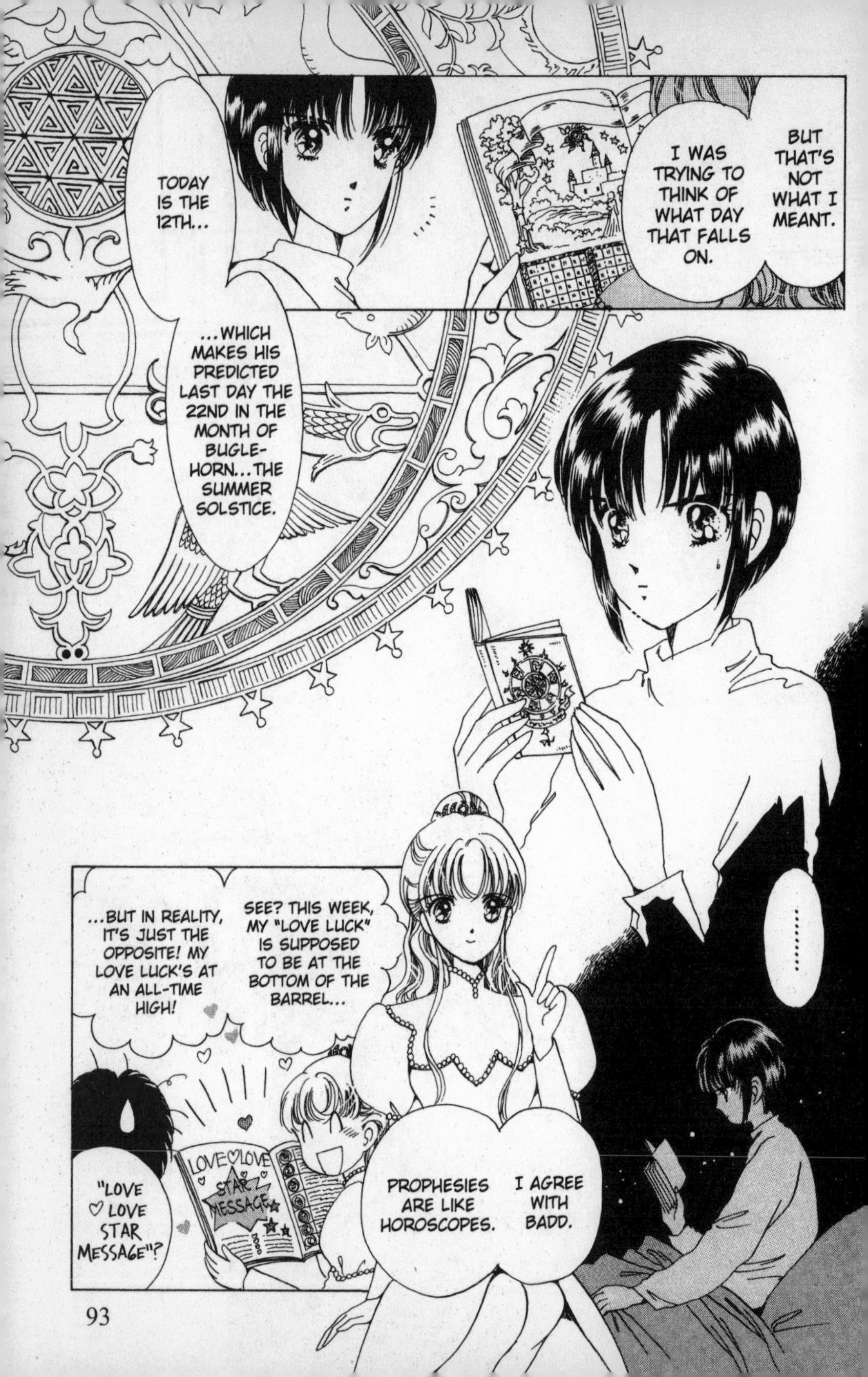
BUT THAT'S NOT WHAT I MEANT.
I WAS TRYING TO THINK OF WHAT DAY THAT FALLS ON.
TODAY IS THE 12TH...
...WHICH MAKES HIS PREDICTED LAST DAY THE 22ND IN THE MONTH OF BUGLE-HORN...THE SUMMER SOLSTICE.
......
SEE? THIS WEEK, MY "LOVE LUCK" IS SUPPOSED TO BE AT THE BOTTOM OF THE BARREL...
...BUT IN REALITY, IT'S JUST THE OPPOSITE! MY LOVE LUCK'S AT AN ALL-TIME HIGH!
I AGREE WITH BADD.
PROPHESIES ARE LIKE HOROSCOPES.
LOVE♡LOVE STAR MESSAGE
"LOVE ♡ LOVE STAR MESSAGE"?

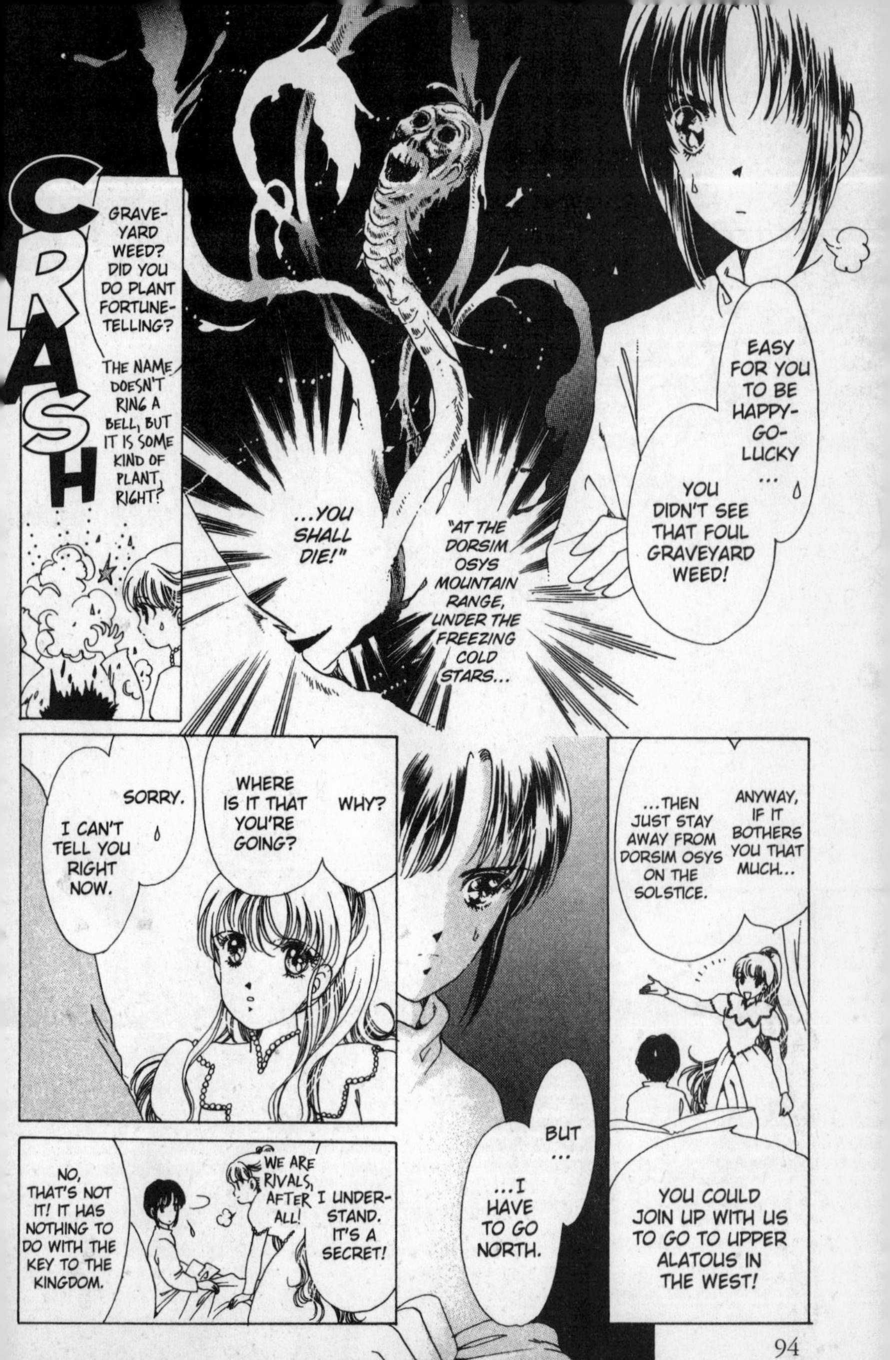
EASY FOR YOU TO BE HAPPY-GO-LUCKY...
YOU DIDN'T SEE THAT FOUL GRAVEYARD WEED!
"AT THE DORSIM OSYS MOUNTAIN RANGE, UNDER THE FREEZING COLD STARS...
...YOU SHALL DIE!"
CRASH
GRAVE-YARD WEED? DID YOU DO PLANT FORTUNE-TELLING?
THE NAME DOESN'T RING A BELL, BUT IT IS SOME KIND OF PLANT, RIGHT?
ANYWAY, IF IT BOTHERS YOU THAT MUCH...
...THEN JUST STAY AWAY FROM DORSIM OSYS ON THE SOLSTICE.
YOU COULD JOIN UP WITH US TO GO TO UPPER ALATOUS IN THE WEST!
BUT...
...I HAVE TO GO NORTH.
WHY?
WHERE IS IT THAT YOU'RE GOING?
SORRY.
I CAN'T TELL YOU RIGHT NOW.
I UNDER-STAND. IT'S A SECRET!
WE ARE RIVALS, AFTER ALL!
NO, THAT'S NOT IT! IT HAS NOTHING TO DO WITH THE KEY TO THE KINGDOM.

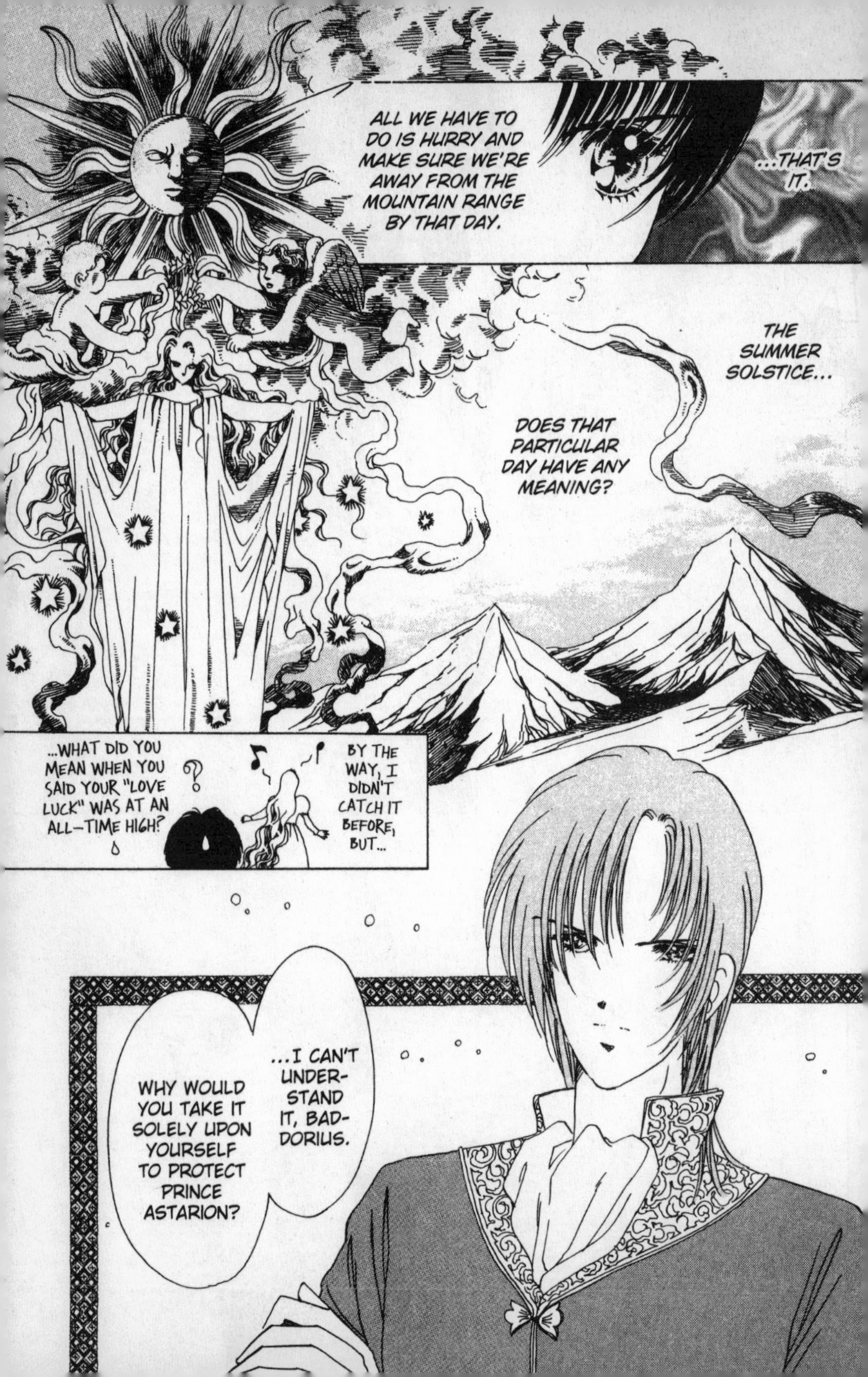
...THAT'S IT.
ALL WE HAVE TO DO IS HURRY AND MAKE SURE WE'RE AWAY FROM THE MOUNTAIN RANGE BY THAT DAY.
THE SUMMER SOLSTICE...
DOES THAT PARTICULAR DAY HAVE ANY MEANING?
BY THE WAY, I DIDN'T CATCH IT BEFORE, BUT...
...WHAT DID YOU MEAN WHEN YOU SAID YOUR "LOVE LUCK" WAS AT AN ALL-TIME HIGH?
...I CAN'T UNDER-STAND IT, BAD-DORIUS.
WHY WOULD YOU TAKE IT SOLELY UPON YOURSELF TO PROTECT PRINCE ASTARION?

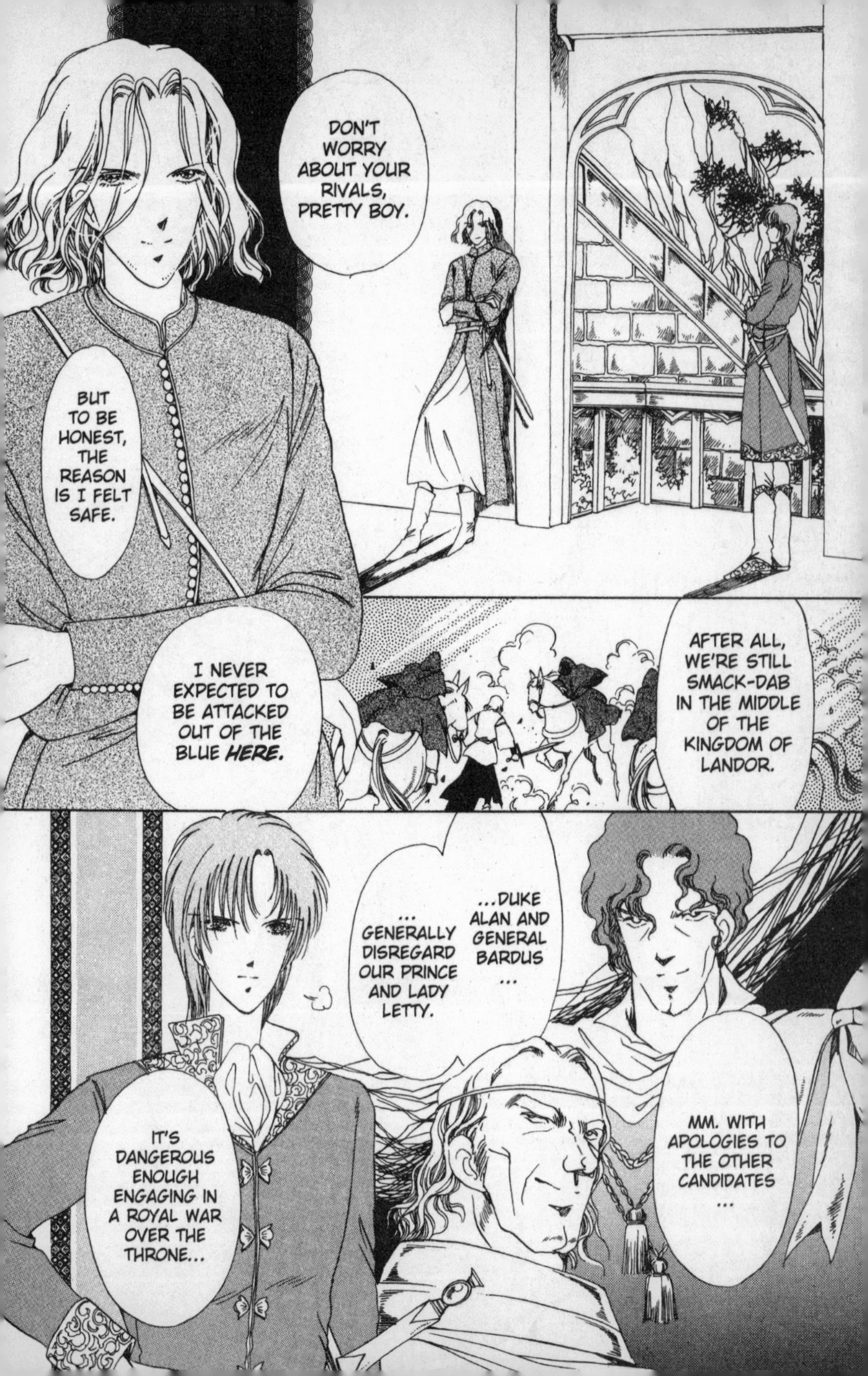
DON'T WORRY ABOUT YOUR RIVALS, PRETTY BOY.
BUT TO BE HONEST, THE REASON IS I FELT SAFE.
AFTER ALL, WE'RE STILL SMACK-DAB IN THE MIDDLE OF THE KINGDOM OF LANDOR.
I NEVER EXPECTED TO BE ATTACKED OUT OF THE BLUE *HERE.*
MM. WITH APOLOGIES TO THE OTHER CANDIDATES...
...DUKE ALAN AND GENERAL BARDUS...
...GENERALLY DISREGARD OUR PRINCE AND LADY LETTY.
IT'S DANGEROUS ENOUGH ENGAGING IN A ROYAL WAR OVER THE THRONE...

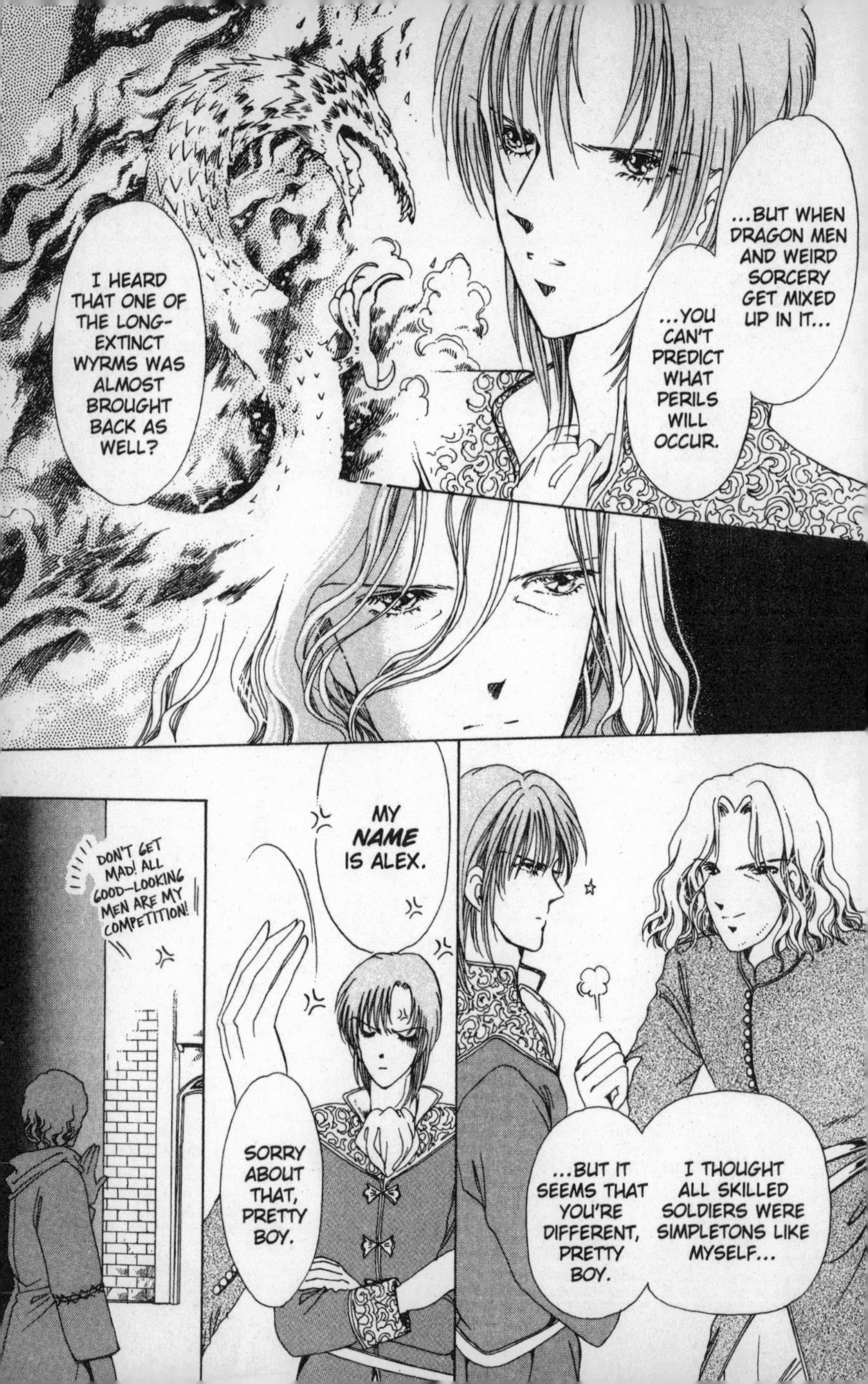
...BUT WHEN DRAGON MEN AND WEIRD SORCERY GET MIXED UP IN IT...
...YOU CAN'T PREDICT WHAT PERILS WILL OCCUR.
I HEARD THAT ONE OF THE LONG-EXTINCT WYRMS WAS ALMOST BROUGHT BACK AS WELL?
I THOUGHT ALL SKILLED SOLDIERS WERE SIMPLETONS LIKE MYSELF...
...BUT IT SEEMS THAT YOU'RE DIFFERENT, PRETTY BOY.
MY *NAME* IS ALEX.
SORRY ABOUT THAT, PRETTY BOY.
DON'T GET MAD! ALL GOOD-LOOKING MEN ARE MY COMPETITION!

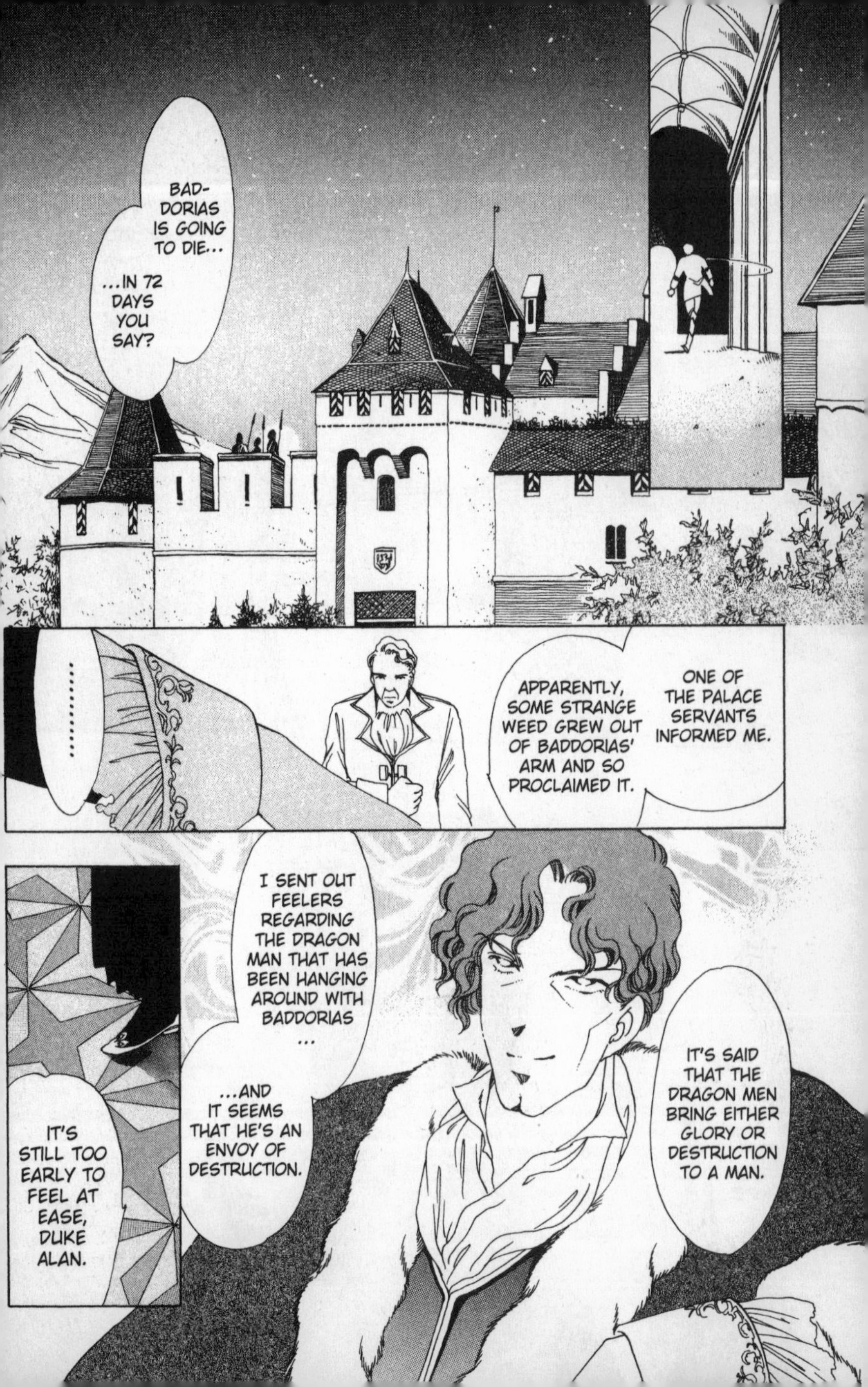
BAD-DORIAS IS GOING TO DIE...
...IN 72 DAYS YOU SAY?
ONE OF THE PALACE SERVANTS INFORMED ME.
APPARENTLY, SOME STRANGE WEED GREW OUT OF BADDORIAS' ARM AND SO PROCLAIMED IT.
......
IT'S SAID THAT THE DRAGON MEN BRING EITHER GLORY OR DESTRUCTION TO A MAN.
I SENT OUT FEELERS REGARDING THE DRAGON MAN THAT HAS BEEN HANGING AROUND WITH BADDORIAS...
...AND IT SEEMS THAT HE'S AN ENVOY OF DESTRUCTION.
IT'S STILL TOO EARLY TO FEEL AT EASE, DUKE ALAN.

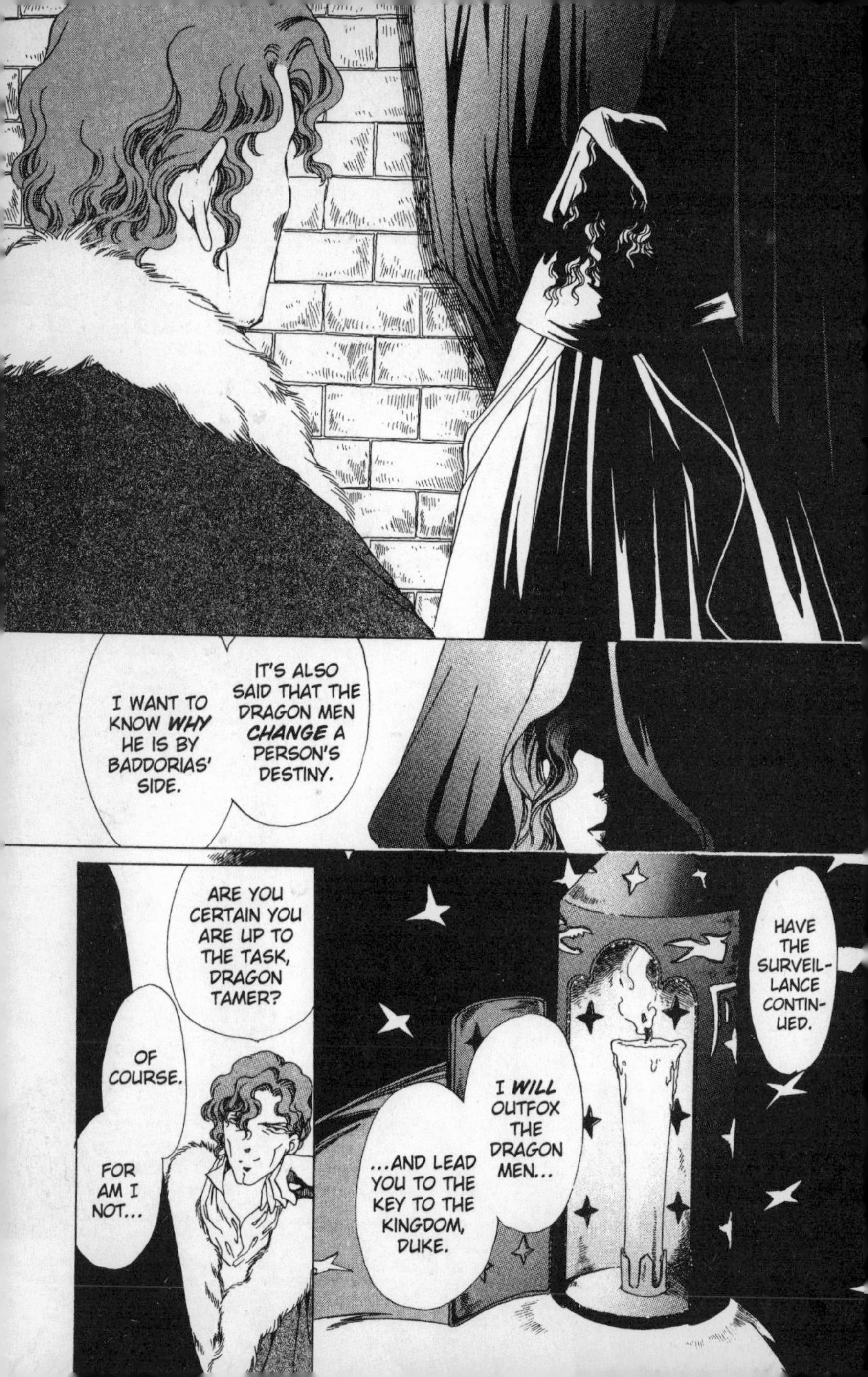
IT'S ALSO SAID THAT THE DRAGON MEN **CHANGE** A PERSON'S DESTINY.
I WANT TO KNOW **WHY** HE IS BY BADDORIAS' SIDE.
HAVE THE SURVEILLANCE CONTINUED.
I **WILL** OUTFOX THE DRAGON MEN...
...AND LEAD YOU TO THE KEY TO THE KINGDOM, DUKE.
ARE YOU CERTAIN YOU ARE UP TO THE TASK, DRAGON TAMER?
OF COURSE.
FOR AM I NOT...

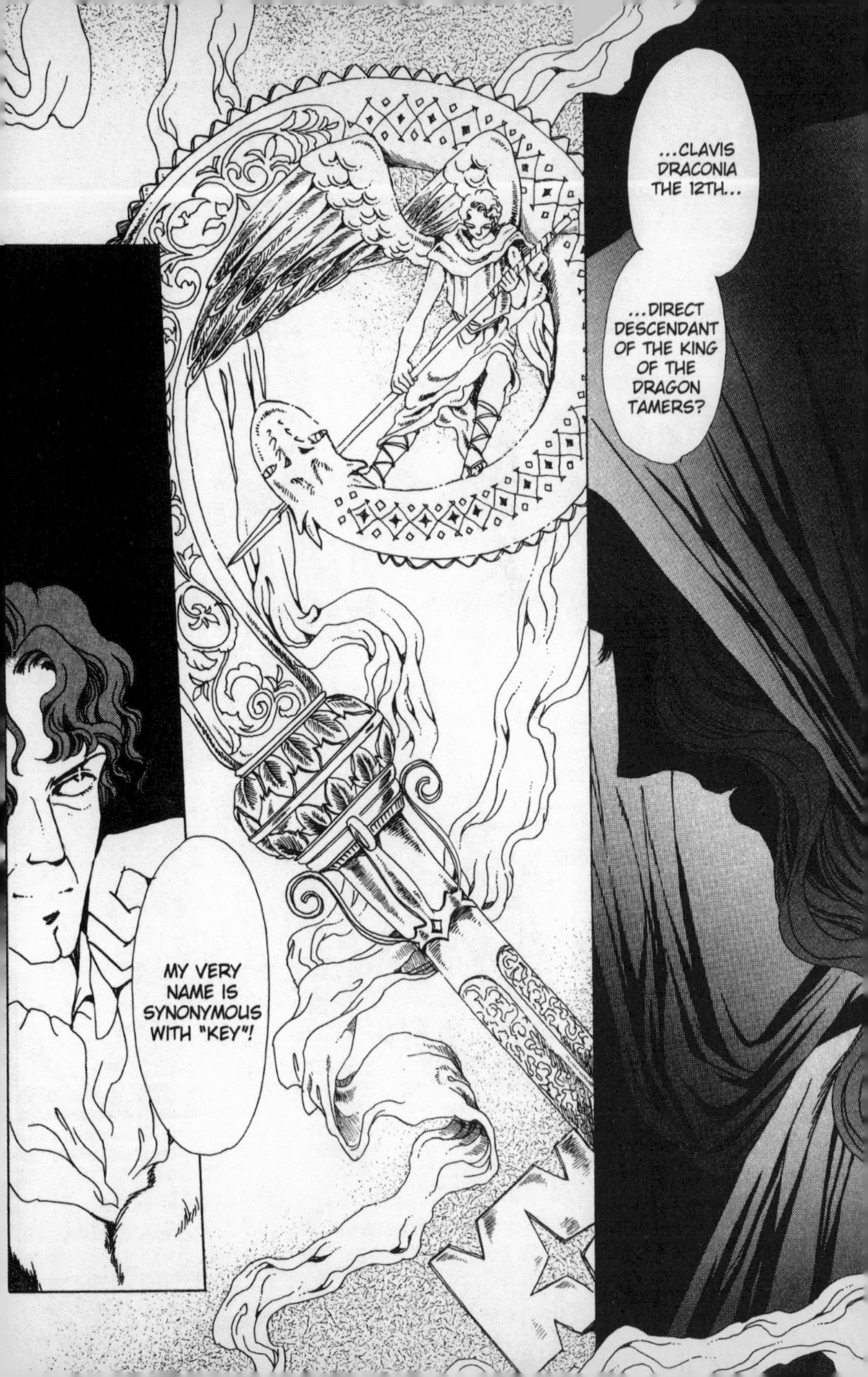
...CLAVIS DRACONIA THE 12TH...
...DIRECT DESCENDANT OF THE KING OF THE DRAGON TAMERS?
MY VERY NAME IS SYNONYMOUS WITH "KEY"!

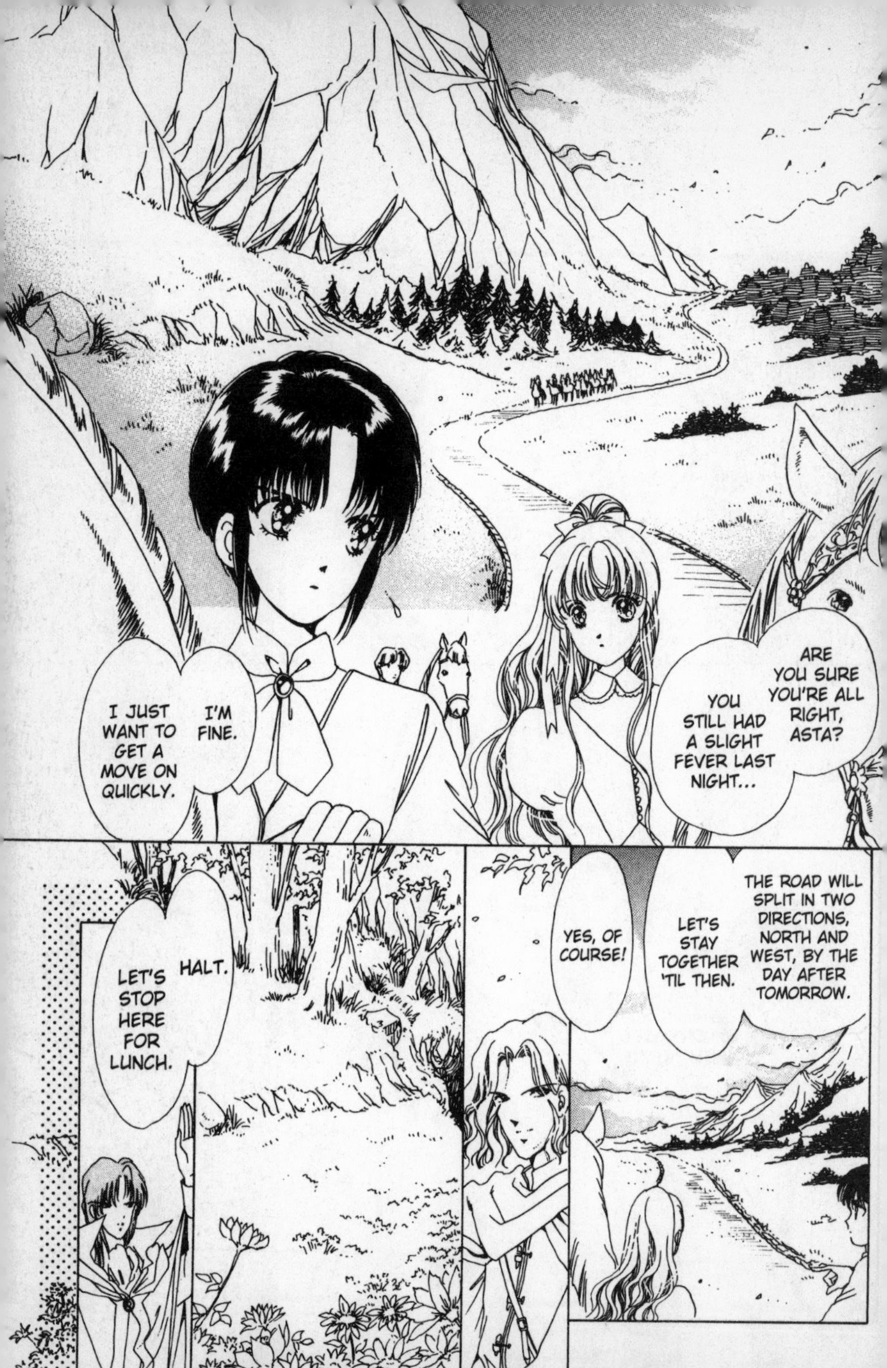
ARE YOU SURE YOU'RE ALL RIGHT, ASTA?
YOU STILL HAD A SLIGHT FEVER LAST NIGHT...
I'M FINE.
I JUST WANT TO GET A MOVE ON QUICKLY.
THE ROAD WILL SPLIT IN TWO DIRECTIONS, NORTH AND WEST, BY THE DAY AFTER TOMORROW.
LET'S STAY TOGETHER 'TIL THEN.
YES, OF COURSE!
HALT.
LET'S STOP HERE FOR LUNCH.

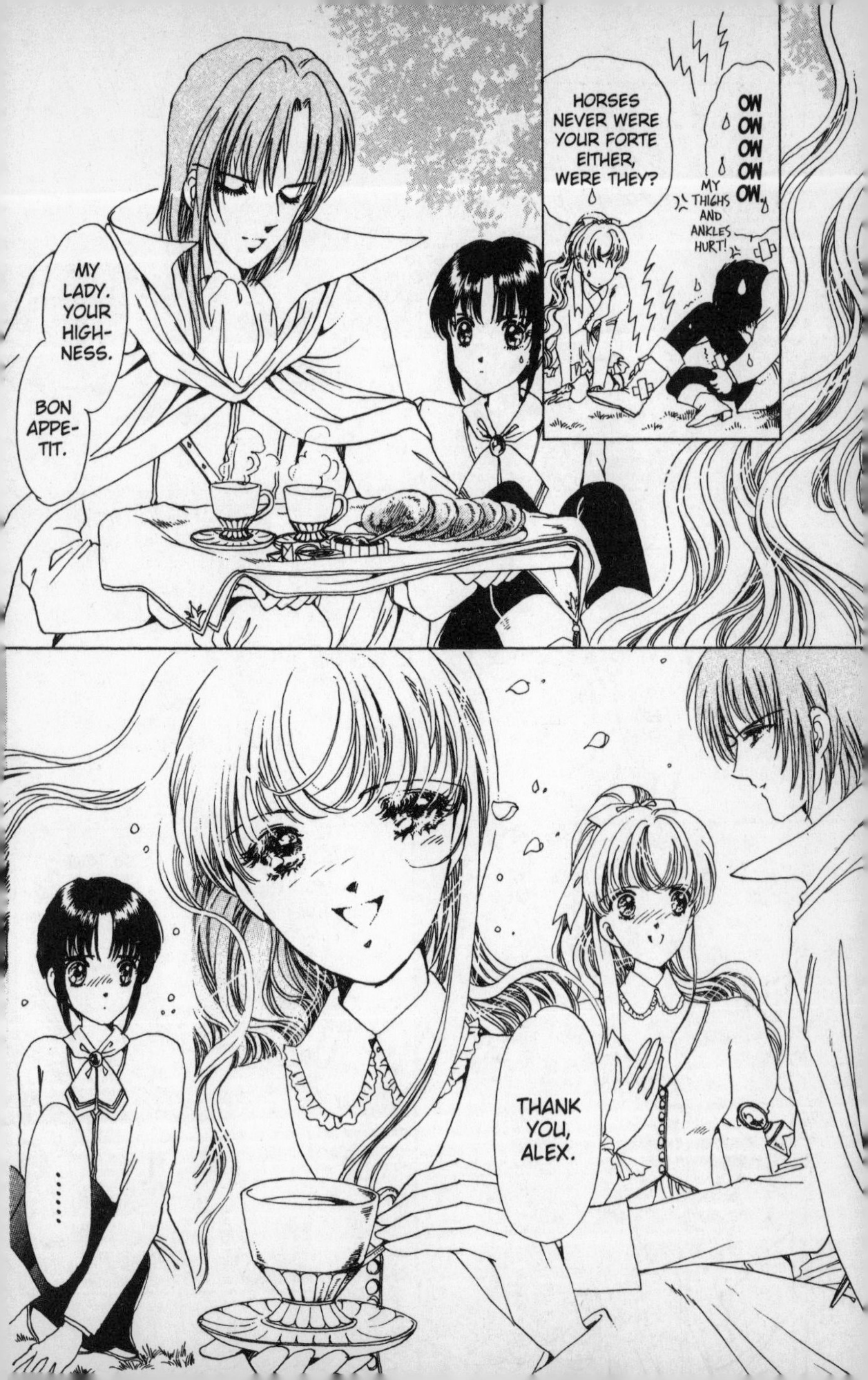
OW OW OW OW OW,
MY THIGHS AND ANKLES HURT!
HORSES NEVER WERE YOUR FORTE EITHER, WERE THEY?
MY LADY. YOUR HIGH-NESS.
BON APPE-TIT.
THANK YOU, ALEX.
......

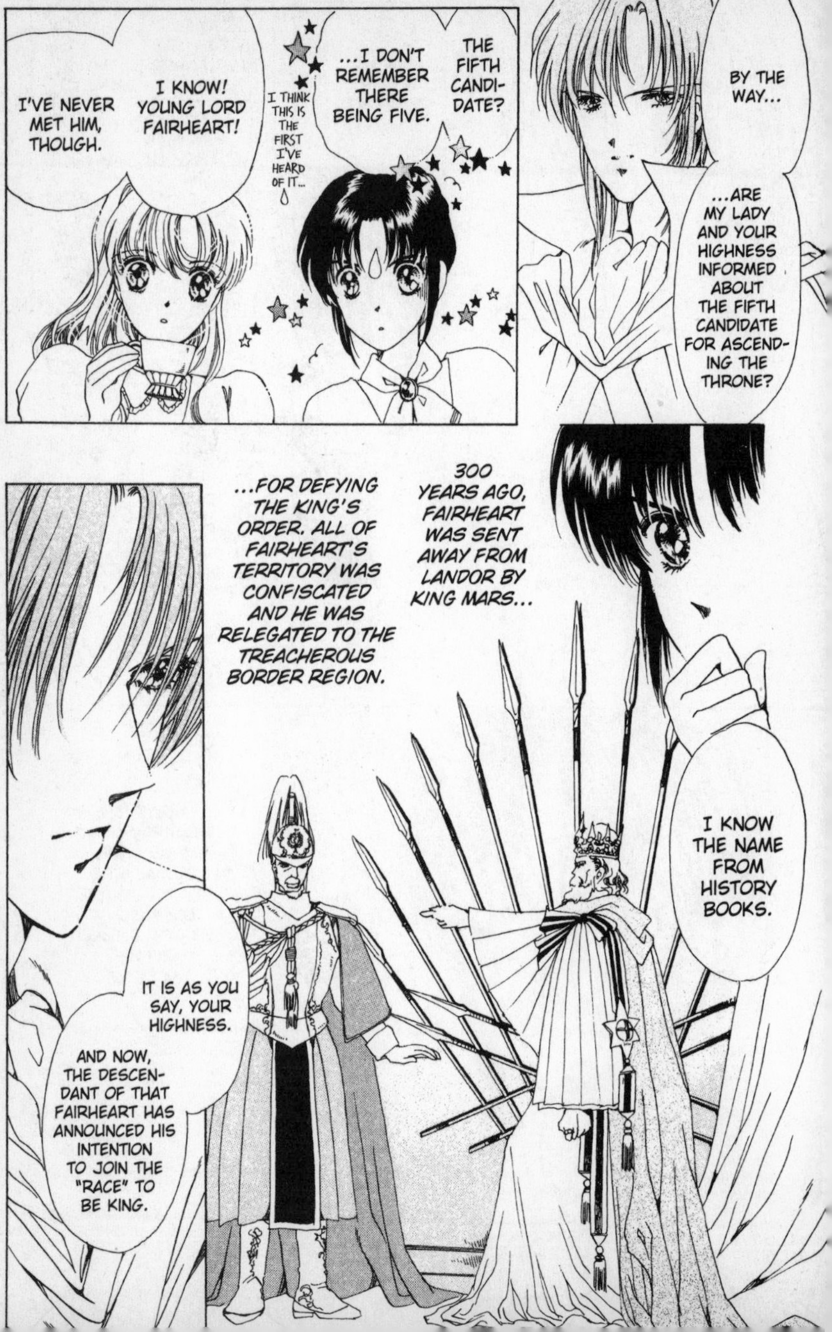
BY THE WAY...
...ARE MY LADY AND YOUR HIGHNESS INFORMED ABOUT THE FIFTH CANDIDATE FOR ASCENDING THE THRONE?
THE FIFTH CANDIDATE?
...I DON'T REMEMBER THERE BEING FIVE.
I THINK THIS IS THE FIRST I'VE HEARD OF IT...
I KNOW! YOUNG LORD FAIRHEART!
I'VE NEVER MET HIM, THOUGH.
I KNOW THE NAME FROM HISTORY BOOKS.
300 YEARS AGO, FAIRHEART WAS SENT AWAY FROM LANDOR BY KING MARS...
...FOR DEFYING THE KING'S ORDER. ALL OF FAIRHEART'S TERRITORY WAS CONFISCATED AND HE WAS RELEGATED TO THE TREACHEROUS BORDER REGION.
IT IS AS YOU SAY, YOUR HIGHNESS.
AND NOW, THE DESCENDANT OF THAT FAIRHEART HAS ANNOUNCED HIS INTENTION TO JOIN THE "RACE" TO BE KING.

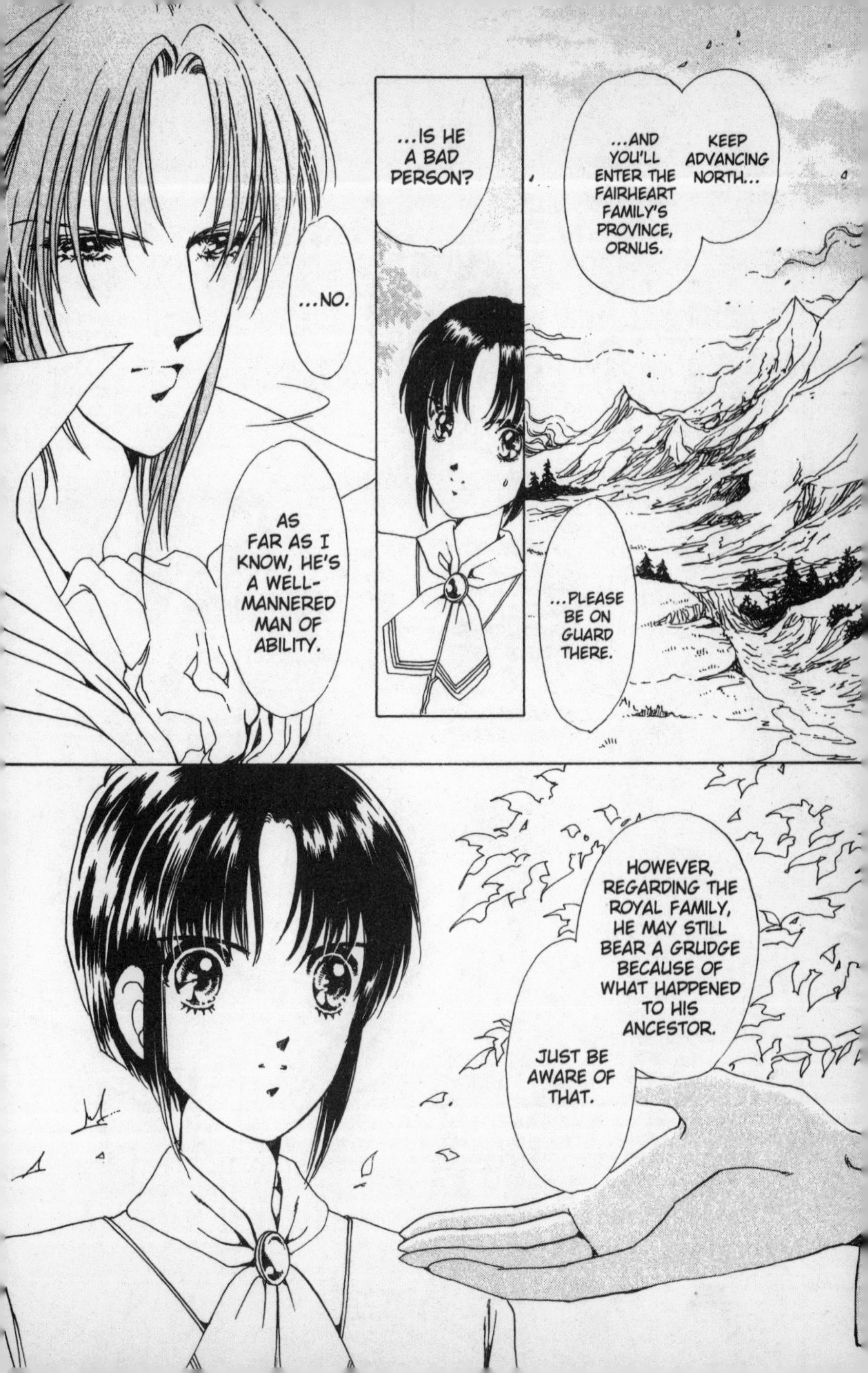
KEEP ADVANCING NORTH...
...AND YOU'LL ENTER THE FAIRHEART FAMILY'S PROVINCE, ORNUS.
...PLEASE BE ON GUARD THERE.
...IS HE A BAD PERSON?
...NO.
AS FAR AS I KNOW, HE'S A WELL-MANNERED MAN OF ABILITY.
HOWEVER, REGARDING THE ROYAL FAMILY, HE MAY STILL BEAR A GRUDGE BECAUSE OF WHAT HAPPENED TO HIS ANCESTOR.
JUST BE AWARE OF THAT.

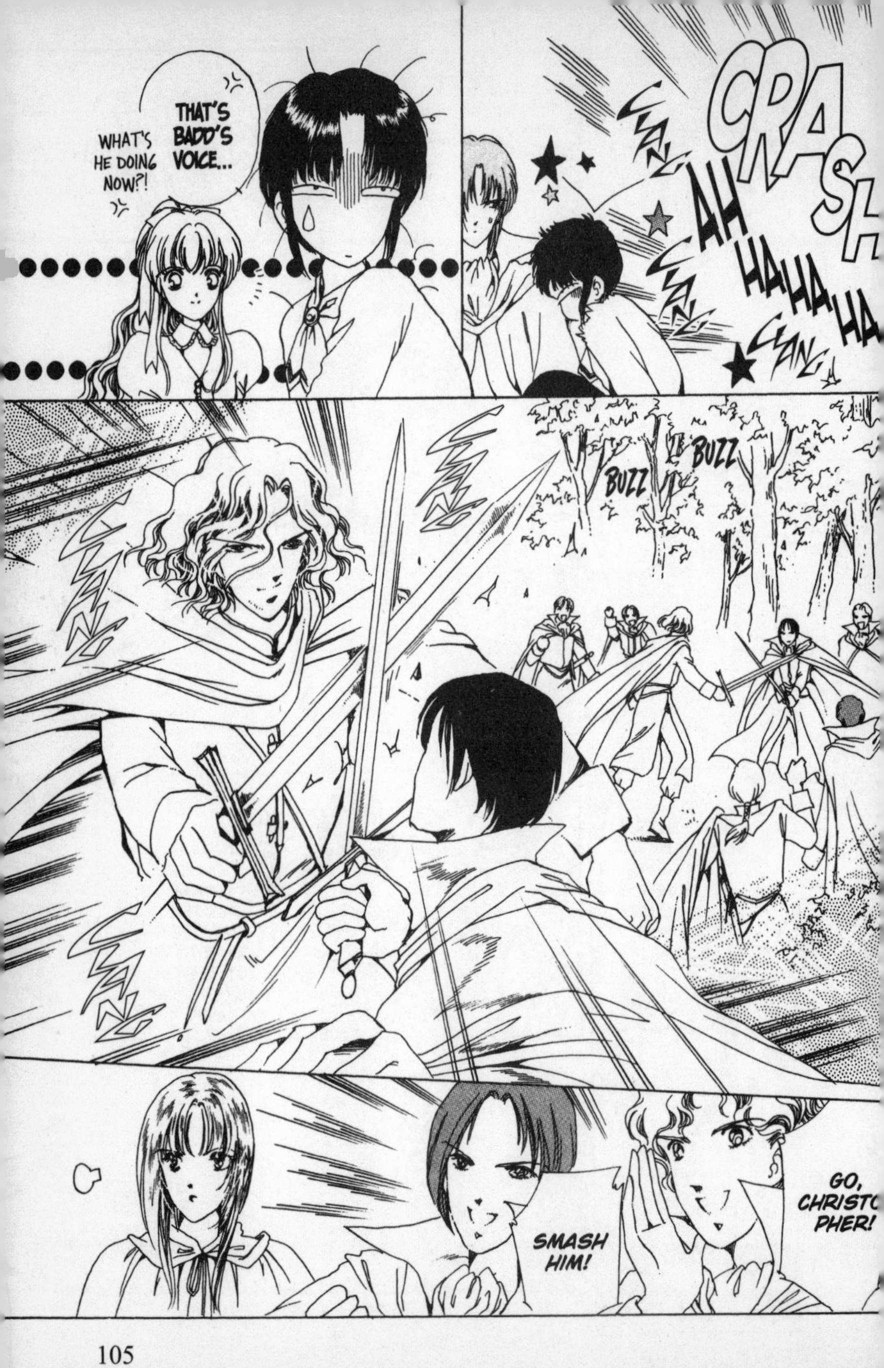
CRASH
AH HA HA HA HA
CLANG
CLANG
CLANG
THAT'S BADD'S VOICE...
WHAT'S HE DOING NOW?!
BUZZ
BUZZ
CLANG
CLANG
CLANG
GO, CHRISTO PHER!
SMASH HIM!

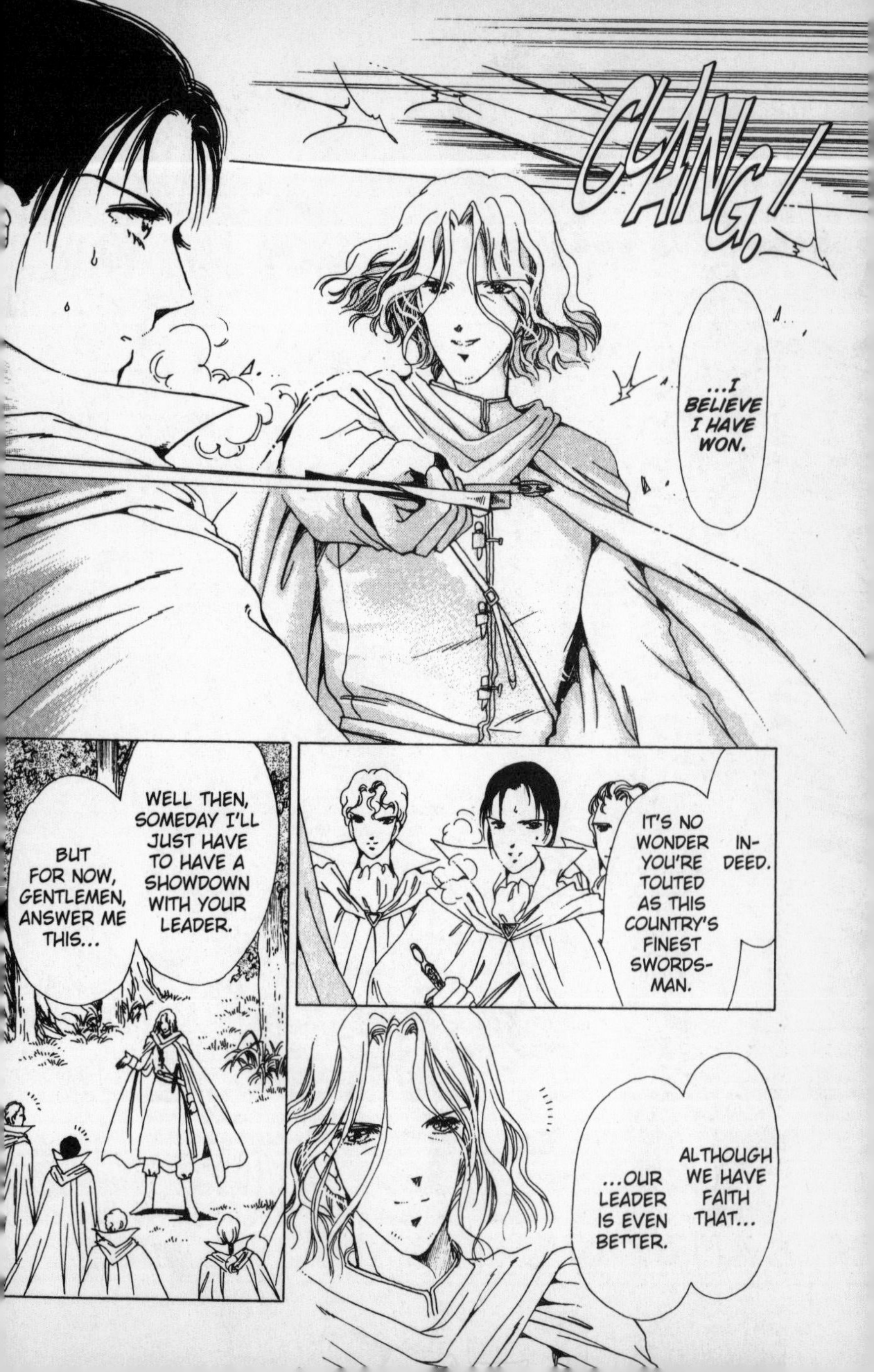
CLANG!
...I BELIEVE I HAVE WON.
INDEED.
IT'S NO WONDER YOU'RE TOUTED AS THIS COUNTRY'S FINEST SWORDSMAN.
ALTHOUGH WE HAVE FAITH THAT...
...OUR LEADER IS EVEN BETTER.
WELL THEN, SOMEDAY I'LL JUST HAVE TO HAVE A SHOWDOWN WITH YOUR LEADER.
BUT FOR NOW, GENTLEMEN, ANSWER ME THIS...

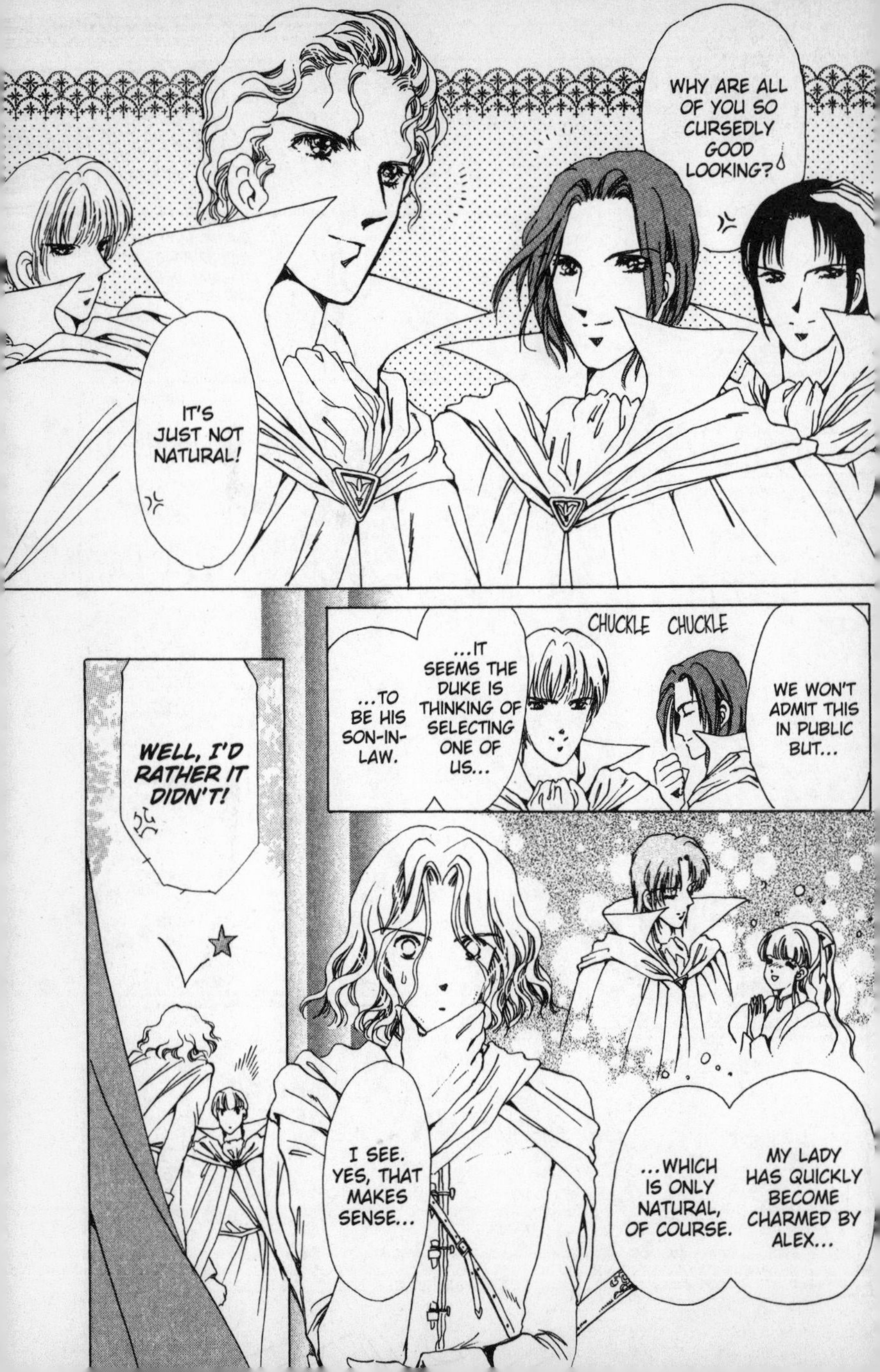
WHY ARE ALL OF YOU SO CURSEDLY GOOD LOOKING?
IT'S JUST NOT NATURAL!
WE WON'T ADMIT THIS IN PUBLIC BUT...
CHUCKLE CHUCKLE
...IT SEEMS THE DUKE IS THINKING OF SELECTING ONE OF US...
...TO BE HIS SON-IN-LAW.
MY LADY HAS QUICKLY BECOME CHARMED BY ALEX...
...WHICH IS ONLY NATURAL, OF COURSE.
I SEE. YES, THAT MAKES SENSE...
WELL, I'D RATHER IT DIDN'T!

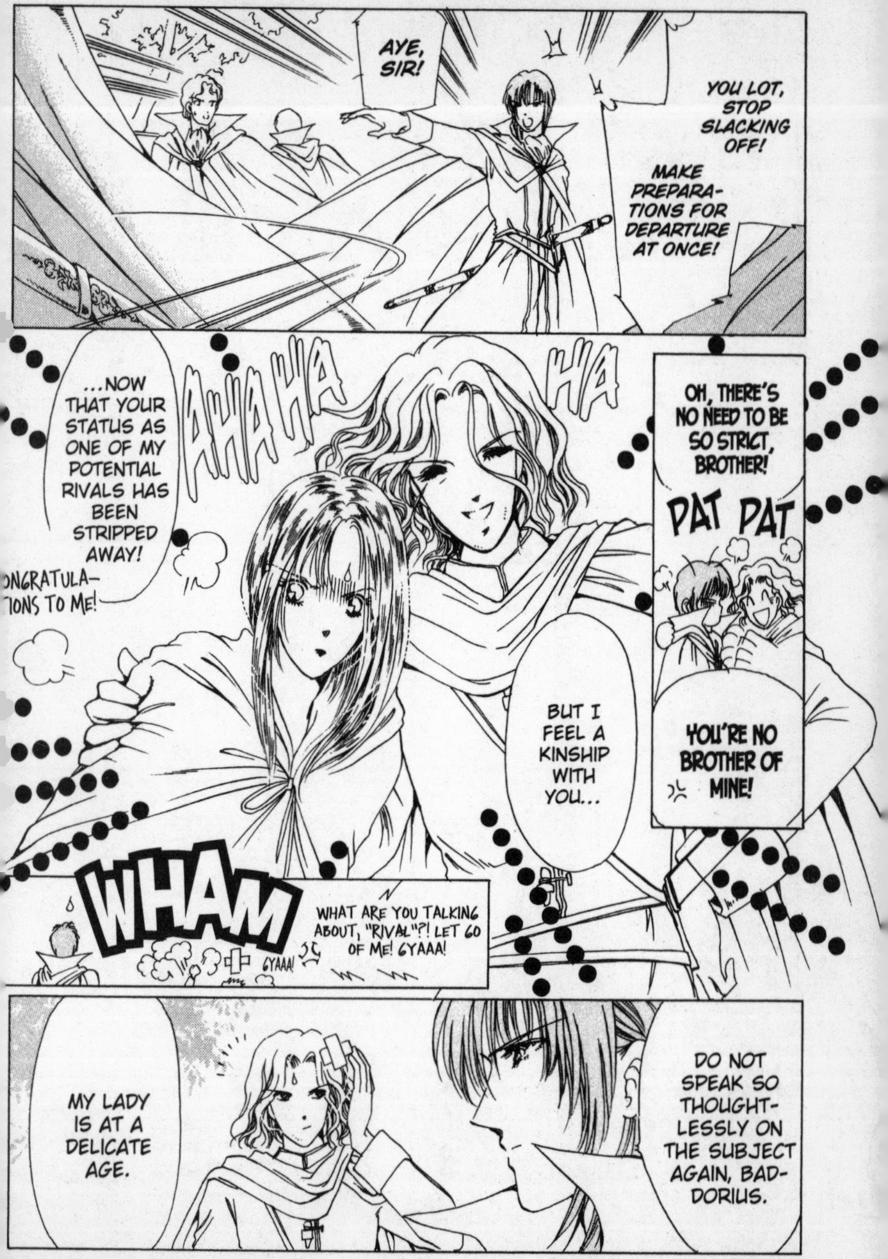
YOU LOT, STOP SLACKING OFF!
MAKE PREPARATIONS FOR DEPARTURE AT ONCE!
AYE, SIR!
OH, THERE'S NO NEED TO BE SO STRICT, BROTHER!
PAT PAT
YOU'RE NO BROTHER OF MINE!
BUT I FEEL A KINSHIP WITH YOU...
AHAHAHA HA
...NOW THAT YOUR STATUS AS ONE OF MY POTENTIAL RIVALS HAS BEEN STRIPPED AWAY!
ONGRATULATIONS TO ME!
WHAT ARE YOU TALKING ABOUT, "RIVAL"?! LET GO OF ME! GYAAA!
GYAAA!
WHAM
DO NOT SPEAK SO THOUGHTLESSLY ON THE SUBJECT AGAIN, BADDORIUS.
MY LADY IS AT A DELICATE AGE.

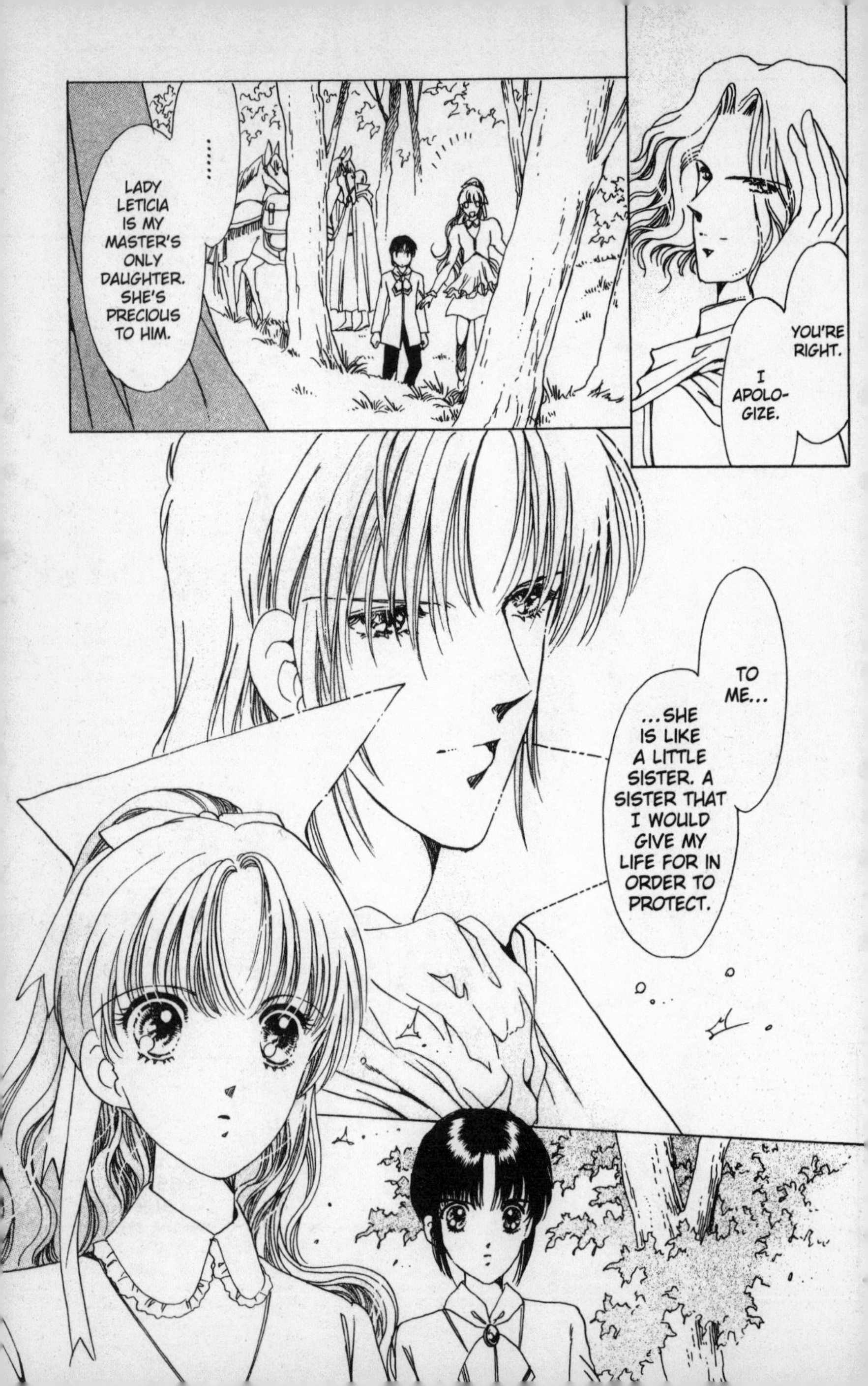
YOU'RE RIGHT.
I APOLOGIZE.
......
LADY LETICIA IS MY MASTER'S ONLY DAUGHTER. SHE'S PRECIOUS TO HIM.
TO ME...
...SHE IS LIKE A LITTLE SISTER. A SISTER THAT I WOULD GIVE MY LIFE FOR IN ORDER TO PROTECT.

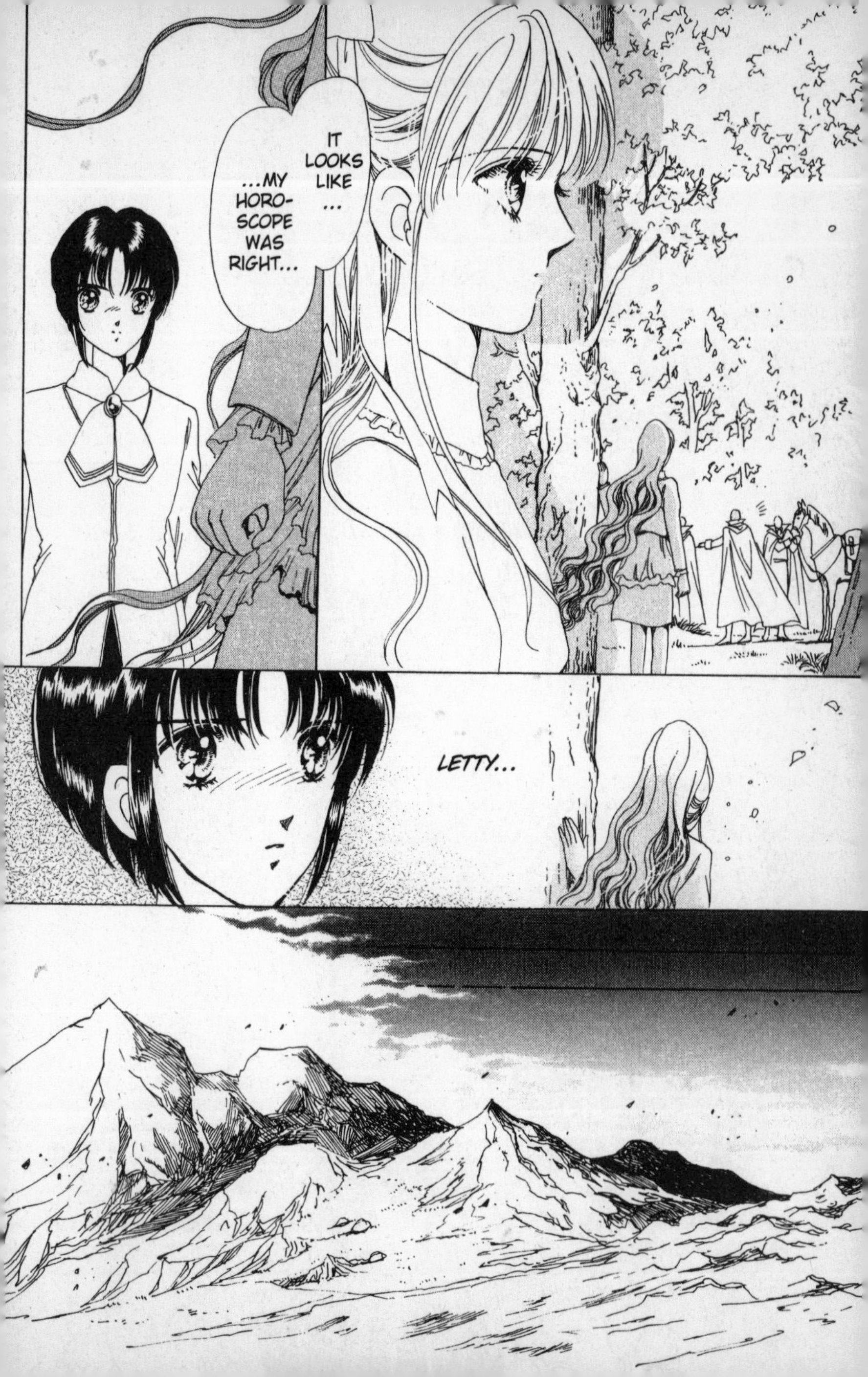
IT LOOKS LIKE ...
...MY HORO-SCOPE WAS RIGHT...
LETTY...

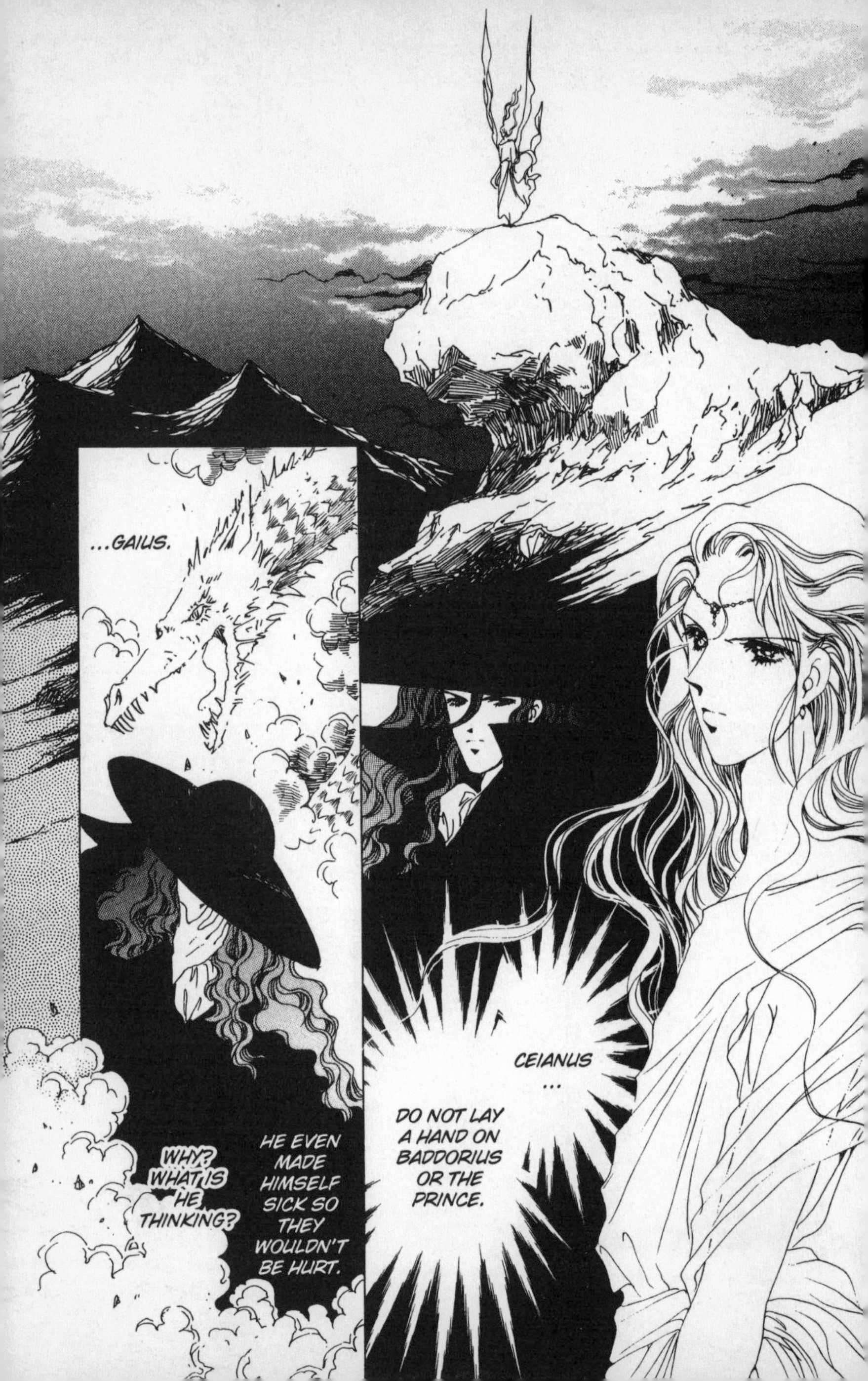
CEIANUS ...
DO NOT LAY A HAND ON BADDORIUS OR THE PRINCE.
HE EVEN MADE HIMSELF SICK SO THEY WOULDN'T BE HURT.
...GAIUS.
WHY? WHAT IS HE THINKING?

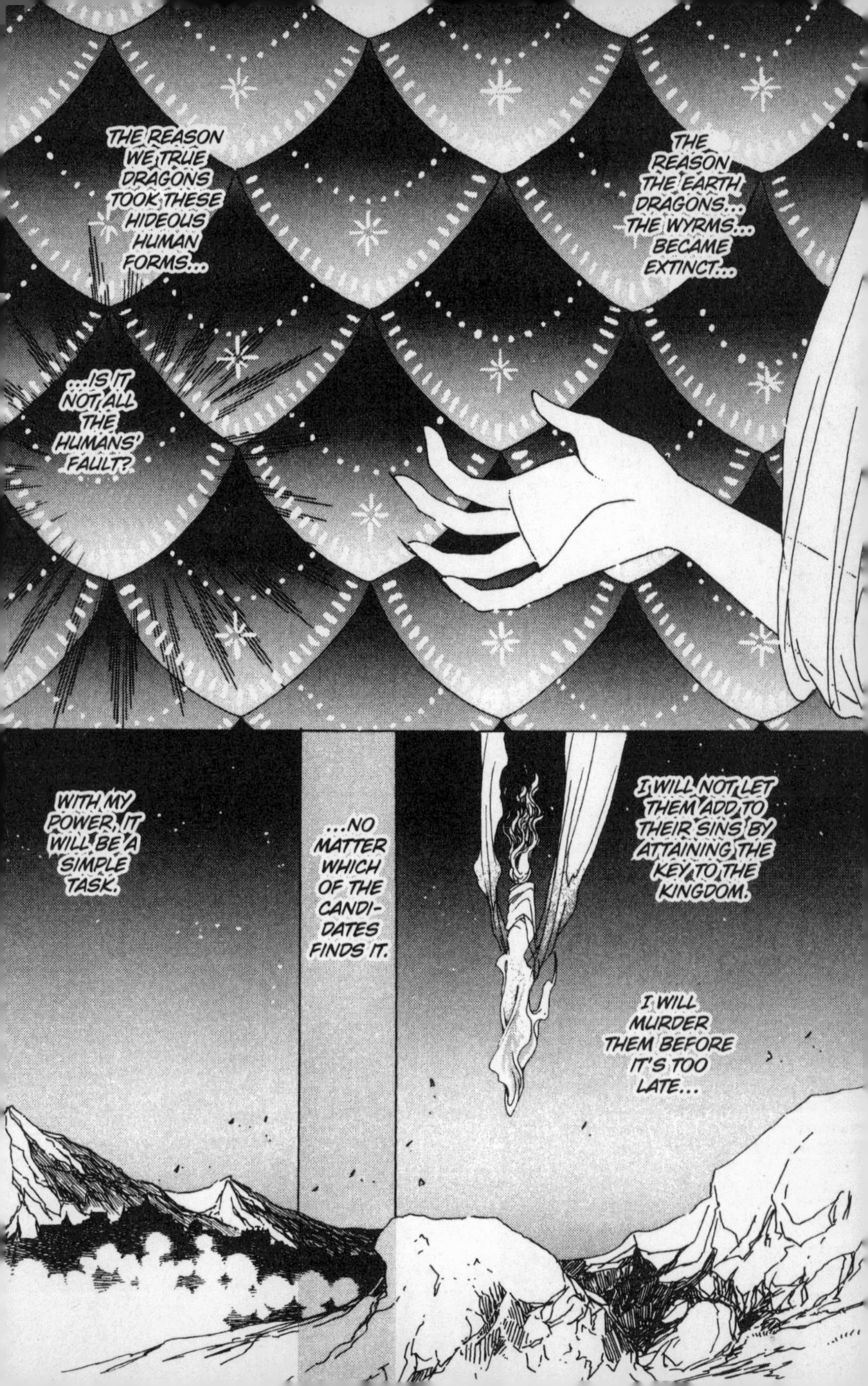
THE REASON THE EARTH DRAGONS... THE WYRMS... BECAME EXTINCT...
THE REASON WE TRUE DRAGONS TOOK THESE HIDEOUS HUMAN FORMS...
...IS IT NOT ALL THE HUMANS' FAULT?
I WILL NOT LET THEM ADD TO THEIR SINS BY ATTAINING THE KEY TO THE KINGDOM.
I WILL MURDER THEM BEFORE IT'S TOO LATE...
...NO MATTER WHICH OF THE CANDIDATES FINDS IT.
WITH MY POWER, IT WILL BE A SIMPLE TASK.

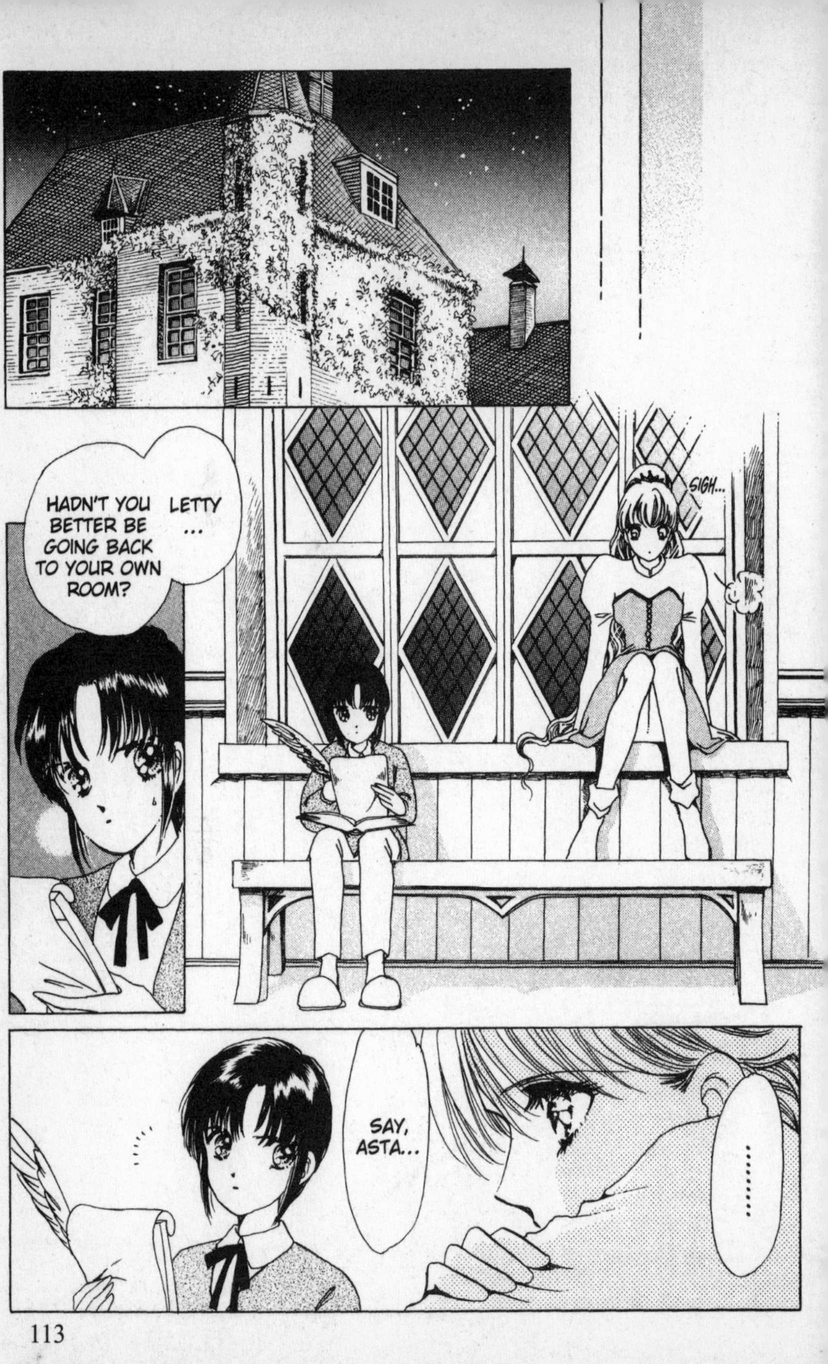
SIGH...
LETTY ...
HADN'T YOU BETTER BE GOING BACK TO YOUR OWN ROOM?
......
SAY, ASTA...
...

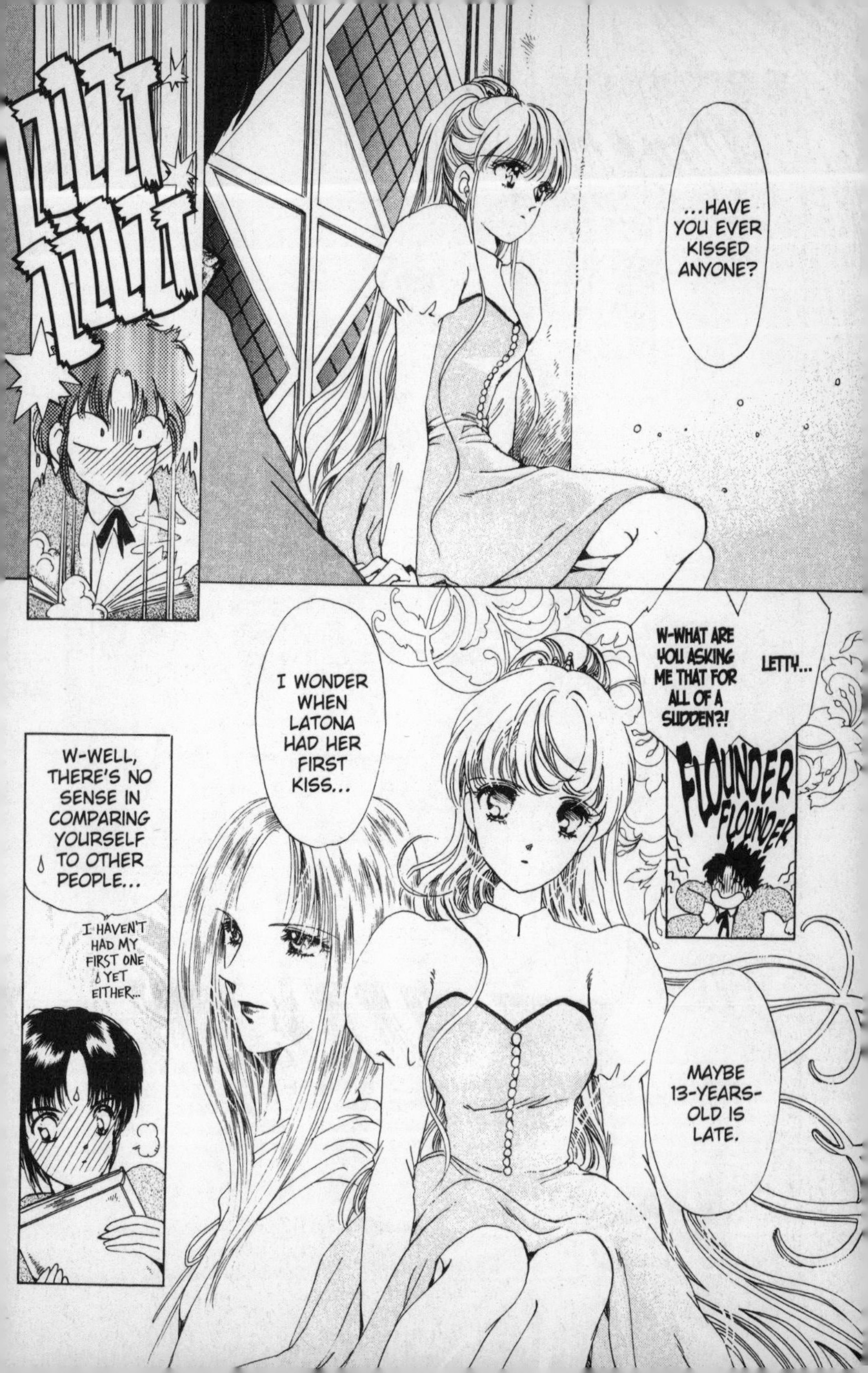
...HAVE YOU EVER KISSED ANYONE?
ZZZT ZZZT
W-WHAT ARE YOU ASKING ME THAT FOR ALL OF A SUDDEN?!
LETTY...
FLOUNDER FLOUNDER
I WONDER WHEN LATONA HAD HER FIRST KISS...
MAYBE 13-YEARS-OLD IS LATE.
W-WELL, THERE'S NO SENSE IN COMPARING YOURSELF TO OTHER PEOPLE...
I HAVEN'T HAD MY FIRST ONE YET EITHER...

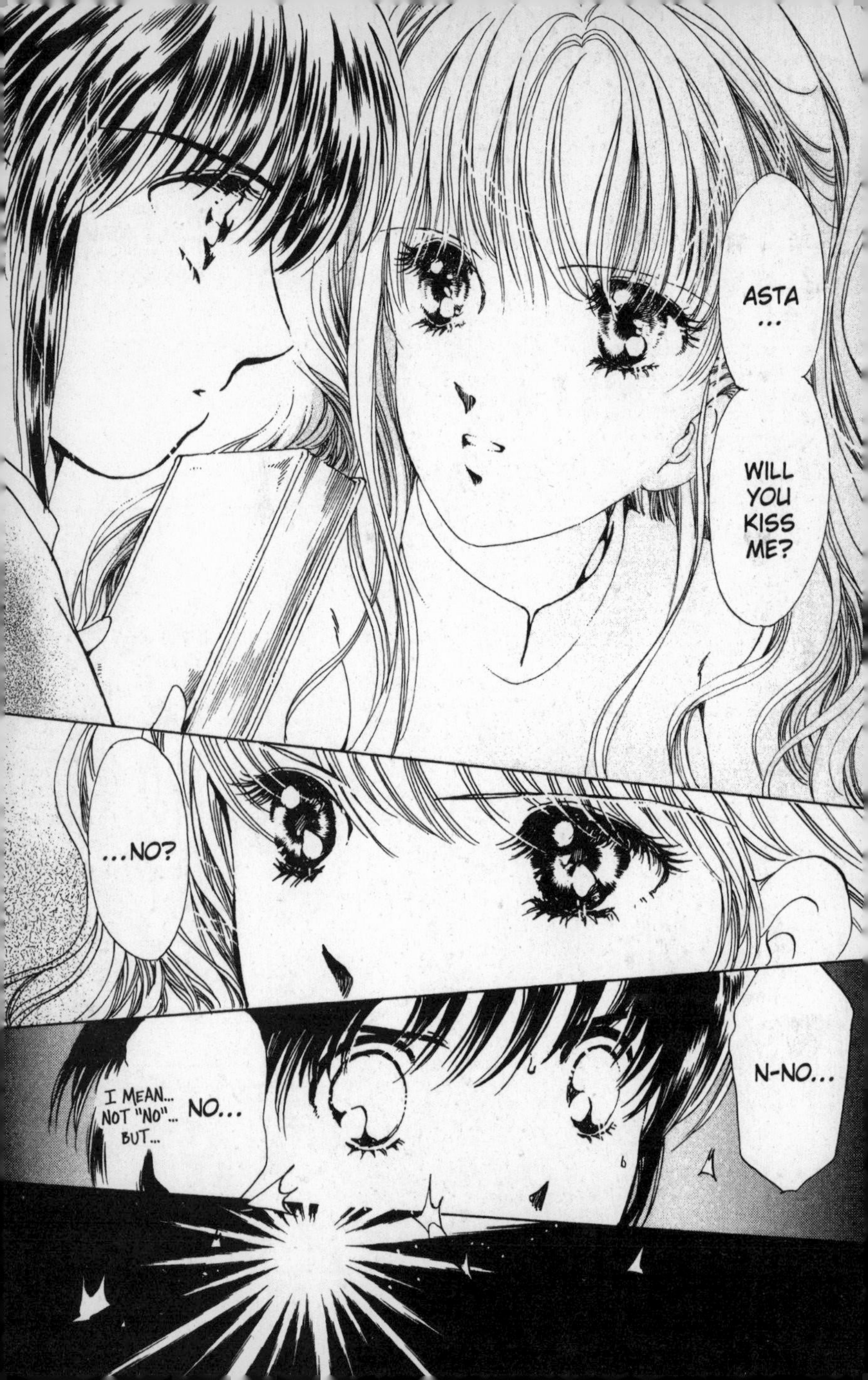
ASTA ...
WILL YOU KISS ME?
...NO?
N-NO...
NO...
I MEAN... NOT "NO"... BUT...

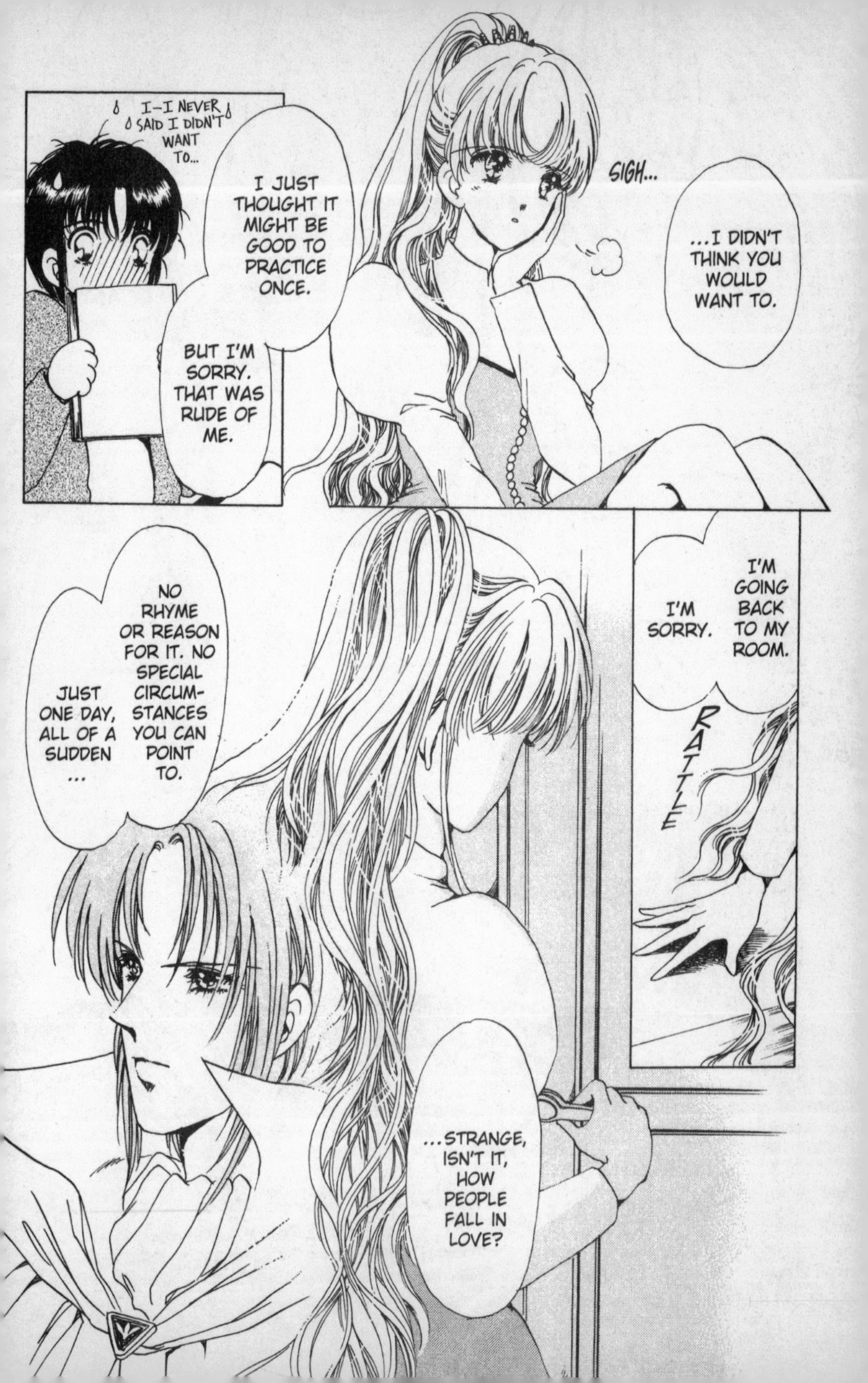
SIGH...
...I DIDN'T THINK YOU WOULD WANT TO.
I JUST THOUGHT IT MIGHT BE GOOD TO PRACTICE ONCE.
I-I NEVER SAID I DIDN'T WANT TO...
BUT I'M SORRY. THAT WAS RUDE OF ME.
I'M GOING BACK TO MY ROOM.
I'M SORRY.
RATTLE
...STRANGE, ISN'T IT, HOW PEOPLE FALL IN LOVE?
NO RHYME OR REASON FOR IT. NO SPECIAL CIRCUMSTANCES YOU CAN POINT TO.
JUST ONE DAY, ALL OF A SUDDEN ...

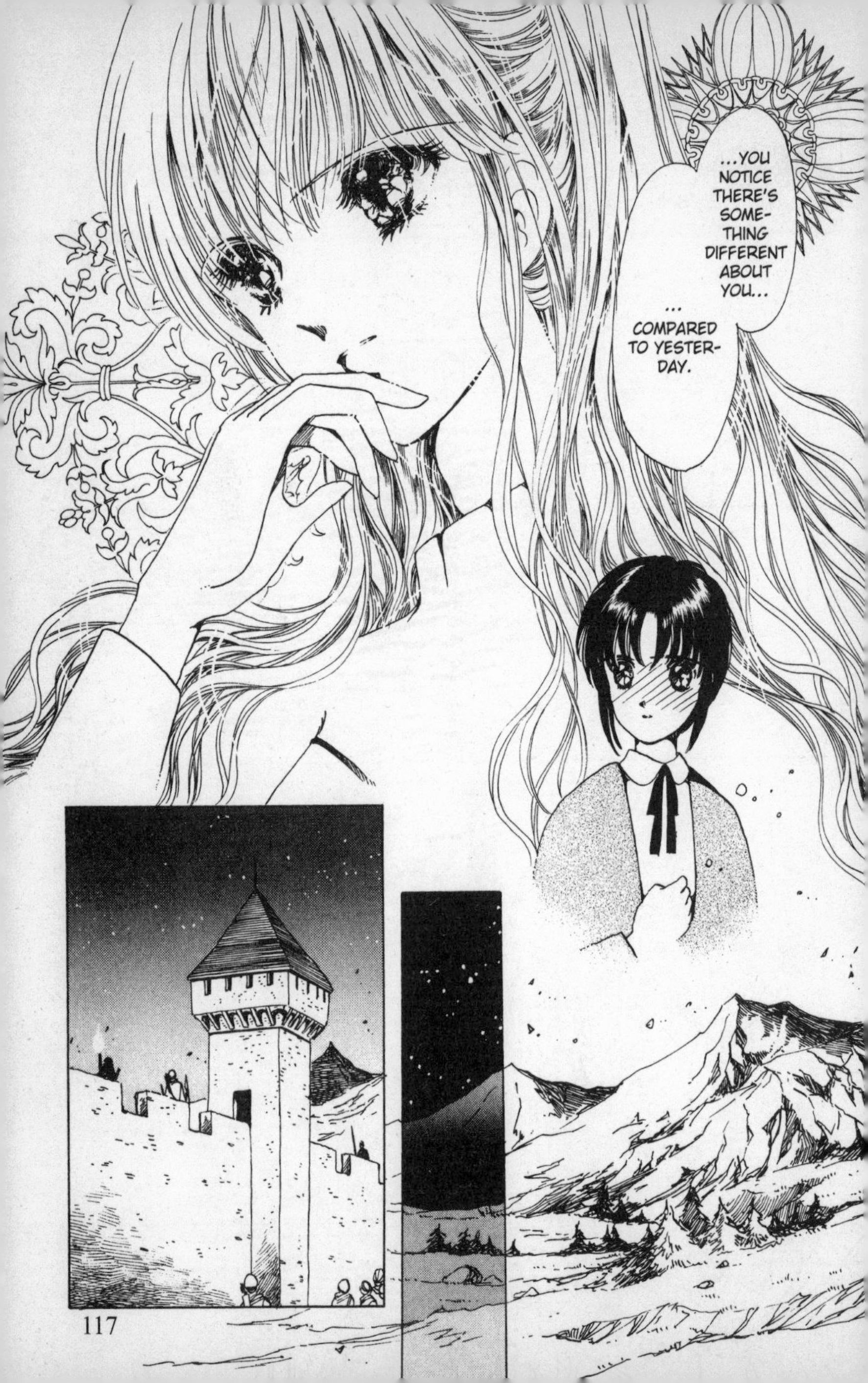
...YOU NOTICE THERE'S SOME- THING DIFFERENT ABOUT YOU...
... COMPARED TO YESTER- DAY.

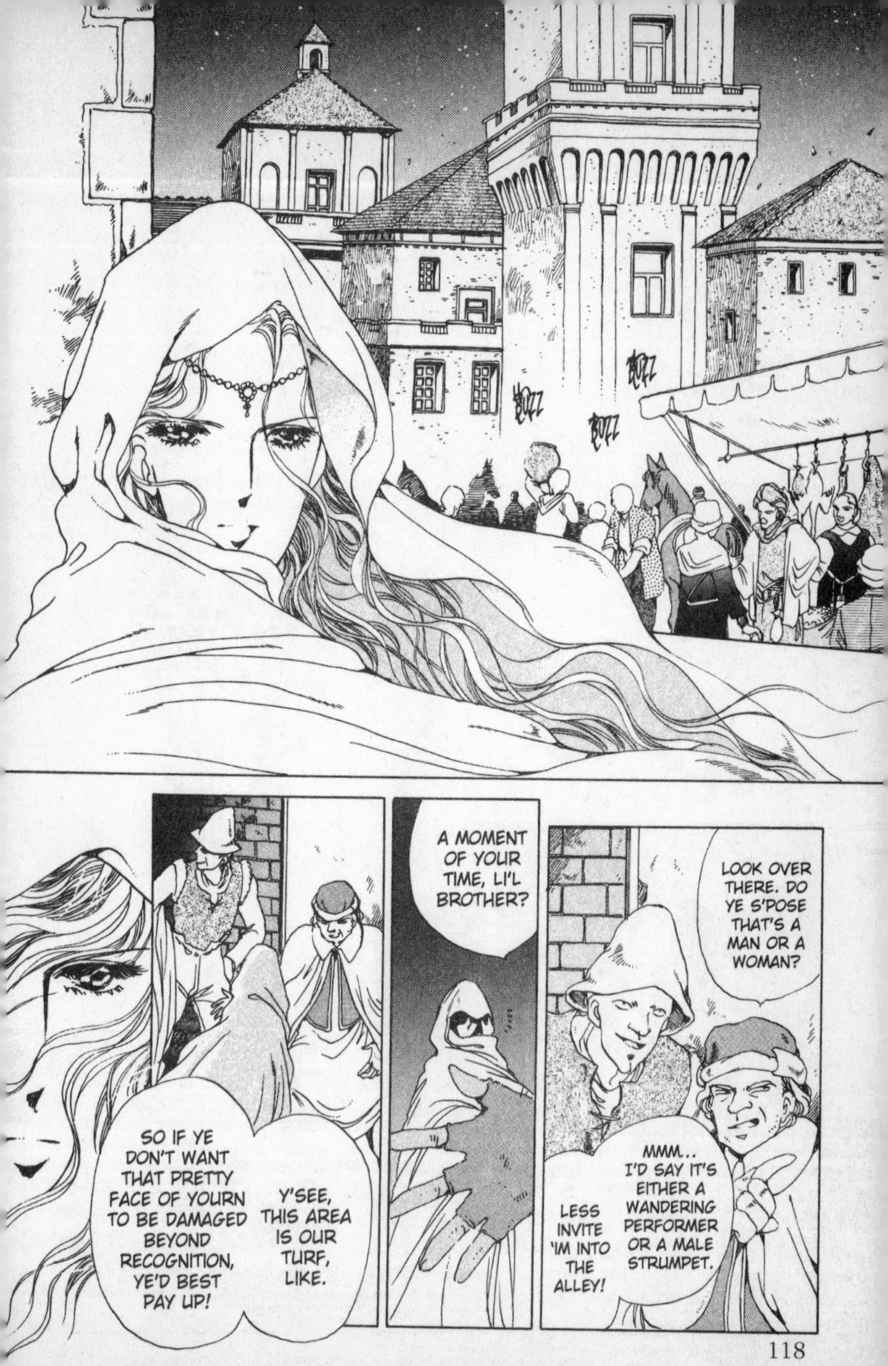
BUZZ
BUZZ
BUZZ
LOOK OVER THERE. DO YE S'POSE THAT'S A MAN OR A WOMAN?
MMM... I'D SAY IT'S EITHER A WANDERING PERFORMER OR A MALE STRUMPET.
LESS INVITE 'IM INTO THE ALLEY!
A MOMENT OF YOUR TIME, LI'L BROTHER?
Y'SEE, THIS AREA IS OUR TURF, LIKE.
SO IF YE DON'T WANT THAT PRETTY FACE OF YOURN TO BE DAMAGED BEYOND RECOGNITION, YE'D BEST PAY UP!

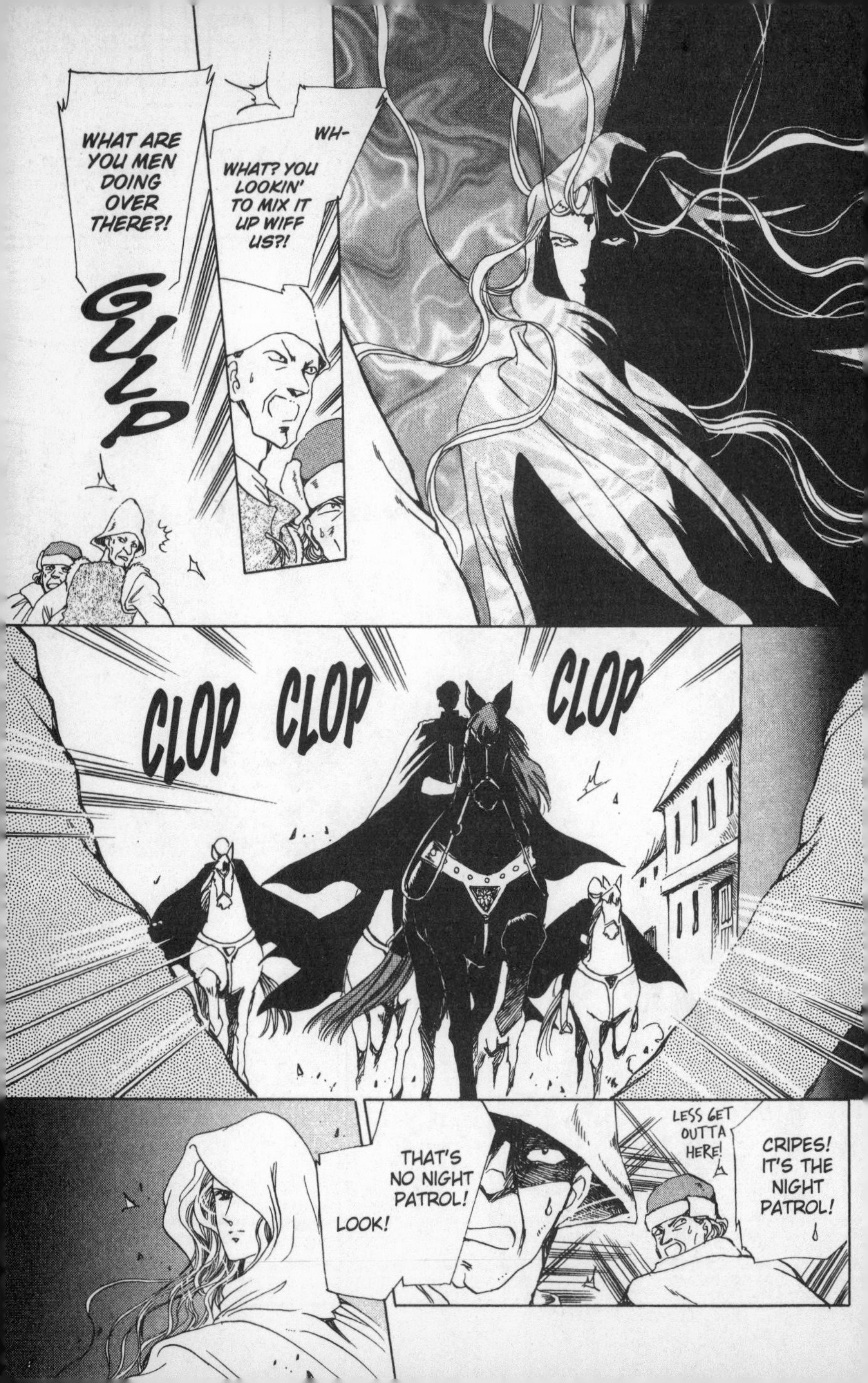
WH- WHAT? YOU LOOKIN' TO MIX IT UP WIFF US?!
WHAT ARE YOU MEN DOING OVER THERE?!
GULP
CLOP CLOP CLOP
CRIPES! IT'S THE NIGHT PATROL!
LESS GET OUTTA HERE!
THAT'S NO NIGHT PATROL!
LOOK!

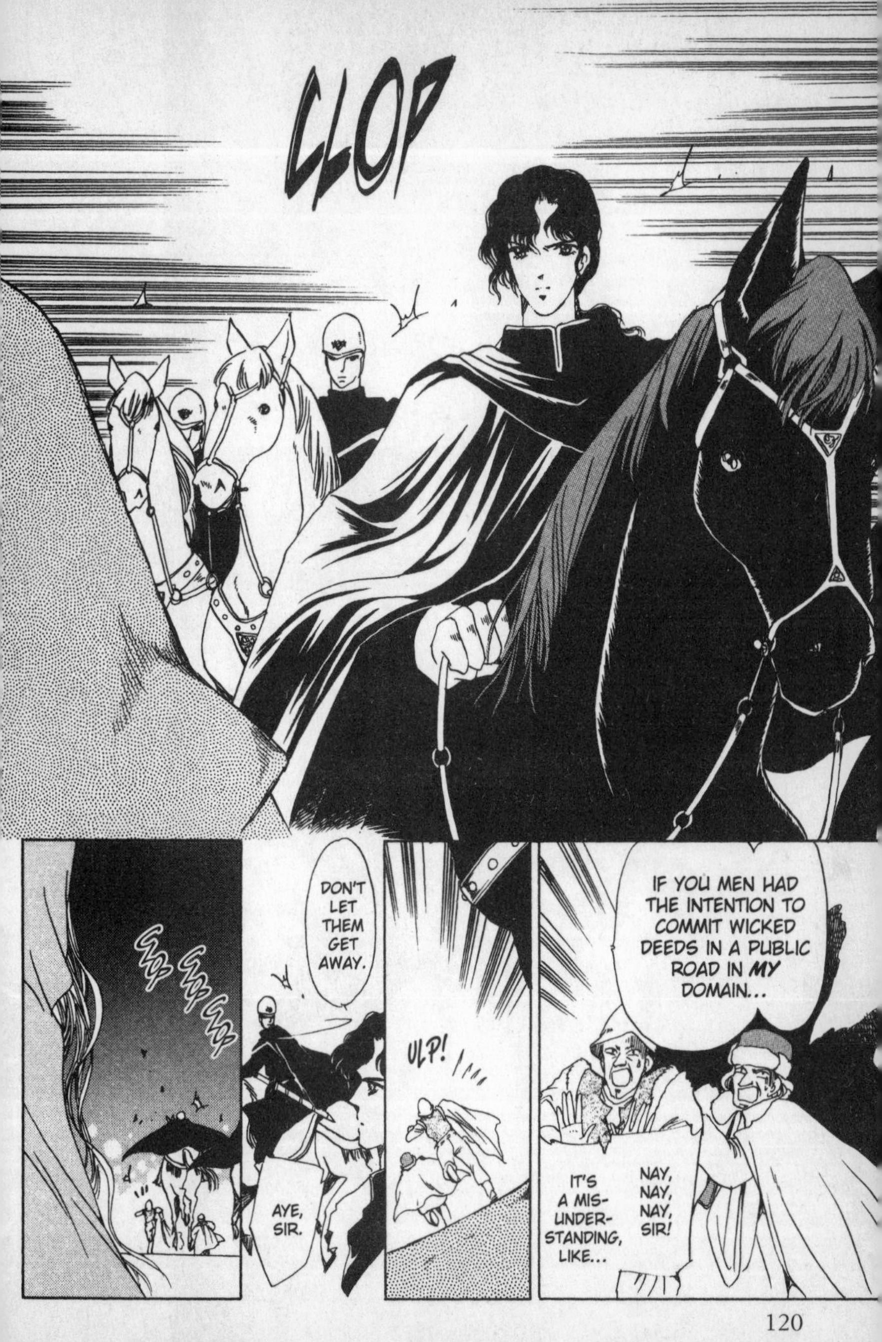
CLOP
IF YOU MEN HAD THE INTENTION TO COMMIT WICKED DEEDS IN A PUBLIC ROAD IN MY DOMAIN...
NAY, NAY, NAY, SIR!
IT'S A MIS-UNDER-STANDING, LIKE...
ULP!
DON'T LET THEM GET AWAY.
AYE, SIR.
CLOP CLOP CLOP

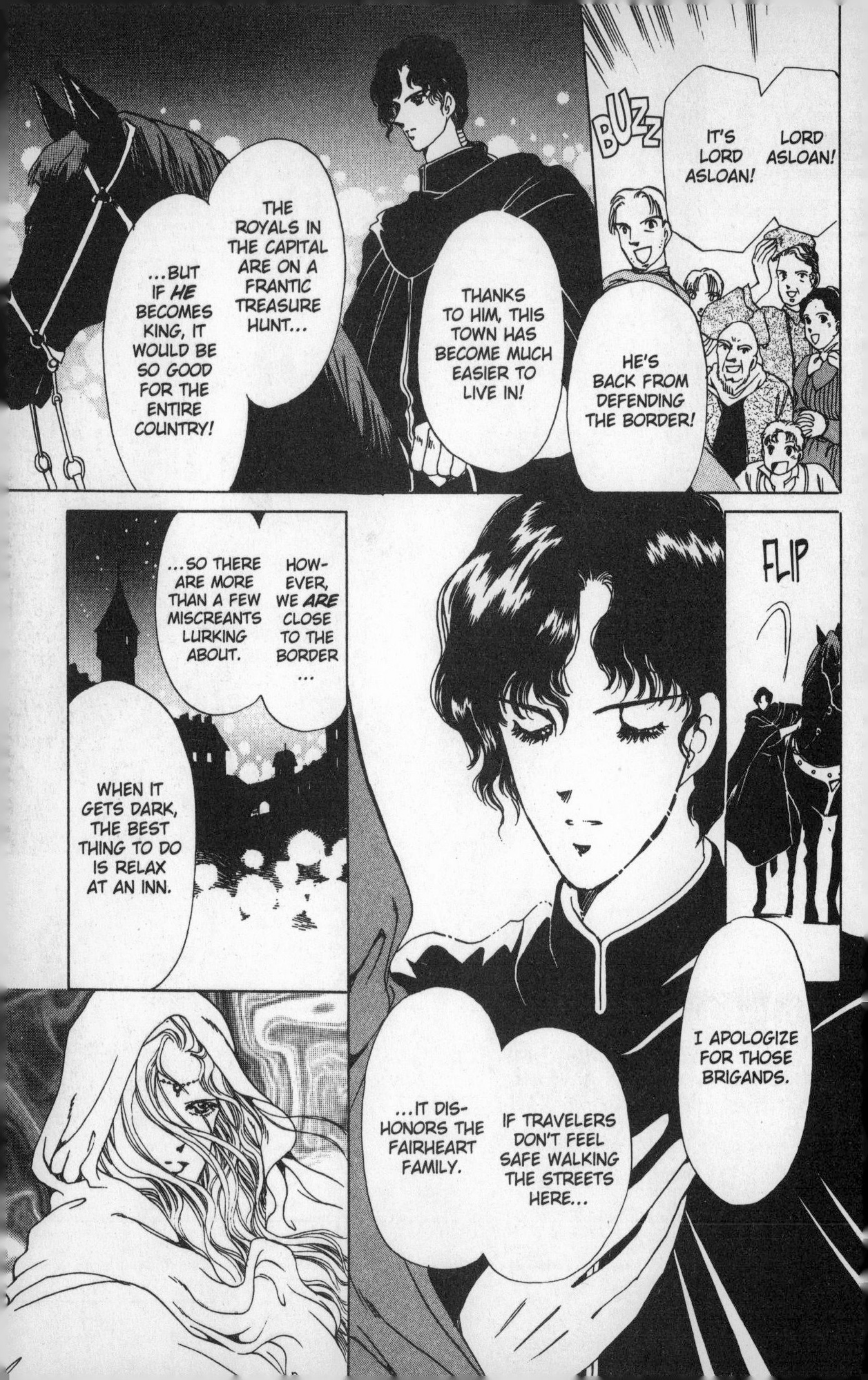
LORD ASLOAN!
IT'S LORD ASLOAN!
BUZZ
HE'S BACK FROM DEFENDING THE BORDER!
THANKS TO HIM, THIS TOWN HAS BECOME MUCH EASIER TO LIVE IN!
THE ROYALS IN THE CAPITAL ARE ON A FRANTIC TREASURE HUNT...
...BUT IF *HE* BECOMES KING, IT WOULD BE SO GOOD FOR THE ENTIRE COUNTRY!
FLIP
I APOLOGIZE FOR THOSE BRIGANDS.
IF TRAVELERS DON'T FEEL SAFE WALKING THE STREETS HERE...
...IT DISHONORS THE FAIRHEART FAMILY.
HOWEVER, WE *ARE* CLOSE TO THE BORDER...
...SO THERE ARE MORE THAN A FEW MISCREANTS LURKING ABOUT.
WHEN IT GETS DARK, THE BEST THING TO DO IS RELAX AT AN INN.

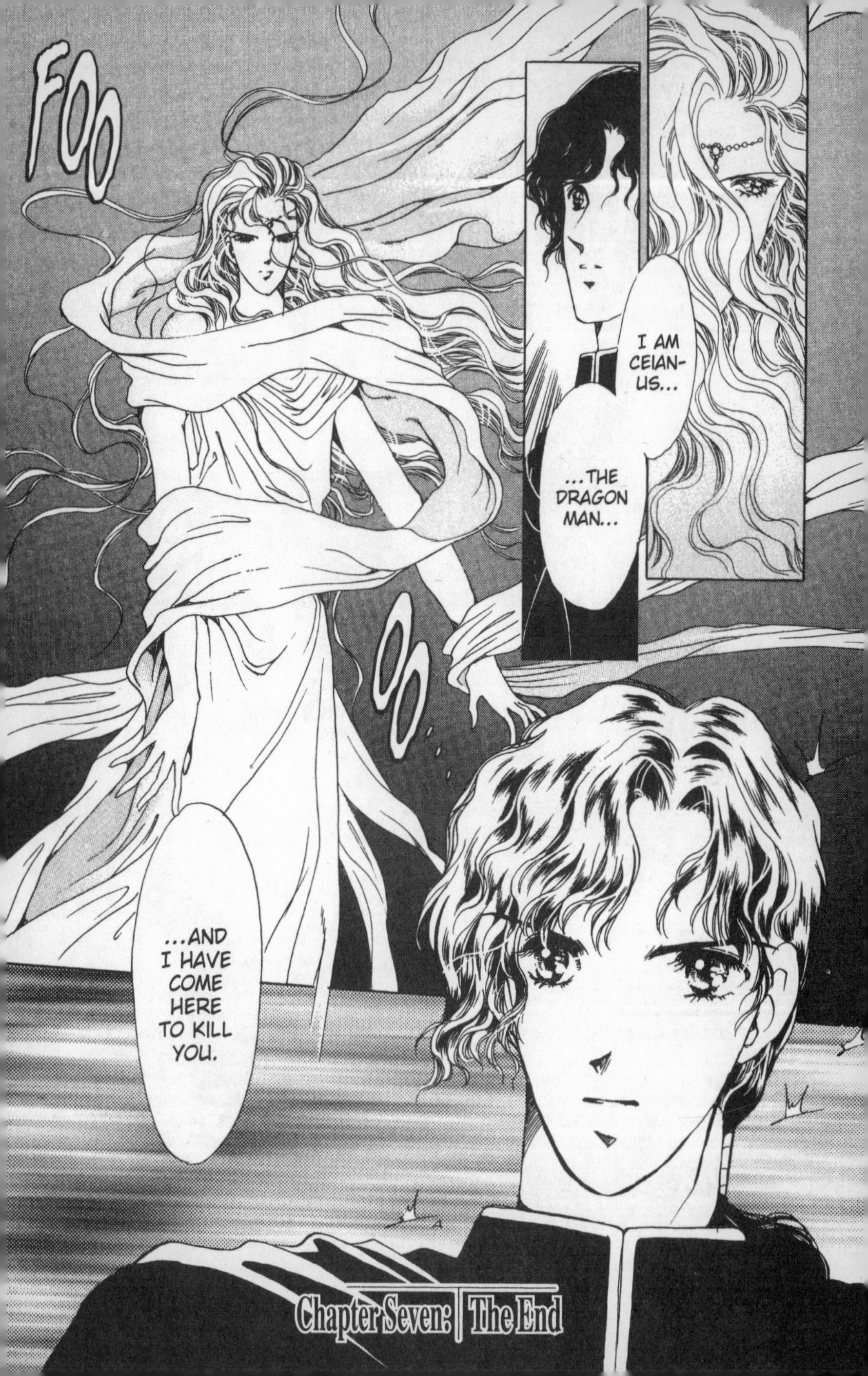
I AM CEIAN-US...
...THE DRAGON MAN...
FOO
OO
...AND I HAVE COME HERE TO KILL YOU.
Chapter Seven: The End

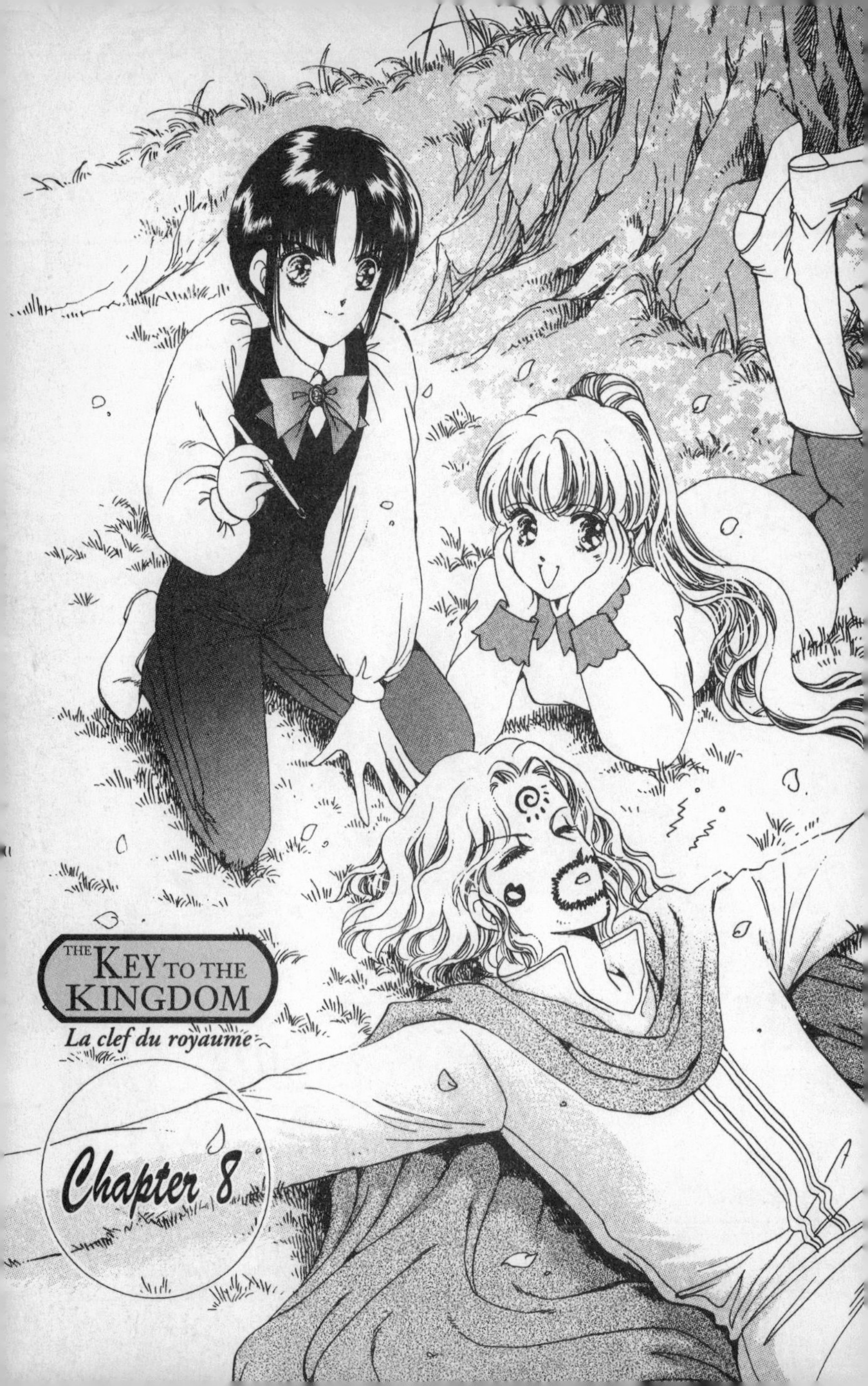
THE KEY TO THE KINGDOM
La clef du royaume
Chapter 8

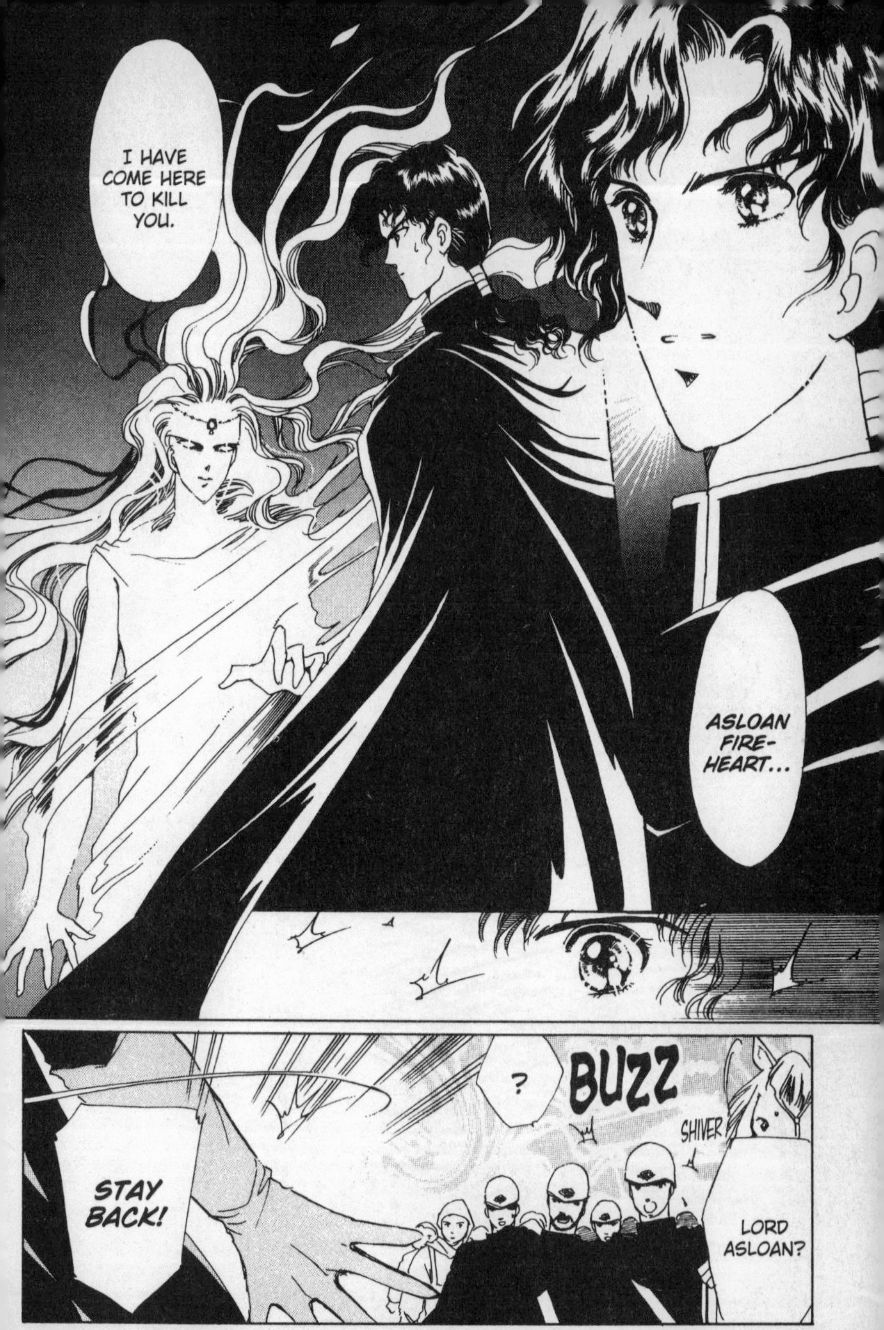
ASLOAN FIRE-HEART...
I HAVE COME HERE TO KILL YOU.
LORD ASLOAN?
SHIVER
BUZZ
?
STAY BACK!

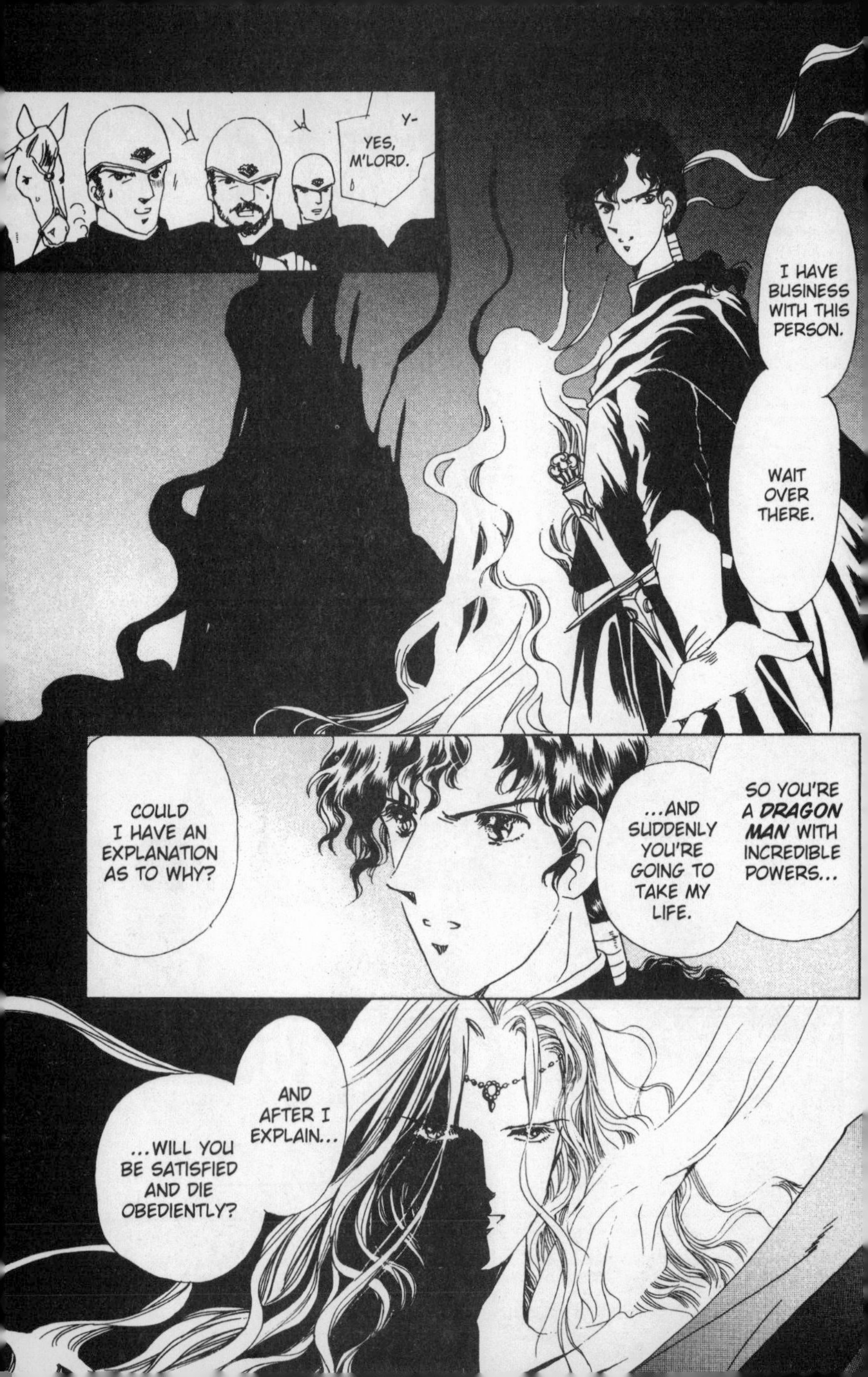
I HAVE BUSINESS WITH THIS PERSON.
WAIT OVER THERE.
Y-
YES, M'LORD.
SO YOU'RE A ***DRAGON MAN*** WITH INCREDIBLE POWERS...
...AND SUDDENLY YOU'RE GOING TO TAKE MY LIFE.
COULD I HAVE AN EXPLANATION AS TO WHY?
AND AFTER I EXPLAIN...
...WILL YOU BE SATISFIED AND DIE OBEDIENTLY?

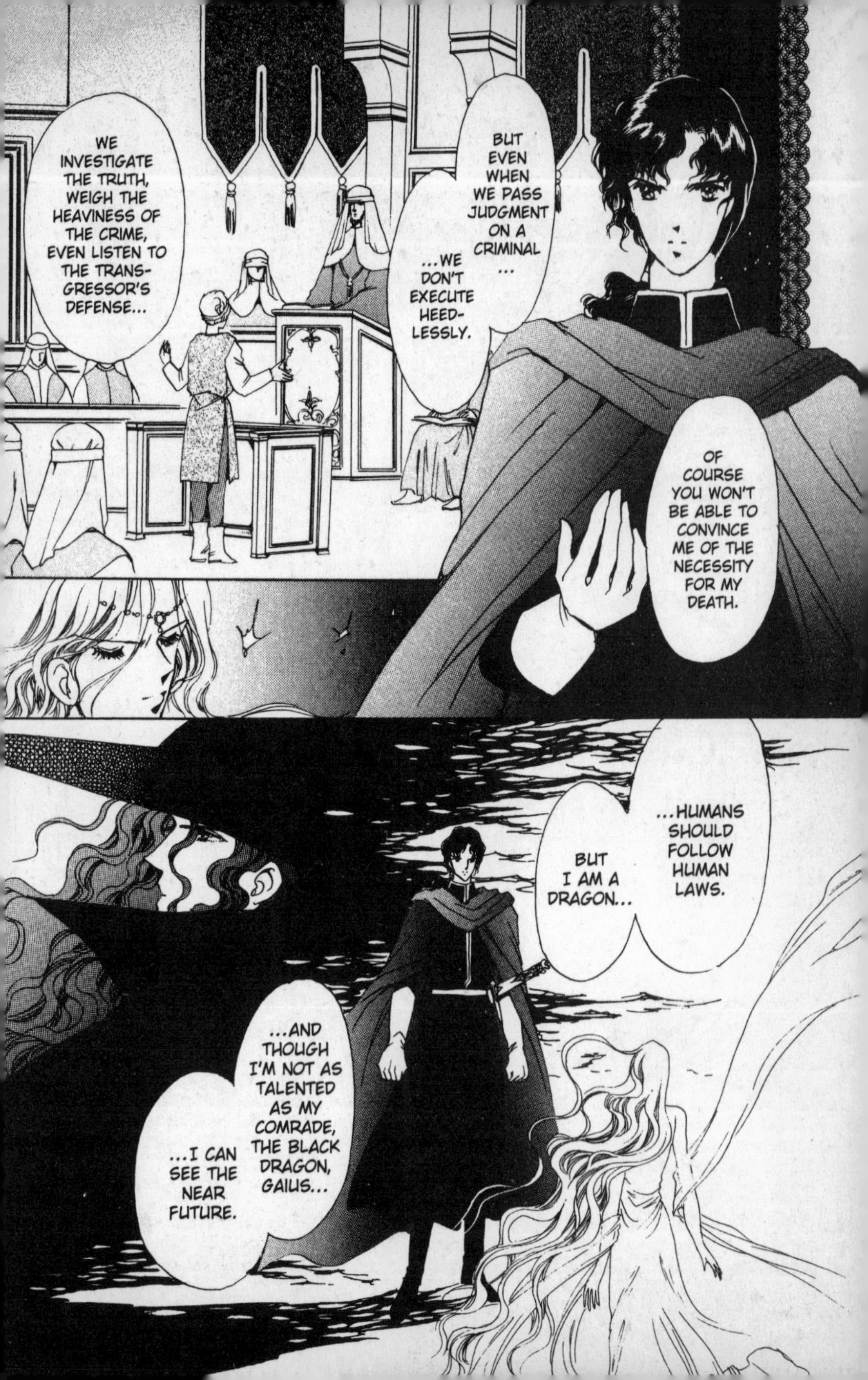
WE INVESTIGATE THE TRUTH, WEIGH THE HEAVINESS OF THE CRIME, EVEN LISTEN TO THE TRANS-GRESSOR'S DEFENSE...
BUT EVEN WHEN WE PASS JUDGMENT ON A CRIMINAL...
...WE DON'T EXECUTE HEED-LESSLY.
OF COURSE YOU WON'T BE ABLE TO CONVINCE ME OF THE NECESSITY FOR MY DEATH.
...HUMANS SHOULD FOLLOW HUMAN LAWS.
BUT I AM A DRAGON...
...AND THOUGH I'M NOT AS TALENTED AS MY COMRADE, THE BLACK DRAGON, GAIUS...
...I CAN SEE THE NEAR FUTURE.

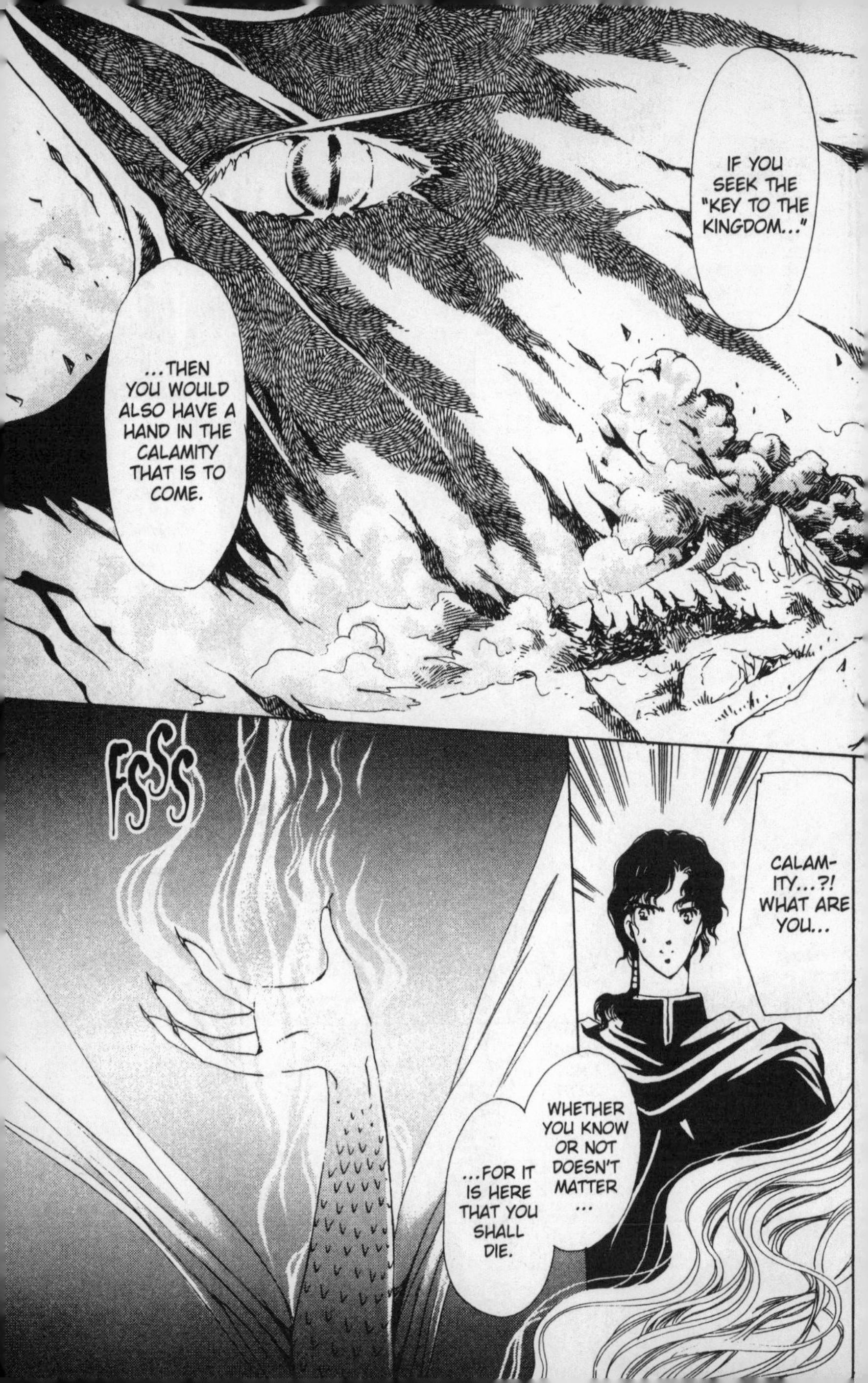
IF YOU SEEK THE "KEY TO THE KINGDOM..."
...THEN YOU WOULD ALSO HAVE A HAND IN THE CALAMITY THAT IS TO COME.
CALAM-ITY...?! WHAT ARE YOU...
FSSS
WHETHER YOU KNOW OR NOT DOESN'T MATTER ...
...FOR IT IS HERE THAT YOU SHALL DIE.

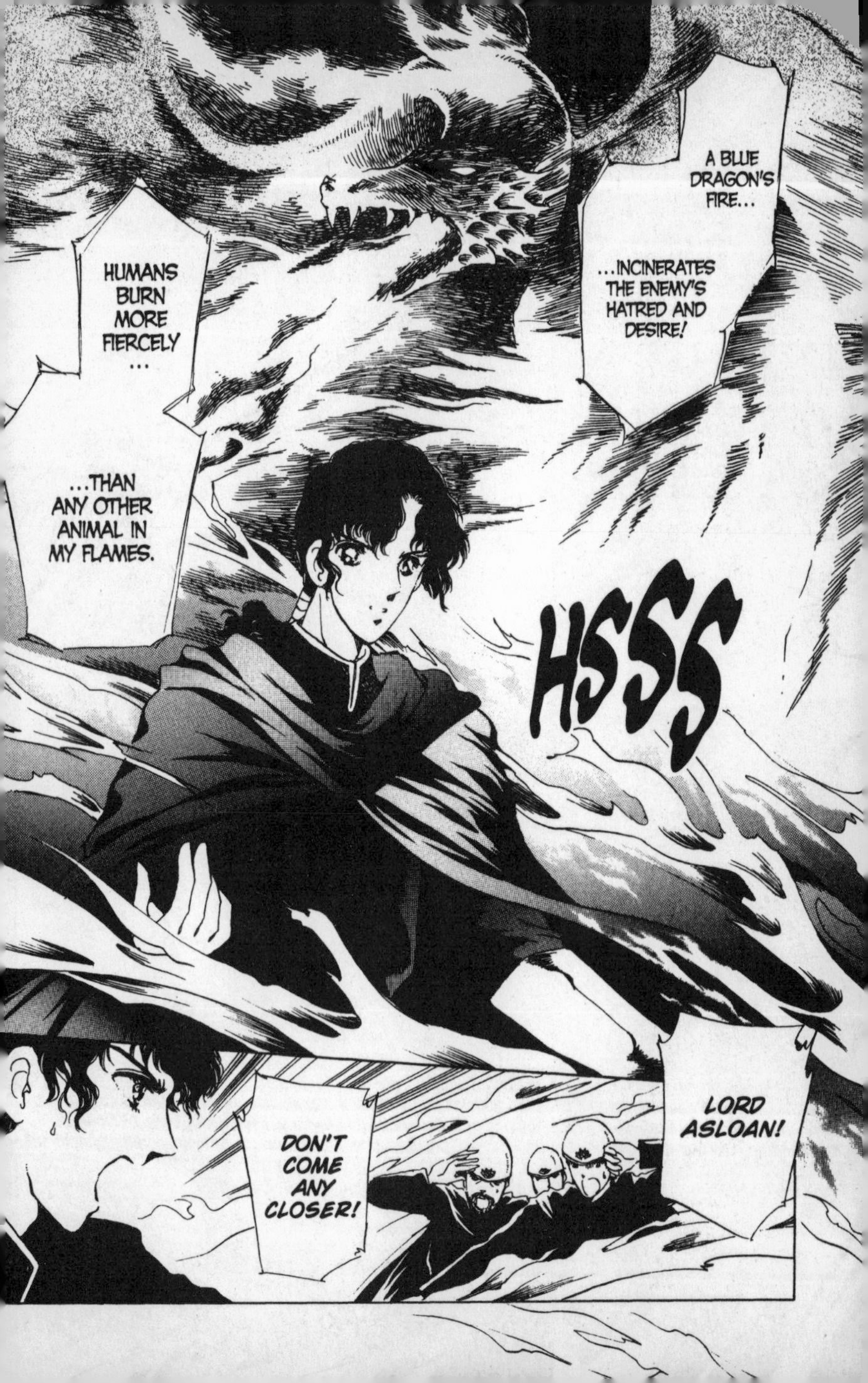
A BLUE DRAGON'S FIRE...
...INCINERATES THE ENEMY'S HATRED AND DESIRE!
HUMANS BURN MORE FIERCELY ...
...THAN ANY OTHER ANIMAL IN MY FLAMES.
HSSS
LORD ASLOAN!
DON'T COME ANY CLOSER!

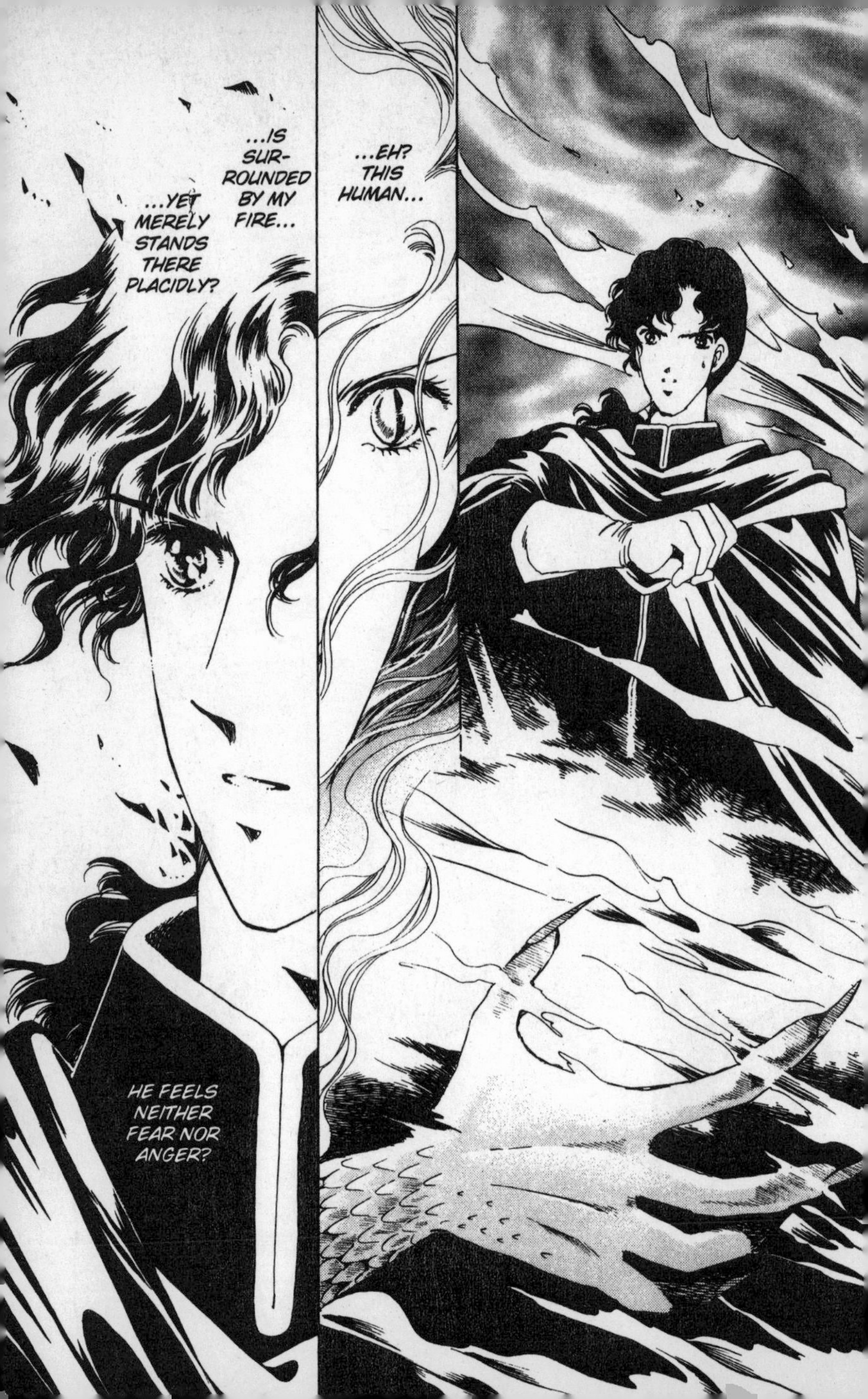
...EH? THIS HUMAN...
...IS SUR-ROUNDED BY MY FIRE...
...YET MERELY STANDS THERE PLACIDLY?
HE FEELS NEITHER FEAR NOR ANGER?

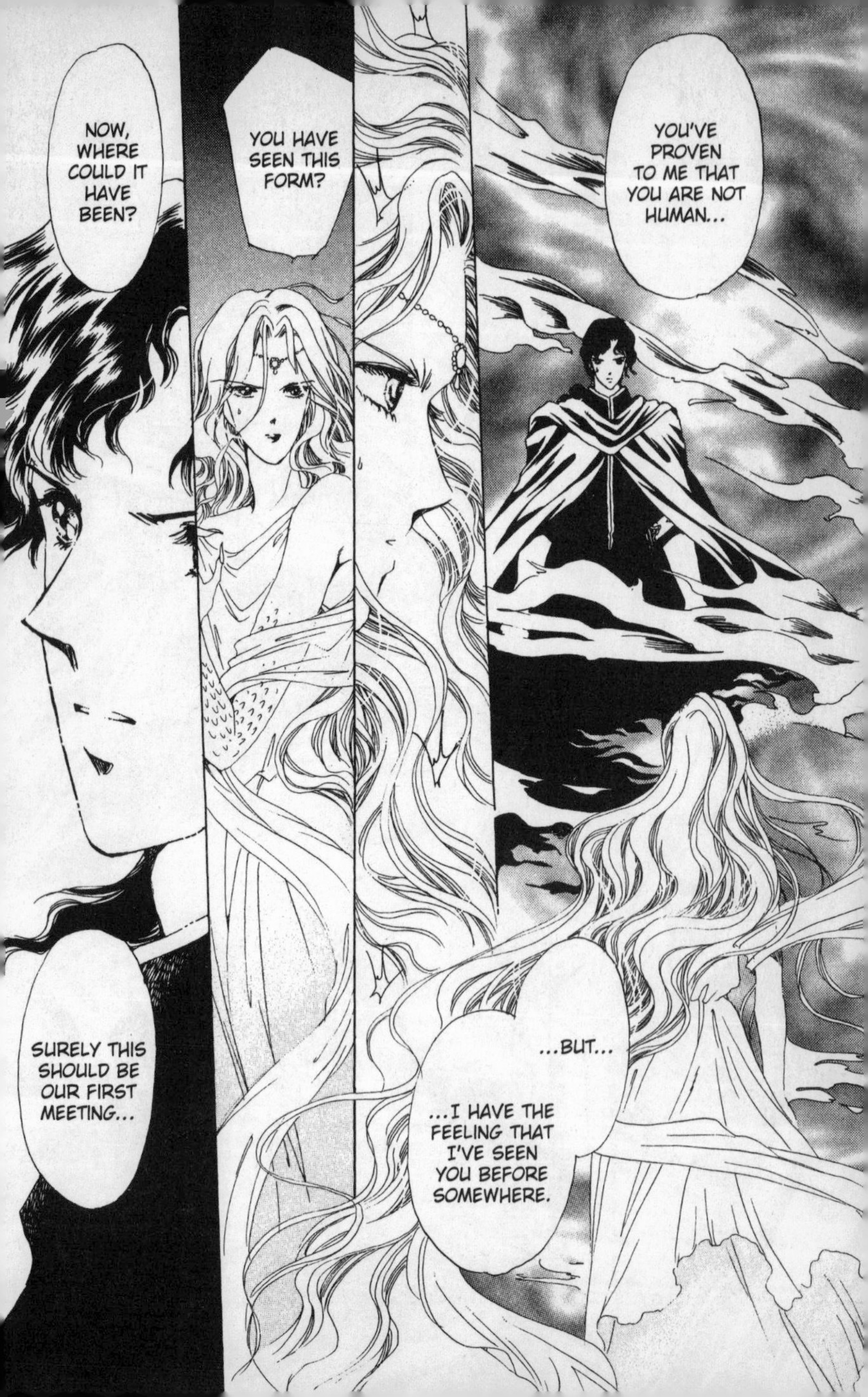
YOU'VE PROVEN TO ME THAT YOU ARE NOT HUMAN...
...BUT...
...I HAVE THE FEELING THAT I'VE SEEN YOU BEFORE SOMEWHERE.
YOU HAVE SEEN THIS FORM?
NOW, WHERE COULD IT HAVE BEEN?
SURELY THIS SHOULD BE OUR FIRST MEETING...

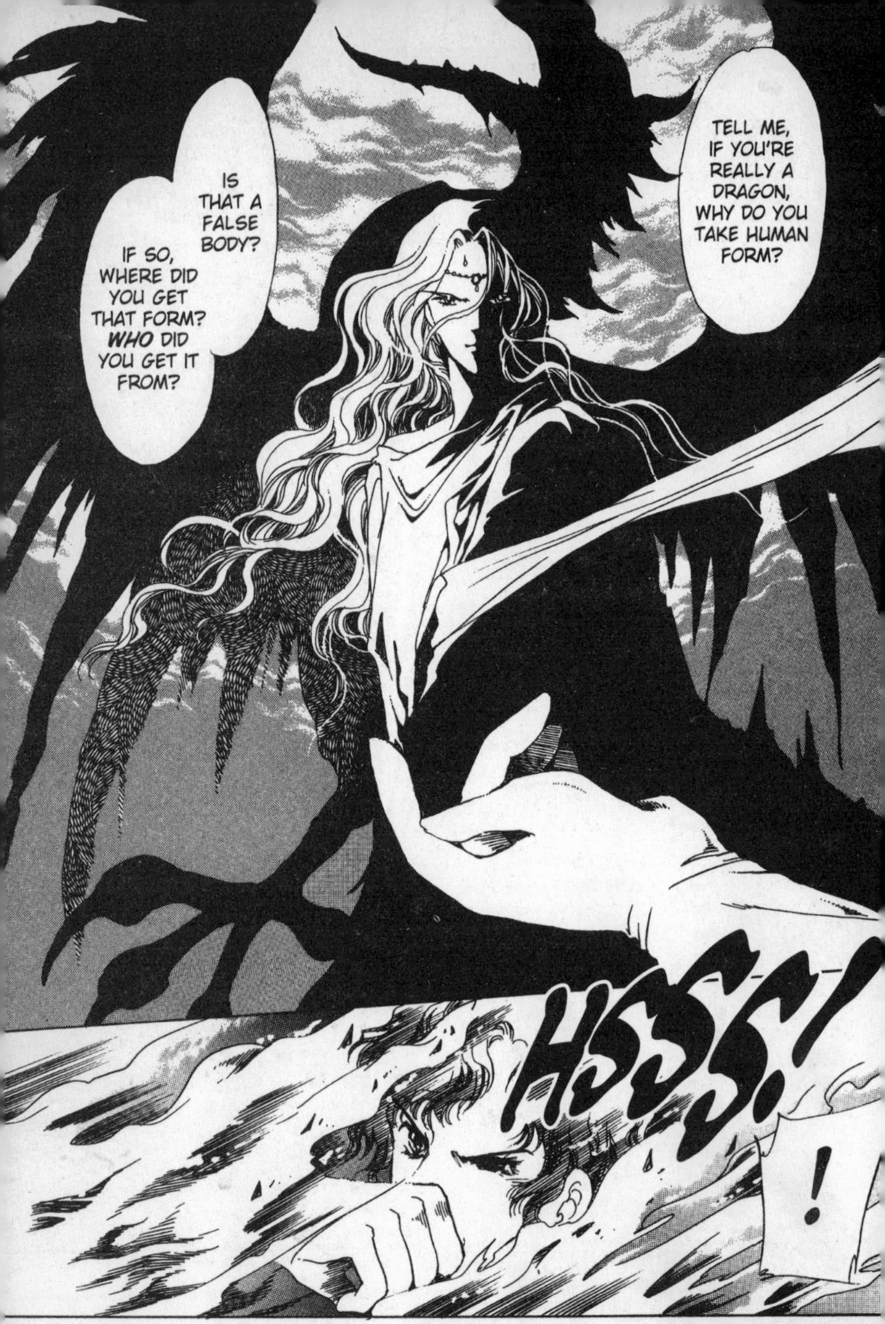
TELL ME, IF YOU'RE REALLY A DRAGON, WHY DO YOU TAKE HUMAN FORM?
IS THAT A FALSE BODY?
IF SO, WHERE DID YOU GET THAT FORM? ***WHO*** DID YOU GET IT FROM?
HSSS!
!

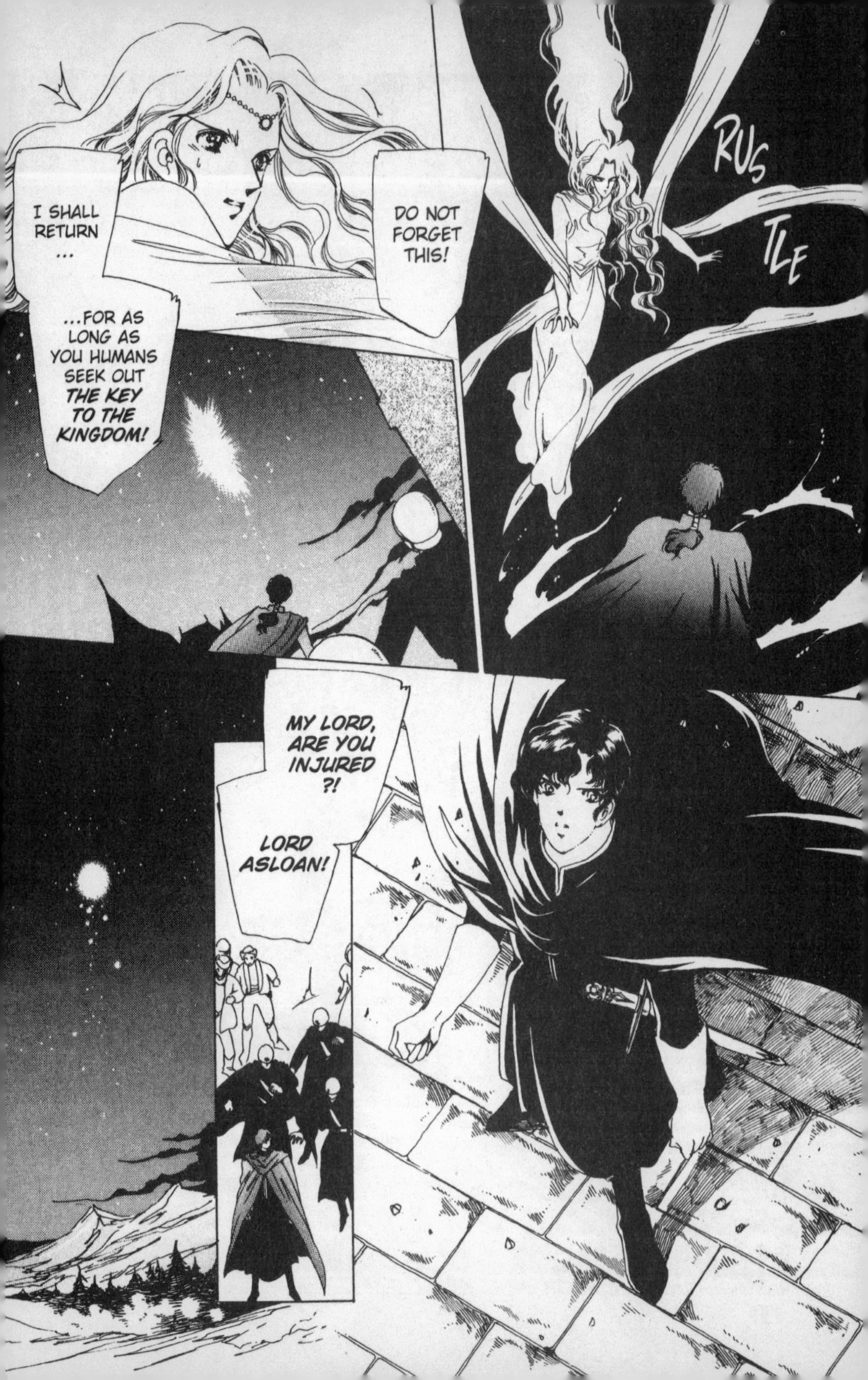
RUSTLE
DO NOT FORGET THIS!
I SHALL RETURN ...
...FOR AS LONG AS YOU HUMANS SEEK OUT THE KEY TO THE KINGDOM!
MY LORD, ARE YOU INJURED ?!
LORD ASLOAN!

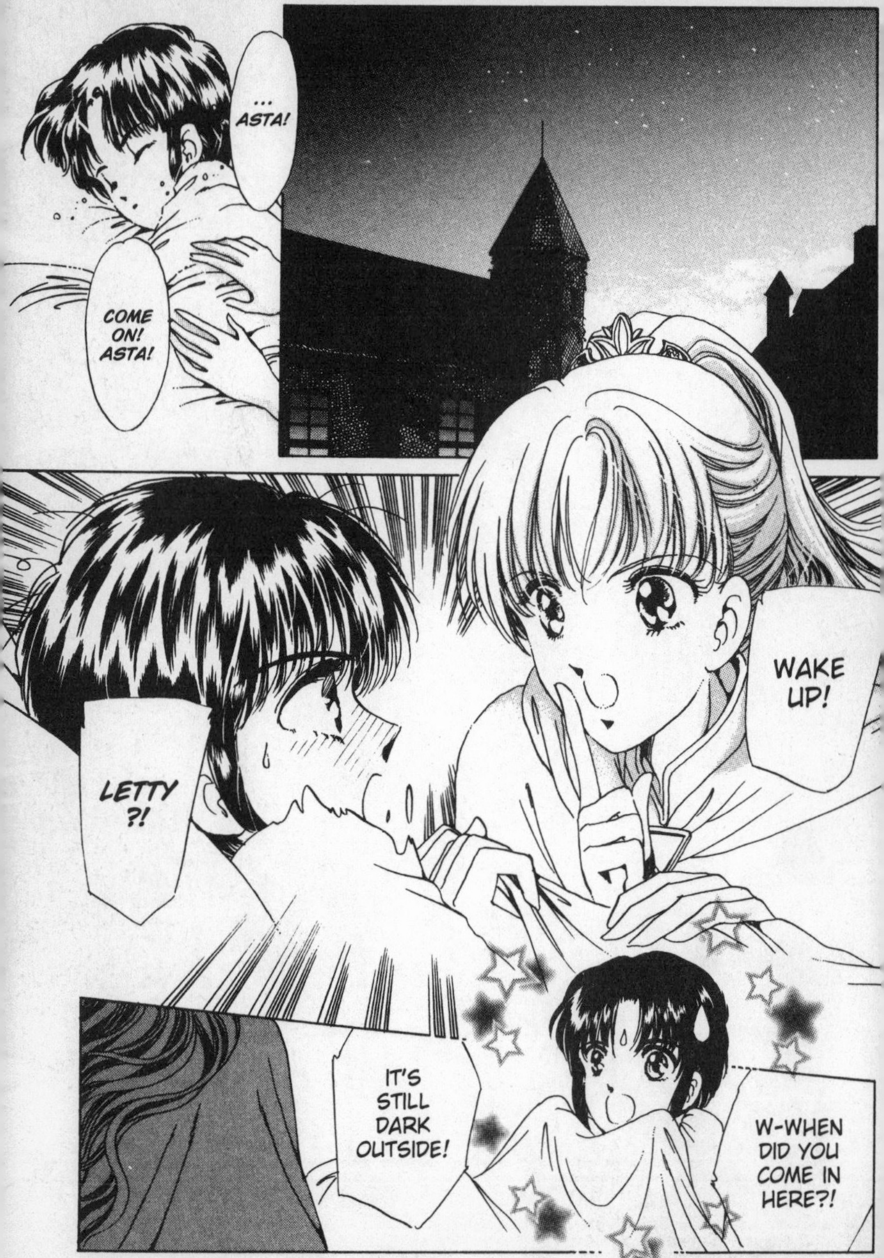

... ASTA!
COME ON! ASTA!
WAKE UP!
LETTY ?!
W-WHEN DID YOU COME IN HERE?!
IT'S STILL DARK OUTSIDE!

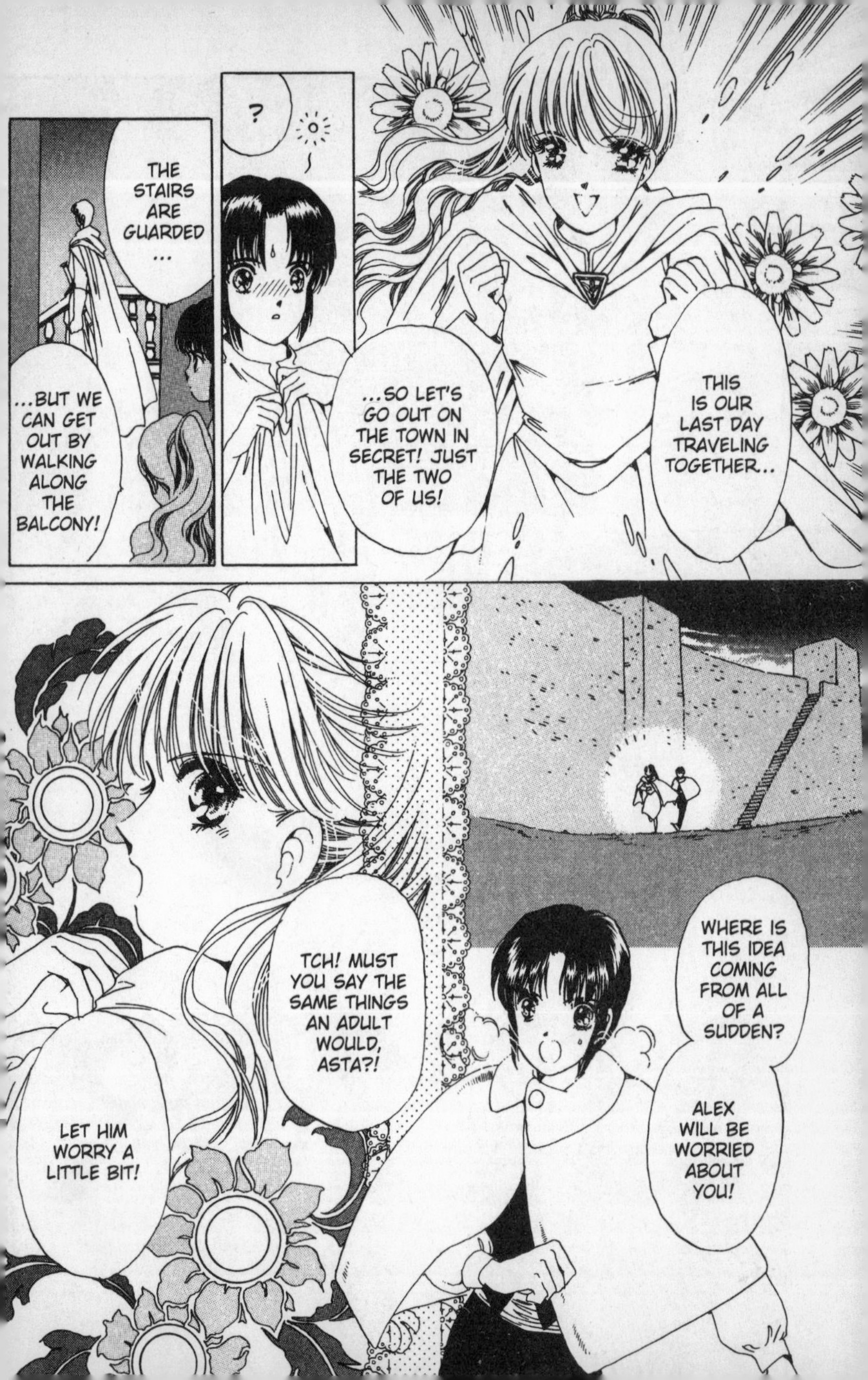
THIS IS OUR LAST DAY TRAVELING TOGETHER...
...SO LET'S GO OUT ON THE TOWN IN SECRET! JUST THE TWO OF US!
?
THE STAIRS ARE GUARDED ...
...BUT WE CAN GET OUT BY WALKING ALONG THE BALCONY!
WHERE IS THIS IDEA COMING FROM ALL OF A SUDDEN?
ALEX WILL BE WORRIED ABOUT YOU!
TCH! MUST YOU SAY THE SAME THINGS AN ADULT WOULD, ASTA?!
LET HIM WORRY A LITTLE BIT!

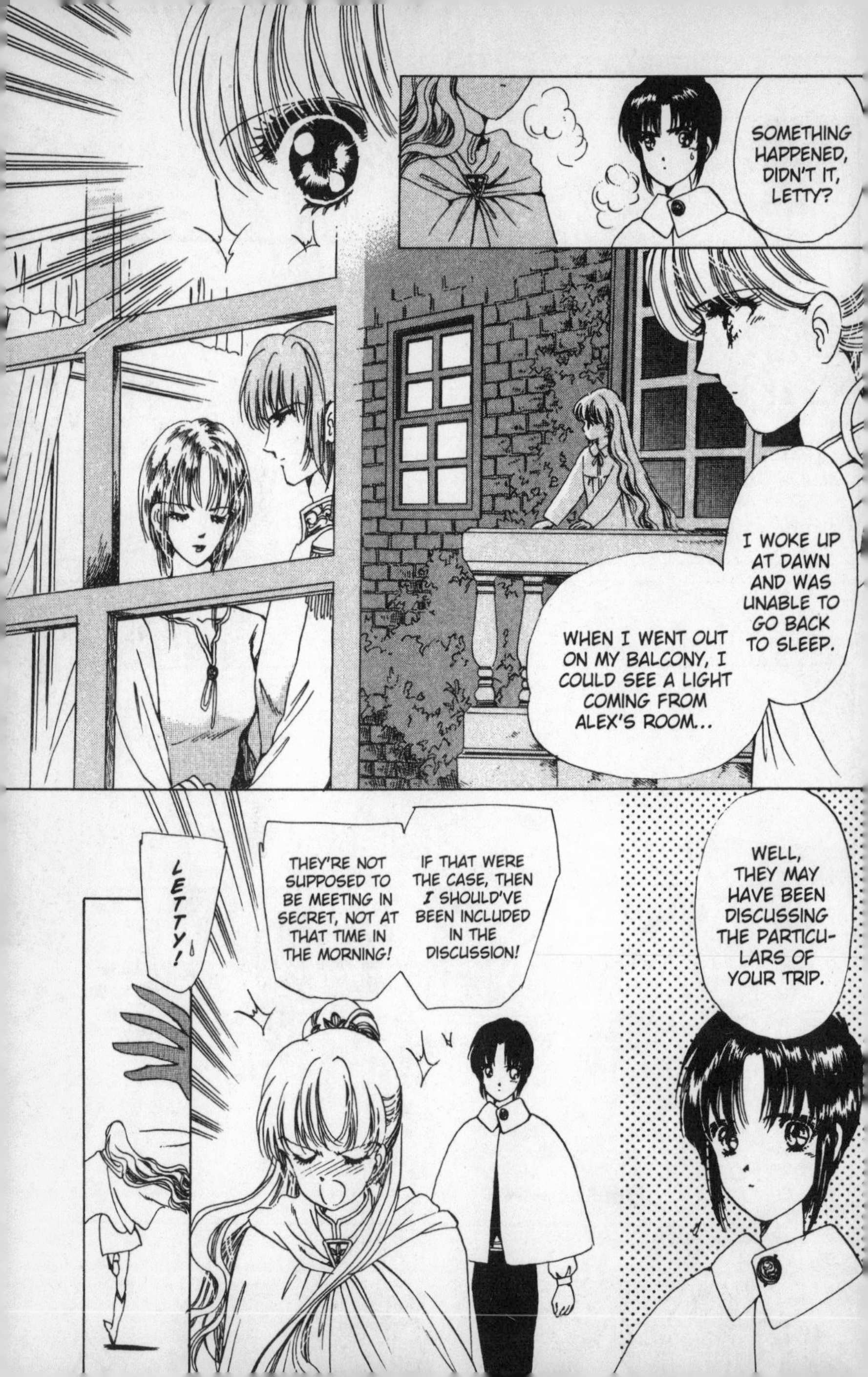
SOMETHING HAPPENED, DIDN'T IT, LETTY?
I WOKE UP AT DAWN AND WAS UNABLE TO GO BACK TO SLEEP.
WHEN I WENT OUT ON MY BALCONY, I COULD SEE A LIGHT COMING FROM ALEX'S ROOM...
WELL, THEY MAY HAVE BEEN DISCUSSING THE PARTICULARS OF YOUR TRIP.
IF THAT WERE THE CASE, THEN I SHOULD'VE BEEN INCLUDED IN THE DISCUSSION!
THEY'RE NOT SUPPOSED TO BE MEETING IN SECRET, NOT AT THAT TIME IN THE MORNING!
LETTY!

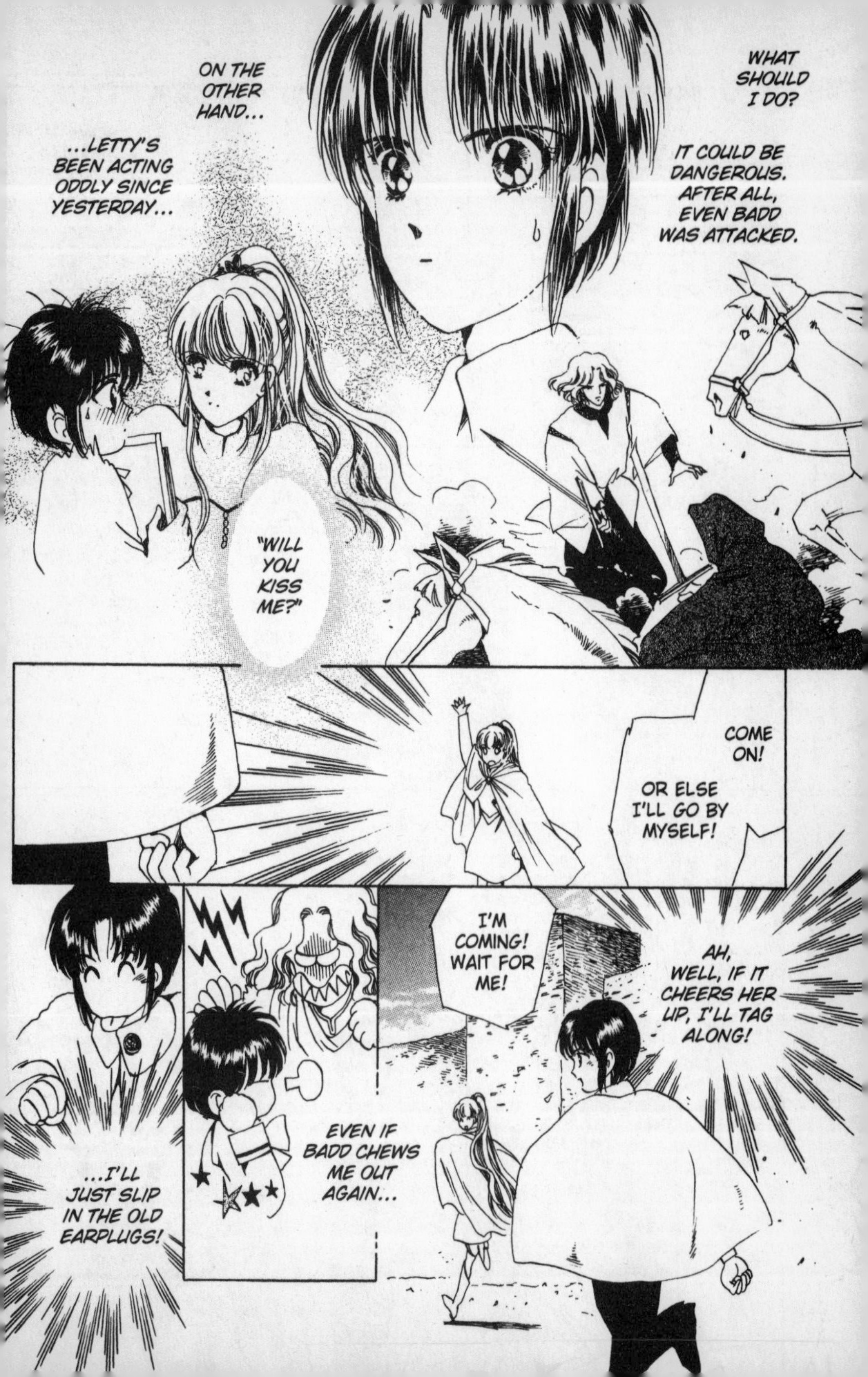
WHAT SHOULD I DO?
IT COULD BE DANGEROUS. AFTER ALL, EVEN BADD WAS ATTACKED.
ON THE OTHER HAND...
...LETTY'S BEEN ACTING ODDLY SINCE YESTERDAY...
"WILL YOU KISS ME?"
COME ON!
OR ELSE I'LL GO BY MYSELF!
AH, WELL, IF IT CHEERS HER UP, I'LL TAG ALONG!
I'M COMING! WAIT FOR ME!
EVEN IF BADD CHEWS ME OUT AGAIN...
...I'LL JUST SLIP IN THE OLD EARPLUGS!

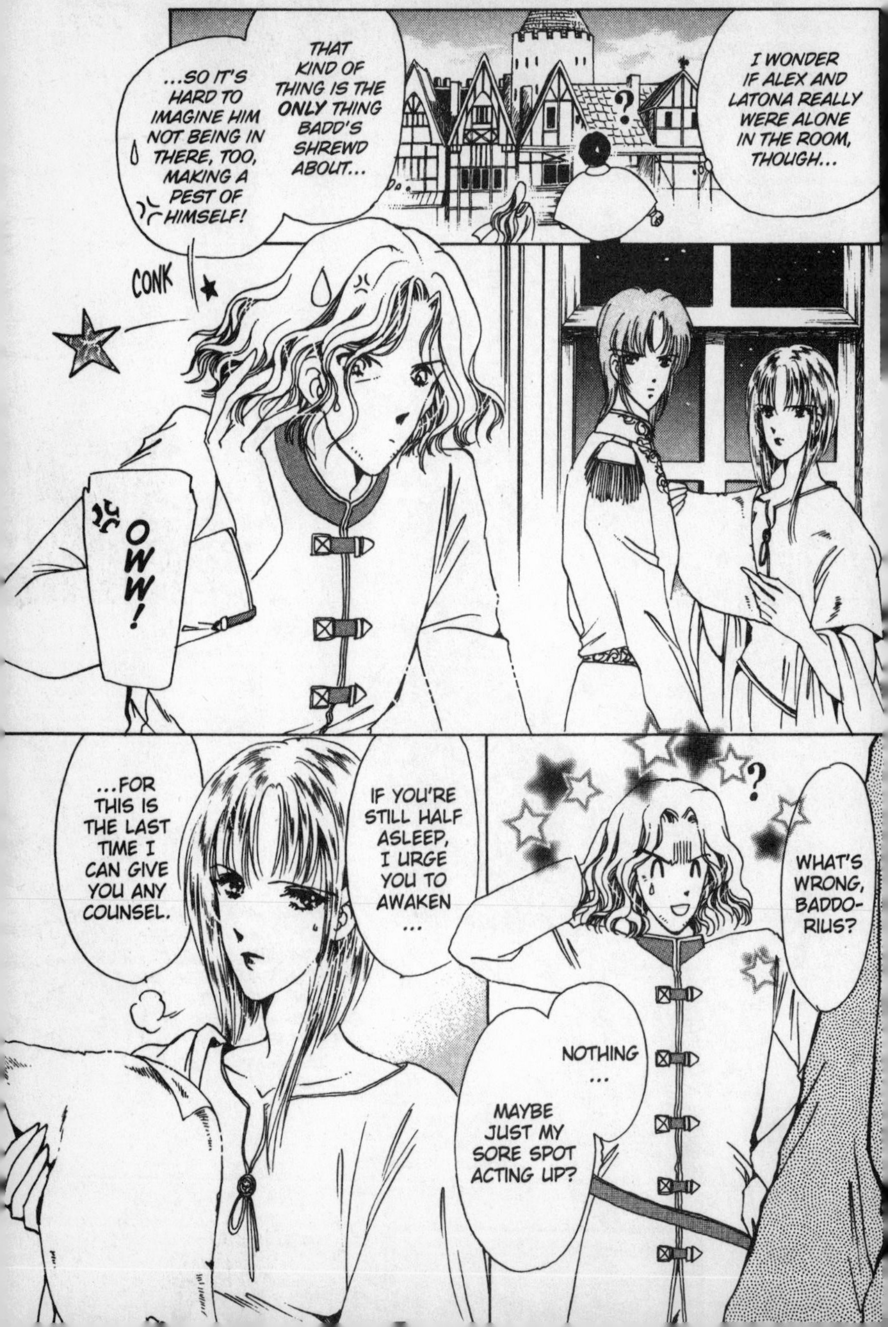
I WONDER IF ALEX AND LATONA REALLY WERE ALONE IN THE ROOM, THOUGH...
THAT KIND OF THING IS THE ONLY THING BADD'S SHREWD ABOUT...
...SO IT'S HARD TO IMAGINE HIM NOT BEING IN THERE, TOO, MAKING A PEST OF HIMSELF!
CONK
OWW!
WHAT'S WRONG, BADDORIUS?
NOTHING...
MAYBE JUST MY SORE SPOT ACTING UP?
IF YOU'RE STILL HALF ASLEEP, I URGE YOU TO AWAKEN...
...FOR THIS IS THE LAST TIME I CAN GIVE YOU ANY COUNSEL.

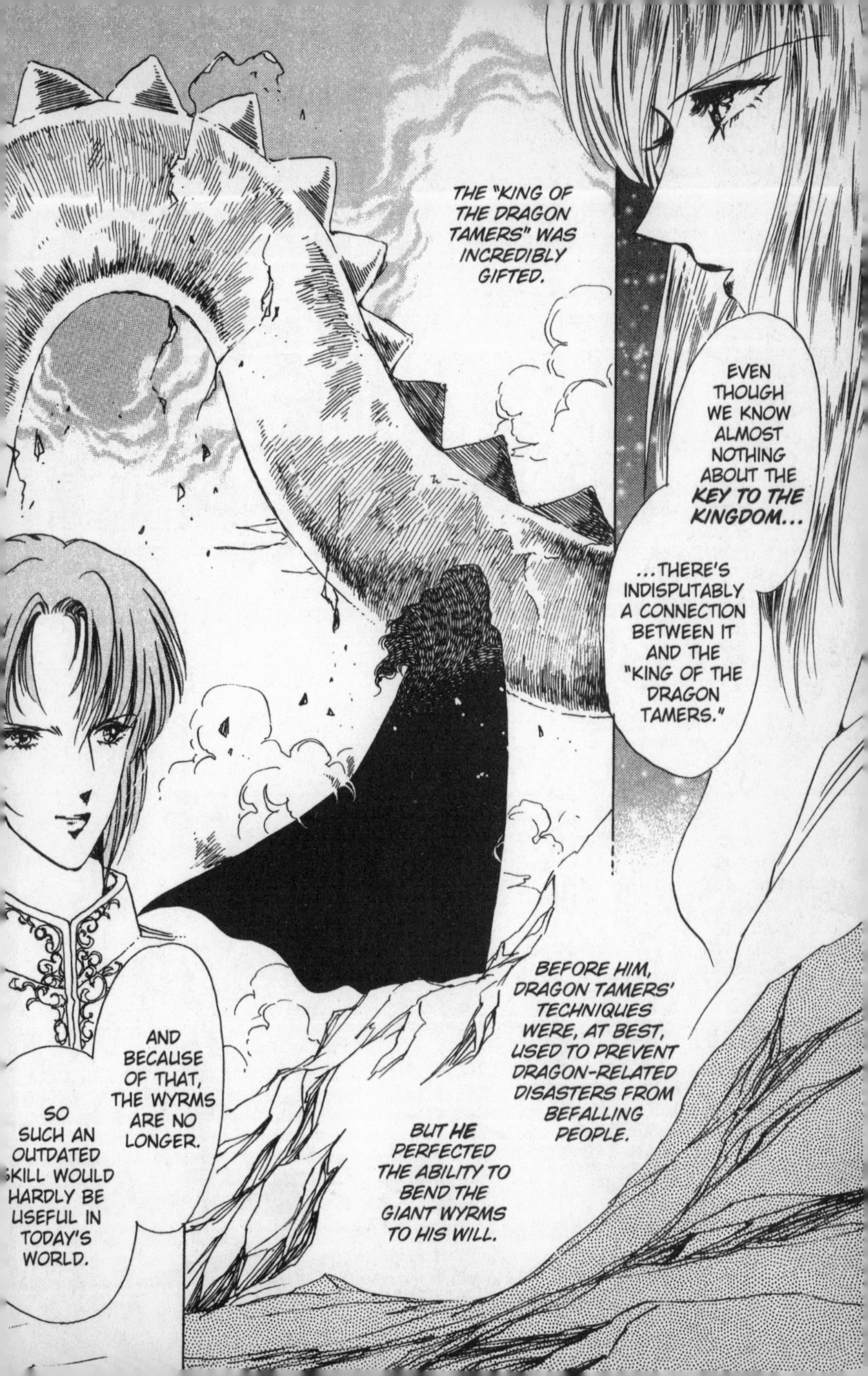
THE "KING OF THE DRAGON TAMERS" WAS INCREDIBLY GIFTED.
EVEN THOUGH WE KNOW ALMOST NOTHING ABOUT THE KEY TO THE KINGDOM...
...THERE'S INDISPUTABLY A CONNECTION BETWEEN IT AND THE "KING OF THE DRAGON TAMERS."
BEFORE HIM, DRAGON TAMERS' TECHNIQUES WERE, AT BEST, USED TO PREVENT DRAGON-RELATED DISASTERS FROM BEFALLING PEOPLE.
BUT HE PERFECTED THE ABILITY TO BEND THE GIANT WYRMS TO HIS WILL.
AND BECAUSE OF THAT, THE WYRMS ARE NO LONGER.
SO SUCH AN OUTDATED SKILL WOULD HARDLY BE USEFUL IN TODAY'S WORLD.

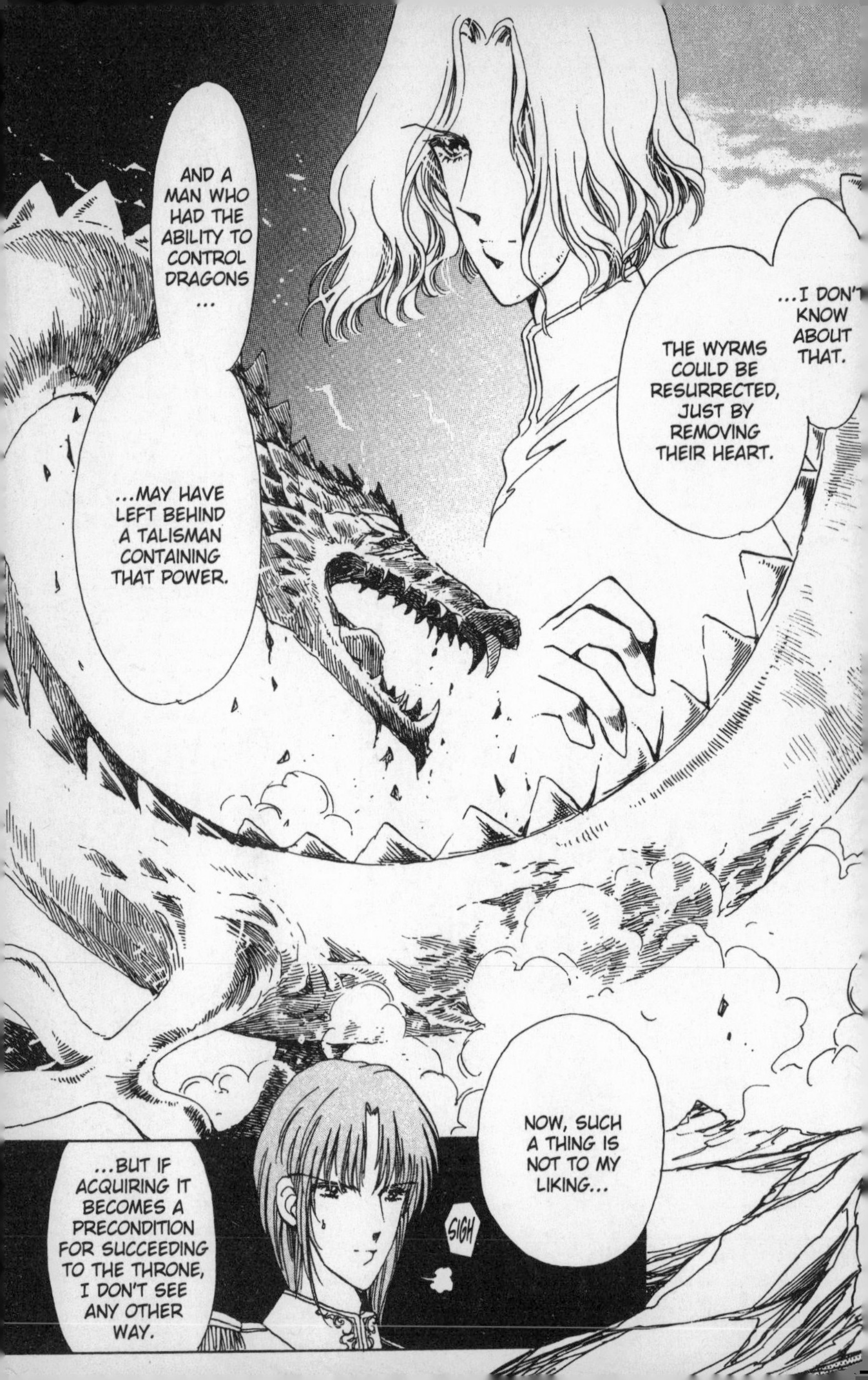
...I DON'T KNOW ABOUT THAT.
THE WYRMS COULD BE RESURRECTED, JUST BY REMOVING THEIR HEART.
AND A MAN WHO HAD THE ABILITY TO CONTROL DRAGONS ...
...MAY HAVE LEFT BEHIND A TALISMAN CONTAINING THAT POWER.
NOW, SUCH A THING IS NOT TO MY LIKING...
SIGH
...BUT IF ACQUIRING IT BECOMES A PRECONDITION FOR SUCCEEDING TO THE THRONE, I DON'T SEE ANY OTHER WAY.

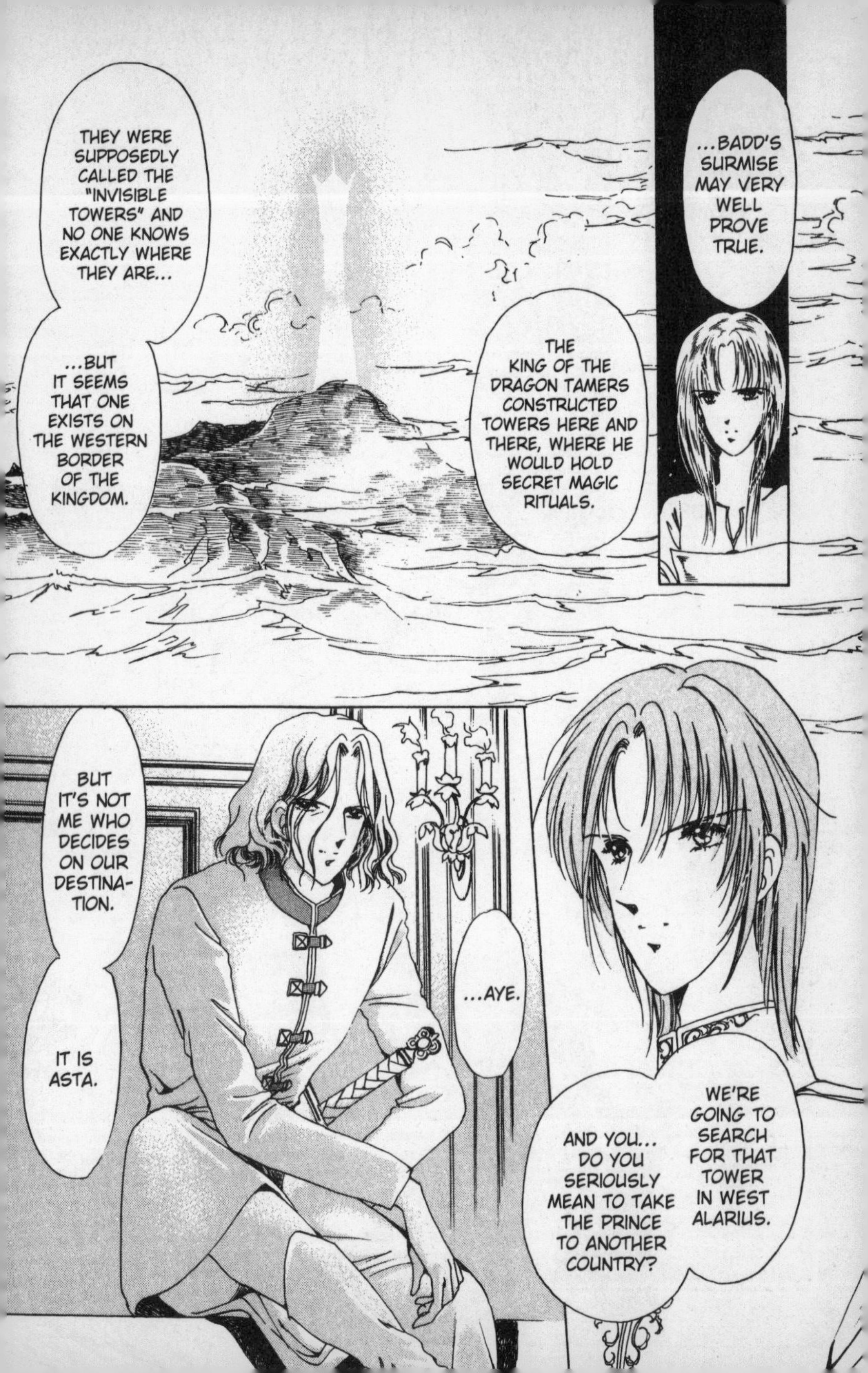
...BADD'S SURMISE MAY VERY WELL PROVE TRUE.
THE KING OF THE DRAGON TAMERS CONSTRUCTED TOWERS HERE AND THERE, WHERE HE WOULD HOLD SECRET MAGIC RITUALS.
THEY WERE SUPPOSEDLY CALLED THE "INVISIBLE TOWERS" AND NO ONE KNOWS EXACTLY WHERE THEY ARE...
...BUT IT SEEMS THAT ONE EXISTS ON THE WESTERN BORDER OF THE KINGDOM.
WE'RE GOING TO SEARCH FOR THAT TOWER IN WEST ALARIUS.
AND YOU... DO YOU SERIOUSLY MEAN TO TAKE THE PRINCE TO ANOTHER COUNTRY?
...AYE.
BUT IT'S NOT ME WHO DECIDES ON OUR DESTINA-TION.
IT IS ASTA.

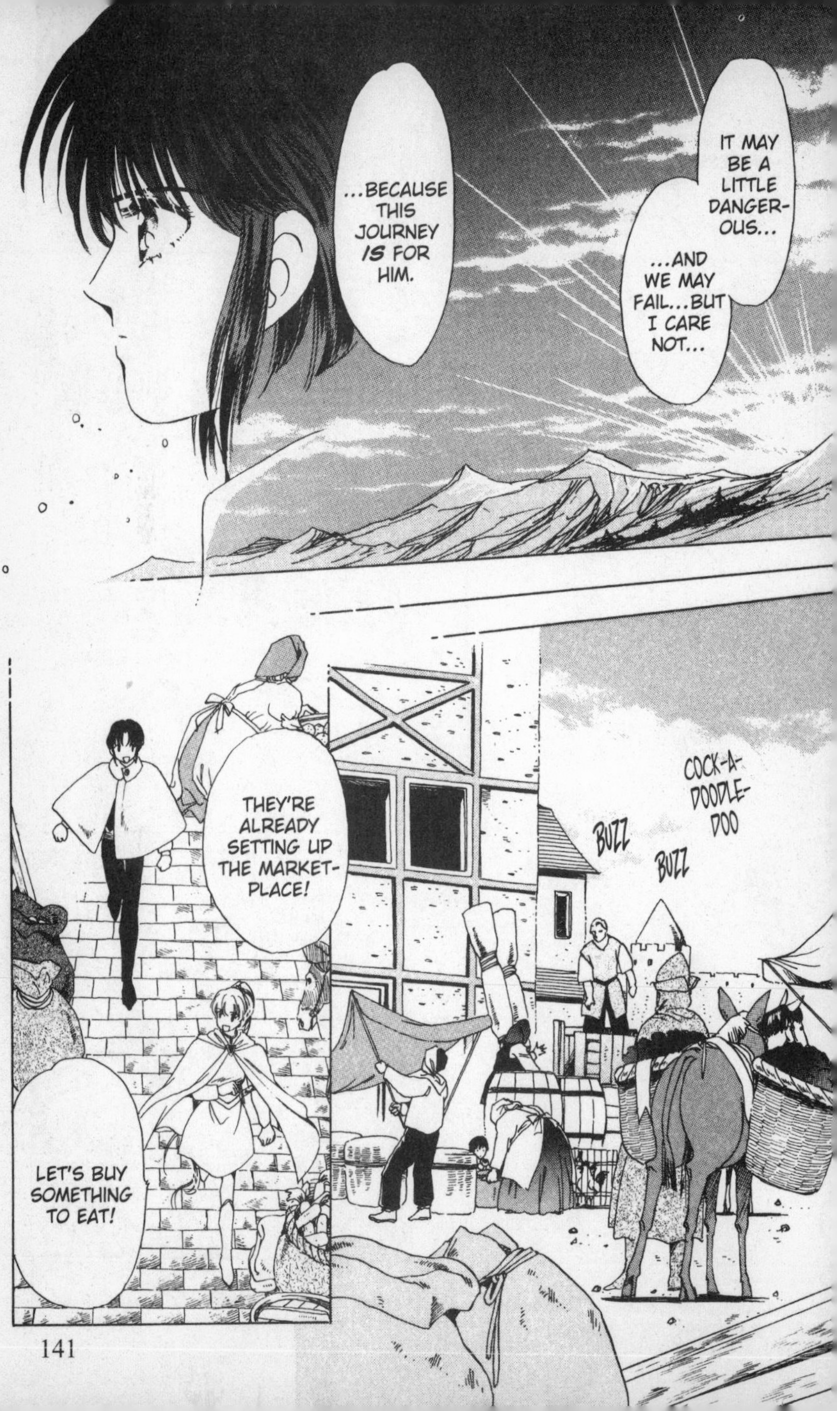
IT MAY BE A LITTLE DANGER-OUS...
...AND WE MAY FAIL...BUT I CARE NOT...
...BECAUSE THIS JOURNEY *IS* FOR HIM.
COCK-A-DOODLE-DOO
BUZZ
BUZZ
THEY'RE ALREADY SETTING UP THE MARKET-PLACE!
LET'S BUY SOMETHING TO EAT!

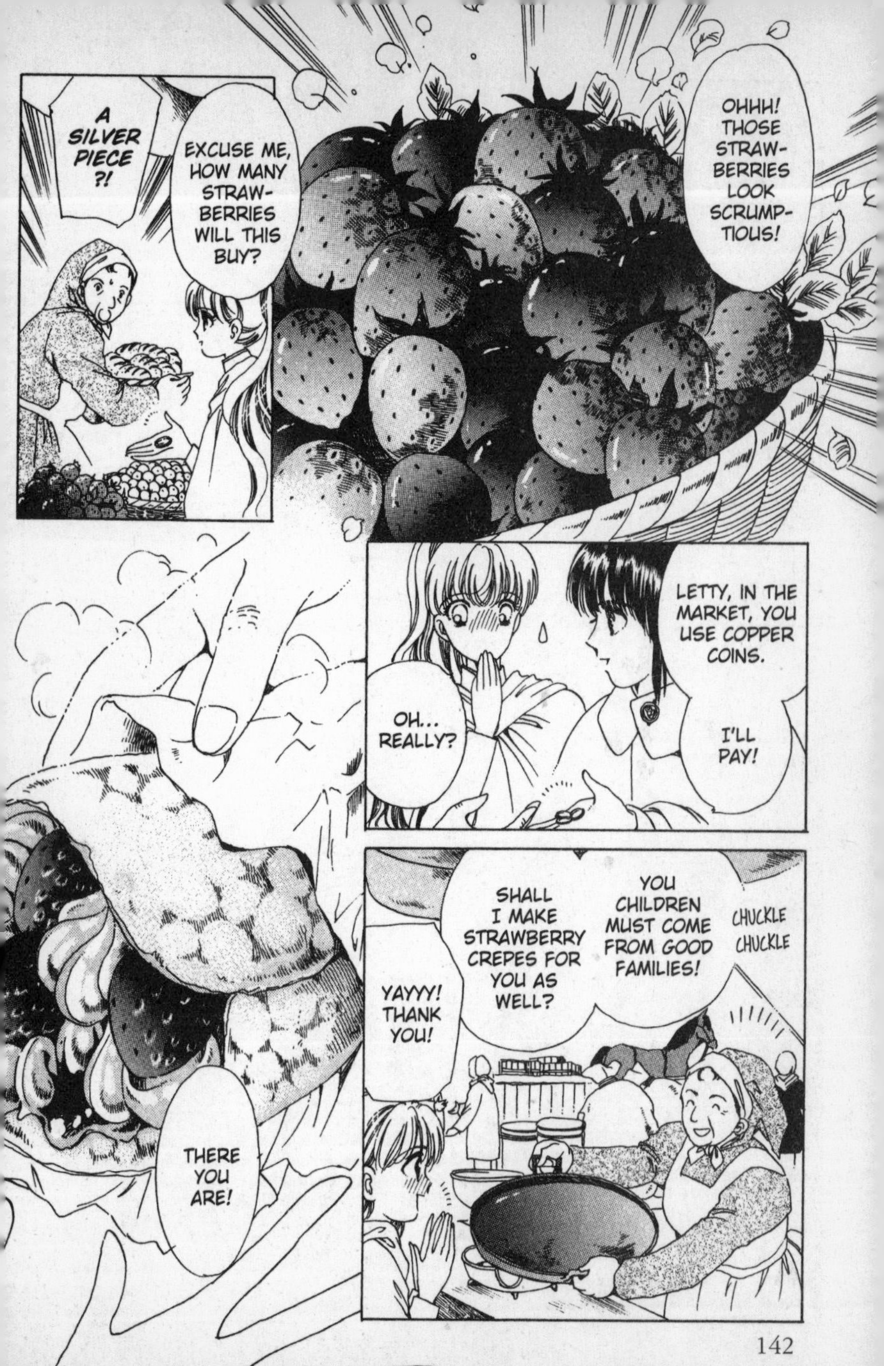
OHHH! THOSE STRAW-BERRIES LOOK SCRUMP-TIOUS!
EXCUSE ME, HOW MANY STRAW-BERRIES WILL THIS BUY?
A SILVER PIECE ?!
LETTY, IN THE MARKET, YOU USE COPPER COINS.
I'LL PAY!
OH... REALLY?
CHUCKLE CHUCKLE
YOU CHILDREN MUST COME FROM GOOD FAMILIES!
SHALL I MAKE STRAWBERRY CREPES FOR YOU AS WELL?
YAYYY! THANK YOU!
THERE YOU ARE!

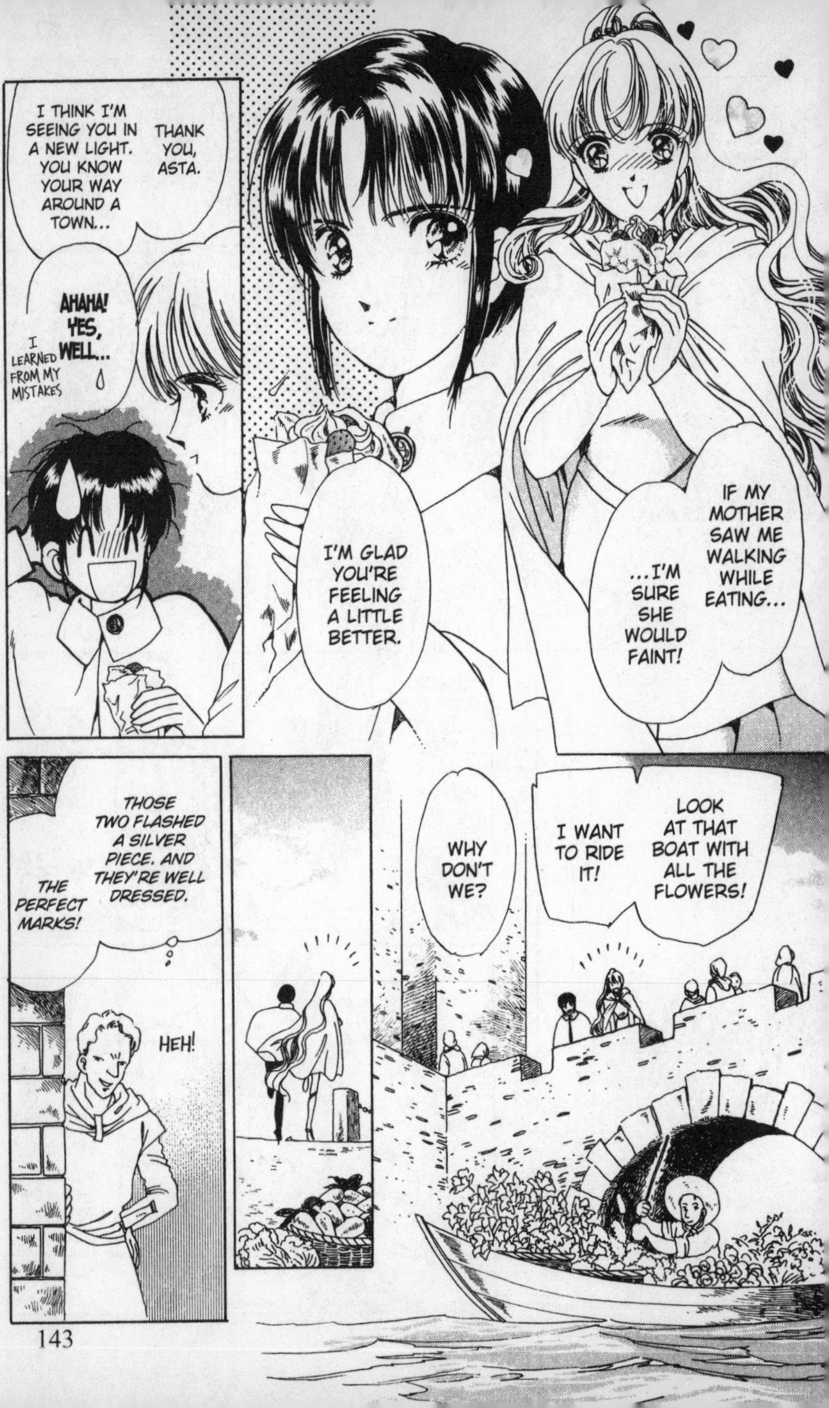
IF MY MOTHER SAW ME WALKING WHILE EATING...
...I'M SURE SHE WOULD FAINT!
I'M GLAD YOU'RE FEELING A LITTLE BETTER.
I THINK I'M SEEING YOU IN A NEW LIGHT. YOU KNOW YOUR WAY AROUND A TOWN...
THANK YOU, ASTA.
AHAHA! YES, WELL...
I LEARNED FROM MY MISTAKES
LOOK AT THAT BOAT WITH ALL THE FLOWERS!
I WANT TO RIDE IT!
WHY DON'T WE?
THOSE TWO FLASHED A SILVER PIECE. AND THEY'RE WELL DRESSED.
THE PERFECT MARKS!
HEH!

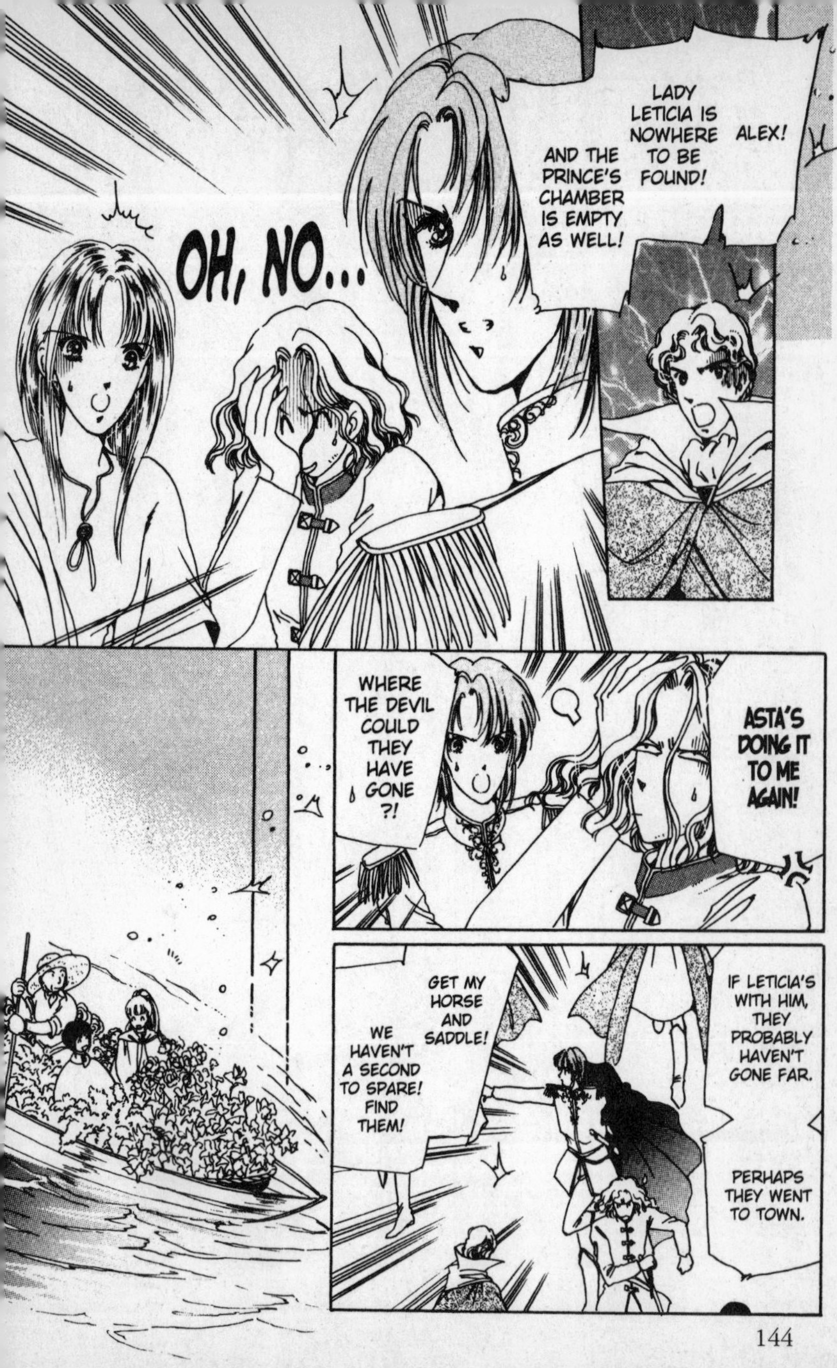
ALEX!
LADY LETICIA IS NOWHERE TO BE FOUND!
AND THE PRINCE'S CHAMBER IS EMPTY AS WELL!
OH, NO...
ASTA'S DOING IT TO ME AGAIN!
WHERE THE DEVIL COULD THEY HAVE GONE ?!
IF LETICIA'S WITH HIM, THEY PROBABLY HAVEN'T GONE FAR.
PERHAPS THEY WENT TO TOWN.
GET MY HORSE AND SADDLE!
WE HAVEN'T A SECOND TO SPARE! FIND THEM!

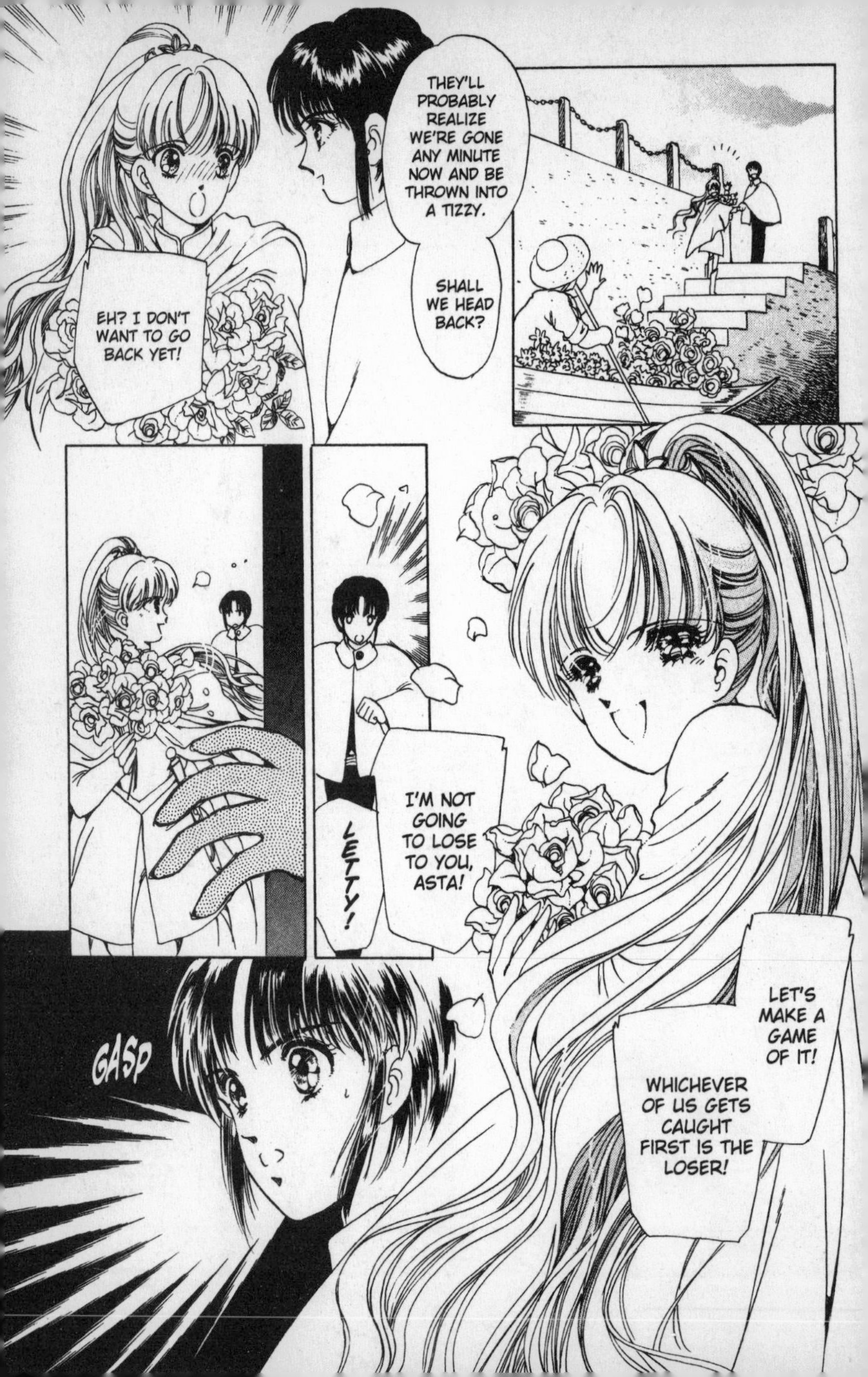
THEY'LL PROBABLY REALIZE WE'RE GONE ANY MINUTE NOW AND BE THROWN INTO A TIZZY.
SHALL WE HEAD BACK?
EH? I DON'T WANT TO GO BACK YET!
I'M NOT GOING TO LOSE TO YOU, ASTA!
LETTY!
LET'S MAKE A GAME OF IT!
WHICHEVER OF US GETS CAUGHT FIRST IS THE LOSER!
GASP

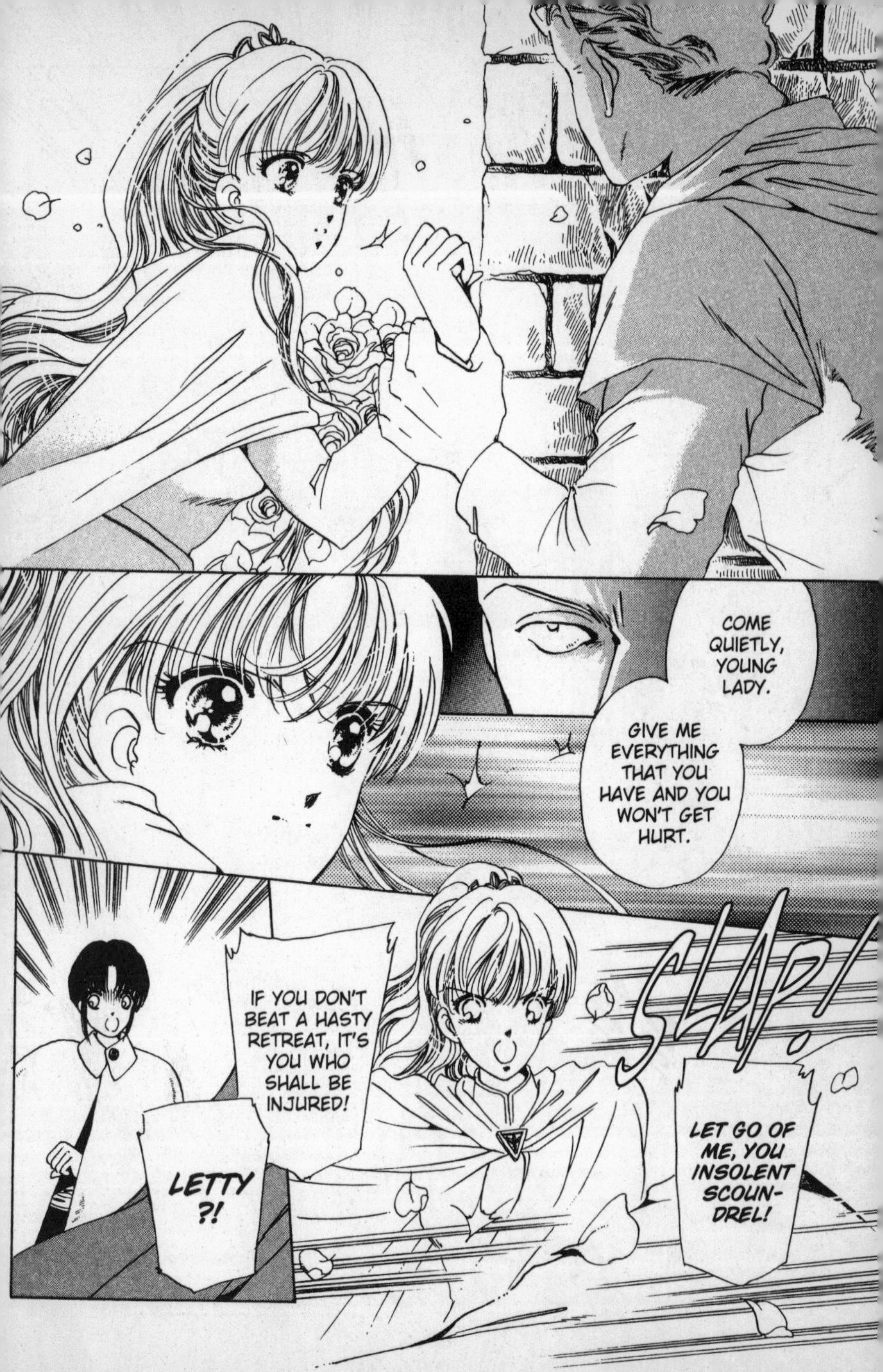
COME QUIETLY, YOUNG LADY.
GIVE ME EVERYTHING THAT YOU HAVE AND YOU WON'T GET HURT.
SLAP!
LET GO OF ME, YOU INSOLENT SCOUN-DREL!
IF YOU DON'T BEAT A HASTY RETREAT, IT'S YOU WHO SHALL BE INJURED!
LETTY ?!

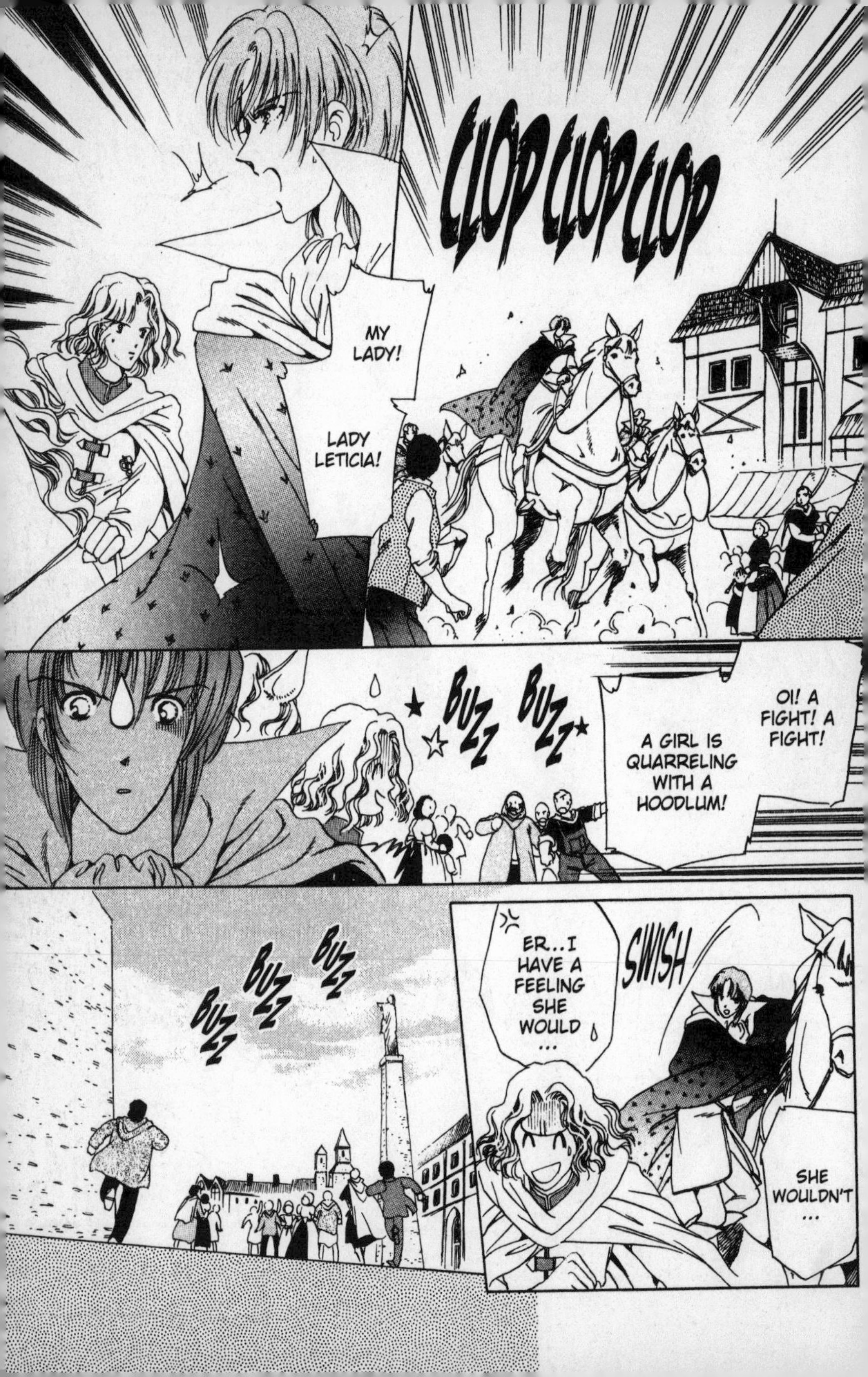
CLOP CLOP CLOP
MY LADY!
LADY LETICIA!
OI! A FIGHT! A FIGHT!
A GIRL IS QUARRELING WITH A HOODLUM!
BUZZ BUZZ
SHE WOULDN'T ...
SWISH
ER...I HAVE A FEELING SHE WOULD ...
BUZZ BUZZ BUZZ

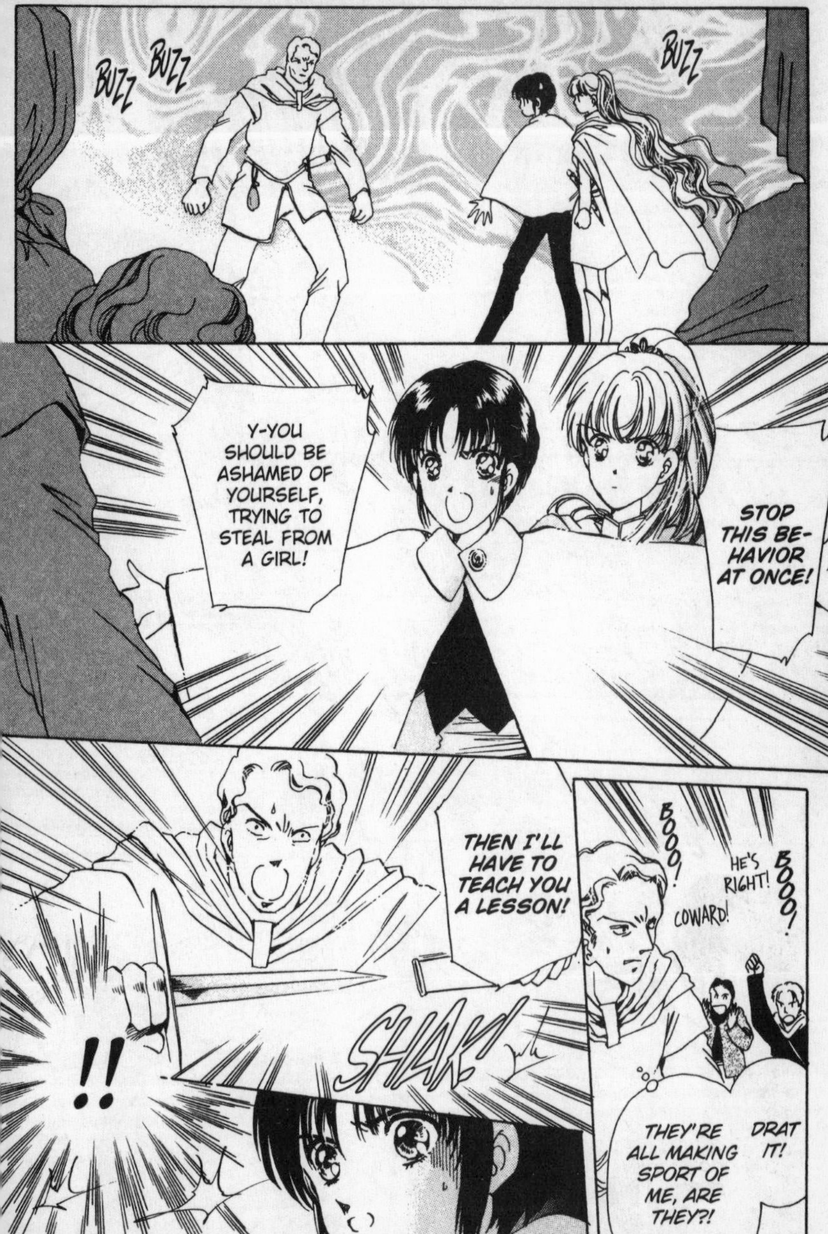
BUZZ
BUZZ
BUZZ
STOP THIS BE-HAVIOR AT ONCE!
Y-YOU SHOULD BE ASHAMED OF YOURSELF, TRYING TO STEAL FROM A GIRL!
BOOO!
HE'S RIGHT!
BOOO!
COWARD!
DRAT IT!
THEY'RE ALL MAKING SPORT OF ME, ARE THEY?!
THEN I'LL HAVE TO TEACH YOU A LESSON!
SHAK!
!!

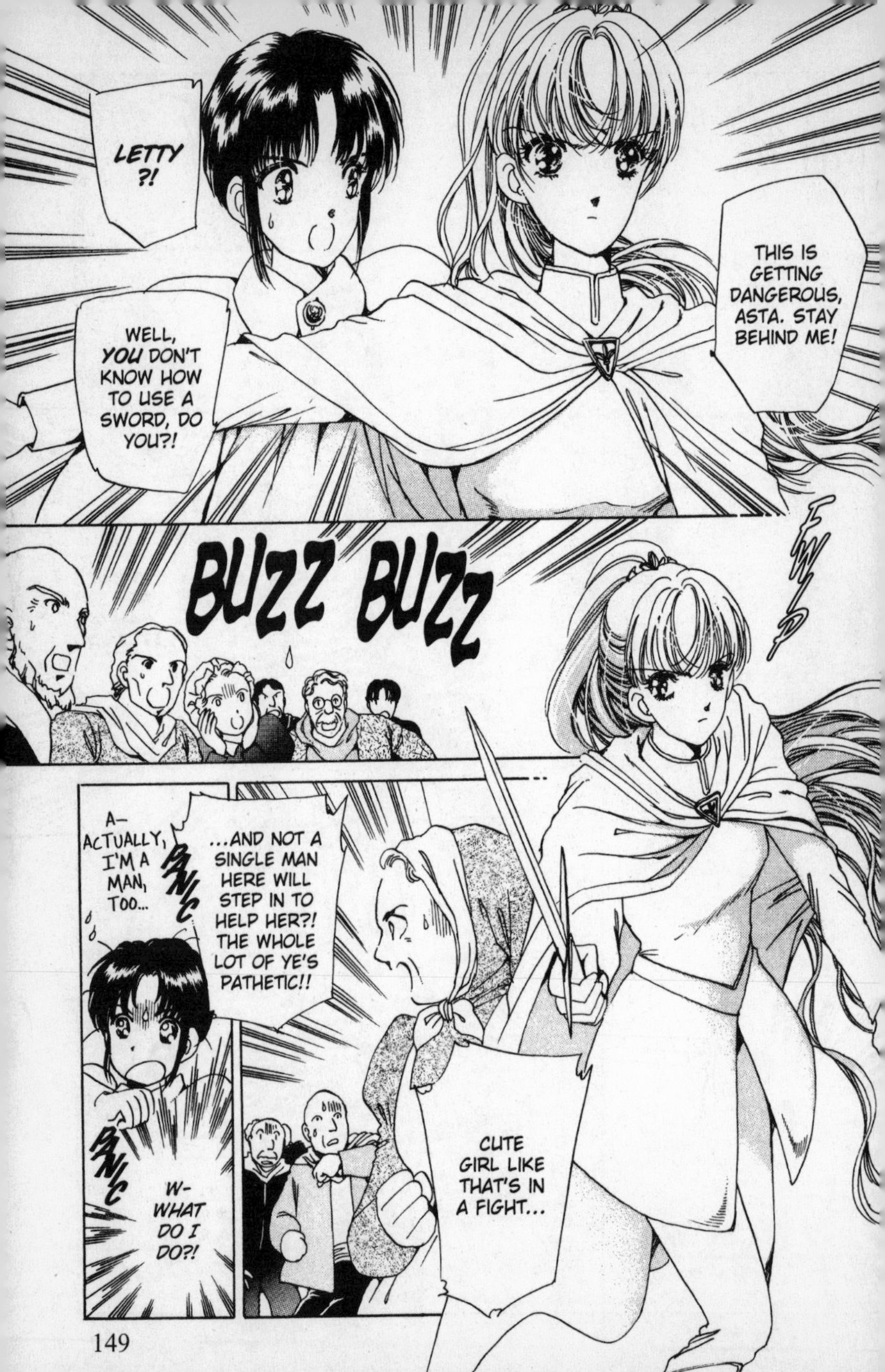
THIS IS GETTING DANGEROUS, ASTA. STAY BEHIND ME!
LETTY ?!
WELL, *YOU* DON'T KNOW HOW TO USE A SWORD, DO YOU?!
FWIP
BUZZ BUZZ
CUTE GIRL LIKE THAT'S IN A FIGHT...
...AND NOT A SINGLE MAN HERE WILL STEP IN TO HELP HER?! THE WHOLE LOT OF YE'S PATHETIC!!
A— ACTUALLY, I'M A MAN, TOO...
PANIC
PANIC
W- WHAT DO I DO?!

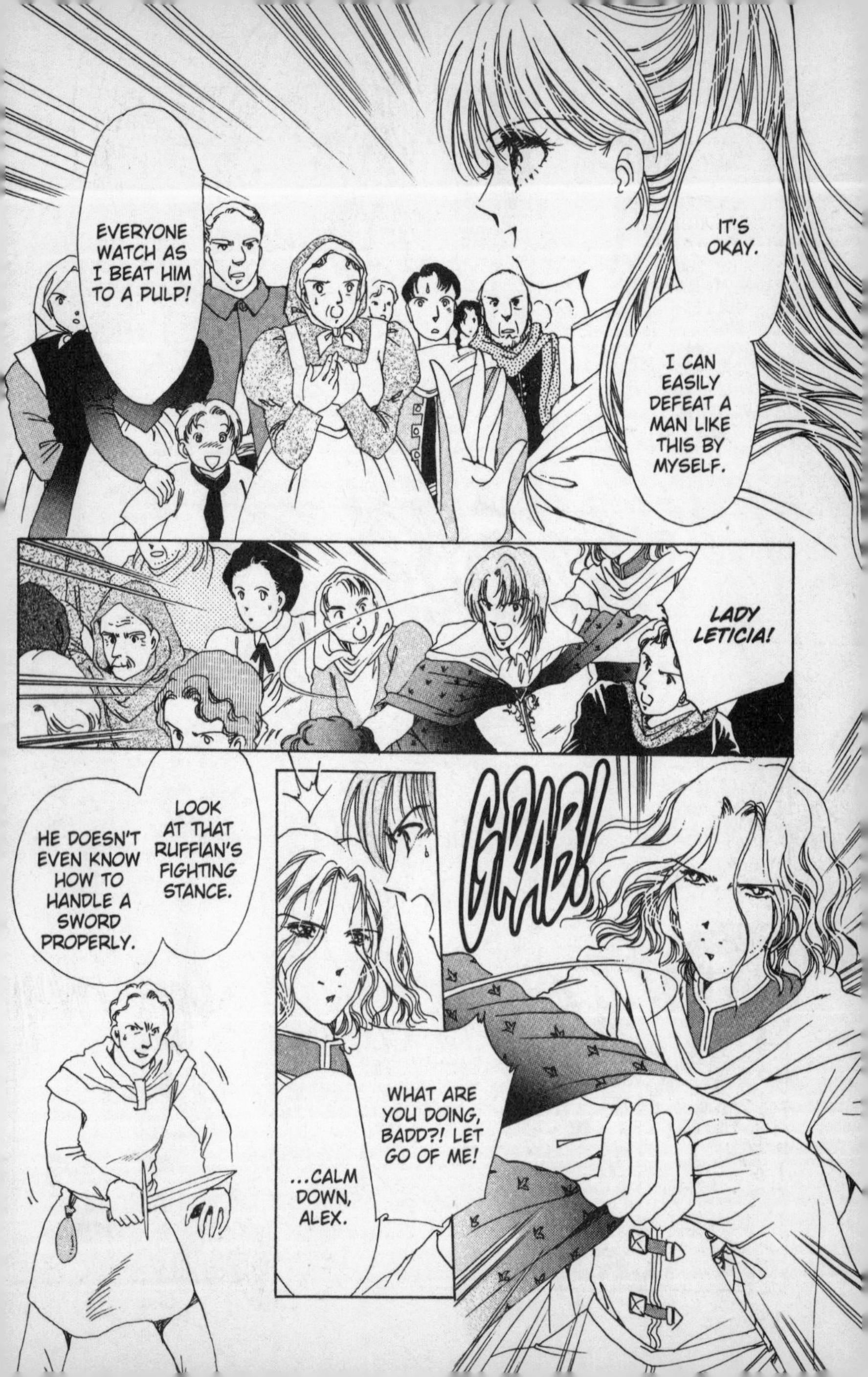
IT'S OKAY.
I CAN EASILY DEFEAT A MAN LIKE THIS BY MYSELF.
EVERYONE WATCH AS I BEAT HIM TO A PULP!
LADY LETICIA!
GRAB!
WHAT ARE YOU DOING, BADD?! LET GO OF ME!
...CALM DOWN, ALEX.
LOOK AT THAT RUFFIAN'S FIGHTING STANCE.
HE DOESN'T EVEN KNOW HOW TO HANDLE A SWORD PROPERLY.

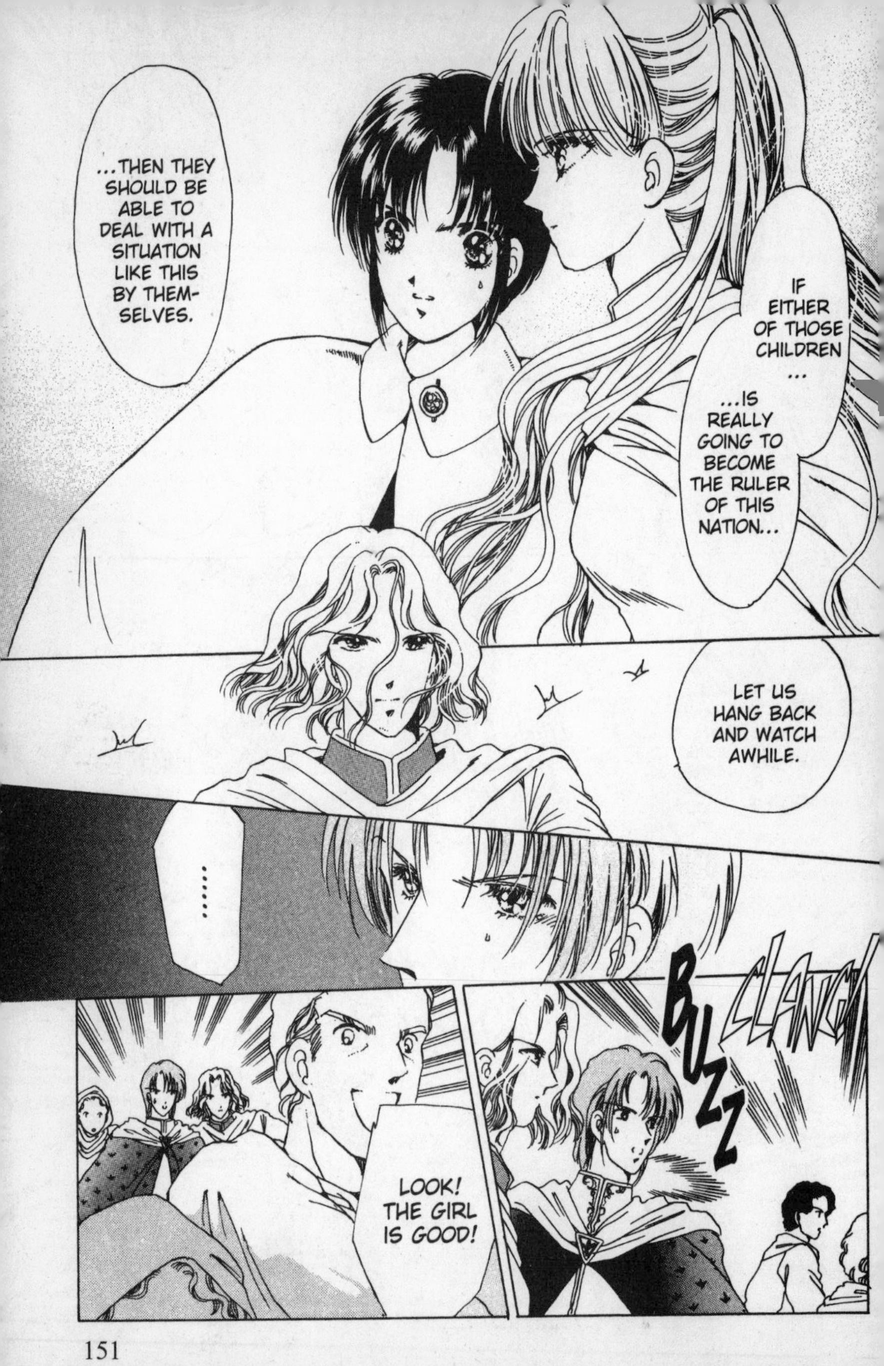
IF EITHER OF THOSE CHILDREN ...
...IS REALLY GOING TO BECOME THE RULER OF THIS NATION...
...THEN THEY SHOULD BE ABLE TO DEAL WITH A SITUATION LIKE THIS BY THEM-SELVES.
LET US HANG BACK AND WATCH AWHILE.
......
CLANG!
BUZZ
LOOK! THE GIRL IS GOOD!

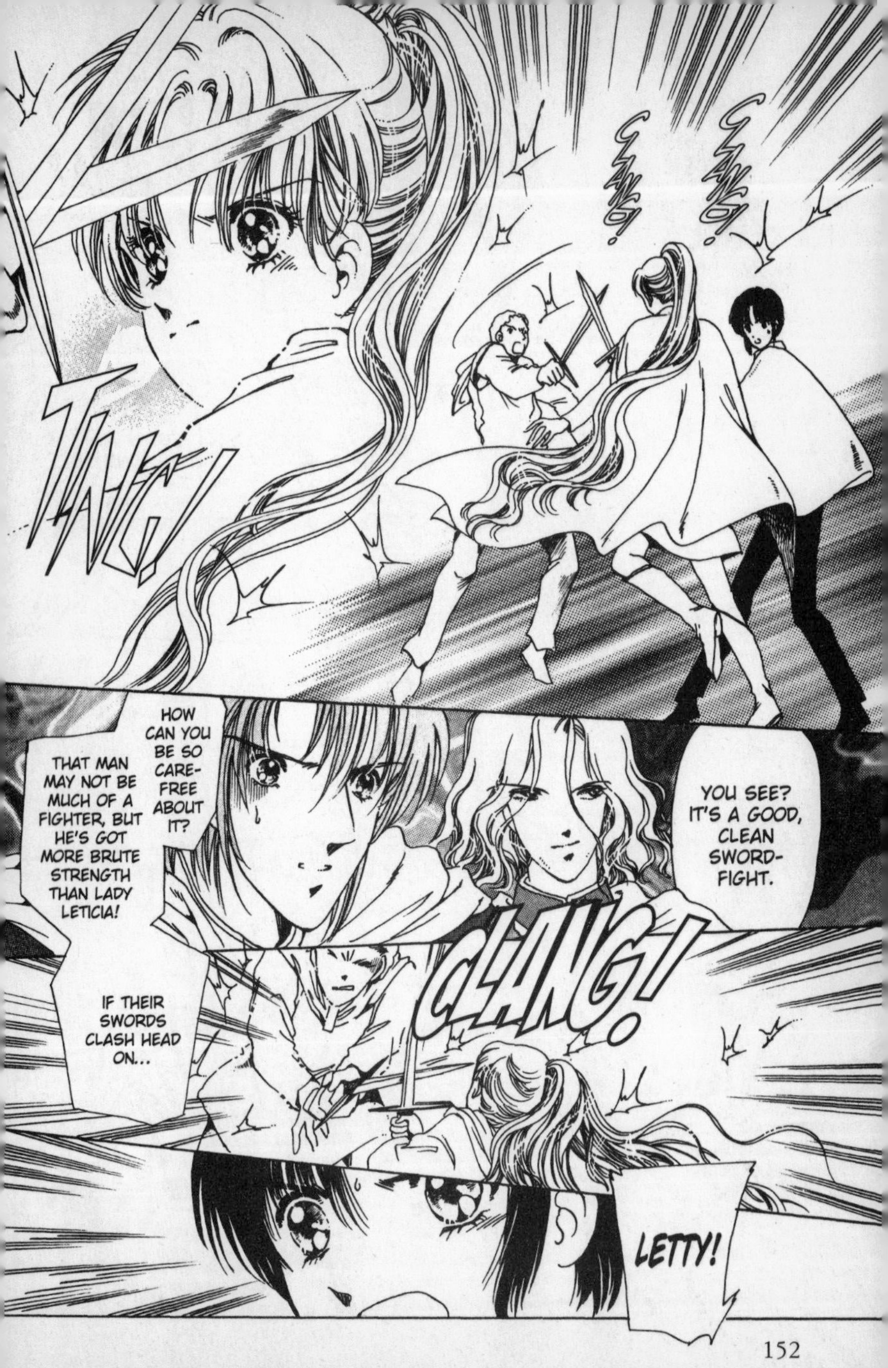
CLANG!
CLANG!
TANG!
YOU SEE? IT'S A GOOD, CLEAN SWORD-FIGHT.
HOW CAN YOU BE SO CARE-FREE ABOUT IT?
THAT MAN MAY NOT BE MUCH OF A FIGHTER, BUT HE'S GOT MORE BRUTE STRENGTH THAN LADY LETICIA!
CLANG!
IF THEIR SWORDS CLASH HEAD ON...
LETTY!

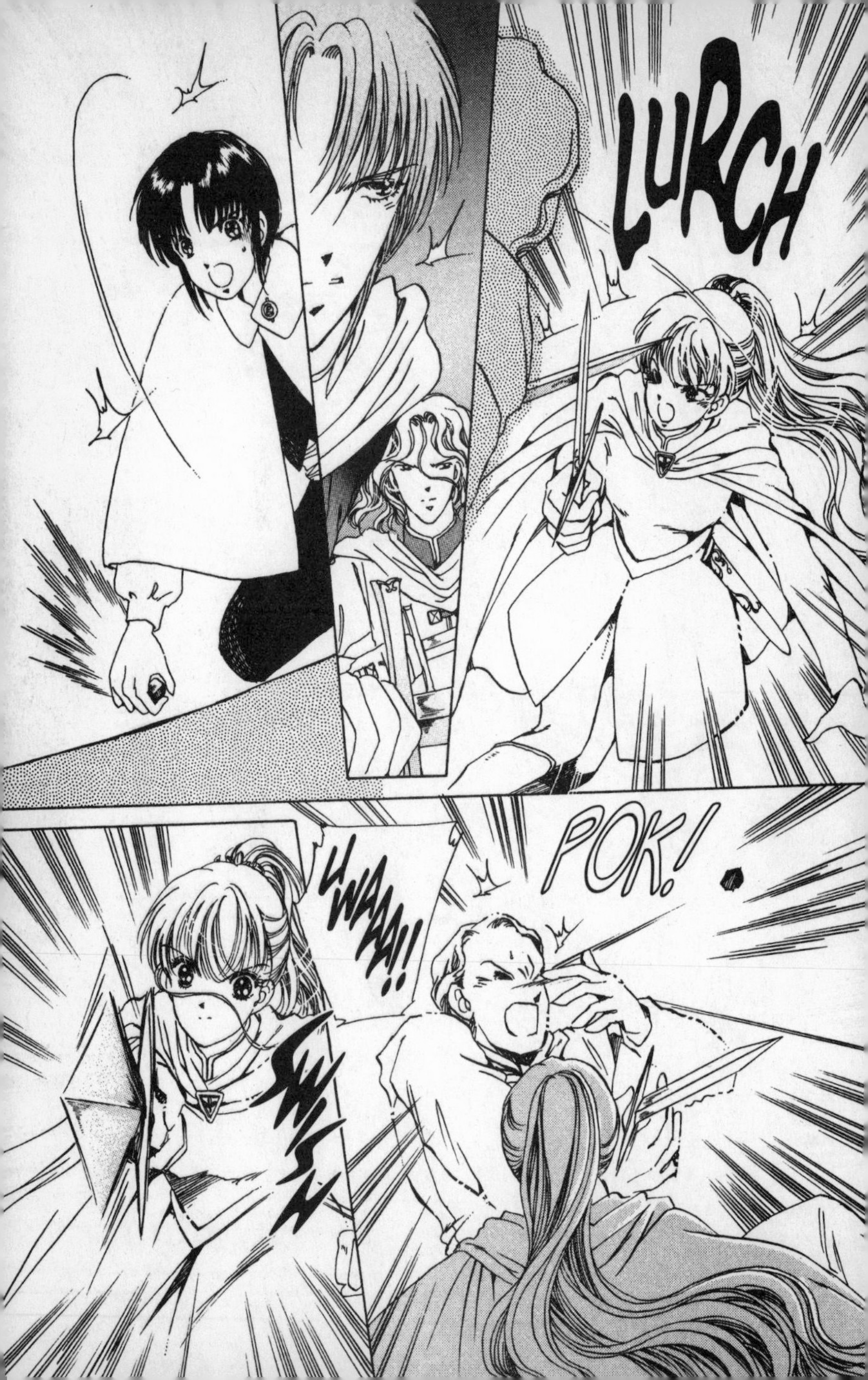
LURCH
POK!
UWAAA!!

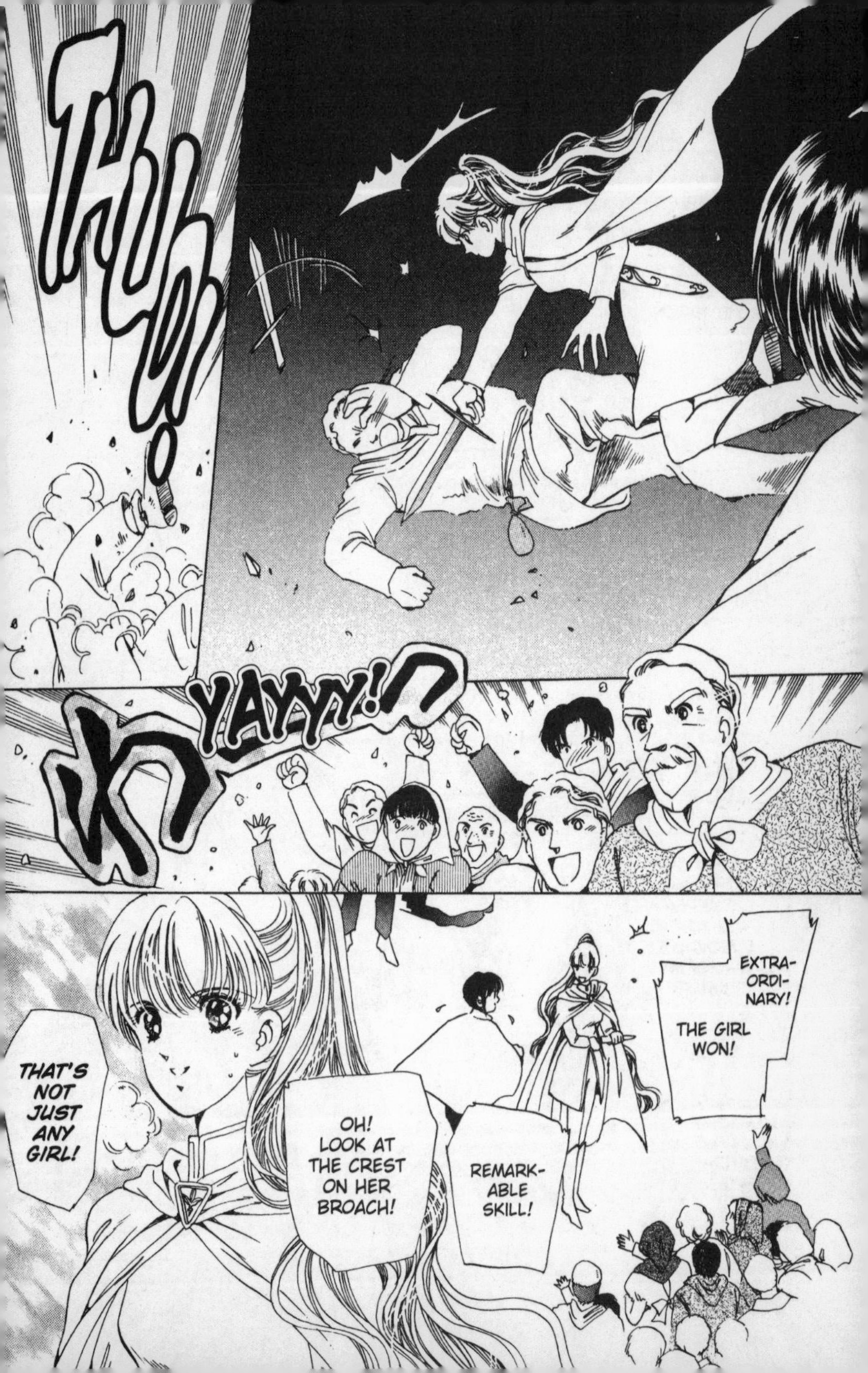
THUD!
わ
YAYYY!
EXTRA-ORDINARY!
THE GIRL WON!
REMARK-ABLE SKILL!
OH! LOOK AT THE CREST ON HER BROACH!
THAT'S NOT JUST ANY GIRL!

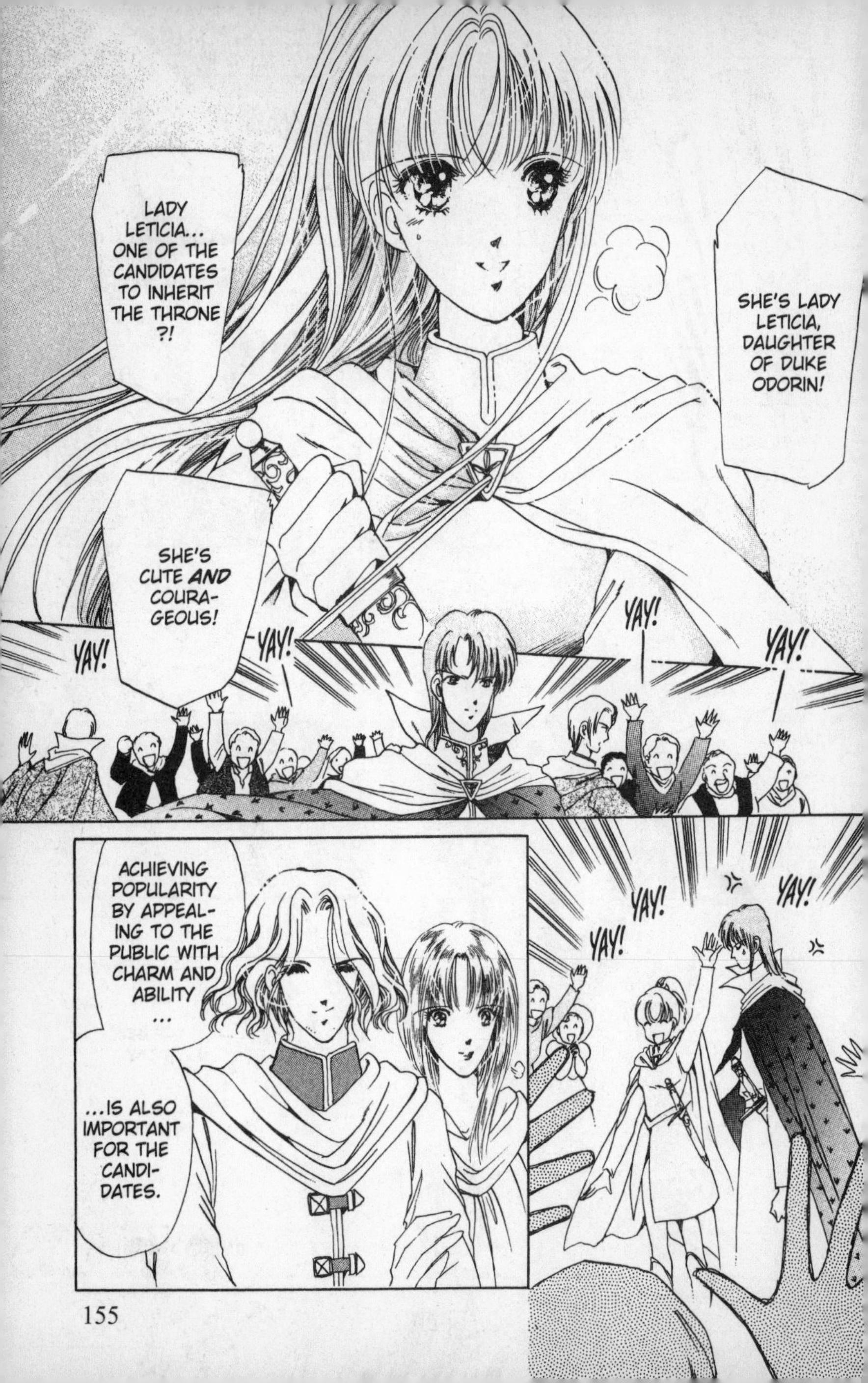
SHE'S LADY LETICIA, DAUGHTER OF DUKE ODORIN!
LADY LETICIA... ONE OF THE CANDIDATES TO INHERIT THE THRONE ?!
YAY!
YAY!
SHE'S CUTE AND COURAGEOUS!
YAY!
YAY!
YAY!
YAY!
YAY!
ACHIEVING POPULARITY BY APPEALING TO THE PUBLIC WITH CHARM AND ABILITY ...
...IS ALSO IMPORTANT FOR THE CANDIDATES.

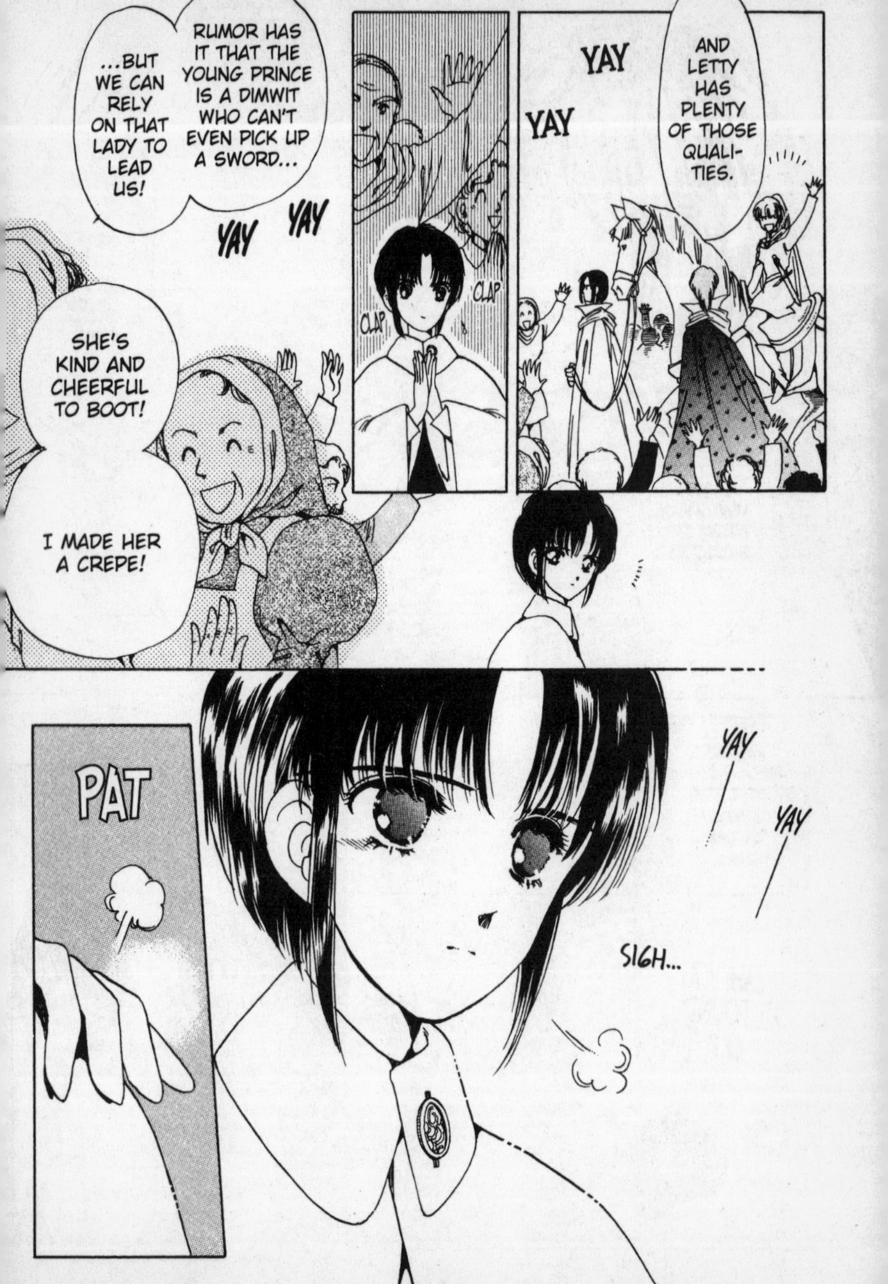
AND LETTY HAS PLENTY OF THOSE QUALI-TIES.
YAY
YAY
CLAP
CLAP
RUMOR HAS IT THAT THE YOUNG PRINCE IS A DIMWIT WHO CAN'T EVEN PICK UP A SWORD...
...BUT WE CAN RELY ON THAT LADY TO LEAD US!
YAY
YAY
SHE'S KIND AND CHEERFUL TO BOOT!
I MADE HER A CREPE!
YAY
YAY
SIGH...
PAT

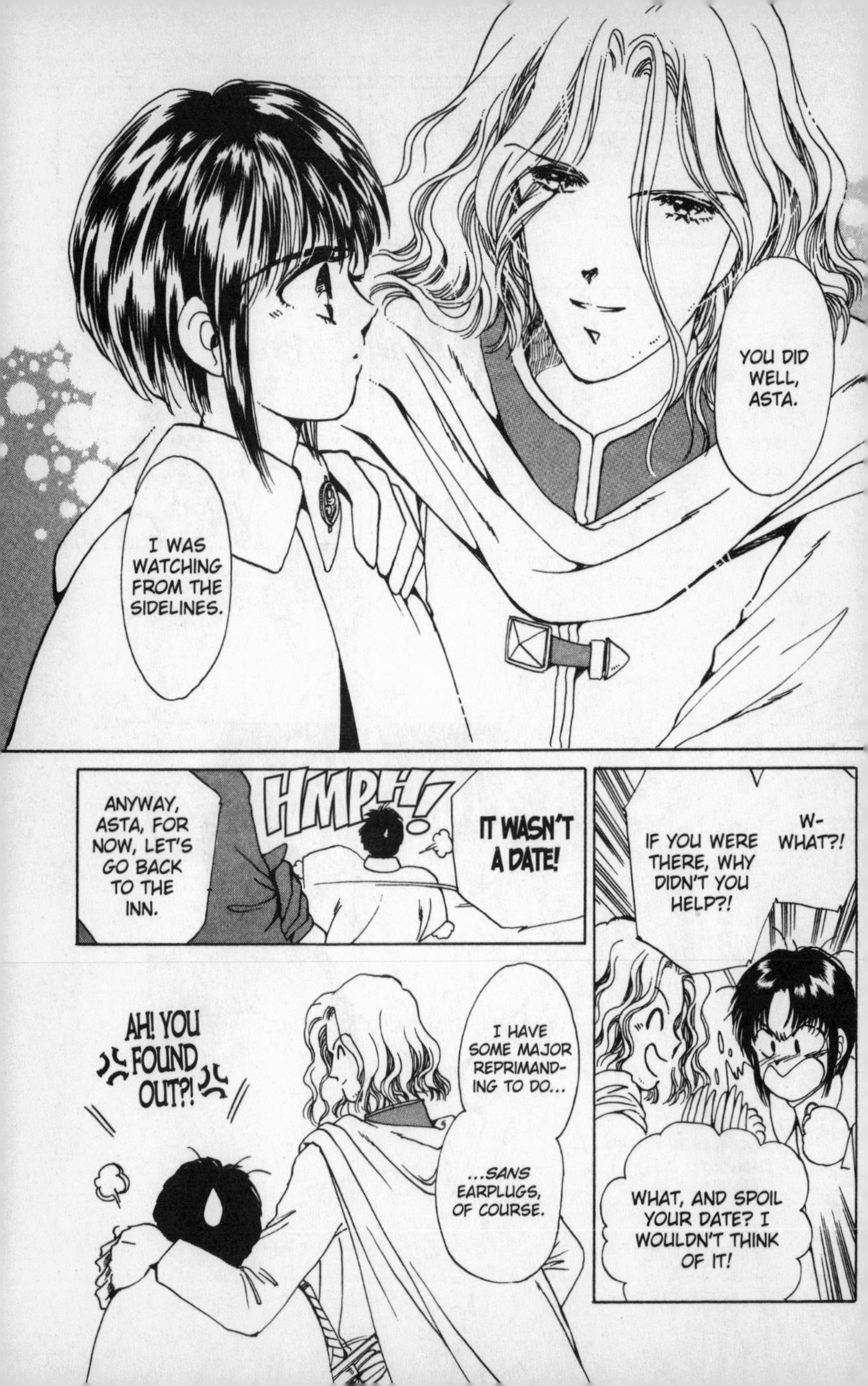
YOU DID WELL, ASTA.
I WAS WATCHING FROM THE SIDELINES.
W-WHAT?!
IF YOU WERE THERE, WHY DIDN'T YOU HELP?!
WHAT, AND SPOIL YOUR DATE? I WOULDN'T THINK OF IT!
IT WASN'T A DATE!
HMPH!
ANYWAY, ASTA, FOR NOW, LET'S GO BACK TO THE INN.
I HAVE SOME MAJOR REPRIMANDING TO DO...
...SANS EARPLUGS, OF COURSE.
AH! YOU FOUND OUT?!

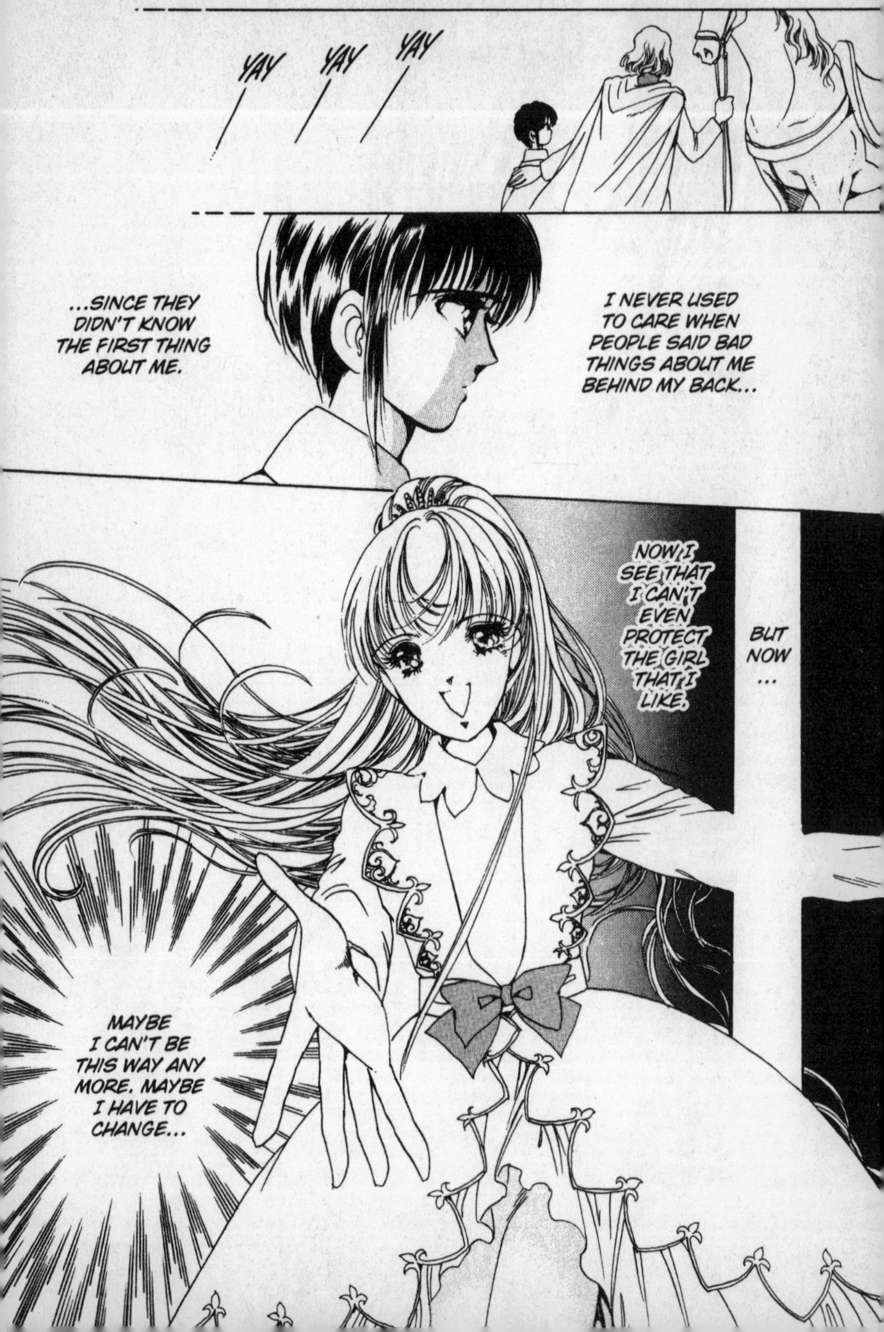
YAY
YAY
YAY
I NEVER USED TO CARE WHEN PEOPLE SAID BAD THINGS ABOUT ME BEHIND MY BACK...
...SINCE THEY DIDN'T KNOW THE FIRST THING ABOUT ME.
BUT NOW...
NOW I SEE THAT I CAN'T EVEN PROTECT THE GIRL THAT I LIKE.
MAYBE I CAN'T BE THIS WAY ANY MORE. MAYBE I HAVE TO CHANGE...

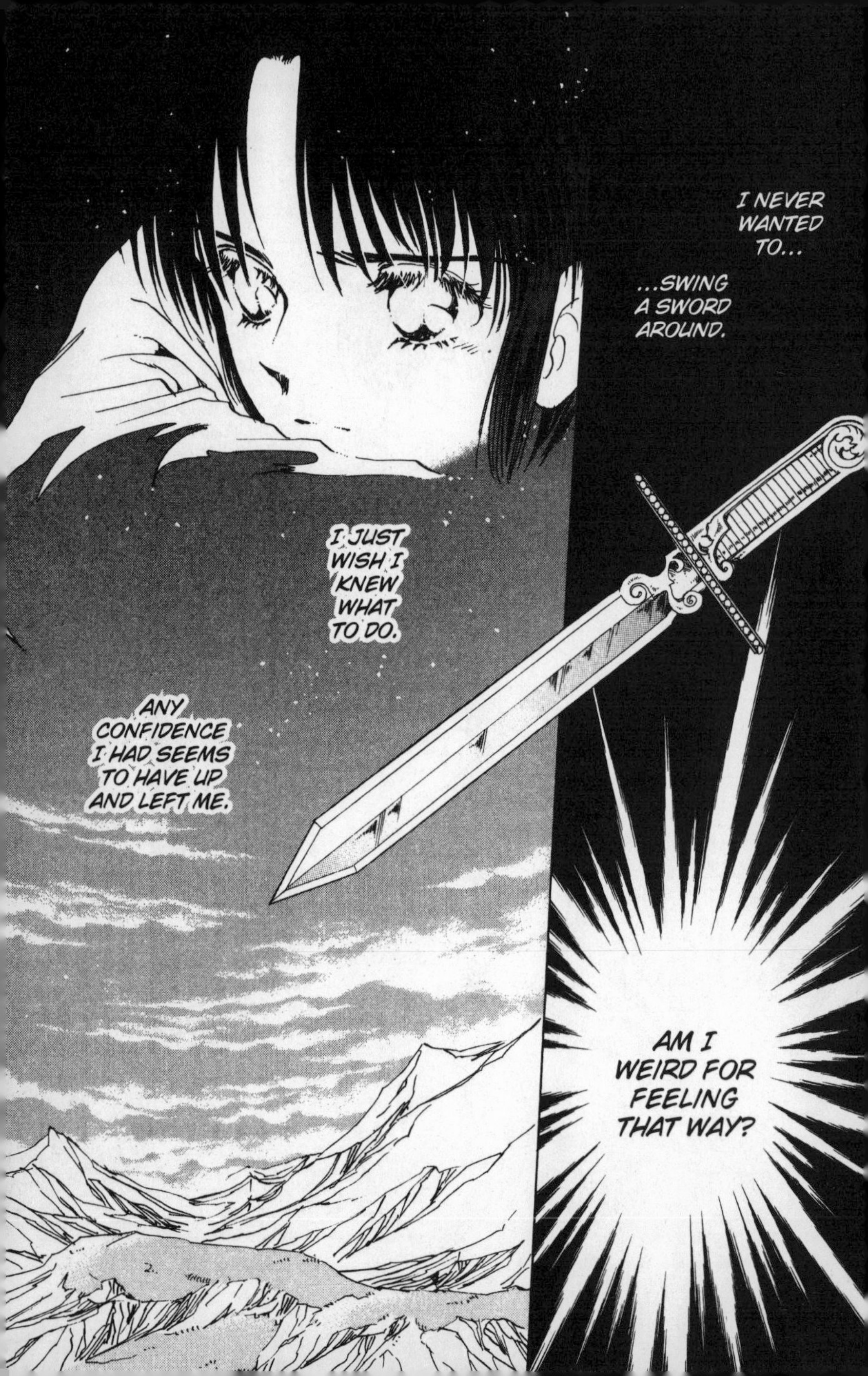
I NEVER WANTED TO...
...SWING A SWORD AROUND.
AM I WEIRD FOR FEELING THAT WAY?
I JUST WISH I KNEW WHAT TO DO.
ANY CONFIDENCE I HAD SEEMS TO HAVE UP AND LEFT ME.

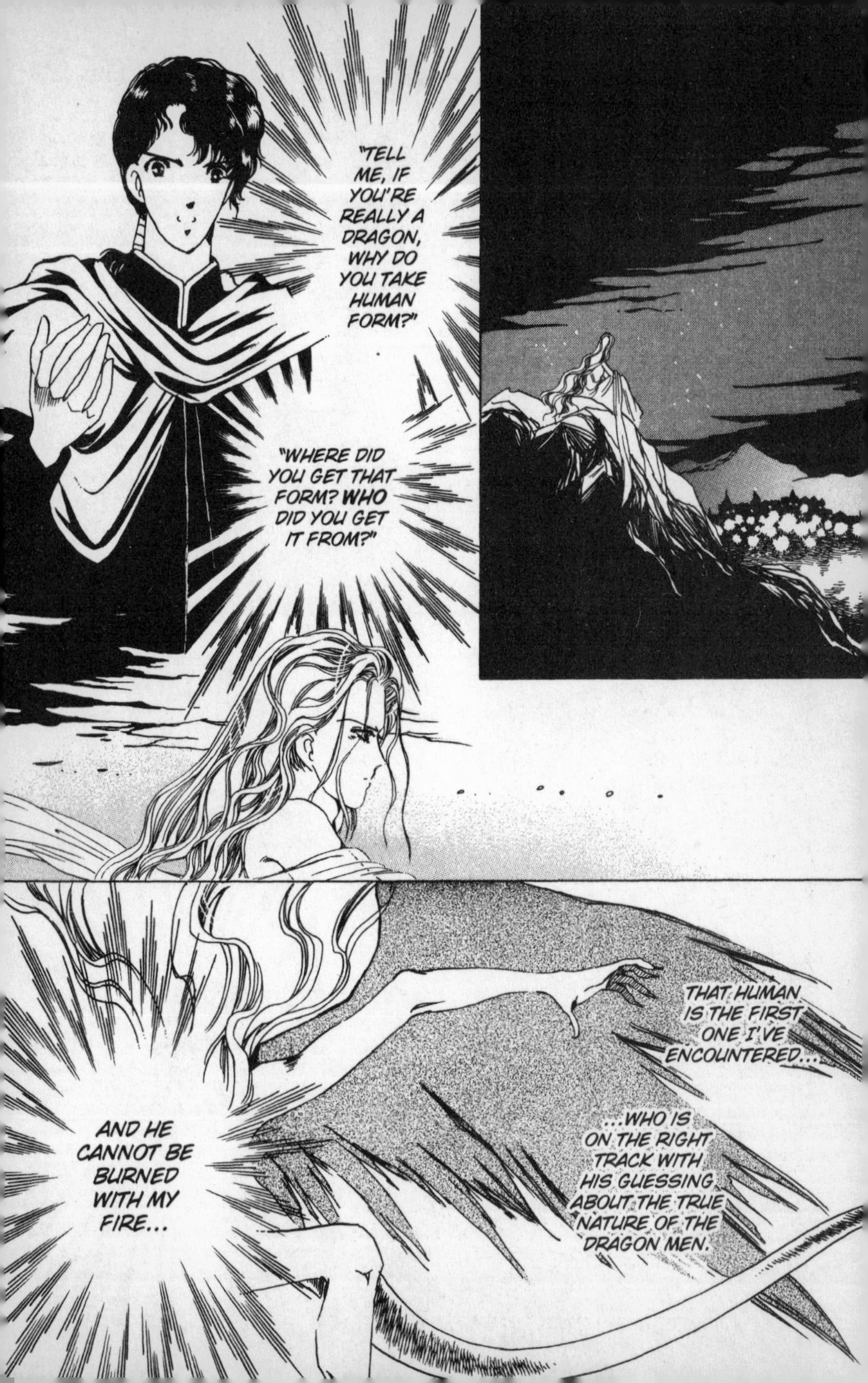
"TELL ME, IF YOU'RE REALLY A DRAGON, WHY DO YOU TAKE HUMAN FORM?"
"WHERE DID YOU GET THAT FORM? WHO DID YOU GET IT FROM?"
THAT HUMAN IS THE FIRST ONE I'VE ENCOUNTERED...
...WHO IS ON THE RIGHT TRACK WITH HIS GUESSING ABOUT THE TRUE NATURE OF THE DRAGON MEN.
AND HE CANNOT BE BURNED WITH MY FIRE...

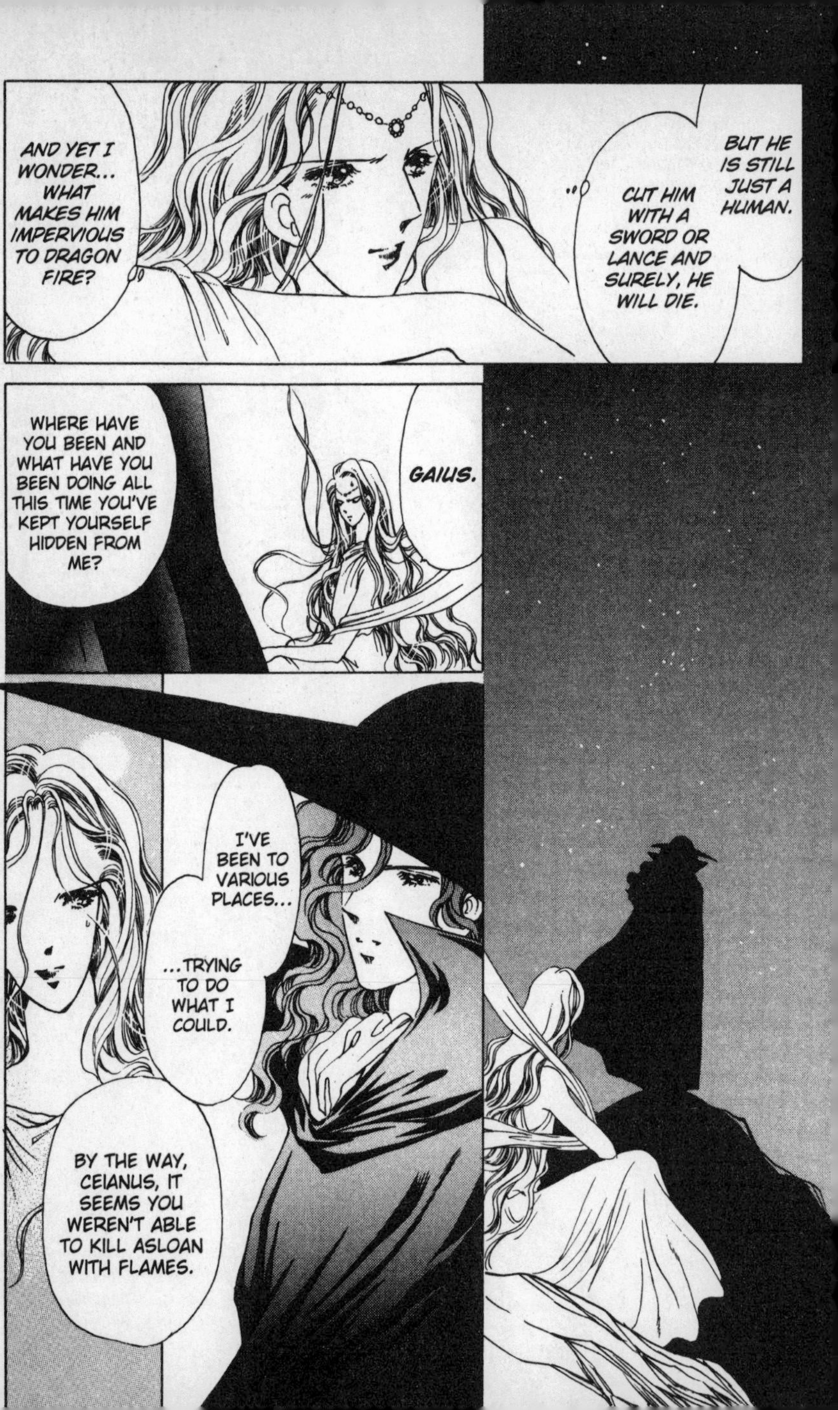
BUT HE IS STILL JUST A HUMAN.
CUT HIM WITH A SWORD OR LANCE AND SURELY, HE WILL DIE.
AND YET I WONDER... WHAT MAKES HIM IMPERVIOUS TO DRAGON FIRE?
GAIUS.
WHERE HAVE YOU BEEN AND WHAT HAVE YOU BEEN DOING ALL THIS TIME YOU'VE KEPT YOURSELF HIDDEN FROM ME?
I'VE BEEN TO VARIOUS PLACES...
...TRYING TO DO WHAT I COULD.
BY THE WAY, CEIANUS, IT SEEMS YOU WEREN'T ABLE TO KILL ASLOAN WITH FLAMES.

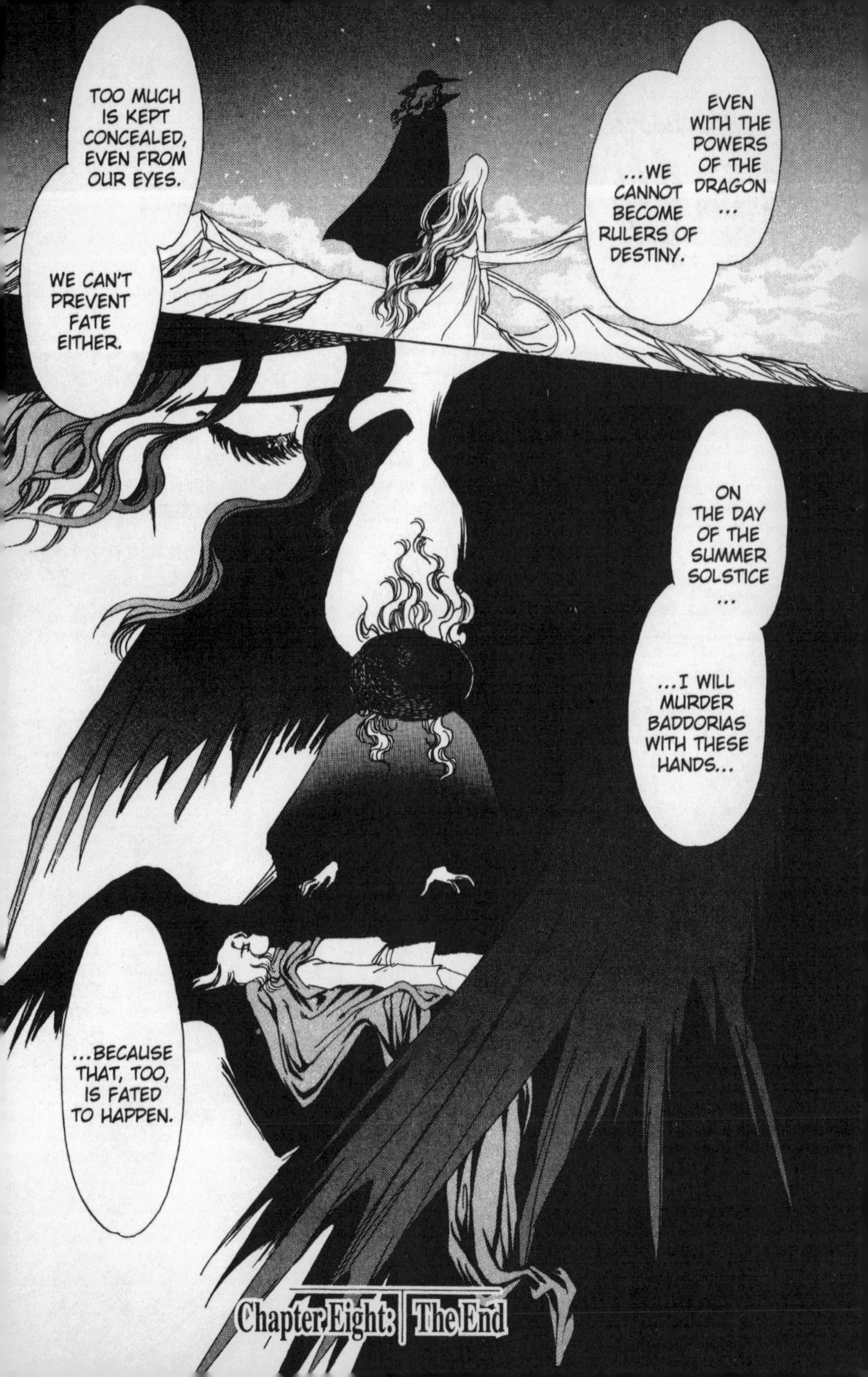
EVEN WITH THE POWERS OF THE DRAGON ...
...WE CANNOT BECOME RULERS OF DESTINY.
TOO MUCH IS KEPT CONCEALED, EVEN FROM OUR EYES.
WE CAN'T PREVENT FATE EITHER.
ON THE DAY OF THE SUMMER SOLSTICE ...
...I WILL MURDER BADDORIAS WITH THESE HANDS...
...BECAUSE THAT, TOO, IS FATED TO HAPPEN.
Chapter Eight: The End

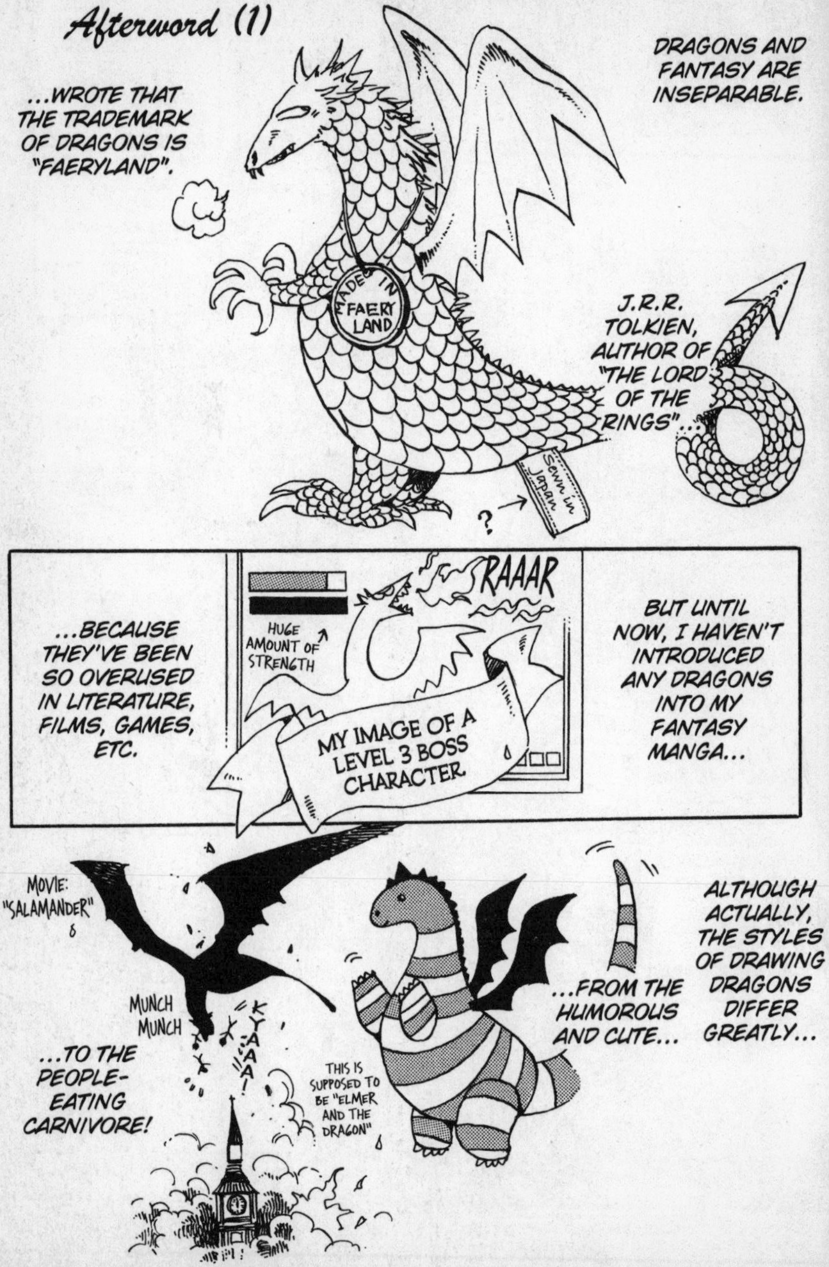
Afterword (1)
DRAGONS AND FANTASY ARE INSEPARABLE.
J.R.R. TOLKIEN, AUTHOR OF "THE LORD OF THE RINGS"...
...WROTE THAT THE TRADEMARK OF DRAGONS IS "FAERYLAND".
MADE IN FAERY LAND
Sewn in Japan
?
BUT UNTIL NOW, I HAVEN'T INTRODUCED ANY DRAGONS INTO MY FANTASY MANGA...
RAAAR
HUGE AMOUNT OF STRENGTH
MY IMAGE OF A LEVEL 3 BOSS CHARACTER
...BECAUSE THEY'VE BEEN SO OVERUSED IN LITERATURE, FILMS, GAMES, ETC.
ALTHOUGH ACTUALLY, THE STYLES OF DRAWING DRAGONS DIFFER GREATLY...
...FROM THE HUMOROUS AND CUTE...
THIS IS SUPPOSED TO BE "ELMER AND THE DRAGON"
MOVIE: "SALAMANDER"
MUNCH MUNCH
KYAAAA!
...TO THE PEOPLE-EATING CARNIVORE!

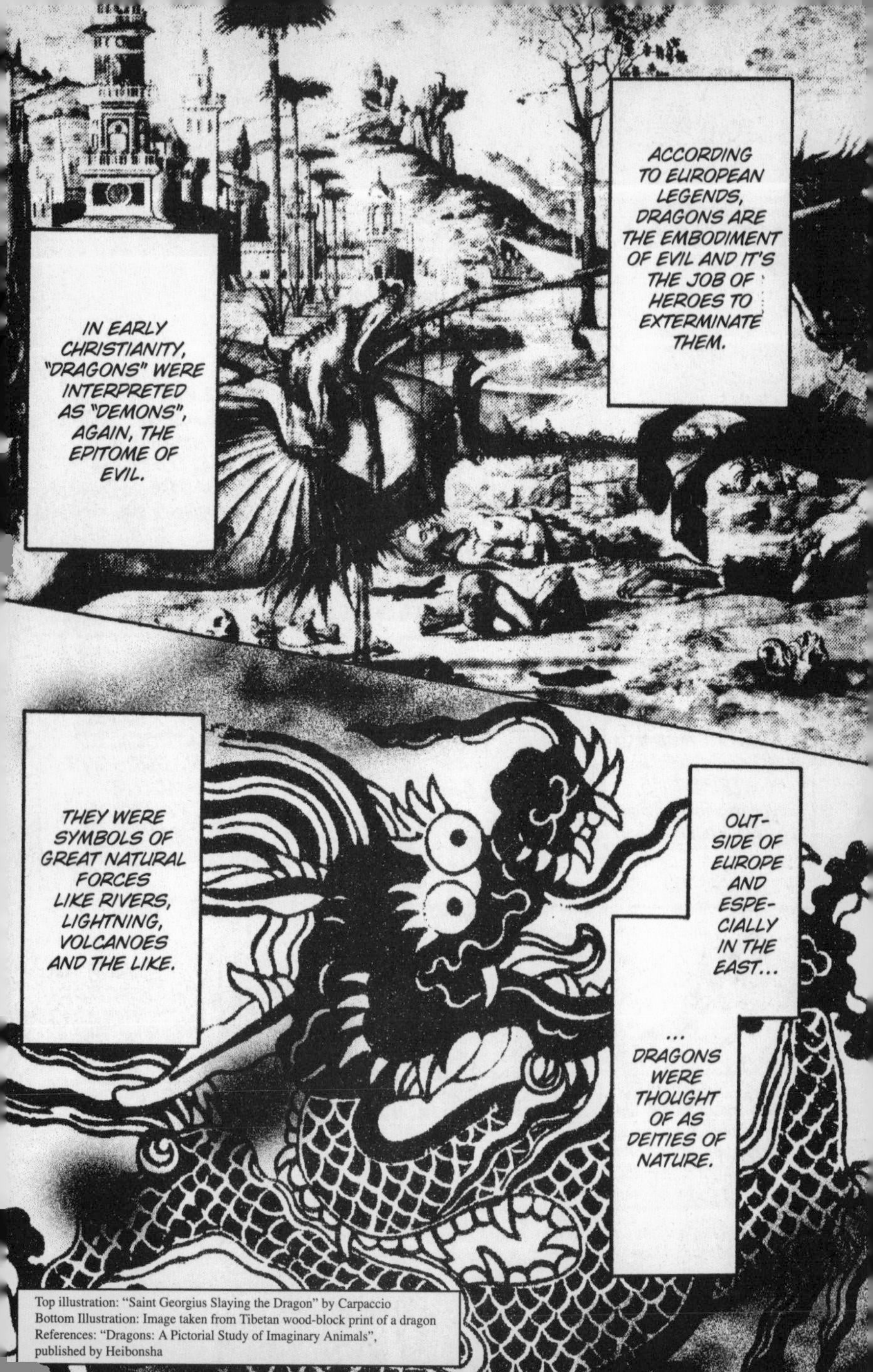
ACCORDING TO EUROPEAN LEGENDS, DRAGONS ARE THE EMBODIMENT OF EVIL AND IT'S THE JOB OF HEROES TO EXTERMINATE THEM.
IN EARLY CHRISTIANITY, "DRAGONS" WERE INTERPRETED AS "DEMONS", AGAIN, THE EPITOME OF EVIL.
OUT-SIDE OF EUROPE AND ESPE-CIALLY IN THE EAST...
...DRAGONS WERE THOUGHT OF AS DEITIES OF NATURE.
THEY WERE SYMBOLS OF GREAT NATURAL FORCES LIKE RIVERS, LIGHTNING, VOLCANOES AND THE LIKE.

Top illustration: "Saint Georgius Slaying the Dragon" by Carpaccio
Bottom Illustration: Image taken from Tibetan wood-block print of a dragon
References: "Dragons: A Pictorial Study of Imaginary Animals", published by Heibonsha

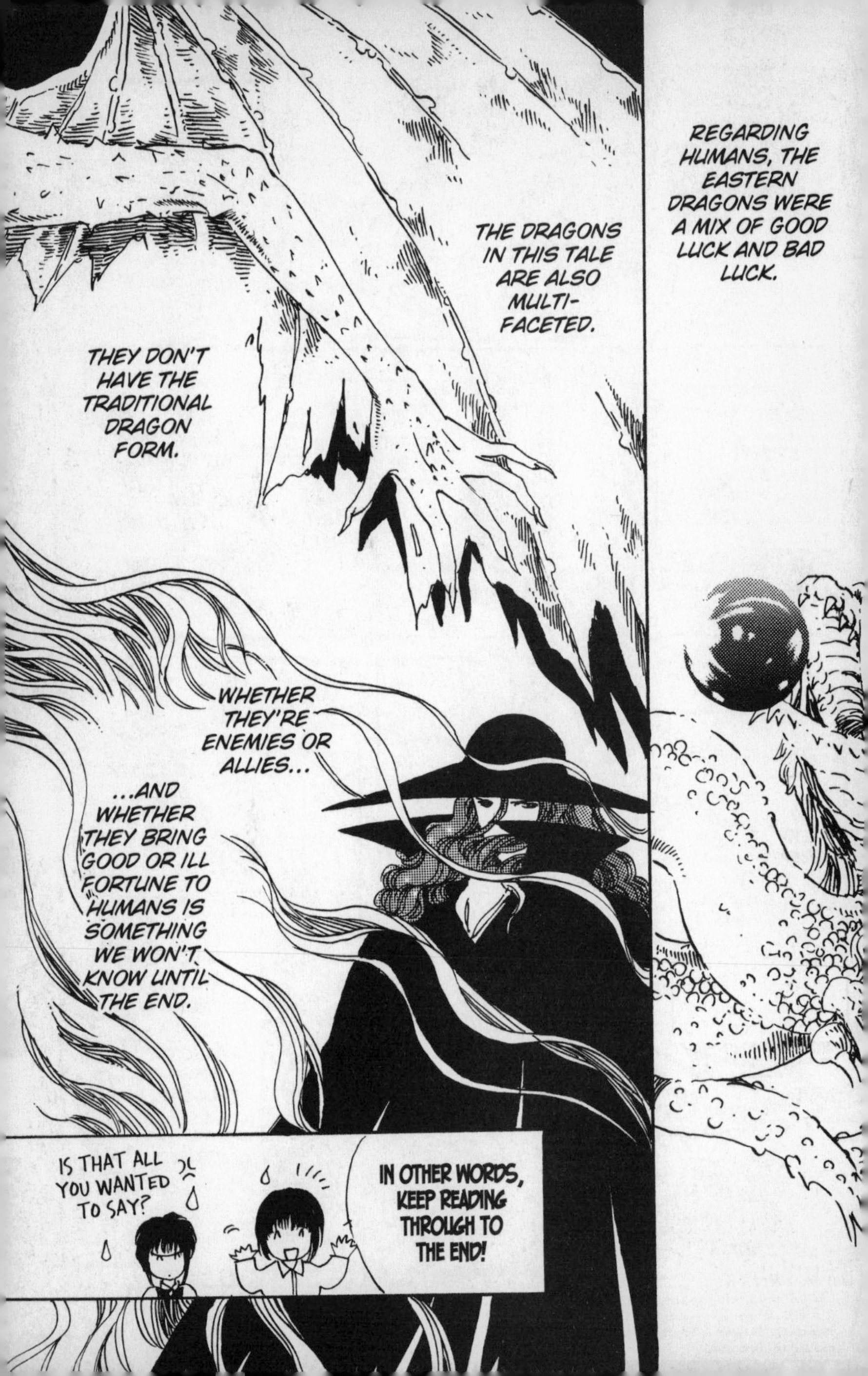
REGARDING HUMANS, THE EASTERN DRAGONS WERE A MIX OF GOOD LUCK AND BAD LUCK.
THE DRAGONS IN THIS TALE ARE ALSO MULTI-FACETED.
THEY DON'T HAVE THE TRADITIONAL DRAGON FORM.
WHETHER THEY'RE ENEMIES OR ALLIES...
...AND WHETHER THEY BRING GOOD OR ILL FORTUNE TO HUMANS IS SOMETHING WE WON'T KNOW UNTIL THE END.
IN OTHER WORDS, KEEP READING THROUGH TO THE END!
IS THAT ALL YOU WANTED TO SAY?

Afterword (2)

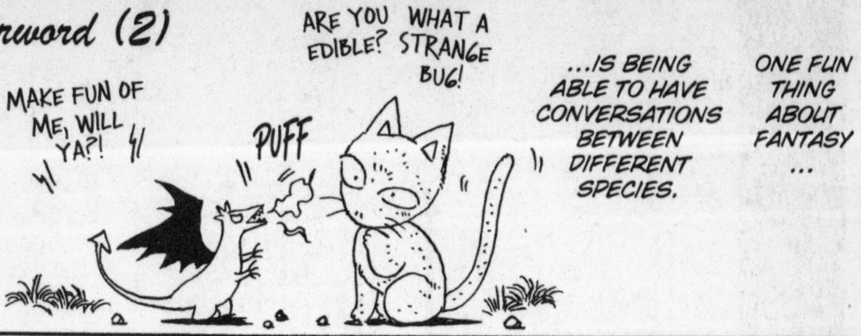
ONE FUN THING ABOUT FANTASY ...
...IS BEING ABLE TO HAVE CONVERSATIONS BETWEEN DIFFERENT SPECIES.
WHAT A STRANGE BUG!
ARE YOU EDIBLE?
PUFF
MAKE FUN OF ME, WILL YA?!

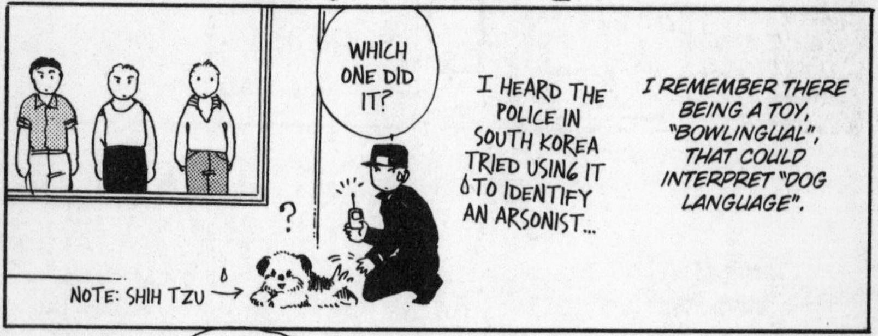
I REMEMBER THERE BEING A TOY, "BOWLINGUAL", THAT COULD INTERPRET "DOG LANGUAGE".
I HEARD THE POLICE IN SOUTH KOREA TRIED USING IT TO IDENTIFY AN ARSONIST...
WHICH ONE DID IT?
?
NOTE: SHIH TZU

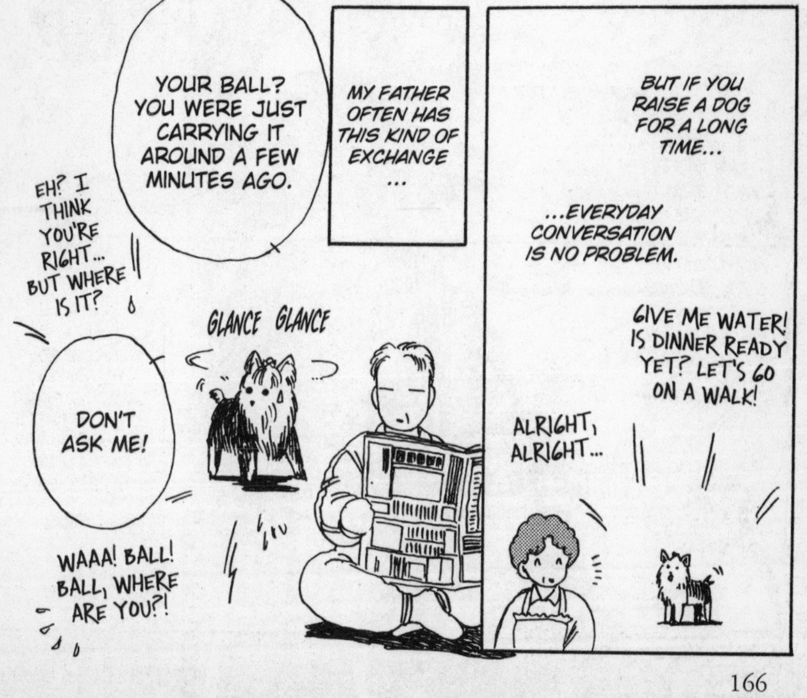
BUT IF YOU RAISE A DOG FOR A LONG TIME...
...EVERYDAY CONVERSATION IS NO PROBLEM.
GIVE ME WATER! IS DINNER READY YET? LET'S GO ON A WALK!
ALRIGHT, ALRIGHT...
MY FATHER OFTEN HAS THIS KIND OF EXCHANGE ...
YOUR BALL? YOU WERE JUST CARRYING IT AROUND A FEW MINUTES AGO.
EH? I THINK YOU'RE RIGHT... BUT WHERE IS IT?
GLANCE GLANCE
DON'T ASK ME!
WAAA! BALL! BALL, WHERE ARE YOU?!

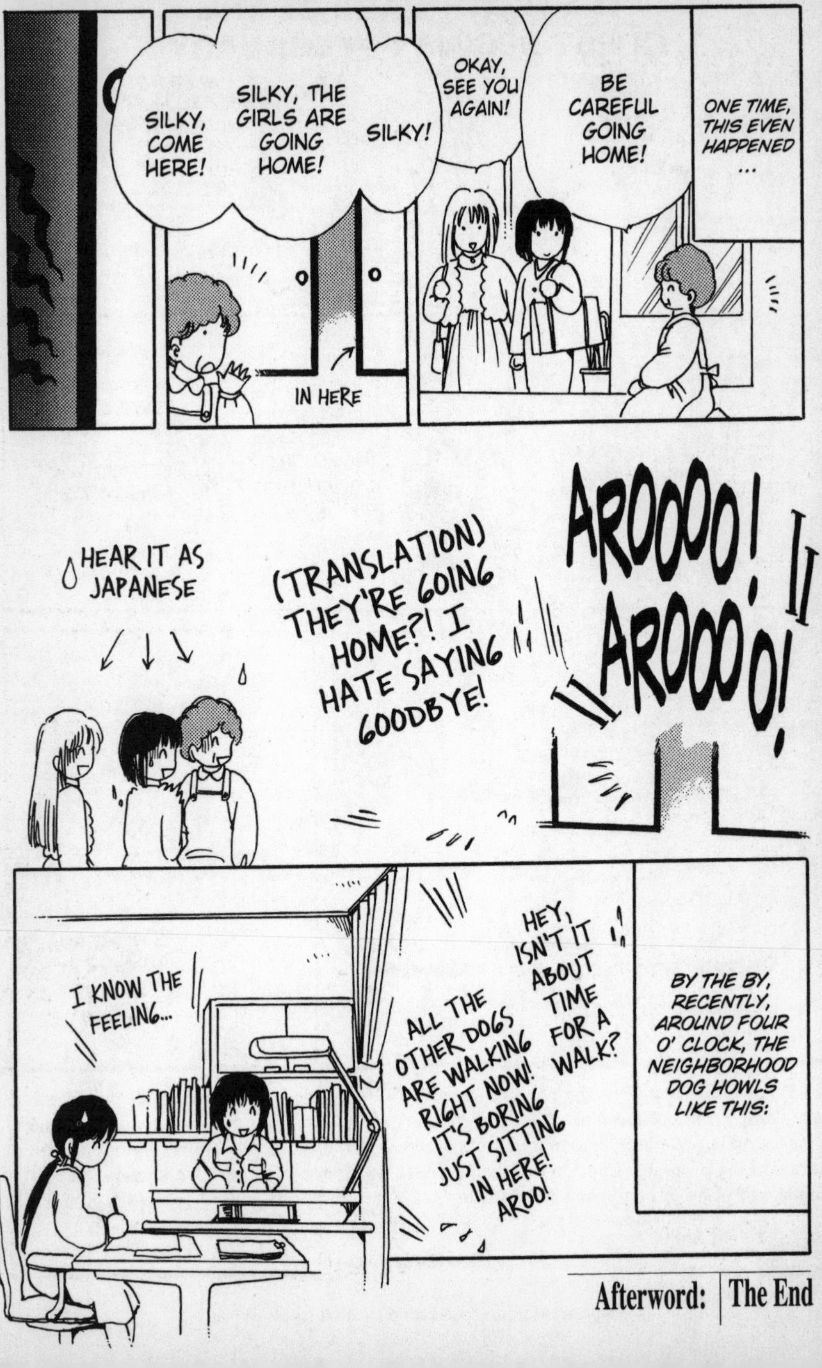
ONE TIME, THIS EVEN HAPPENED ...
BE CAREFUL GOING HOME!
OKAY, SEE YOU AGAIN!
SILKY!
SILKY, THE GIRLS ARE GOING HOME!
SILKY, COME HERE!
IN HERE
AROOOO! AROOOO!
(TRANSLATION) THEY'RE GOING HOME?! I HATE SAYING GOODBYE!
HEAR IT AS JAPANESE
BY THE BY, RECENTLY, AROUND FOUR O' CLOCK, THE NEIGHBORHOOD DOG HOWLS LIKE THIS:
HEY, ISN'T IT ABOUT TIME FOR A WALK?
ALL THE OTHER DOGS ARE WALKING RIGHT NOW! IT'S BORING JUST SITTING IN HERE! AROO!
I KNOW THE FEELING...

Afterword: The End

THE NEXT PHASE OF THE QUEST BEGINS IN FEBRUARY!

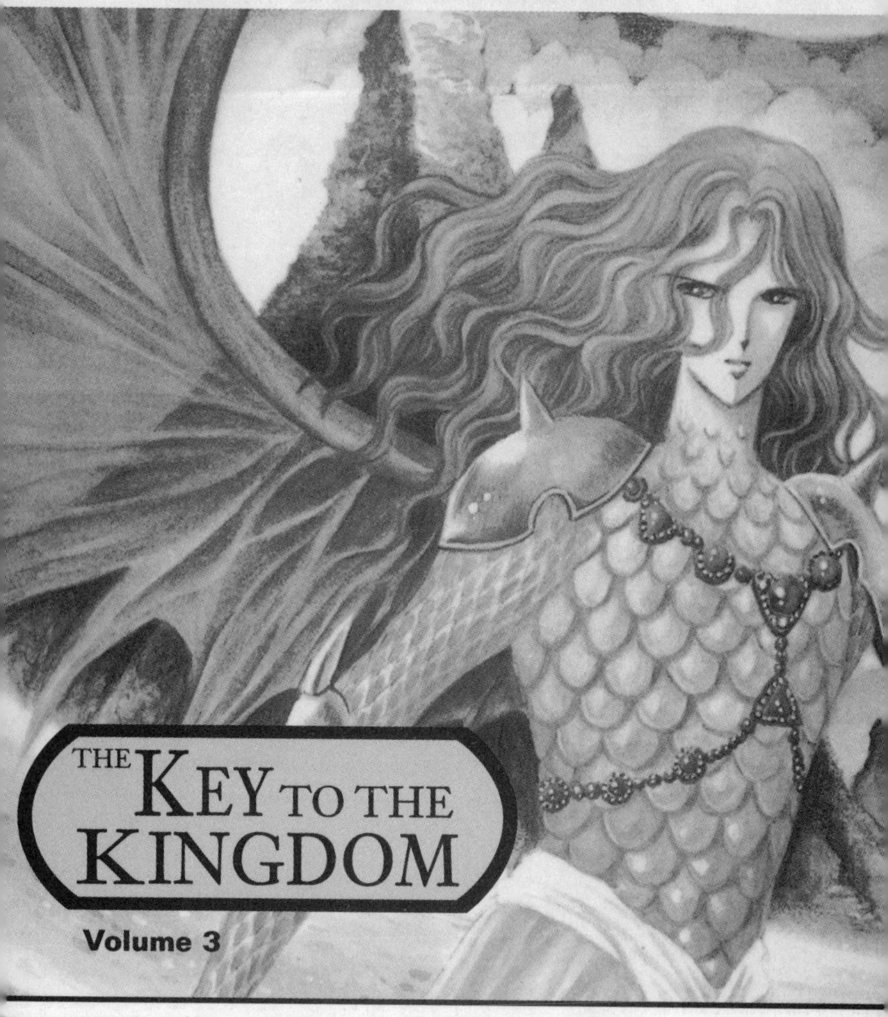
THE KEY TO THE KINGDOM
Volume 3

By Kyoko Shitou. The competitors search for "The Invisible Tower," an elusive location containing an important clue about the quest. A new competitor enters the ring: Fairheart, a man who is seemingly impervious to the flames of the Dragon Men. He welcomes Prince Asta and his protector Badd to his castle. There he shares with Asta his knowledge of a family secret he learned from Asta's father – the late King of Landor – just before he died.

CLASS IS NOW IN SESSION!
IN STORES EVERYWHERE!

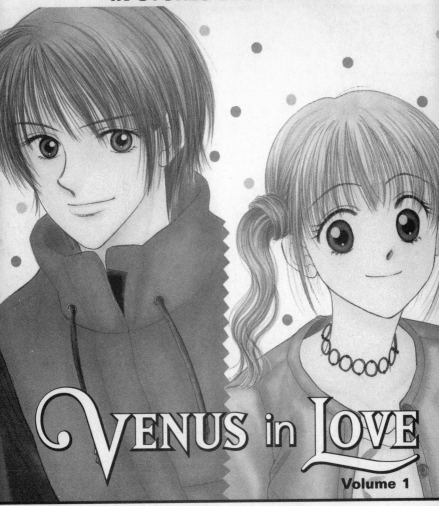

Venus in Love

Volume 1

By Yuki Nakaji. As a college freshman, Suzuna is looking forward to making friends, joining a club and hopefully getting a boyfriend! She develops a crush on Fukumi—charismatic tennis player and friend of her neighbor, Eichi. But her other new friend—the beautiful Hinako—has some interesting information regarding Eichi that's going to force Suzuna to take a second look at the whole situation. She's about to discover that love can come with some unexpected competition.

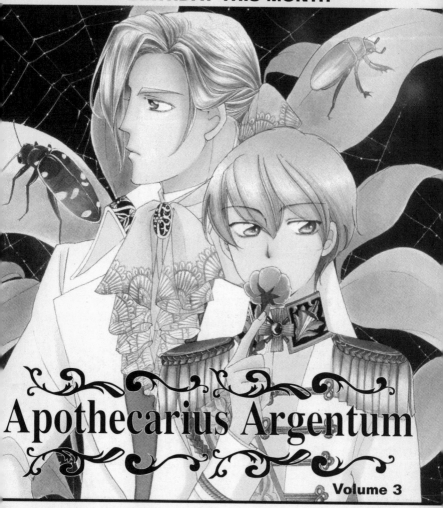

Apothecarius Argentum

Volume 3

By Tomomi Yamashita. Various merchants from across the country have gathered around the castle to bring supplies for the celebration. However, this is not an ordinary birthday dinner. Princes from other nations have gathered to ask for Primula's hand in marriage! A mysterious blonde boy not only crashes the engagement party, but also reveals his shocking identity and makes a surprising offer!

WILL MANAMI BE READY TO TAKE ON JAPAN'S NUMBER ONE PLAYER? IN STORES NOW!

KING OF CARDS

Volume 2

By Makoto Tateno. A lovesick Manami passes out when she sees the object of her affection with another girl. When she wakes up, she finds herself in the world of the cards, where she is forced to compete against Sahgan, her usual ally. In this realm, the matches aren't simply imagined: players summon actual monsters and gods to do physical battle!

DON'T MISS THESE OTHER GREAT SERIES!

By Yasuko Aoike
10 Volumes Available

By Kyoko Ariyoshi
11 Volumes Available

By Minako Narita
9 Volumes Available

By Reiko Shimizu
8 Volumes Available

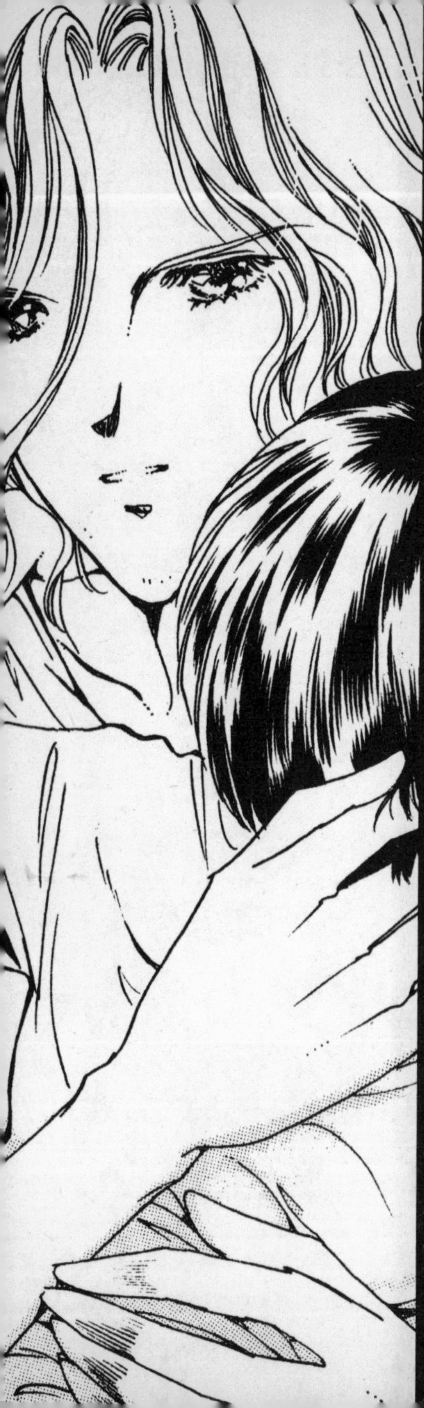

KNOW WHAT'S INSIDE

With the wide variety of manga available, CMX understands it can be confusing to determine age-appropriate material. We rate our books in four categories: EVERYONE, TEEN, TEEN + and MATURE. For the TEEN, TEEN + and MATURE categories, we include additional, specific descriptions to assist consumers in determining if the book is age appropriate. (Our MATURE books are shipped shrink-wrapped with a Parental Advisory sticker affixed to the wrapper.)

E

EVERYONE

Titles with this rating are appropriate for all age readers. They contain no offensive material. They may contain mild violence and/or some comic mischief.

T

TEEN

Titles with this rating are appropriate for a teen audience and older. They may contain some violent content, language, and/or suggestive themes.

T+

TEEN PLUS

Titles with this rating are appropriate for an audience of 16 and older. They may contain partial nudity, mild profanity and more intense violence.

M

MATURE

Titles with this rating are appropriate only for mature readers. They may contain graphic violence, nudity, sex and content suitable only for older readers.

cmx

OUKOKU NO KAGI Vol. 2 © Kyoko SHITOU 2003. First
Published in Japan in 2003 by KADOKAWA SHOTEN PUB-
LISHING CO., LTD., Tokyo.

The Key to the Kingdom, Volume 2, published by WildStorm
Productions, an imprint of DC Comics, 888 Prospect St.
#240, La Jolla, CA 92037. English Translation © 2008. All
Rights Reserved. English translation rights in U.S.A.
arranged with KADOKAWA SHOTEN PUBLISHING CO.,
LTD., Tokyo, through TUTTLE-MORI AGENCY, INC., Tokyo.
CMX is a trademark of DC Comics. The stories, characters,
and incidents mentioned in this magazine are entirely fic-
tional. Printed on recyclable paper. WildStorm does not
read or accept unsolicited submissions of ideas, stories or
artwork. Printed in Canada.

DC Comics, a Warner Bros. Entertainment Company.

Sheldon Drzka – Translation and Adaptation
AndWorld Design – Lettering
Larry Berry – Design
Jim Chadwick – Editor

ISBN:1-4012-1394-4
ISBN-13: 978-1-4012-1394-7

All the pages in this book were created—and are printed here—in Japanese RIGHT-to-LEFT format. No artwork has been reversed or altered, so you can read the stories the way the creators meant for them to be read.

RIGHT TO LEFT?!

Traditional Japanese manga starts at the upper right-hand corner, and moves right-to-left as it goes down the page. Follow this guide for an easy understanding.

For more information and sneak previews, visit cmxmanga.com. Call 1-888-COMIC BOOK for the nearest comics shop or head to your local book store.

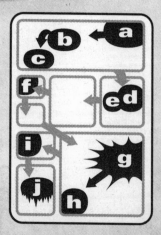